This Book is Only the Beginning.

For every kind of computer user, there is a SYBEX book.

All computer users learn in their own way. Some need straightforward and methodical explanations. Others are just too busy for this approach. But no matter what camp you fall into, SYBEX has a book that can help you get the most out of your computer and computer software while learning at your own pace.

Beginners generally want to start at the beginning. The **ABC's** series, with its step-by-step lessons in plain language, helps you build basic skills quickly. Or you might try our **Quick & Easy** series, the friendly, full-color guide.

The **Mastering** and **Understanding** series will tell you everything you need to know about a subject. They're perfect for intermediate and advanced computer users, yet they don't make the mistake of leaving beginners behind.

If you're a busy person and are already comfortable with computers, you can choose from two SYBEX series—**Up & Running** and **Running Start**. The **Up & Running** series gets you started in just 20 lessons. Or you can get two books in one, a step-by-step tutorial and an alphabetical reference, with our **Running Start** series.

Everyone who uses computer software can also use a computer software reference. SYBEX offers the gamut—from portable **Instant References** to comprehensive **Encyclopedias, Desktop References**, and **Bibles**.

SYBEX even offers special titles on subjects that don't neatly fit a category—like **Tips & Tricks**, the **Shareware Treasure Chests**, and a wide range of books for Macintosh computers and software.

SYBEX books are written by authors who are expert in their subjects. In fact, many make their living as professionals, consultants or teachers in the field of computer software. And their manuscripts are thoroughly reviewed by our technical and editorial staff for accuracy and ease-of-use.

So when you want answers about computers or any popular software package, just help yourself to SYBEX.

For a complete catalog of our publications, please write:

SYBEX Inc. 2021 Challenger Drive Alameda, CA 94501
Tel: (510) 523-8233/(800) 227-2346 Telex: 336311
Fax: (510) 523-2373

SYBEX is committed to using natural resources wisely to preserve and improve our environment. As a leader in the computer book publishing industry, we are aware that over 40% of America's solid waste is paper. This is why we have been printing the text of books like this one on recycled paper since 1982.

This year our use of recycled paper will result in the saving of more than 15,300 trees. We will lower air pollution effluents by 54,000 pounds, save 6,300,000 gallons of water, and reduce landfill by 2,700 cubic yards.

In choosing a SYBEX book you are not only making a choice for the best in skills and information, you are also choosing to enhance the quality of life for all of us.

THE SOUND BLASTER™ BOOK

Josha Munnik
Eric Oostendorp

SYBEX®
San Francisco • Paris • Düsseldorf • Soest

Acquisitions Editor: David Clark
Developmental Editor: Steve Lipson
Project Editor: Kristen Vanberg-Wolff
Editor: Peter Weverka
Technical Editor: Erik Ingenito
Book Series Designer/Production Artist: Suzanne Albertson
Technical Art/Screen Graphics: John Corrigan
Typesetter: Thomas Goudie
Proofreader/Production Assistant: Sarah Lemas
Indexer: Nancy Guenther
Cover Designer: Ingalls + Associates
Cover Illustrator/Photographer: Max Seabaugh

Authorized translation from Dutch Language Edition.
Original copyright © SYBEX Uitgeverij b.v., Soest 1992.
Translation copyright © SYBEX Inc. 1994.

Library of Congress Card Number: 93-87420
ISBN: 0-7821-1320-6

Manufactured in the United States of America
10 9 8 7 6 5 4 3 2 1

ACKNOWLEDGMENTS

First of all, we would like to thank our colleagues at Ultra Force Development—Arjan Brusse, Michel Hooymans, Eric Soonius, and Remco de Berk—for their criticism, insights, and support.

Thanks are also due to our parents. They were very helpful during the writing of this book.

We wish to thank Walop Electronics B.V. for putting the necessary hardware at our disposal, and especially Ferry ten Brink for the many contacts he gave us. We thank everyone who contributed to this book, particularly Frank van Tol and the employees of Black Pearl Music.

Finally, we would like to thank the people at SYBEX and Fontline, without whom it would have been impossible to publish this book. Thanks especially to Tim Tully for writing the material concerning Sound Blaster 16.

CONTENTS AT A GLANCE

TABLE OF CONTENTS

INTRODUCTION

For a long time the internal speaker was the only sound source for the PC. Unfortunately, the internal speaker's repertoire consists of a few simple beeps. Not until 1987, when audio adapter cards began appearing on the market, did PC users get an opportunity to hear and create true sound.

In 1987, the AdLib Music Synthesizer card was put on the market. Soon AdLib became the standard card for computer games. Besides graphical capabilities, sound effects and music became a part of computer games thanks to this sophisticated new card.

The year 1989 saw the first release of the Sound Blaster card from Creative Labs. Whereas AdLib is built around a synthesizer chip, which limits its sound capabilities, Sound Blaster offers more possibilities for creating sound. With Sound Blaster you can digitally record and play sound. Thanks to Sound Blaster's digital capabilities, you can use speech and sound effects in programs.

More and more games and programs support the Sound Blaster. Sound Blaster has ousted AdLib from the sound card market.

The original release of Sound Blaster was followed in succession by Sound Blaster Pro, which has enhanced stereo capabilities and can be combined with a CD-ROM; by Sound Blaster MCV, a version for IBM PS/2 model 50 and higher; and by Sound Blaster 16, the newest and most advanced version of the Sound Blaster card. Microsoft has chosen Sound Blaster Pro as its standard multimedia sound card.

> **NOTE**   This book covers Sound Blaster and Sound Blaster Pro in great detail. Sound Blaster 16 is being released as of the writing of this book, and it is discussed in Appendix A. Sound Blaster MCV, designed solely for the PS/2, was a bit of a bust. It is not covered in this book because so few people use it.

What You'll Learn from This Book

This book was written for Sound Blaster users who want to tap the creative potential of the Sound Blaster card. It covers everything from the basics of installation to programming the timer chip, the FM chip, and CMS chips.

The book consists of two parts: "Sound Blaster Hardware and Software Basics," and "Programming the Sound Blaster." Part II is much longer than Part I.

Chapter-by-chapter, here is what you will find in Part I of this book:

- Chapter 1, "Installing Sound Blaster Hardware and Software," explains how to install your Sound Blaster card, how to test it, and how to make it compatible with your system. It also looks briefly at the software that accompanies the card.

- Chapter 2, "A Tour of the Sound Blaster Cards," looks closely at the five extension cards that "make up" the Sound Blaster card—the CMS Game Blaster card, the AdLib Music Synthesizer card, the Digital Sound Processing (DSP) card, the MIDI card, and the joystick card.

- Chapter 3, "Making Music with Sound Blaster," explains some of the most important aspects of creating music with Sound Blaster. It also describes a few programs for creating music.

- Chapter 4, "Sound Blaster Extensions," discusses extensions you can use, including the MIDI Connector Box, CMS chips, and CD-ROM drives.

- Chapter 5, "Understanding the MIDI Interface," explains what MIDI is and takes a close look at connecting MIDI devices, at MIDI instruments, and at MIDI software.

And in Part II:

- Chapter 6, "Programming the Timer Chip," explains how the timer chip functions with Sound Blaster, timer channels, and ports and counters for the timer chip.

- Chapter 7, "Programming the FM Chip," is particularly helpful for AdLib users because it explores not only the CMF format, but also the ROL format. Moreover, it describes how to program the FM chip—and therefore AdLib—to make it produce sound.

- Chapter 8, "Programming CMS Chips," discusses programming the CMS chip and using the CMS driver. It looks at CMS chip functions, how to create sounds and noises with CMS chips, and how to program the tone, pitch, and duration of notes.

- Chapter 9, "Programming the Digital Sound Processor," examines the DSP. It discusses Sound Blaster Pro's stereo sound processor, covers how sample files are structured, and describes the CT-VOICE driver. It also describes how to record and play back samples without using this driver.

- Chapter 10, "Programming with MIDI," discusses the MIDI language in general, as well as the actual MIDI file format. It explains how messages are transferred through the Sound Blaster and out of the MIDI port. It also explains how to send MIDI information to external synthesizer modules.

- Chapter 11, "Sound Blaster Pro's Mixer Chip," explains how to change the volume settings on the Sound Blaster Pro, as well as how to set the input and output levels of the various parts of the Pro, including Line In, Mic In, and CD-ROM In.

The book also includes seven appendices:

- Appendix A, "Sound Blaster 16 Hardware and Software," explains how to install the Sound Blaster 16 card and how to use its accompanying software. It also looks at some enhancements to SB16, including the Wave Blaster and Creative WaveStudio.

- Appendix B, "DMAs, IRQs, and I/O Addresses," explains what DMA channels, IRQ numbers, and I/O addresses are for. It also explains how they interact with the Sound Blaster card.

- Appendix C, "Sound Blaster Port Addresses," lists the port addresses for registers that control various parts of the Sound Blaster.

- Appendix D, "Mixer Chip Registers," lists registers for controlling the operation of the mixer chip.

- Appendix E, "DSP Commands," discusses all the DSP commands.
- Appendix F, "ID Codes for MIDI Instrument Manufacturers," lists the ID codes for various MIDI instrument manufacturers. These codes are used in system exclusive messages.
- Appendix G, "MIDI Status and Data Bytes," lists the byte values of various MIDI messages.

Every part of the Sound Blaster has its own unique features and settings, which makes it possible to treat every part of the sound card in a separate chapter. The parts are independent of each other, but that doesn't mean you cannot combine them. For example, by combining the FM chip and the DSP, you can enrich FM music with samples, with voices, with a bass drum, or with all three. Furthermore, you can also make use of the CMS chips to add stereo effects.

A Word about the Program Listings

All chapters in this book, and especially Chapters 6 through 11, include program listings. The listings are in Pascal, C, and sometimes in Assembly language. The Assembly programs usually support the C and Pascal programs. Sometimes examples are presented in Assembly simply because that language has a higher code speed.

Don't be alarmed if you are not an ace at C or Pascal, and if you're not an Assembly ace don't worry at all, because most examples are presented in the form of independent libraries, or units. A *library* consists of a number of functions that are followed by a short explanation. With libraries, you can use various functions without knowing how they are set up and how they work.

Besides libraries, this book provides simple example programs that use the functions of a particular library and illustrate how you can use these functions yourself.

The programs use Turbo C, Turbo Pascal, and Turbo Assembler for the simple reason that we, the authors, are familiar with these programming environments. On occasion we took advantage of the benefits that these environments offer (including units in Pascal). An average programmer, however, will find no difficulty in converting the programs to his or her own Pascal or C compiler. All programs are quite easy and linear; no complicated techniques or tricks are applied.

Tips for Using the Listings

Before you can use the programs, you have to enter the listings in the compiler environment in question. Here are some useful tips to follow when typing these listings:

- Don't type the comments unless you need them for explanatory purposes. This will save you half the typing time.
- In Turbo Pascal, you can type everything in lowercase to save time, as Turbo Pascal makes no distinction between upper- and lowercase. If you do make all entries in lowercase, however, your listings will be harder to understand.
- C does distinguish between upper- and lowercase. In C, functions and variables are in lowercase, and macro names are in uppercase. In C, you must consider case as you enter program code.

Conventions Used in This Book

This book was designed and written to help you, the reader, learn and be able to reference Sound Blaster programming techniques quickly and easily. To that end, we have:

- Included more than the usual number of headings. We want you to be able to look up information quickly.
- Included numerous tables, each of which provides succinct information about Sound Blaster.
- Included illustrations where necessary to help you learn to use Sound Blaster, its extensions, and its software programs.

For your benefit, we have also included Notes, Tips, and Warnings in this book.

NOTE   Notes tell you where to go elsewhere in the book for further information about a topic.

TIP   Tips give you insights into using Sound Blaster.

WARNING   Warnings tell you when you must make a crucial decision or choice that could affect, for example, how well a program runs or how well the card will produce sound.

PART I

Sound Blaster Hardware and Software Basics

CHAPTER

ONE

Installing Sound Blaster Hardware and Software

- Choosing address, port, and connector settings for your system

- Attaching the card to your computer

- Testing the card to see if it was configured properly

- Installing the Sound Blaster Software

This chapter explains how to install the Sound Blaster card and the Sound Blaster software on your PC. It tells you how to test the card to make sure you've installed it properly. It explains how to make your card compatible with your system. It also looks briefly at the software that accompanies the card so you can get an idea of what Sound Blaster does.

Installing Sound Blaster requires three steps: selecting the right settings for the card, attaching the card to your PC, and testing Sound Blaster. Choosing the right settings is examined first.

> **NOTE** Where installation instructions for Sound Blaster and Sound Blaster Pro are different, we will explain them. Otherwise, unless noted, the techniques for installing Sound Blaster and Sound Blaster Pro are the same.

> **NOTE** As this book is being written, Creative Labs is introducing its newest release, Sound Blaster 16. See Appendix A for information about installing the Sound Blaster 16 card and Sound Blaster 16 hardware.

Choosing Jumper Settings for Your System

To make the card settings, you use *jumpers*. Jumpers are the small plastic and metal blocks that connect pairs of pins on the card. By selecting jumpers, you configure Sound Blaster so it will work on your system.

All settings with Sound Blaster are made on the card itself by means of the jumpers. You cannot change settings with software, so before you install Sound Blaster, you must consider how your system is configured. If you make settings that conflict with other cards on your computer, you won't find out until you've attached the card, at which time you'll have to take the card off again and change the settings. The following sections of the chapter explain how to make jumper settings, and which settings to select or not select to make Sound Blaster work with your system.

How to Change Jumper Settings

Before you choose settings, you need to know how jumpers work, since all settings are made with jumpers.

Figure 1.1 shows three jumper settings—not selected, selected, and not selected with the block on one pin for storage.

- A jumper is *not selected* when the plastic and metal block is not connecting the two pins. When a jumper is not selected, the corresponding setting will not be used by your card.

- A *selected* jumper has the plastic and metal block over the two pins. In effect, the pins are "connected" and activated when the jumper is set this way. With the block on, the setting will be used by your system.

TIP

To store jumper blocks in case you need them later, place the block over one of the pins, not both, in the jumper. This way the setting will not be selected but you'll still have the jumper block in case you need it later.

Jumper Settings for Configuring Sound Blaster

Figure 1.2 shows the jumper settings on the Sound Blaster card. There are four sets of settings, one each for

- I/O addresses
- IRQ numbers
- the joystick
- DMA settings

You can select one setting from each set.

FIGURE 1.1:

Jumper settings. A jumper is selected when the plastic block is placed over the two pins.

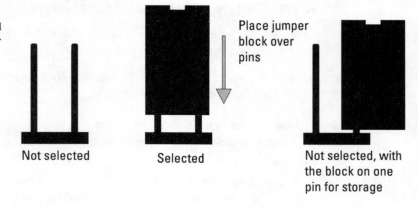

Not selected

Place jumper block over pins

Selected

Not selected, with the block on one pin for storage

NOTE   IRQ, DMA, and I/O address settings are explained in detail in Appendix B.

Figure 1.3 shows the Sound Blaster Pro card. On the Sound Blaster Pro, the IRQ settings are made with DACK and DRQ jumpers, there is a Speaker Input jumper and a Remote Speaker Enable jumper, and a CD-ROM audio input.

Let's look at the settings one at a time.

The I/O Address Jumper

The *I/O (input/output) address* jumper establishes the basic port for the card. All communication with the card takes place through this address. The default port is 220H, but if this address is already used by another card, you must select another port for the Sound Blaster.

The value of the I/O address port must be between 210H and 260H.

Sound Blaster Pro I/O Address   For the Sound Blaster Pro, you can only select 240H as the alternative port if you can't use the 220H default. However, we suggest changing the port on the other card before using the 240H alternative. Some software for the Sound Blaster was written for the 220H port and won't permit you to change ports. Most devices do not use port 220H, so you likely don't have to change to 240H.

FIGURE 1.2:

Settings on the Sound Blaster card

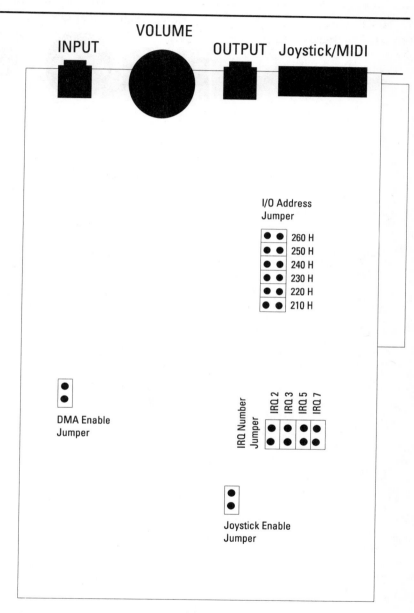

FIGURE 1.3:

Settings on the Sound Blaster Pro card

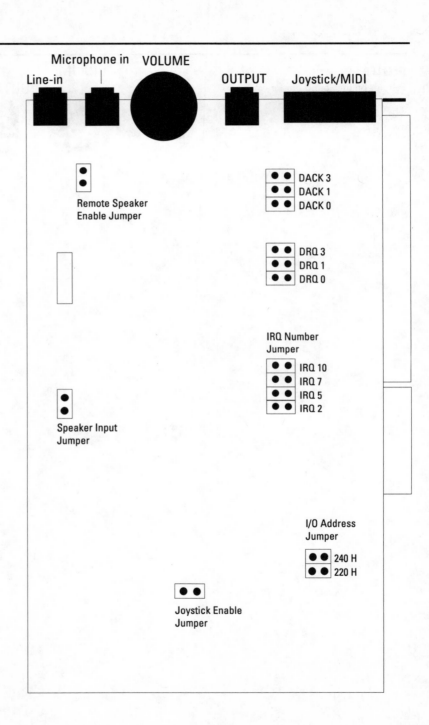

The Interrupt (IRQ) Jumper

The *interrupt* (IRQ) *jumper* sets the hardware interrupt numbers for the card. IRQ stands for *interrupt request*. Other devices may already be using an IRQ number, so you have to choose one for Sound Blaster carefully. The default number is IRQ 7.

Table 1.1 describes the available IRQ numbers. Both Sound Blaster and Sound Blaster Pro can use 2, 5, and 7, but only Sound Blaster can use 3 as well, and only Sound Blaster Pro can use 10.

If you use a printer and a sound card at the same time, you have to select another setting besides the default 7. If you have a PS/2, use another setting besides 7.

TIP Try to avoid using IRQ 10. Ten, a new IRQ number, is not supported by older Sound Blaster software.

The DMA Enable Jumper

Sound Blaster uses the *direct memory access* (DMA) channel for sound input and output. This jumper is enabled in Sound Blaster. Sound Blaster Pro does not have a DMA Enable jumper, but DMA is used by default.

TABLE 1.1: Sound Blaster IRQ Numbers

IRQ Number	Description
2	Used by ATs to daisy-chain.
3	Used by COM2 (if this port is present and used).*
5	Used by some XTs for the hard disk and for the parallel port.
7	The default. Used by the parallel port. On a Tandy 1000, this number is used internally and may not be selected.
10	Free for use.**

* Only available with Sound Blaster, not Sound Blaster Pro.

** Only available with Sound Blaster Pro.

PC-XT DMA Channels   The PC-XT has four DMA channels:

0	Used for memory refresh
1	Free for use by other cards
2	Used by the disk drives
3	Used by the hard disk

PC-AT and PS/2 DMA Channels   The PC-AT and PS/2 have eight channels each:

0	Free for use by other cards
1	Free for use by other cards
2	Used by disk drives
3	Used by the hard disk
4	Used as a passage which enables Channels 5, 6, and 7
5	Free for use by other cards
6	Free for use by other cards
7	Free for use by other cards

NOTE   The DMA Enable jumper is only available on the Sound Blaster, not the Sound Blaster Pro.

Enabling the DMA jumper shortens the amount of processing time needed for sound input and output. If the DMA channel is already being used consistently by another device, you can disable the DMA channel by removing the jumper.

Keep in mind, however, that the Sound Blaster only uses the DMA channel when there is actual sound input or output. The rest of the time the channel is free for use by other cards. So if your devices use the DMA channel infrequently, you can still enable the DMA jumper.

If you think enabling the DMA jumper will lead to conflicts with your other cards, try changing the DMA channel on the other cards. However, because most software produces sound input and output with the DMA channel, we suggest *not* removing the DMA jumper so you can use this software. Most devices use a DMA channel different from the one Sound Blaster uses, so you don't really have to remove this jumper.

The Joystick Enable Jumper

All Sound Blaster cards have a joystick connection. If you already have a joystick hooked up, remove Sound Blaster's joystick enable jumper. Because the joysticks will conflict, you have to disable one of them.

NOTE   Disconnecting the Joystick Enable jumper doesn't affect the MIDI connection. You can still use MIDI devices after disabling your joystick port.

Sound Blaster Pro Settings

Three more settings are available for Sound Blaster Pro. They are the DACK and DRQ settings, the Remote Speaker (RSPK EN) enable jumper, and the Speaker Input jumper.

DACK and DRQ Settings   The DMA defaults for Sound Blaster Pro are DMA1 (DACK1 and DRQ1). The DMA is enabled automatically. Keep in mind, however, that the Sound Blaster only uses DMA channels when there is actual sound input or output. Two devices can share the same DMA channel as long as they are not doing it at the exact same time.

If you think enabling the DMA Select jumper will lead to conflicts with your other cards, try changing the DMA channel on the other cards. Because most software written for Sound Blaster produces sound input and output with DMA Channel 1, we strongly suggest *not* changing the DMA jumper setting. If one of the DMA channels is already being used consistently by another device, use Channel 0.

If you change the DMA setting, you have to adjust the *DMA request line* (DRQ) and *DMA acknowledge line* (DACK) settings (see Figure 1.3). Choose DRQ 0 and DACK 0 for Channel 0. You must choose these DACK and DRQ settings.

The Speaker Input Jumper   You can connect the speaker output from your PC's motherboard to the Speaker Input jumper on the Sound Blaster. When you do this, all your PC sounds will be played through Sound Blaster, which means you can adjust the volume of the sounds your PC makes. However, making this connection requires soldering and should perhaps be done by a professional. The speaker's ground wire connects to the right pin of the jumper, and the 5-volt connection connects to the left pin.

The Remote Speaker Enable Jumper   If connecting the speaker output from your PC's motherboard to the Speaker Input jumper on the Sound Blaster creates problems, you can disable this option with the Remote Speaker Enable jumper.

Installing the Card

Once you've configured the card, you can install it:

1. Turn the PC's power off, but do not disconnect its power cable—you want the PC to stay grounded.

2. Remove the screws that hold the cover. If you need help doing this, consult your computer's manual.

3. Slowly remove the cover of an empty slot. As you remove the cover, make sure it doesn't get snagged on any cables.

4. Connect the internal speaker to Sound Blaster Pro if you choose to.

5. Place the card in the empty slot and screw down the top.

The Sound Blaster Pro is a 16-bit card and can only be installed in PC-ATs in a 16-bit slot. Figure 1.4 shows the difference between an 8- and a 16-bit slot. Sound Blaster can go in an 8- or 16-bit slot.

6. Put back the cover of the computer.

Testing the Card

Now that the card has been configured and installed, it is time to test it. To test the card, you have to connect it to an input and output device. Then you run the test utility programs to make sure your card has been installed correctly and that it works with your system.

Plugging In the Input and Output Devices   First thing you must do is plug in an input device. Sound Blaster has only one audio input plug (see Figure 1.2), but Sound Blaster Pro has two (see Figure 1.3). You can plug in an amplifier, speaker, or headphones as the output device.

The maximum power of the card is:

- 4 watts per channel if you use 4 ohms speakers, or
- 2 watts per channel if you use 8 ohms speakers.

TIP   If you don't have a microphone, try connecting an amplifier to the line-in or microphone connection. The sound quality, though not very high, is high enough for testing purposes. Adjust the volume control to midrange.

FIGURE 1.4:
An 8- and a 16-bit slot

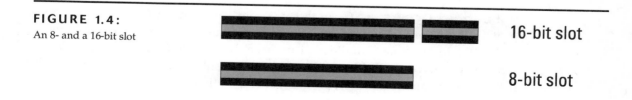

16-bit slot

8-bit slot

Running the Test Programs

To run the test programs and see whether Sound Blaster has been installed properly:

1. Switch on the computer.

2. Put disk 1 in one of the drives and go to the root directory of your disk.

3. Depending on whether you have Sound Blaster or Sound Blaster Pro, type

   A:TEST-SBC

   (assuming you are using the A drive) for Sound Blaster, or type

   A:TEST-SBP

   (assuming you are using the A drive) for the Pro card.

The test program will tell you if there are any hardware conflicts, and if there are any, what they are.

> **TIP**   Make note of where the test program finds the conflicts so that you can make port and connector changes later on.

If, during the testing procedure, your program freezes, try running the test program with the /M switch (you can only do this with Sound Blaster Pro):

1. Type

   TEST-SBP /M

   at the DOS prompt.

2. A series of prompts appears so you can tell the program how you set your card—that is, how you have set the I/O address, DMA channel, and interrupts.

If a Conflict Occurs...   If the test program discovers an I/O address, Interrupt, or DMA conflict, you will have to take the card off and change the settings. Follow the instructions found earlier in this chapter to do this. To change jumper settings, you have to take the card out of the computer. Make the changes, install the card again, and run the test program one more time.

Installing Sound Blaster Software

The Sound Blaster software is stored in compressed files. Sound Blaster includes an INST-HD (Install Hard Disk) program for decompressing the software and copying it to your hard disk. INST-HD is found on Disk 1, the same disk as TEST-SBC. To run the Sound Blaster installation program, you must use DOS commands, as the program runs under DOS.

WARNING Before you install the software, be sure to make backup copies of the disks. Use the copies instead of the originals to install the software.

To install the Sound Blaster hardware:

1. Insert Disk 1 into drive A or B.

2. Type

   ```
   INST-HD D:
   ```

   and press Enter, where D is the drive letter of your hard disk (enter C, for example, if C is your hard drive).

The files will be copied to a new subdirectory called \SB (or \SBPRO if you have Sound Blaster Pro). The \SB directory will include a few subdirectories for Sound Blaster drivers and utilities. *Drivers* are programs in separate files that control how the audio cards and the software communicate.

Updating the AUTOEXEC.BAT File

The INST-HD program makes a few changes to the AUTOEXEC.BAT file. Specifically, it adds two lines, SET SOUND and SET BLASTER:

- SET SOUND points to the directory where you just installed the software with INST-HD. If you change the directory name, you must change this statement accordingly.

- SET BLASTER points to the settings of the Sound Blaster card. The parameters and their functions are as follows:

  SET BLASTER=A*nnn* I*n* D*n* T*n*

A*nnn*	The port. For example, A220 represents port 220H.
I*n*	The IRQ number. For example, I10 represents IRQ number 10.
D*n*	The DMA channel. For example, D1 represents channel 1.
T*n*	The type of card. T1 stands for the standard Sound Blaster and T2 for the Sound Blaster Pro.

Installing the Drivers   The included software uses various drivers. If the cards are modified, you have to use the INST-DRV (Install Drivers) program to adjust the drivers. The INST-DRV program recognizes which drivers are located in the directory and it tells you which ones can be changed.

Type

INST-DRV /?

for a list of all drivers INST-DRV can modify.

Type

INST-DRV

to change the driver in the current directory.

Type

INST-DRV *name*

to change one or more drivers in the subdirectory *name*.

The subdirectories VOXKIT and FMORGAN both contain a driver for the Sound Blaster. The subdirectory DRV contains a driver for the Sound Blaster Pro that has to be modified. Finally, the CMS driver (CMSDRV.COM) can be changed. This is a driver that works with the CMS chips of the standard Sound Blaster.

A Quick Tour of Sound Blaster Programs

To help you get familiar with Sound Blaster, following is a short description of some software programs. These programs can be started from the \SB or \SBPRO directory. In the case of Sound Blaster, each program can also be started from disk.

Talking Parrot

The Talking Parrot, as you might expect, repeats what you say into your system's microphone. If you don't have a microphone, you can still make the parrot talk with your keyboard.

To try out the Talking Parrot:

1. Type

   PARROT

   from the SB or SBPRO directory and press Enter.

An oscilloscope appears showing how much environmental noise is being picked up by your microphone.

2. Talk into the microphone to see how loud you have to talk.

3. You are asked to enter a value. Choose a value that is approximately 10 counts above the noise the environment makes.

A parrot appears on screen to welcome you.

4. Talk into the microphone. The parrot will repeat what you say. If you don't have a microphone, you can "tickle" the parrot by pressing a key on the keyboard.

5. Press Esc to quit the program.

FM Organ

The FM Organ resembles a simple keyboard synthesizer. With it, you can play a song, replay it, and save the song on disk. The Sound Blaster Pro FM Organ has stereo FM capabilities.

To start the FM Organ:

1. Switch the SB or SBPRO directory, if necessary.

2. Type the following for Sound Blaster:

   FMORGAN

   or following for Sound Blaster Pro:

   PRO-ORG

For a complete description of how to operate the organ, see the documentation. Meanwhile, here are some useful key combinations for playing the organ:

Key	Use
F1	Provides help information for using the keys when composing.
F2	Begins recording a new song.
F3	Lets you replay a song you have just recorded.
F4	Exits the program.
F6	Lets you load a previously saved song.
F7	Lets you store a song on disk after you have recorded it.

VOXKIT

The VOXKIT program lets you *sample* sound—that is, record and play back sound. This program stores sound in digital form so it can be stored in your computer's memory and played back later.

NOTE   The VOXKIT program comes with Sound Blaster, not Sound Blaster Pro. However, Sound Blaster Pro's VEDIT program includes all the functions of VOXKIT, but only works in graphics mode.

To see how VOXKIT works:

1. Go to the SB directory, if necessary.
2. Type

   VOXKIT

   and press Enter.

The VOXKIT Main menu offers the following options:

Record Sample	Lets you record a sample. When you make this choice, VOXKIT gives you the option of sampling at a prechosen rate or changing the sampling rate.

NOTE   The *sampling rate* is the speed at which the program records sound. The higher the speed, the better the quality, but high-speed samples require more memory.

Play Sample	Lets you play a sample you have recorded with the microphone.
Save Sample	Lets you write samples to disk.
Load Sample	Lets you load a sample on disk. Samples are stored in VOC files.

Use Disk	Lets you record the sample directly on a diskette or on the hard disk instead of in internal memory. By storing samples this way, you can create larger (and therefore longer) samples.

PLAYCMF

PLAYCMF plays CMF songs through the 11-voice FM part of the Sound Blaster. CMF stands for *creative music files*. Similar to MIDI files, CMF files are audio files that Creative Labs, the maker of Sound Blaster, invented.

To play PLAYCMF:

1. Switch to the SB or SBPRO directory.

2. Type

   SBFMDRV

   and press Enter to load the SM synthesizer driver.

3. Type

   CD PLAYCMF

   and press Enter to go to the PLAYCMF directory.

4. Type

   PLAYCMF *name*.CMF

   where *name* is the name of the file you want to hear.

NOTE The difference between PLAYCMF and FMORGAN is that PLAYCMF uses all eleven voices, whereas FMORGAN can only play one note at a time and contains a limited number of rhythms and instruments.

Doctor SBAITSO

Doctor Sbaitso demonstrates the voice capabilities of Sound Blaster. The program actually reads the words you enter with your keyboard and responds to them.

To start Doctor Sbaitso:

1. Go to the proper directory and type either

   SBAITSO

   for Sound Blaster or

   SBAITSO2

   for Sound Blaster Pro.

At the beginning the program asks you for your name and for a sentence. After you enter the sentence, the program analyses it and gives an "intelligent" answer. Use the Help command to get information about how to change settings. Use the Exit command to stop the program.

Additional Programs for Sound Blaster Pro

With the exception of VOXKIT, which is found only in Sound Blaster, both Sound Blaster and Sound Blaster Pro come with the programs mentioned above. However, the following programs work only with Sound Blaster Pro.

VEDIT

The VEDIT (or VOC editor) program is only included in Sound Blaster Pro. With it, you can combine samples you have recorded with the VOXKIT. You can also record samples and edit them in several different ways.

To start VEDIT, go to the SBPRO directory and type

VEDIT2

Multimedia Player

Sound Blaster Pro includes a demo that shows the capabilities of the multimedia extension (a combination of graphics and sound). The graphics files are created with *presentation programs*, programs that combine graphics and text. The multimedia manager determines which sound is played with what demo.

To try out the multimedia demo, type

MMDEMO

at the SBPRO directory.

Tetra Compositor Demo

The Tetra Compositor demo plays Noise Tracker music through the Sound Blaster. The Noise Tracker format is a popular one for the Amiga and is used in a lot of demos and games. Music is created by playing samples of musical instruments or other sounds at different frequencies. By playing different samples at the same time and by adding effects to these samples, you can create all kinds of music, from classical to hip-hop and heavy metal. On the Amiga, this takes very little time because the Amiga has four independent channels for voice input and output. The Sound Blaster only contains one channel, so playing this format takes more time.

To try out the Tetra Compositor demo, type

TDEMO

at the SBRPRO directory.

Windows Software

Three Sound Blaster programs can be used with MS-Windows 3.0:

Program	Use
SBMIXER	Controls the volume of different parts on the Sound Blaster card.
JUKEBOX MIDI player	Plays MIDI files on the FM part in the background.
SETUP	Can be used to modify the default settings.

The WINDOWS directory also contains the SOUND.DLL file that is required for these three programs. This file can also be used by other software that is developed for MS-Windows.

CHAPTER

TWO

A Tour of the Sound Blaster Cards

- How sound waves work

- CMS and FM stereo chips

- The Digital Sound Processor for handling digital sound

- The MIDI interface for communication between hardware devices

- Comparing Sound Blaster and Sound Blaster Pro capabilities

The Sound Blaster card is really an amalgamation of five extension cards:

- A CMS Game Blaster card, whose stereo chips can be found on the Sound Blaster card

- An AdLib Music Synthesizer card, whose FM chip (the heart of the AdLib card) is used by the Sound Blaster

- A Digital Sound Processing (DSP) card for working with digital and analog sounds

- A MIDI card for communicating with, among other things, synthesizers

- A joystick card for playing games

This chapter looks at all these functions. It also offers a very basic course in the physics of sound.

The Physics of Sound

Sound is produced by vibrations called *sound waves*. When a sound wave is produced repeatedly and regularly, the sound acquires a fixed pitch, just like a musical note. When a sound wave has an irregular pattern, it has little or no pitch and produces an irregular sound, such as a loud bang or a gurgle.

The *frequency* of a sound is determined by the number of times the sound wave is repeated during a given period. *Pitch* is determined by frequency. As frequency rises, the pitch gets higher. The unit for measuring frequency is called *Hertz* and is abbreviated Hz. Hertz is the number of sound waves per second. A healthy human ear can recognize sounds between 20Hz and 20kHz (about 20,000 vibrations per second).

To get a better understanding of a sound wave and how it works, look at Figure 2.1. This figure shows a chart of a sound wave with a sine curve. In the figure, differences in sound vibrations are plotted. This chart, for example, could represent the sound wave produced by a flute. Whistle into the microphone of an oscilloscope and you will see a wave similar to the one in Figure 2.1.

A sine waveform

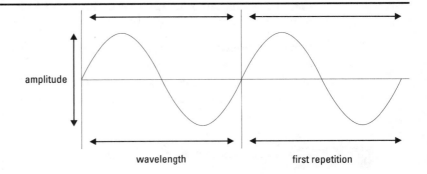

In the figure, the X axis measures the time and the Y axis measures the amplitude in order to gauge the intensity of the sound wave. The higher the amplitude, the louder the sound.

Sound Blaster Functions

The following sections discuss the functions of the Sound Blaster in detail. Because the joystick port is not used for musical applications, these sections describe the CMS, FM, DSP, and MIDI functions only.

NOTE Except for the discussion of CMS stereo chips, the following information about Sound Blaster functions also applies to Sound Blaster Pro. A later section in this chapter, "Sound Blaster Pro Functions," describes Pro functions in detail.

CMS Stereo Chips

The Sound Blaster was not the first sound card developed by Creative Labs. The company's first sound card was the Game Blaster, a card that employed AM (amplitude modulation) synthesis. The Game Blaster card was released in 1987 and was one of the first audio adapter cards for the IBM PC and compatible machines. In terms of sales, this card lost out to the AdLib card and never became popular.

However, Sound Blaster inherited one important element from its Game Blaster prototype—the CMS, or *creative music system,* stereo chip. CMS chips employ AM technology for synthesizing sound. When Sound Blaster 1.0 was introduced, the CMS chips were included. Version 1.5 does not include CMS chips.

NOTE   **Chapter 8 explains how to program CMS chips.**

While CMS chips offer 12 independent voices and a stereo effect, you can not really modify the timbre of the sound with these chips. All you can do is adjust the volume and the frequency. You can adjust the volume of the left and right output of each voice. By making the left and right volume unequal during the reproduction of the sound, you can create a stereo effect.

CMS chips do not have a built-in clock, so you have to program the duration of the notes yourself. Despite the lack of a clock, you can still use the stereo chips in combination with FM music.

Lack of Support for CMS   If you don't have the CMS chips, here are two reasons to purchase some:

- If you are a programmer and you want to support your software with CMS.
- If you have games that support CMS.

However, support for CMS chips is sparse as of the writing of this book. CMS chips were invented to make the Sound Blaster compatible with its prototype, Game Blaster. Because support for CMS chips is lacking, you likely will not need to add them.

FM Chips for Changing Sound Frequency

The *FM* in the FM chips's name stands for *frequency modulation.* With this chip, you can change the frequency of sound by manipulating the sine waves produced by

FM signals. The sound frequency produced by an instrument can be divided into three elements: the pitch, timbre, and amplitude. With the FM chip, you can create your own "instruments" by editing these elements.

NOTE   See Chapter 7 for information about programming the FM chip.

NOTE   Because the AdLib card also supports FM chips, Sound Blaster and AdLib are fully compatible and can be used together.

The FM chip has two settings:

- The 11-voice setting, consisting of 6 voices for FM sound and 5 percussion voices. On each of the 6 voices you can create virtually any instrument you like. The 5 percussion voices represent fixed instruments that can be edited in a limited way.

- The 9-voice FM audio setting. All 9 voices can be used to your liking.

The FM chip can reproduce 11 different instruments with high fidelity at the same time.

The Digital Sound Processor for Handling Digital Sound

In their natural state, sound waves are *analog*. They rise and fall, changing in frequency and amplitude in smooth progressions. Obviously, the computer cannot store sound itself. In order to store sound, the format for the information needs to be changed in order for the computer to store or manipulate it as data in memory. In other words, the information needs to be *digitized*. It needs to be converted into digital numbers that the computer can work with.

ADC   In order to digitize the sound waves, the computer's *analog-to-digital converter* (ADC) samples the sound over and over, each time taking a reading of the sound's volume and pitch. The ADC converts this information to numbers. By doing this over and over, at thousands of times per second, the computer can build up a *sample*—that is, a digital representation—of an analog waveform.

Sampling   During sampling, some information is necessarily lost. Because the ADC cannot sample continuously, small changes in volume or pitch that occur in the periods between samples are not recorded. This is why higher sampling rates make for more accurate readings. The *sampling rate* is the number of times per second the sound wave is read. For example, if a sound wave is read at $\frac{1}{8000}$ of a second, the sampling rate is 8000.

DAC   For the reproduction of a sample, you need a *digital-to-analog converter* (DAC), pronounced "dack." The DAC converts a number to an analog signal, a voltage, and sends this signal to the audio port. First the voltage passes the audio connection, and then it passes an amplifier (if desired). It ends up at the speakers, which convert the voltage to an audible vibration.

The higher the sampling rate, the more carefully the sound wave is read. Figure 2.2 shows the same sample taken at a high sampling rate and at a low sampling rate. As you can see, a low sampling rate mutilates the waveform. The only advantage of low sampling rates is that the samples they produce require less memory to store.

The ADC is for recording and storing analog sounds (the recorder function), and the DAC is for reproducing those recordings. Together they make up the DSP, or *Digital Sound Processor.*

FIGURE 2.2:
Differences in sampling rates

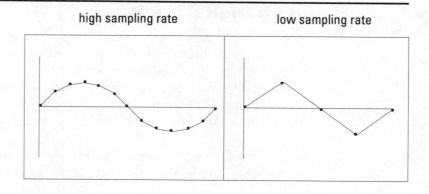

high sampling rate   low sampling rate

NOTE The acronym DSP is normally used to describe a "digital signal processor." Creative Labs' use of the letters DSP to designate its Digital Sound Processor has created some confusion. Be aware of this in your work with Sound Blaster.

MIDI for Communication between Devices

MIDI (Musical Instrument Digital Interface), pronounced "middy," is a serial interface standard for connecting synthesizers, musical instruments, and computers. The MIDI standard helps ensure that music and sound are encoded correctly for communication between devices.

NOTE See Chapter 10 for a thorough discussion of programming with MIDI.

Nowadays most composers work with synthesizers. In fact, for the purposes of composition, the computer and synthesizer have become indispensable. Musicians and composers often own several synthesizers. Before the MIDI standard, manufacturers produced different connections for communication purposes, and synthesizers had trouble communicating. However, the MIDI standard has been adopted world-wide. This is why MIDI is now a central element of almost all music and sound cards—and why Sound Blaster supports the MIDI standard.

WARNING The Sound Blaster cannot transmit and receive data at the same time through its MIDI interface. It can only transmit *or* receive data, unlike the Sound Blaster Pro, which can do both at once.

MIDI Connector Box Module The MIDI Connector Box module can be plugged into the joystick port. It can play 6 MIDI instruments at a time. Five of these 6 MIDI instruments are able to receive all MIDI data. These 5 instruments are called *slaves* because they can only reproduce the received MIDI data. The sixth MIDI instrument, called the *master,* is for use by you.

When the musician plays, the master converts the notes into MIDI codes. The MIDI instrument sends these MIDI codes to the MIDI Connector Box, after which they reach the Sound Blaster.

A MIDI instrument always contains two MIDI ports:

- MIDI In, for receiving MIDI codes
- MIDI Out, for transmitting MIDI codes

The MIDI cables connecting two MIDI devices are also standard: they have 5-pin DIN connectors.

MIDI can also be used to program your synthesizer. For example, with MIDI you can create your own instruments and "play" them with you synthesizer.

Sound Blaster Pro Functions

The chief difference between Sound Blaster and Sound Blaster Pro is that the Pro version provides for stereo sound. Sound Blaster Pro, which includes all the functions found in the Sound Blaster except for CMS stereo chips, offers the following functions as well:

- Two FM chips, which we will call FM *stereo* chips to distinguish them from the mono chip found in Sound Blaster.
- A modified DSP chip. This chip can record and play stereo sound.
- Improvements to the MIDI interface.
- Support for CD-ROM drives.
- Extra connections for line-in input and CD audio. These connections are supported by a mixer that can merge all sounds generated by the card.

In the next sections, we describe these functions in greater detail.

Stereo FM

In order to produce stereo sound, Creative Labs included two identical FM chips on the Pro. One chip is used for the left channel and one chip is used for the right channel. Because the Pro card is fully compatible with the standard Sound Blaster card, the Pro can also operate in mono mode. In mono mode, identical commands and data are transmitted to the left and the right channel. You can, however, change the volume of each channel to produce a semblance of stereo sound.

With the two FM stereo chips, 9 different instruments can be defined on both the left and the right channel, making a total of 18 instruments. In the 11-voice FM audio setting, each voice can hold 6 instruments as well as 5 percussion instruments. Therefore, the left and the right channels can produce 22 instruments in all.

With stereo sound, you have many capabilities unavailable with mono sound. For example, you can make the sound of a racing car or make unusual "pings" and "dings" to show directional movements in a maze game.

Pro's Stereo Digital Sound Processor

The Sound Blaster Pro uses a more advanced DSP chip than the Sound Blaster does. Pro's chip is capable of recording stereo sound and reproducing stereo samples. While this improvement is welcome, it does tax memory resources. During sampling, the Pro reads or reproduces one byte for the left channel and one byte for the right channel, so twice as much memory space is needed.

The standard Sound Blaster has a limited sampling rate of 13kHz for recording and 23kHz for reproducing sound. The sampling rate, in mono mode, of the Pro for both recording and reproducing sound has been increased to 44kHz. The stereo mode has a maximum sampling rate of 22kHz; half the rate of the mono mode.

Pro's MIDI Capabilities

With its MIDI interface, the Sound Blaster can read or transmit a signal originating from an external MIDI device. However, unlike Sound Blaster Pro, Sound Blaster cannot read and transmit at the same time. In this regard, the Sound Blaster can be described as a *half-duplex* device. (This term, often used to describe modems, refers to devices that cannot transmit and receive data at the same time.) An interface is called *full-duplex* if it can send and receive data at the same time.

Full-Duplex Device   The MIDI interface in the Sound Blaster Pro is full-duplex. You no longer have to switch between the read mode and the write mode of the MIDI interface. This is a blessing for the programmer and gives the Pro more professional capabilities.

Furthermore, the Pro comes with the MIDI time-stamp protocol. Thanks to this protocol, external devices that are connected to a MIDI network can be synchronized. In other words, a program can tell a connected MIDI device when it has to execute a certain instruction. For example, during a concert, the time-stamp protocol could switch on a spotlight at the same time the keyboard player plays the first note of the third song. This is a very powerful function, especially as it applies to multimedia.

CD-ROMs and the Pro

CD-ROM drives for personal computers have been around for some time, but only in the last couple of years has the price of CD-ROMs come down far enough for the average user to consider buying one.

More and more manufacturers are producing CD-ROM drives, which is bringing prices down. Moreover, games manufacturers such as Sierra and LucasArts are starting to release games on CD-ROM. If you don't have a CD-ROM and you are a serious games player, you by all means need to get one.

A CD-ROM (the name is an acronym for *Compact Disk-Read Only Memory*) works with compact disks (CDs). These disks can store as much as 552MB of data. A CD cannot be written to. The contents of a CD are read-only memory.

Specifications for Using CD-ROMs with Pro   The CD-ROM drive you connect to the Sound Blaster Pro must have the following hardware characteristics:

- It must be able to play audio CDs.
- It has to meet the High Sierra standard for CD-ROM drives. (This standard was named after the hotel where the people who developed it stayed, not after the superb movie starring Humphrey Bogart.)

- It needs a connector that can be plugged into the CD-ROM interface of the Pro. Unfortunately, this is a proprietary interface developed exclusively for Creative Labs CD-ROM drives. This is not a SCSI interface. Call Creative Labs for further information.

- It needs a 4-pin audio connector that can be plugged into the CD Audio In of the Pro.

- It has to be accompanied by drivers (programs) so the CD-ROM drive can be read.

CD-ROM is destined to play a very significant role in what is likely to be the foremost learning and entertainment phenomenon of the future, multimedia. Multimedia combines images, sounds, information, and interactive programs to create an all-out info-assault on the user. Multimedia is sure to generate large files, and these files will have to be stored in CD-ROM drives.

CHAPTER

THREE

Making Music with Sound Blaster

- The CDMS Composer

- The Visual Composer

- The Voice Editor (Vedit)

- Sequencer Plus Junior

Besides playing games, making music is one of the most popular pastimes with Sound Blaster. In fact, much of Sound Blaster's popularity comes from the fact that, of all the sound cards, Sound Blaster is the one most suitable for making music. The Sound Blaster breaks all the barriers inherent in the small PC speaker. It adds a dose of realism to your games and lets you hear the type of soundtrack music you would expect from a movie. When you play games, you can hear explosions as the sheriff gets shot down on Main Street. You can hear the funeral dirge playing as they carry him off to the undertaker's.

But Sound Blaster is more than just a great toy. Thanks to the FM and MIDI support, you can compose serious music at home. One result of Sound Blaster's success is that more and more music programs are being released that support the Sound Blaster card. Sound Blaster is here to stay.

This chapter explains some of the most important aspects of creating music with Sound Blaster. It also describes a few of the programs for creating music. Composing your own songs is much more fun than listening to prerecorded music. Fortunately, because the Sound Blaster includes CMS chips, the FM synthesizer, the DSP chip, and MIDI connections, you have a lot of possibilities for experimenting with sound. For each of these music sources—CMS, FM, DSP, and MIDI—there are many software programs you can use. The four covered in this chapter are:

- the CDMS Composer for CMS
- the Visual Composer for FM
- Vedit for DSP
- Sequencer Plus Junior for MIDI

The following sections look at each of these composers to show you what they can do.

CDMS Composer

With most software composers, you enter the notes with the mouse or with menu commands, but CDMS (Creative Digital Musical Score) lets you enter notes with a text editor. You can use any editor or word processor that exports ASCII files. With CDMS, which was developed by Creative Labs, you can use a text editor of your choice. All the notes and notations that can be placed on a standard music staff—including clefs, flats, sharps, quarter notes, and rests—can be entered with the text editor and translated directly into CDMS language.

NOTE If you want to use the CDMS Composer with the Sound Blaster, make sure the CMS stereo chips are installed on the Sound Blaster and that CMSDRV.COM has been loaded. This program is found on the master disk that accompanies Sound Blaster.

CDMS Composer was originally developed by Creative Labs to accompany its Game Blaster card. The CDMS Composer makes use of the CMS stereo chips that are present on the Game Blaster and on early versions of Sound Blaster.

NOTE See "CMS Stereo Chips" in Chapter 2 for further information about these chips.

CDMS Composer Notation

CDMS Composer has its own unique notation system. The CDMS notations are modeled after real music notations.

Dot Commands for General Information   You can place dot commands at the top of a file to provide general information. Information following a dot command is not read by the program as a musical notation. CDMS uses the following dot commands:

Dot Command	Use
.TITLE	Indicates the title of the song. Song titles can be up to 32 characters long.
.COMPOSER	Indicates the name of the person who wrote the song.

Dot Command	Use
.MESSAGE	Lets you enter a message to the reader.
.LINE5	Changes modes so you can enter notes as letters (the traditional way) instead of numbers. Normally, you enter notes as numbers. As you would expect, the eight letters are c, d, e, f, g, a, b and 0. The 0 signifies a rest.

Code Sample   To give you an idea of what a song looks like, consider the following two code examples. The first is in normal mode (with the notes entered as numbers), and the second is in LINE5 mode, with the notes entered as letters.

In normal mode:

```
m1 ¦ [1=C]   1 2 3 4 ¦ 5 6 7 +1 ¦
m2 ¦ _       7 1 2 3 ¦4 5 6 7    ¦
```

In LINE5 mode:

```
.LINE5
m1 ¦ [1=C]   c d e f ¦ g a b +c ¦
m2 ¦ _       b c d e ¦ f g a b   ¦
```

Notes   CDMS recognizes eight notes and a rest. In normal mode, notes are numbered, but in LINE5 mode you can use normal musical notation, with letters. The following list shows the musical notes and their corresponding numbers:

Note	Number
C	1
D	2
E	3
F	4
G	5
A	6

Note	Number
B	7
rest	0

Sharps and flats are entered with the pound sign (#) and at sign (@) respectively. These symbols are placed before the notes, like so:

#G @A @B

Voices   The CMS chips offer twelve voices. You can define a different instrument for each voice. In CDMS language, voices are numbered m1 through m12, as shown in the code sample above. Voices are placed one below the other on lines, with each line containing no more than six measures.

Clef Notation   At the beginning of song comes a clef notation, which is marked with 1= in brackets. In the above example, the C clef was used, and the notation read [1=C]. Other possible clefs are:

A, B, C, D, E, F, G

#A, #B, #C, #D, #E, #F, #G

@A, @B, @C, @D, @E, @F, @G

A keyboard is divided into seven octaves indicated by the letters A to G, with A being the lowest octave and G the highest.

Measures   In CDMS language, measures are separated by a vertical sign (¦). Measures must all be the same size. In the above example, each measure comprised four beats. Each line can contain six measures.

Table 3.1 shows the various notations you use in CDMS Composer.

To give you an idea of what CDMS Composer files look like and how they function, following are two example files. Listing 3.1 demonstrates converting an .ABC file into a .CMS file. The example consists of the DANCE.ABC file, the accompanying TANGO1.BCD file, and the compilation of these two files into a .THM file, the DANCE.THM file, and the final compilation of this .THM file to a .CMS file.

Listing 3.2 shows the song SPRING.THM. This example is included because it includes many different tricks.

TABLE 3.1: Notations Used in CDMS Composer

Notation	Use
+	Indicates that the note should be played one octave higher.*
_	Indicates that the note should be played one octave lower.*
/	If a note is less than one beat, divides the note into two. For example, in $\frac{4}{4}$ time an eighth note would be entered as 1/, and a sixteenth note would be written as 1//. (A quarter note would be written simply as 1.) The slash can also serve to keep a group of notes together. For example, in $\frac{4}{4}$ time, 1234// indicates four quarter notes comprising a measure.
--	Enters a whole note. For example, in $\frac{4}{4}$ time, a whole note comprises four beats and is written as 1--.
^	Indicates a slur. The ^ should be placed in front of the last note.
%	When placed inside a measure, indicates that the measure doesn't take a time signature but contains parameters only. This notation is used when a lot of parameters have to be added at once. If you use this parameter, all voices have to be preceded by this measure.
T	Indicates triplets. For example, in $\frac{4}{4}$ time, 123T// is a triplet comprising three notes of half a beat each.
[s=..]	Indicates an instrument selection.
[t=..]	Indicates the time signature. The default is 4/4, with four beats to the measure and the quarter note equaling one beat. Other available time signatures are 1/4, 2/4, 3/4, 4/4, 3/8, 6/8, and 9/8.
[v=..]	Determines the volume level.
[x=..]	Selects the output for the stereo effect, where = L is for the left, = R is for right, and = B is for both.

* If you are entering these symbols before sharps or flats, place the + or the _ in front of the # and @ symbols.

Listing 3.1: Compiling a .CMS File

```
{ dance.abc }
;
.copy m1-m3
m1 ¦ [t=2/4,s=120,1=C,r=tango1] D 5+111 / ¦ _76/ 5 ¦ 5+222/ ¦ 32/ 1 ¦
AA ¦                               C         ¦ G        ¦           ¦ C      ¦
m1 ¦ _5+111/ ¦ _76/ 5 ¦ 5567/ ¦ +11/ 1 ¦
AA ¦ C       ¦ G      ¦ Gs     ¦ C       ¦
m1 ¦ 1555/ ¦ 65/ 4 ¦ 4566/ ¦ 54/ 5 ¦
AA ¦       ¦ F     ¦        ¦ Gs     ¦
```

```
m1 ¦  2555/  ¦43/ 2   ¦  5./4// 32/  ¦ 1 1 ¦
AA ¦ G       ¦ Gs      ¦ G           ¦ C   ¦
{ tango1.bcd }
; Tango Rhythm  - variation #1
B ¦[p=3]C 1   5   1   5   ¦ 11/  05/  1   5   ¦
C ¦ [p=4,v=180] z0z0/ z0zz/  ¦  zz0z/ z0z0/    ¦
R ¦ [v=180] xxyx/ xx/ xy/¦ x0/ x0/ x0/ x0/¦
{ compile dance.abc }
Creative CMS Auto Bass Chord Generator Version 3.00
Copyright (c) Creative Music Lab., 1987. All rights reserved.
Reading DANCE.ABC... Line # 12345678910111213 1415
  Auto bass/chord TANGO1.BCD
Job done.
{ dance.thm }
;
M1¦ [t=2/4,2=120,1=C,r=tango1]  D 5+111/  ¦ _76/ 5 ¦ 5+222/ ¦ 32/ 1 ¦
M2¦                             D 5+111/  ¦ _76/ 5 ¦ 5+222/ ¦ 32/ 1 ¦
M3¦                             D 5+111/  ¦ _76/ 5 ¦ 5+222/ ¦ 32/ 1 ¦
M6¦[p=4,v=180]%¦ 1010/ ¦ 5505/ ¦ 5050/ ¦ 1101/ ¦
M7¦[p=4,v=180]%¦ 3030/ ¦ 7707/ ¦ 7070/ ¦ 3303/ ¦
M8¦[p=4,v=180]%¦ 5050/ ¦ +2202/ ¦ 2020/ ¦ _5505 ¦
M9¦[p=4,v=180]%¦ +1010/ ¦ 5505/ ¦ 5050/ ¦ 1101/ ¦
M10¦[v=180]%¦ xxyx/ ¦ x0x0/ ¦ xxyx/ ¦ x0x0/ ¦
M11¦[p=3]%¦C_15¦ 550+2/ ¦C_5+2¦ _1105/ ¦
M12¦[p=3]%¦C15¦ 550+2/ ¦C_5+2¦ _1105/ ¦
M1¦ _5+111/ ¦ -76/ 5 ¦ 5567/ ¦ +11/ 1 ¦
M2¦ _5+111/ ¦ -76/ 5 ¦ 5567/ ¦ +11/ 1 ¦
M3¦ _5+111/ ¦ -76/ 5 ¦ 5567/ ¦ +11/ 1 ¦
M6¦ 1010/ ¦ 5505/ ¦ 5050/ ¦ 1101/ ¦
M7¦ 3030/ ¦ 7707/ ¦ 7070/ ¦ 3303/ ¦
M8¦ 5050/ ¦ +2202/ ¦ 2020/ ¦ _5505 ¦
M9¦ 1010/ ¦ 5505/ ¦ 4040/ ¦ 1101/ ¦
M10¦ xxyx/ ¦ x0x0/ ¦ xxyx/ ¦ x0x0/ ¦
M11¦C_15¦ 550+2/ ¦C_5+2¦ _1105/ ¦
M12¦C15¦ 550+2/ ¦C5+2¦ _1105/ ¦
M1¦ 1555/ ¦ 65/ 4 ¦ 4566/ ¦ 54/ 5 ¦
M2¦ 1555/ ¦ 65/ 4 ¦ 4566/ ¦ 54/ 5 ¦
M3¦ 1555/ ¦ 65/ 4 ¦ 4566/ ¦ 54/ 5 ¦
M6¦ 1010/ ¦ 4404/ ¦ 4040/ ¦ 5505/ ¦
M7¦ 3030/ ¦ 6606/ ¦ 6060/ ¦ 7707/ ¦
M8¦ 5050/ ¦ +1101/ ¦ 1010/ ¦ 2202 ¦
M9¦ 1010/ ¦ 4404/ ¦ 4040/ ¦ 4404/ ¦
M10¦ xxyx/ ¦ x0x0/ ¦ xxyx/ ¦ x0x0/ ¦
M11¦C_15¦ 440+1/ ¦C_4+1¦ _550+2/ ¦
M12¦C15¦ 440+1/ ¦C4+1¦ _550+2/ ¦
```

```
M1¦ 2555/  ¦ 43/ 2  ¦ 5./4//  32/  ¦ 1 1  ¦
M2¦ 2555/  ¦ 43/ 2  ¦ 5./4//  32/  ¦ 1 1  ¦
M3¦ 2555/  ¦ 43/ 2  ¦ 5./4//  32/  ¦ 1 1  ¦
M6¦ 5050/  ¦ 5505/  ¦ 5050/  ¦ 1101/  ¦
M7¦ 7070/  ¦ 7707/  ¦ 7070/  ¦ 3303/  ¦
M8¦ 2020/  ¦ 2202/  ¦ 2020/  ¦ _5505  ¦
M9¦ 5050/  ¦ 4404/  ¦ 5050/  ¦ 1101/  ¦
M10¦ xxyx/  ¦ x0x0/  ¦ xxyx/  ¦ x0x0/  ¦
M11¦C_5+2¦  _550+2/  ¦C_5+2¦  _1105/  ¦
M12¦C5+2¦  _550+2/  ¦C5+2¦  _1105/  ¦
{ compile dance.thm }
Creative CMS Music Composer Version 3.00
Copyright (c) Creative Music Lab., 1987. All rights reserved.
Reading source file DANCE.THM - 46 lines read.
Master Bar: 1234567891011121314151617
Writing CMS file DANCE.CMS...
```

Listing 3.2: The Song of Spring

```
{ spring.thm }
.title SONG OF SPRING
; Enter by Jessie Tan   21st August 1987
.message edited by WH Sim
m1 ¦% [1=A,s=120,p=13,t=2/4 ] ¦
m2 ¦% [p=4 ]¦
m3 ¦% [p=4 ] ¦
m4 ¦% [p=4] ¦
m5 ¦% [p=3] ¦
m1 ¦F 3 ^ 34#45// ¦ +1_5/43/ ¦ 2. 4/ ¦ 6. 4/ ¦
m2 ¦E 3 ^ 34#45// ¦ +1_5/43/ ¦ 2. 4/ ¦ 6. 4/ ¦
m3 ¦D 05/5 ¦ 01/1 ¦ 02/2 ¦ 06/6 ¦
m4 ¦D 03/3 ¦ 0_5/5 ¦ 06/6 ¦ 0+4/4 ¦
m5 ¦C 1 0 ¦ _3 0 ¦ 4 0 ¦ +2 0 ¦
m1 ¦ 2 ^ 2#12#2// ¦ 35/43/ ¦ 21/_7+1/ ¦ 3 2_5/ ¦
m2 ¦ 2 ^ 2#12#2// ¦ 35/43/ ¦ 21/_7+1/ ¦ 3 2_5/ ¦
m3 ¦ 05/5 ¦ 05/5 ¦ 0#4/4 ¦ 05/5 ¦
m4 ¦ 04/4 ¦ 03/3 ¦ 02/2 ¦ 01/_7 ¦
m5 ¦ _7 0 ¦ +1 0 ¦ _6 0 ¦ 5 0 ¦
m1 ¦ +3 ^ 34#45// ¦ +1_5/43/ ¦ 2. 4/ ¦ 6. 5/ ¦
m2 ¦ +3 ^ 34#45// ¦ +1_5/43/ ¦ 2. 4/ ¦ 6. 5/ ¦
m3 ¦ 05/5 ¦ 01/1 ¦ 06/6 ¦ 06/6 ¦
m4 ¦ +03/3 ¦ _05/5 ¦ +02/2 ¦ 03/3 ¦
m5 ¦ +1 0 ¦ _3 0 ¦ 4 0 ¦ #1 0 ¦
m1 ¦ #4~4/32/ ¦ 1_7/+32/ ¦ 2 1_5/ ¦ +5 ^ 5#4~43// ¦
m2 ¦ #4~4/32/ ¦ 1_7/+32/ ¦ 2 1_5/ ¦ +5 ^ 5#4~43// ¦
```

```
m3  |  06/6   |  04/4   |  05/5   |  01/+1  |
m4  |  04/4   |  02/_7  |  +04/3  |_05/5    |
m5  |  2 0   |  5 0   |  +1 0   |  _3 0   |
m1  |  2_7/65/   |  +5 ^ 5#4~43//   |  2_7/65   |  7+1/51/   |
m2  |  2_7/65/   |  +5 ^ 5#4~43//   |  2_7/65   |  7+1/51/   |
m3  |  0_2/2   |  01/1   |  02/2   |  01/1   |
m4  |  05/7   |  05/5   |  05/7   |  05/5   |
m5  |  4 0   |  3 0   |  4 0   |  3 0   |
m1  |  _7.7/   |  6@7/57/   |  6. 6/   |  76/7+1/   |
m2  |  _7.7/   |  6@7/57/   |  6. 6/   |  76/7+1/   |
m3  |  02/2   |  05/@7   |  05/5   |0#4/4   |
m4  |  05/5   |  +05/5   |  03/3   |  02/2   |
m5  |  2 0   |  +2 0   |  #1 0   |  1 0   |
m1  |  2. 2/   |  5432/   |  2 #13/   |  6#432/   |
m2  |  2. 2/   |  5432/   |  2 #13/   |  6#432/   |
m3  |  05/5   |  05/5   |  05/5   |  02/2   |
m4  |  02/2   |  02/2   |  02/2   |  01/1   |
m5  |  _7 0   |  @7 0   |  6 0   |  #4 0   |
m1  |  75#43/   |  2_6/  7/+2///1.//   |  _7. +2/   |  6#432/   |
m2  |  75#43/   |  2_6/  7/+2///1.//   |  _7. +2/   |  6#432/   |
m3  |  02/2   |  01/_6   |  0+2/2   |  02/2   |
m4  |  _07/7   |  04/4   |  07/7   |  +01/1   |
m5  |  5 0   |  2 0   |  5 0   |  #4 0   |
m1  |  75#43/   |  2_6/  +1_#4/   |  5. #5/   |  6. 7/   |
m2  |  75#43/   |  2_6/  +1_#4/   |  5. #5/   |  6. 7/   |
m3  |  020#1/   |  0101/   |  0204/   |  0304/   |
m4  |  _070@7/   |  0#406/   |  070+2/ 0102/   |
m5  |  5050/   |  3030/   |  5050/   |  5050/   |
m1  |  +1.#1/   |  321_6/ 5. #5/   |  6. 7/|
m2  |  +1.#1/   |  321_6/ 5. #5/   |  6. 7/|
m3  |  0503/   |  0101/   |  _57+24/   |  0 4@6/   |
m4  |  030_@7/   |  0#404/   |  57+24/   |  0 4@6/   |
m5  |  5050/   |  2020/   |  5+2/0   |  13/0   |
m1  |  +1. #1/   |  2. 3/   |  4 ^ 4345//   |  6 ^ 6345//   |
m2  |  +1. #1/   |  2. 3/   |  4 ^ 4345//   |  6 ^ 6345//   |
m3  |  0 5@7/   |  0 @7+@2/   |  01/_6   |  0+1/6   |
m4  |  0 5@7/   |  0 @7+@2/   |  01/_6   |  06/4   |
m5  |  35/0   |  46/0   |  6 0   |  4 0   |
m1  |  6 ^ 6#123//   |  4 ^ 4#123//   |  4#123// 4123//   |  4#45#5//7623//   |
m2  |  6 ^ 6#123//   |  4 ^ 4#123//   |  4#123// 4123//   |  4#45#5//7623//   |
m3  |  06/4   |  0@6/4   |  05/0   |  0 0   |
m4  |  04/2   |  04/2   |  04/0   |  0 0   |
m5  |  2 0   |  +1 0   |  _7 0   |  0 0   |
m1  |  54_7+1..32_75//   |  +3 ^ 34#45//   |  +1_543/   |  2. 4/   |
m2  |  54_7+1..32_75//   |  +3 ^ 34#45//   |  +1_543/   |  2. 4/   |
```

```
m3  ¦ 0 0  ¦ 05/5  ¦ 01/1  ¦ 02/2  ¦
m4  ¦ 0 0  ¦ 03/3  ¦ _05/5  ¦ 06/6  ¦
m5  ¦ 0 0  ¦ 1 0  ¦ _3 0  ¦ 4 0  ¦
m1  ¦ 6. 4/  ¦ 2 ^ 2#12#2//  ¦ 3543/  ¦ 21_7+1/  ¦
m2  ¦ 6. 4/  ¦ 2 ^ 2#12#2//  ¦ 3543/  ¦ 21_7+1/  ¦
m3  ¦ 06/6  ¦ 05/5  ¦ 05/5  ¦ 0#4/4  ¦
m4  ¦ +04/4  ¦ 04/4  ¦ 03/3  ¦ 02/2  ¦
m5  ¦ +2 0  ¦ _7 0  ¦ +1 0  ¦ _6 0  ¦
m1  ¦ 3 2_5/  ¦ +3 ^ 34#45//  ¦ +1_543/ 2. 4/  ¦
m2  ¦ 3 2_5/  ¦ +3 ^ 34#45//  ¦ +1_543/ 2. 4/  ¦
m3  ¦ 05/5  ¦ 05/5  ¦ 01/1  ¦ 02/2  ¦
m4  ¦ 01/_7  ¦ +03/3  ¦ _05/5  ¦ 06/6  ¦
m5  ¦ 5 0  ¦ +1 0  ¦ _3 0  ¦ 4 0  ¦
m1  ¦ 6. 4/  ¦ 2. #4/  ¦ 6. 2/  ¦ +1_765/  ¦
m2  ¦ 6. 4/  ¦ 2. #4/  ¦ 6. 2/  ¦ +1_765/  ¦
m3  ¦ 02/2  ¦ 01/1  ¦ 02/2  ¦ 04/4  ¦
m4  ¦ 06/6  ¦ 06/6  ¦ +01/1  ¦ 02/_7  ¦
m5  ¦ 4 0  ¦ #4 0  ¦ 2 0  ¦ 5 0  ¦
m1  ¦ +31_76/  ¦ 52/3/5//4.//  ¦ 3 05/  ¦ +1_765  ¦
m2  ¦ +31_76/  ¦ 52/3/5//4.//  ¦ 3 05/  ¦ +1_765  ¦
m3  ¦ 03/3  ¦ 04/2  ¦ 01/1  ¦ 04/4  ¦
m4  ¦ +01/1  ¦ _07/7  ¦ 05/5  ¦ +02/2  ¦
m5  ¦ 5 0  ¦ 5 0  ¦ 1 0  ¦ 5 0  ¦
m1  ¦ +31_76/  ¦ 524_7/  ¦ +1. #1/  ¦ 2. 3/  ¦
m2  ¦ +31_76/  ¦ 524_7/  ¦ +1. #1/  ¦ 2. 3/  ¦
m3  ¦ 0101@3/  ¦ 0204/  ¦ 030@7/  ¦ 060@7/  ¦
m4  ¦ _050+1/  ¦ 0_70+2/  ¦ 0305/  ¦ 0405/  ¦
m5  ¦ 3 #4/  ¦ 5 5  ¦ +1 1  ¦ 1 1  ¦
m1  ¦ 4. #4/ 6542/  ¦ 1. #1  ¦ 2. 3/  ¦
m2  ¦ 4. #4/ 6542/  ¦ 1. #1  ¦ 2. 3/  ¦
m3  ¦ 0606/  ¦ 0204/  ¦ 0503/  ¦ 0205/  ¦
m4  ¦ 040@3/  ¦ 0_70+2/  ¦ 030_@7/  ¦ 060+@2/  ¦
m5  ¦ 1 1  ¦ _5 5  ¦ +1 _5  ¦ 4 @7  ¦
m1  ¦ 4. #4/  ¦ 6542/  ¦ 135+1/  ¦ _7542/  ¦
m2  ¦ 4. #4/  ¦ 6542/  ¦ 135+1/  ¦ _7542/  ¦
m3  ¦ 0406/  ¦ 0204/  ¦ 05/5  ¦ 04/2  ¦
m4  ¦ 010@3/  ¦ 0_707/ +03/3  ¦ _07/7  ¦
m5  ¦ 6 +1  ¦ _5 5  ¦ +1 0  ¦ _5 0  ¦
m1  ¦ 135+1/  ¦_ 7542/  ¦ 3 ^ 34#45//  ¦ +1 _02#23//  ¦
m2  ¦ 135+1/  ¦_ 7542/  ¦ 3 ^ 34#45//  ¦ +1 _02#23//  ¦
m3  ¦ 05/5  ¦ 04/2  ¦ 05/5  ¦ 05/5  ¦
m4  ¦ +03/3  ¦ _07/7  ¦ +03/3  ¦ 03/3  ¦
m5  ¦ +1 0  ¦ _5 0  ¦ +1 0  ¦ 1 0  ¦
m1  ¦ 5 0_67+1//  ¦ 3 0_4#45//  ¦ +1_35+1/  ¦ 35+13/  ¦
m2  ¦ 5 0_67+1//  ¦ 3 0_4#45//  ¦ +1_35+1/  ¦ 35+13/  ¦
```

```
m3 ┊ 05/5 ┊ 05/3 ┊ _0535/ ┊ +0535/ ┊
m4 ┊ 03/3 ┊ 03/3 ┊ _0535/ ┊ +0535/ ┊
m5 ┊ 1 0 ┊ 1 0 ┊ _1 0 ┊ +1 0 ┊
m1 ┊ 5010/ ┊ 10/ 0 ┊
m2 ┊ 5010/ ┊ 10/ 0 ┊
m3 ┊ 3050/ ┊ 50/0 ┊
m4 ┊ 3050/ ┊ 30/0 ┊
m5 ┊ 0 10/ ┊ 10/0 ┊
```

Visual Composer

Each composer described in this chapter makes use of specific hardware in the Sound Blaster card. Visual Composer, which was written by the creators of the Ad-Lib card, makes use of the FM chip. The program is rather old, but Sound Blaster aficionados seem to be quite satisfied with it. New versions have never been released, nor have programs similar to Visual Composer appeared on the market yet.

The program has only one screen and a handful of pull-down menus. Personally, we like this because it means never having to switch screens. Because Visual Composer is graphically oriented, a mouse is indispensable.

The Visual Composer Screen

As shown in Figure 3.1, the screen is composed of a large "drawing sheet" similar to the piano-rolls found in player pianos. On the left side of the drawing sheet is a vertical keyboard. The horizontal lines in the sheet correspond to the black keys on the keyboard. Each continuous vertical line marks the start of a measure. Dotted horizontal lines in the measures mark the beat.

There are more keys on the keyboard than can be shown on screen. To see more keys, use the vertical scroll bar on the right side of the sheet to scroll up and down. With the horizontal scroll bar at the bottom of the screen you can scroll the sheet to the left or right.

Figure 3.2 shows the Visual Composer drawing screen after a musical composition has been entered. Now the screen is really looking like a piano roll! The rectangles on the screen mark where notes are to be played. Notice that each rectangle lines

FIGURE 3.1:

The Visual Composer screen

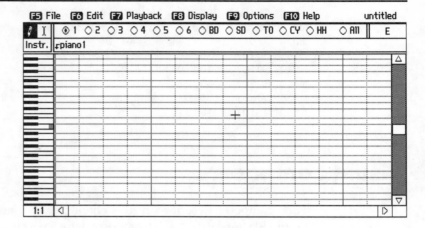

FIGURE 3.2:

The Visual Composer with a musical
composition entered

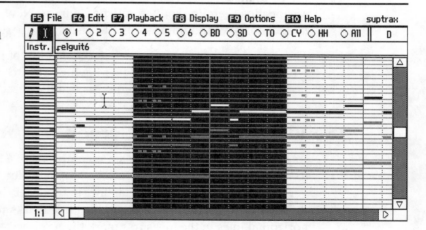

up with a keyboard position. Horizontally, the note is measured in time: each note
"occupies" one or more beats or measures.

Composing Music

Because Visual Composer takes advantage of the FM chip, you can enter several
different instruments on the sheet. The second row on the screen—right below the
main menu options—lists all the instruments with a number or a two-letter code.

The two letter codes representing percussion instruments are:

BD	Bass drum
DB	Snare drum
TO	Tom-tom
CY	Cymbals
HH	High hat

You can select one instrument at a time or all the instruments at once with the All option on the right side of the second row.

In the drawing sheet you always edit one instrument at a time. Once you've selected an instrument, the notes of the other instruments on the sheet are grayed to tell you that they cannot be changed. By placing a black rectangle on top of a gray one, you can have more than one instrument play the same note. In fact, you can make eleven instruments play the same note or notes if you want to.

Selecting Instruments and Entering Notes   Notice the pen and the hook on the left side of the second line on screen. Select the pen to enter notes in the sheet. When you select the pen, the mouse pointer on the sheet changes into a cross-hair. You place a note or a series of notes on the sheet by pressing the left mouse button.

Select the hook to change to cut and paste mode. When the mouse pointer changes into a hook, select a block by pressing and holding down the mouse button and moving the mouse to the left or to the right. The black notes will be selected. If you also want to select the gray notes in the block, select All (all instruments) before performing the cut and paste.

Menu Options

Following is a brief description of the various options on the pull-down menus.

File Menu   The File menu offers the following options:

Option	Use
New	Deletes the current song from memory so you can start a new composition.
Open	Lets you select a file that is loaded in memory.
Save	Lets you store a song with the current name on disk.
Save As	Lets you save the file under a name you choose. Choose this option the first time you save the file.
Revert	Restores the song to the way it was before you loaded it. Choose this option when you don't like a change you made in a song.
Instrument Bank File	Lets you select the file that contains the instruments. This file usually has the extension .BNK.
Quit	Leaves Visual Composer and returns you to DOS.

Edit Menu   The Edit menu has the following options:

Option	Use
Copy	Copies the selected block to a buffer.
Cut	Removes the selected block and places it in a buffer. The notes to the right of the block move to the left.
Paste	Inserts the contents of the buffer at the position of the mouse pointer.
Clear	Deletes the contents of a selected block.
Semitone Up	Raises the notes of a selected block by a semitone.
Semitone Down	Lowers the notes of a selected block by a semitone.

Option	Use
Octave Up	Raises the notes of a selected block by one octave.
Octave Down	Lowers the notes of a selected block by one octave.

Playback Menu   Following are the options presented on the Playback menu:

Option	Use
Play	Plays the song with all instruments.
Play Voice	Plays the song with one selected instrument.
Interrupt	Stops playing the song.
Basic Tempo	Sets the number of beats per minute. The BPM (beats per measure) in the Display menu determines the tempo.

Display Menu   Here are the Display menu options:

Option	Menu
Tempo	Lets you set the tempo of the song.
Instrument	Lets you change instruments.
Volume	Sets the volume of the song.
Pitch Accuracy	Sets the pitch of the song.
Large Grid	Changes the screen to a large drawing sheet with big notes.
Medium Grid	Changes to a medium drawing sheet.
Small Grid	Changes to a small drawing sheet with a lot of notes in one sheet.
Ticks per Beat	Sets the number of ticks per beat.
Beats per Measure	Sets the number of beats per measure.

Options Menu   The Options menu gives you these choices:

Option	Use
With Percussion	Selects the 11-voice mode.
Without Percussion	Selects the 9-voice mode.
Audio Feedback	When enabled, lets you hear each note you enter in the sheet.
MIDI Input	Switches from normal input of notes to MIDI input of notes.

Vedit

Creative Labs' Vedit, also called the Voice Editor, is an all-purpose recording and editing program. The program makes use of the DSP chip. With Vedit you can record analog sounds and store them digitally. With the sample in digital form, you can cut and paste it for use elsewhere. You can also fill and echo the digital sample. Vedit provides many options for enhancing samples.

NOTE   Sound Blaster Pro's version of Vedit is called Vedit2. For the most part, the following discussion of Vedit also applies to Vedit2.

The program is graphics based. To make option selections, you use a mouse and pull-down menus. Key combinations are also available. Once you have pulled down a menu, press Alt and the underlined letter in the menu to activate an option.

Recording, Playing, and Editing Samples

As soon as you run Vedit, you see the main menu. This menu consists of five pull-down menus: File, Record, Play, Pack, and Edit, as shown in Figure 3.3.

FIGURE 3.3:

The Vedit main menu

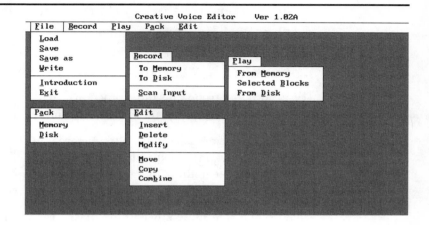

Loading and Saving Samples

With the File menu you can load and save samples. The File menu offers these options:

Option	Use
Load	Loads a sample from disk. After you select this option, you'll see a File Directory screen with a list of .VOC files. When you select a file, the Block Information screen appears with the file's blocks. From here you can delete, move, play, or modify them.

NOTE   The .VOC format is discussed in greater detail in Chapter 9.

Save	Writes a previously loaded sample to the same file.
Save as	Performs the same function as Save, except that you can enter a different name for the file.
Write	Writes a selected block from a sample to the disk.

| Introduction | Displays information about the author. |
| Exit | Returns you to DOS. |

Recording a Sample

The Record menu contains three functions: To Memory, To Disk, and Scan Input. As the menu names imply, you can record sound to memory or to disk.

You can select the Scan Input option before you start recording to check if the microphone input of the Sound Blaster actually receives a signal. If no signal is received, you'll see nothing but a straight line in the Input window, but if a signal is being received the window displays a waveform, as in Figure 3.4.

Once you've determined that Sound Blaster is receiving a signal, select To Memory or To Disk to start recording the signal. Sound Blaster will ask you to enter a sampling rate before the recording can begin. If you select To Disk you also have to enter a name for the file.

**TIP** Use high sampling rates for music. For voices, use low sampling rates. Remember that the higher the sampling rate, the more memory is used.

FIGURE 3.4:

The Scan Input screen

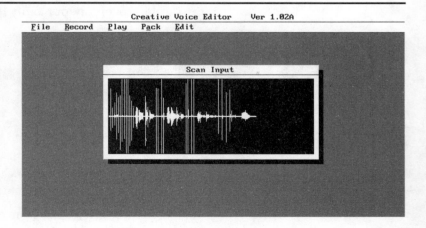

If everything works correctly and you are able to load the sample, you should see a window showing the different blocks in the sample. Such a window is shown in Figure 3.5. As the figure shows, a sample always ends with a *terminator block*.

You can select blocks with the mouse and perform operations on the blocks. For example, by selecting blocks and choosing the Selected Blocks option on the Play menu, you can play selected blocks only.

- To select an active block, press the left mouse button once. The active block is always highlighted.

- To select several blocks at once, press and hold down the mouse button. Selected blocks appear in outline.

Playing Samples

You can play the blocks you've selected. The Selected Blocks option on the Play menu, for example, allows you to play only the selected blocks. From the Play menu you can also play an entire sample from memory (with the From Memory option) or play a sample from disk (with the From Disk option).

FIGURE 3.5:

Block information with a sample loaded

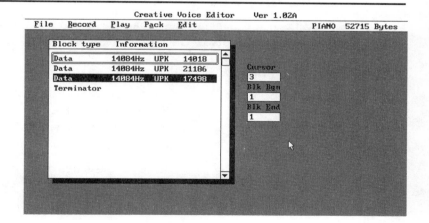

Conserving Disk Space with the Pack Options

Samples can take up a lot of disk space, so Vedit includes a Pack menu for "packing" blocks together and saving disk space. *Packing* is when two, three, or four successive sample values are compressed into one value. Packing can reduce the size of a file by as much as two-thirds. Vedit offers two choices on its Pack menu:

- *Memory* packs the digital audio stored in memory.
- *Disk* packs the digital audio stored on disk files.

There are two types of packing, *silence block packing* and *data block packing*. With silence block packing, the silence between words or notes is compressed. In data block packing, the files are simply compressed.

WARNING There are some tradeoffs involved in packing audio files. The sound quality can suffer, and you cannot edit packed files.

Editing Recorded Samples

Edit is the last menu on the main menu bar. This menu is where the real cutting and pasting takes place. The Edit menu offers the following functions:

Option	Use
Insert	Lets you place silence, marker, ASCII, or repeat blocks in front of the active block in the Block Information window (see Figure 3.5). These blocks are explained below.
Delete	Removes the active block from the sample.
Modify	Opens the Modify menu so you can change the waveform of the sample. The options on the Modify menu are explained below.
Move	Places the selected blocks in front of the active blocks.

Option	Use
Copy	Copies the selected blocks after the active block.
Combine	Merges the selected blocks to one block. The blocks are pasted together, not mixed.

Types of Blocks   Four types of blocks can be inserted in front of the active block in the Block Information window:

- A *silence block* is a period of silence. By replacing low levels of sound with a silence block, you can conserve disk space.

- An *ASCII block* is simply ASCII text. Insert an ASCII block for documentation purposes to label a sound block.

- A *repeat block* duplicates a sample block or several sample blocks that you've selected.

- A *marker block* is used for the handling of animation in multimedia presentations. The Multimedia Player can read these blocks and uses them to synchronize sound and animation.

Selecting a Data Block   Selecting Modify on the Edit menu brings up an Editing screen similar to the one in Figure 3.6. With this screen, you can select a data block and edit it. To select and edit a data block:

1. Move the mouse arrow to the desired position in the waveform.

2. Press the left mouse button. A vertical line appears.

3. To select a data block, press and hold down the mouse button, and release it at the position where you want to place the end of the block.

Editing a Data Block   Now that you have selected the data block, it is time to edit it. Notice the Play button and the Zoom bar on the Editing screen (see Figure 3.6):

- Play plays the waveform.

- Zoom zooms in on the waveform when the bar is moved to the left and zooms out when the bar is moved to the right.

Use these tools to view and play the waveform as you edit it.

FIGURE 3.6:

Editing a data block

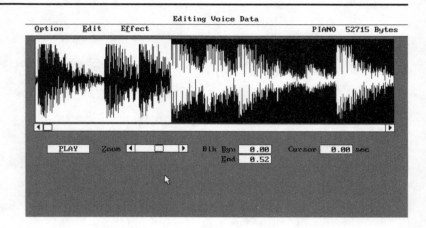

To help you edit the waveform, the Editing screen has three menus on its menu bar: Option, Edit, and Effect.

The Option menu offers three choices:

Option	Use
Split block	Divides the waveform into two blocks at the position of the pointer.
Edit Sampling Rate	Allows you to enter a different sampling rate.
Exit	Returns you to the main menu.

The Edit menu offers the following choices:

Option	Use
Save	Writes a selected data block to a file.
Cut	Removes a selected block from the waveform and places it in a buffer so you can paste it elsewhere.
Paste	Inserts the contents of the buffer at the pointer position.
Fill	Fills a selected data block with one value.

Option	Use
Insert	Works the same as Fill but fills the block with the value the pointer indicates in the waveform.

The Effect menu, an amusing one, offers the following choices:

Option	Use
Amplify	Lets you amplify the block and thereby make it louder and more robust. When you choose this option, a small dialog box appears for entering the percentage by which you want to amplify the block. Fifty percent lowers the amplitude by half; 200 percent doubles the amplitude.

WARNING   Amplifying voice recordings too much can cause distortion.

Echo	Allows you to create echo sounds. When you select this option, a small dialog box appears for entering two parameters, Percentage and Delay, as shown in Figure 3.7. The first parameter is the volume of the echo and the second parameter is the time that has to pass before a new echo starts.

Sequencer Plus Junior

Sequencer Plus Junior (SpJr), which was created by Voyetra, is a software MIDI *sequencer*. The program can record, arrange, manipulate, and reproduce MIDI data. More comprehensive versions of SpJr, called Sequencer Plus and Sequencer Plus Gold, are also available. Sequencer Plus Junior is covered here because it accompanies the Sound Blaster MIDI Kit.

FIGURE 3.7:
Creating an echo effect

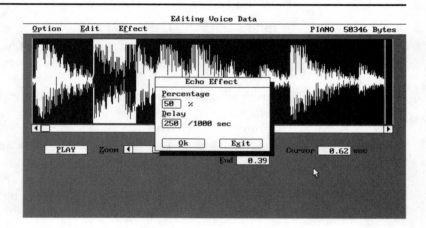

NOTE For a detailed discussion of MIDI, see Chapter 10.

If you want to play bass and percussion at the same time on one keyboard, you are in trouble. You could resolve this problem with a few tricks, but if you also want to play the piano, tricks won't work. With sequencers, playing several instruments at once is no longer a problem. SpJr contains 64 music tracks. These tracks are similar to the tracks found on a multitrack audio tape: on each track of an audio tape you can record an instrument, and the same is true of a sequencer track. With a MIDI instrument you can record a different sound on each track.

However, a MIDI instrument only has sixteen channels. It can send and receive no more than sixteen sounds at the same time. So why the 64 tracks in Sequencer Plus Junior? Here's why: Track 1 to 4 are assigned to MIDI channel 1, for example. Track 1 contains a bass, track 2 a snare drum, track 3 a low tom-tom and track 4 cymbals. Since one second is divided into four (or more) pieces, by assigning the first piece to track 1, the second piece to track 2, etc., you can play 1 MIDI channel with four tracks. If you do this to every MIDI channel, you will use all 64 tracks.

The Main Screen

After starting SpJr, you see a screen similar to the one in Figure 3.8. Notice the menu options at the bottom of the screen. Notice, on the right side, the track numbers and instrument names. Next to the tracks are the different options you can assign.

The status bar at the top shows the name of the song and other general information:

- BPM (beats per minute) is the tempo of the song. The tempo can range from 16 to 255 BPM.
- MIDI IN or OUT refers to the MIDI status.
- REC appears when a recording is being made.

To record, press R. The status bar should show the letters REC. For a recording to start, MIDI must be set to IN. With these conditions met, you can play the MIDI instrument and fill the selected track with MIDI data.

Apart from the main menu the program contains four other menus: Edit, Files, Options, View.

Options Menu   The Options menu, shown in Figure 3.9, offers the following options:

Options	Use
Metronome	Lets you hear the beats of the tempo through your PC's internal speaker. The Metronome can be a useful accompaniment when you're playing a MIDI instrument.
Lead-In	Indicates the number of measures that SpJr counts before playing or recording.
TS (Time Signal)	Indicates how the tracks should be synchronized so they play and record simultaneously.
MIDI	Indicates whether the accessories that may be connected to the MIDI instrument have to be dealt with.

FIGURE 3.8:

The main screen of Sequencer Plus Junior

```
Song BRAND1AD                                    STOP    Mem 221648
Tk  2 ------------------- BPM  90  MIDI:IN        1:0   THRU:OFF

Trk Name                 Port Chan Prg  Transpose  Quantize  Loop   Mute
  1 TRUMPET                 3   5   37   0: 5↑       ---      ---    ----
  2 -------------------     1   1    2   -----       ---      ---    MUTE
  3 FLUTE                   2   5    4   -----       ---      ---    ----
  4 OBOE                    3   4   21   -----       ---      ---    ----
  5 -------------------     1   1    2   -----       ---      ---    MUTE
  6 VIOLIN SOLO             2   4   40   -----       ---      ---    ----
  7 -------------------     1   1    2   -----       ---      ---    MUTE
  8 VIOLIN I                3   3   10   -----       ---      ---    ----
  9 VIOLIN II               2   3    2   -----       ---      ---    ----
 10 VIOLA                   3   2   11   -----       ---      ---    ----
 11 VIOLONE                 2   2    3   -----       ---      ---    ----
 12 CELLO                   3   1    3   1: 0↓       ---      ---    ----
 13 -------------------     1   1    2   -----       ---      ---    MUTE
 14 HARPSICHORD             2   1   17   -----       ---      ---    ----
 15 harp (double)           3   6   17   -----       ---      ---    ----
 16 -------------------     1   1    2   -----       ---      ---    ----
 17 -------------------     1   1    2   -----       ---      ---    ----
 18 -------------------     1   1    2   -----       ---      ---    ----
 19 -------------------     1   1    2   -----       ---      ---    ----
 20 -------------------     1   1    2   -----       ---      ---    ----
 21 -------------------     1   1    2   -----       ---      ---    ----
 22 -------------------     1   1    2   -----       ---      ---    ----
 23 -------------------     1   1    2   -----       ---      ---    ----
 24 -------------------     1   1    2   -----       ---      ---    ----
 25 -------------------     1   1    2   -----       ---      ---    ----
 26 -------------------     1   1    2   -----       ---      ---    ----
 27 -------------------     1   1    2   -----       ---      ---    ----
 28 -------------------     1   1    2   -----       ---      ---    ----
 29 -------------------     1   1    2   -----       ---      ---    ----
 30 -------------------     1   1    2   -----       ---      ---    ----
 31 -------------------     1   1    2   -----       ---      ---    ----
 32 -------------------     1   1    2   -----       ---      ---    ----
 33 -------------------     1   1    2   -----       ---      ---    ----
 34 -------------------     1   1    2   -----       ---      ---    ----
 35 -------------------     1   1    2   -----       ---      ---    ----
 36 -------------------     1   1    2   -----       ---      ---    ----
 37 -------------------     1   1    2   -----       ---      ---    ----
 38 -------------------     1   1    2   -----       ---      ---    ----
 39 -------------------     1   1    2   -----       ---      ---    ----
 40 -------------------     1   1    2   -----       ---      ---    ----
 41 -------------------     1   1    2   -----       ---      ---    ----
Main Menu
  Delete  Loop  Mute  Name  Quit  Record  Solo  Tempo  EDIT  FILES  OPTIONS

  VIEW
```

FIGURE 3.9:

The Options menu

```
Main
Song BRAND1AD                                             STOP    Mem 221648
Tk   2 ------------------- BPM  90  MIDI:IN          1:0   THRU:OFF

Trk Name                 Port Chan Prg    Transpose  Quantize  Loop   Mute
  1 TRUMPET                 3   5   37     0: 5       ---       ---    ----
  2 --------------------    1   1    2     -----      ---       ---    MUTE
  3 FLUTE                   2   5    4     -----      ---       ---    ----
  4 OBOE                    3   4   21     -----      ---       ---    ----
  5 --------------------    1   1    2     -----      ---       ---    MUTE
  6 VIOLIN SOLO             2   4   40     -----      ---       ---    ----
  7 --------------------    1   1    2     -----      ---       ---    MUTE
  8 VIOLIN I                3   3   10     -----      ---       ---    ----
  9 VIOLIN II               2   3    2     -----      ---       ---    ----
 10 VIOLA                   3   2   11     -----      ---       ---    ----
 11 VIOLONE                 2   2    3     -----      ---       ---    ----
 12 OPTIONS -      ----
 13 ┌─────────────────────── OPTIONS ───────────────────┐ -      MUTE
 14 │Metronome       OFF        M BENDERS etc.   NO PRESS│ -      ----
 15 │                           I                        │ -      ----
 16 │Lead-in         OFF        D PROGRAMS       ON       │ -      ----
 17 │                           I                        │ -      ----
 18 │ ┌SOURCE        SMART     X-PEDALS Up      ON       │ -      ----
 19 │T S                                                 │ -      ----
 20 │i i┤ DEFAULT    4/4        MIDI THRU       OFF      │ -      ----
 21 │m g                                                 │ -      ----
 22 │e └FIXED Trk 1             VELOCITY filter  OFF      │ -      ----
 23 └────────────────────────────────────────────────────┘ -      ----
 24-       ----
 25 --------------------    1   1    2     -----      ---       ---    ----
 26 --------------------    1   1    2     -----      ---       ---    ----
 27 --------------------    1   1    2     -----      ---       ---    ----
 28 --------------------    1   1    2     -----      ---       ---    ----
 29 --------------------    1   1    2     -----      ---       ---    ----
 30 --------------------    1   1    2     -----      ---       ---    ----
 31 --------------------    1   1    2     -----      ---       ---    ----
 32 --------------------    1   1    2     -----      ---       ---    ----
 33 --------------------    1   1    2     -----      ---       ---    ----
 34 --------------------    1   1    2     -----      ---       ---    ----
 35 --------------------    1   1    2     -----      ---       ---    ----
 36 --------------------    1   1    2     -----      ---       ---    ----
 37 --------------------    1   1    2     -----      ---       ---    ----
 38 --------------------    1   1    2     -----      ---       ---    ----
 39 --------------------    1   1    2     -----      ---       ---    ----
 40 --------------------    1   1    2     -----      ---       ---    ----
 41 --------------------    1   1    2     -----      ---       ---    ----
Options Menu
Bender  Default  Fixed  Kill-controllers  Lead-in  Metronome  Omni-off
Prgrms  Source  Thru  Velocity  Xped  HARDWARE
```

Options	Use
MIDI THRU	Passes the data that are received by the MIDI port on to the FM chip. With MIDI THRU enabled, you can hear the result of the song through the Sound Blaster FM even as you record the song.
VELOCITY Filter	Assigns all notes the highest velocity. Certain MIDI keyboards are not velocity-sensitive. This means they cannot register the velocity at which a key is pressed. Enable this option to assign all notes the highest velocity.

Files Menu   The Files menu, shown in Figure 3.10, is for saving and loading songs. From this menu you can also execute almost all functions regarding file management without having to return to DOS. The options on this menu are self-explanatory.

Note that SpJr can handle three song formats: SNG, MID, and ROL:

- SNG is Voyetra's own song format.
- MID is the standard MIDI file format.
- ROL is the format used by the creators of the AdLib card.

TIP   SND and MID files can be loaded and saved. A ROL file can only be loaded.

View Menu   The View menu, shown in Figure 3.11, lets you get an overall look at the various tracks. The measures (called *bars*) are indicated at the right of the tracks. An empty measure is marked with a minus sign and a nonempty measure is marked with a rectangle. The points indicate the measures that have not been recorded yet.

FIGURE 3.10:

The Files menu

```
Files
BRAND1AD C:\VOYETRA\SONGS\
Mem 221648  Ext.SNG        BPM  90   MIDI:IN        1:0    THRU:OFF

SONG       Size    Date     Time  SONG       Size    Date      Time
[A:]                               TEST       19610  8/16/91  16:58
[B:]
[C:]
[D:]
.
  7/25/91 22:28
..
  7/25/91 22:28
2GUITARS  15819 12/24/90  0:49
ALLTIME   16907 12/15/90 21:55
BRAND-AD  17531  5/29/90 16:53
BRAND1AD  80619  5/30/90 12:14
CANCAN    21259 12/08/90 21:30
CHEERS3   22091  2/24/91 22:37
CMLCHEER  15163  7/17/90 12:16
CMLDISCO  15467  2/19/91 14:00
CMLJING   18075  7/17/90 12:22
CMLNUTS   13096  7/17/90 13:19
CMLSATIN  27400  7/17/90 13:34
CMLSWING  18059  5/31/90 13:58
CMLTECH   13355  5/30/90 17:46
DAARGAAT  51531  2/24/91 16:37
DEMO       9707  3/09/91 12:08
DEMOSONG  22379 10/16/90 14:04
FANTASIA   7707 12/08/90 16:14
HAPPY#42  21611  3/13/91 12:25
HAVANAG   13387 12/02/90 18:32
HOLDHAND  14333  1/25/90 15:51
HOLYCITY  16619 12/28/90 23:05
HORN      22763  5/27/91 18:13
HORNSBY   22333  6/04/90 17:54
INVITE    23499  3/09/91 12:08
LARGO     10203 12/05/90  0:47
LAVIE     24155 12/18/90  0:20
LDYMDONA  15869  1/21/90 18:04
LEFREAKC  56315  2/24/91 16:32
LETITBE   29965  8/15/89 20:48
LIT_HELP  15677  8/15/89 22:21
LONESOME  19229  1/20/90 17:32
LUCY_SKY  16285  8/19/89 14:03
MAPLERAG  17883 11/29/90 11:09
MINUETG   13003 11/29/90 11:10
SPTUTOR    5915 11/29/90  9:07
Files Menu
Buffers-clear  Create-dir  Delete  Free   Load  Mode  New  Path  Quick-find
Rename  Save
```

FIGURE 3.11:

The View menu

```
Song BRAND1AD                                            STOP      Mem 221648

Tk   2 -------------------- BPM  90   MIDI:IN          1:0   THRU:OFF


Trk  Name                Port Chan Prg Bars*       ↓8     ↓16    ↓24    ↓32
      1  TRUMPET             3    5  37  1 --*
      4  OBOE                3    4  21  4 ----------------------*
      9  VIOLIN II           2    3   2  9 --*
     10  VIOLA               3    2  11 10 -----*
     12  CELLO               3    1   3 12 ----------------*
     13  --------------------  1    1   2 13
     18  --------------------  1    1   2 18
     21  --------------------  1    1   2 21
     24  --------------------  1    1   2 24
     27  --------------------  1    1   2 27
     30  --------------------  1    1   2 30
     33  --------------------  1    1   2 33
     36  --------------------  1    1   2 36
     39  --------------------  1    1   2 39
View Menu
Add   Copy   Delete  Goto-bar   Insert  Loop  Mute  Name  Replace  Solo  Width
Zap   EDIT   FILES   OPTIONS
```

This View menu offers a number of useful functions. In addition to options also available on the main menu, this menu offers these options:

Option	Use
Goto-bar	Lets you move to a track measure you indicate.
Width	Fills the total width of the screen with measures only.
Copy	Copies the measures you indicate to one of the three available buffers. These buffers are called 0, 1, and temp.
Zap	Provides the same service as Copy, except that the copied measures are deleted.
Delete	Works the same as Zap, but in this case the measures to the right of the deleted area are moved to the left.
Insert	Inserts the contents of the buffer at the cursor position.

Option	Use
Replace	Replaces an indicated part of the measure with the contents of the buffer.
Add	Adds an empty measure.

Recording and playing in the View menu starts at the position of the cursor. If you save an SNG file, the buffers 0, 1, and temp are saved together with the file.

Editing Sounds

From the View menu, you can go directly to the Edit menu if you need to. For example, if you were on the View menu, you could enlarge a particular measure in one of the tracks pressing the E for Edit.

On the Edit menu, the pitch of the notes is indicated vertically on the left side. In the Edit screen you can add and remove notes. Just like in the View menu, you can select notes to be copied, removed, or replaced.

The duration of a note is measured in *clicks*. A click is the smallest unit of time you can work with and is equal to $\frac{1}{192}$ of a quarter note. You can enter successively the Length, the Pitch, and the Start of a note. Length and Start are measured in clicks.

Because the screen is too small to represent all notes in clicks, you can use the Units option. Use this option to tell Sequencer Plus Junior the number of clicks that have to be added when the cursor is moved one position. The Track function allows you to enter another track number to edit.

Note Edit Menu   Unlike the Edit menu, which displays several notes in one measure, the Note Edit menu—shown in Figure 3.12—shows only one selected note. The Note Edit menu presents the following options:

Option	Use
Length and Pitch	These options are the same as their namesakes in the Edit menu.
Start	Lets you enter a combination of notes and clicks. For example, 10:+6 means that the note starts 6 clicks after the tenth unit note (the value of this unit note is indicated in Units).

Option	Use
Velocity	Indicates the volume of the note. The term "velocity" is used because the velocity at which a note is pressed also determines the volume of the note.
Off Velocity	Is the value of the velocity at which the pressed key is released.
Accidentals	Lets you change the vertical pitches at the left. You can choose between displaying piano keys, numbers, notes, and flats.
Freeze	Prevents you from scrolling up or down. With this option enabled, you stay in one octave.
Note-trig	Ensures that every selected note is automatically played.

FIGURE 3.12:

The Note Edit menu

```
dit
Song BRAND1AD                                        STOP    Mem 59228

Tk   1 TRUMPET              BPM  90    MIDI:IN        2:0   THRU:OFF


Environment                           CURRENT NOTE      Units: 16th  Fine
Time Sig:    4/4    Sharps            Pitch:  G  5    Start:    3     0
Time Units:  16th                     Velocity: 127   Length:   1   - 8
Freeze:      OFF    Note-trig: ON     Off Vel:   64
!!%%((,,//11
                    BAR  2    OCTAVE  5
  b
  a#
  a
  g#
  g
  f#
  f
  e
  d#
  d
  c#
  c
```

The QWERTY Synthesizer

You can activate the QWERTY synthesizer from every menu in Sequencer Plus Junior. To activate the synthesizer, simply press Shift-F1. The QWERTY synthesizer is a synthesizer you can play by using your computer keyboard—you can play your keyboard like a real MIDI instrument. You can record the notes you play and even play along with a song.

It is also possible to set the velocity, the duration, and the octave of the notes.

CHAPTER

FOUR

Sound Blaster Extensions

- Installing the MIDI Connector Box

- Installing CMS chips in order to acquire more stereo voices

- Uses of a CD-ROM drive with Sound Blaster and how to install a CD-ROM

- Using two Sound Blasters at once

Y ou can boost the capabilities of the Sound Blaster and the Sound Blaster Pro by installing extension hardware. Which extensions you can add, however, has to do with whether you have the Sound Blaster or Sound Blaster Pro.

This chapter discusses the following extensions:

- The MIDI Connector Box for connecting other MIDI devices. This box is included with Sound Blaster Pro. You can connect one to the Sound Blaster.

- CMS chips so you can have 12 stereo voices in Sound Blaster. You can add CMS chips to Sound Blaster, but not to Sound Blaster Pro. In the Pro version, stereo FM chips are used instead.

- A CD-ROM drive. This extension is only available with Sound Blaster Pro.

- Using two Sound Blasters at once.

The MIDI Connector Box

The MIDI Connector Box is for connecting standard MIDI cables to Sound Blaster. It contains one MIDI In and five MIDI Out connectors. A compact version is included with Sound Blaster Pro; it has only one MIDI In and one MIDI Out cable.

Plug the MIDI Connector Box into the joystick connection of the card. The joystick can be plugged into the box and will still function properly.

> **NOTE** See "MIDI for Communication between Devices" in Chapter 2 for more information about MIDI connections. For information about programming with MIDI , see Chapter 10.

CMS Chips

CMS chips are required if you want to have the twelve stereo voices of the Sound Blaster. These chips are included in early versions of the Sound Blaster, but the latest versions of the Sound Blaster cards do not come with CMS chips. You have to purchase them.

Installing CMS chips involves four steps:

1. Removing the Sound Blaster card from the PC.
2. Placing the chips in the proper sockets.
3. Placing the Sound Blaster card back in the PC.
4. Installing the CMS driver with the INST-DRV program.

Because CMS is only supported to a certain degree (usually together with an Adlib=FM option, which produces higher-quality albeit mono music), we advise listening to a Sound Blaster that has CMS chips before installing any. Find out before you buy CMS chips whether the purchase would be worthwhile.

NOTE   See "CMS Stereo Chips" in Chapter 2 for more information about these chips.

Substituting with the SAA 1099   In place of CMS chips, you can use the Phillips chip SAA 1099. Just like CMS chips, you need two 1099s. These chips are functionally the equivalent of CMS chips. Moreover, they usually cost less.

CD-ROM Drives

You can use a CD-ROM drive with the Sound Blaster Pro. At the time of this book's writing, only one type of drive can be used with the Pro: the Matsushita CT-521 CD-ROM drive. Besides providing the usual advantages of having a CD-ROM—namely, being able to store music files without overburdening your hard disk—you can also play commercial CDs and record them by means of the Sound Blaster Pro. Sound Blaster Pro produces high-quality recordings.

One CD can contain hundreds of programs as well as data. It is possible to store about 560MB of data, or roughly 6 million characters, on a CD. CDs are now being released that store entire encyclopedias and dictionaries. CDs can also store music.

Installing the CD-ROM Drive

The CD-ROM drive is easy to connect. You install the CD-ROM drive in the computer by placing it in a 5.25 floppy drive bay. Next, the CD-ROM has to be connected to the power supply and of course to the Sound Blaster Pro. To connect it to the Pro, plug the small white 4-pin connector into the little white socket. Plug the large connector into the back of the Sound Blaster Pro.

NOTE   For more information about CD-ROMs, see "CD ROMs and the Pro" in Chapter 2.

Installing the Drivers

Next you have to install two drivers, SBPCD.SYS and MSCDEX.EXE.

SBPCD in CONFIG.SYS   Add the SBPCD.SYS driver to CONFIG.SYS with the following line:

```
DEVICE = SBPCD.SYS /D:MSCD0001 /P:220 or /P:240
```

Following is an explanation of what this line means:

SBPCD.SYS	The driver file. This file must be located in the root directory of the boot diskette.
/D	Indicates the name of the device SBPCD can be addressed with (in this case MSCD0001).
/P	Indicates the I/O Address.

The SBPCD.SYS device driver enables the CD-ROM hardware to communicate with Microsoft's CD-ROM interface program MSCDEX.EXE. The MSCDEX.EXE driver must be placed in the AUTOEXEC.BAT file.

MSCDEX.EXE in AUTOEXEC.BAT   The MSCDEX driver takes care of the interface between DOS and the SBPCD.SYS driver and contains standard functions that can be used by other programs.

Following is an example of a MSCDEX.EXE line in AUTOEXEC.BAT:

```
MSCDEX.EXE /D:MSCD0001 /L:e /M:10 /E /V
```

Following is an explanation of what this line means:

/D:*xxx*	This is where you put the name of the device. This name must match the drive name in the CONFIG.SYS /D line.
/L:*x*	The drive letter (*E* in the example above). This works just like a DOS drive letter. You can go to this drive letter and run files from your CD-ROM. If you already have a drive E, change the /L switch to an unused drive letter (for example /L:f to use drive F).
/M:*x*	The number of sectors to buffer in memory. A large number of buffers makes for quicker processing and less mistakes but also requires more memory. The MSCDEX will use ten buffers and will keep these buffers in expanded memory if possible. If no expanded memory is available, the driver will use standard memory.
/E	The switch that tells MCSDEX to use expanded memory for storing the buffers. If you do not have expanded memory, you can leave out the option /E.
/V	The switch that tells MCSDEX to give a detailed message about how much memory it is using when it loads.

NOTE When you choose a higher drive with /L, choose a drive that MS-DOS allows you to use. With LASTDRIVE=d in CONFIG.SYS, you can set the number of drives MS-DOS supports. In the case of =d, D is the last drive admitted, but you can change this to LASTDRIVE=Q or higher if you want to.

CDPLYR.EXE for Playing CDs   The Sound Blaster Pro software includes the CDPLYR.EXE program. This program uses the drivers mentioned above to play an ordinary CD. If you use CDPLYR to start playing the CD, it will be played until the end. If you quit CDPLYR without stopping the CD, it will continue playing. This way you can listen to a CD while using other software.

NOTE   CDPLYR is *not* memory resident.

Installing a Second Sound Blaster Card

You can install more than one Sound Blaster card in your computer. Two Sound Blaster cards gives you twice as many opportunities. For instance, by connecting one Sound Blaster to the left channel and one to the right, you can create a stereo effect: stereo DSP and stereo FM. You could do this both with the Sound Blaster and with Sound Blaster Pro.

As this book is being written, and as far as we know, no one has yet tried using two Sound Blasters. Having two Sound Blasters going at once does pose one problem: you cannot use the DMA to control both cards (the DMA can only control one card). In any case, one of the cards has to be programmed directly. This requires processor time and considerably slows down the program.

Installing Two Sound Blasters   If you want to install two Sound Blasters in your PC, pay attention to the following:

- Set a different basic port for each Sound Blaster. If you don't, the cards cannot be programmed separately.

- For safety reasons, remove the DMA Enable jumper from one of the Sound Blasters. Preferably, you should remove the jumper from the card with the highest basic port. Most Sound Blaster detecting programs do not check whether a second Sound Blaster is present, so they don't report an error message when the DMA is not functioning. During the search for the Sound Blaster card, a program usually passes the ports from low to high.

It is possible to install a third, fourth, fifth, and sixth card as long as you choose a different port for the card and remove the DMA Enable jumper. However, only consider using several Sound Blasters at once if you need several independent channels and if you are capable of writing your own software (as far as we know, software is not available for running several Sound Blasters).

If you already own a Sound Blaster card and you want to purchase the Sound Blaster Pro, you might consider keeping the old Sound Blaster card and running it alongside Pro instead of selling it. This way, you will still have the CMS chip at your disposal, which is reason enough to keep the Sound Blaster card.

If you run two Sound Blasters, it could be that both cards perform voice input/output with the DMA. If that is the case, you can use different sampling rates for the cards. By connecting the Sound Blaster to the left channel and the Sound Blaster Pro to the right channel, you can play stereo samples with different sampling rates. This is not possible with the stereo DSP on the Sound Blaster Pro; it uses the same sampling rate for both the left and the right channel.

Installing Sound Blaster and Sound Blaster Pro   If you install both the Sound Blaster and the Sound Blaster Pro, keep this advice in mind:

- The Sound Blaster and the Sound Blaster Pro have to be installed on different ports. Bear in mind that the Sound Blaster Pro uses the seventeen ports following the selected basic port, so it is possible for the last two ports (which are used for the CD-ROM) to overlap the port set on the Sound Blaster. Aside from the same ports, the following settings are not possible:

     220H on the Sound Blaster Pro and 230H on the Sound Blaster
     240H on the Sound Blaster Pro and 250H on the Sound Blaster

  Apart from these settings, every selection is possible.

- Because the default setting of the Sound Blaster is DMA channel 1, the setting of the Sound Blaster Pro has to be changed in order to keep Pro from using DMA channel (DMA 0 for VOICE and DMA 3 for CD-ROM or vice versa).

You can't install two Sound Blaster Pro cards in one PC. The two DMA selections will overlap and it is not yet possible to disable the DMA. Besides, this would be rather expensive and the combination will probably never be supported by any programs.

CHAPTER

FIVE

Understanding the MIDI Interface

- Connecting MIDI devices

- Understanding the MIDI Thru port

- Looking at sequencers

- What you can do with MIDI and the Sound Blaster

MIDI stands for *Musical Instrument Digital Interface* and is pronounced "middy." The MIDI standard allows different instruments and synthesizers to connect to each other and exchange musical information. To play a MIDI instrument you do not have to be familiar with the MIDI language. You only have to connect the cables in the right way.

This chapter explains what MIDI is and takes a close look at connecting MIDI devices, at MIDI instruments, and at MIDI software.

NOTE	For detailed information about the MIDI language, see Chapter 10.

What Is MIDI?

MIDI is an "international language" in the sense that it allows instruments manufactured in different countries and by different manufacturers to communicate with each other. Apart from synthesizers, all kinds of instruments are equipped with MIDI and can communicate thanks to the MIDI standard. These days instruments as diverse as guitars, saxophones, electric pianos, and drum machines have built-in MIDI interfaces.

MIDI Hardware Specifications   MIDI hardware specifications dictate how standard connectors should be designed and how they should work. The MIDI hardware standard defines types of input and output channels (called *MIDI ports*), types of cables, and types of plugs. The three types of ports are MIDI In, MIDI Out, and MIDI Thru.

MIDI Messages   Musical information is exchanged by way of MIDI *messages*. MIDI messages are codes that contain information about such musical elements as volume, pitch, note duration, and of course the notes themselves. For example, a MIDI message could tell a device to "play note C4 at velocity 74."

Connecting MIDI Devices

Every MIDI instrument—whether it be a synthesizer, keyboard, or guitar—has a MIDI In, a MIDI Out, and sometimes a MIDI Thru port:

- The MIDI In port receives the MIDI data. In effect, this connection is the device's "ear." A synthesizer, keyboard, or other MIDI device receives MIDI messages by way of its MIDI In port. The Out cable of the Sound Blaster MIDI interface connects to the In port of the synthesizer, keyboard, or other MIDI device.

- The MIDI Out port sends the MIDI data out and is, to continue the metaphor, the "mouth" of the device. A synthesizer, keyboard, or other MIDI device sends MIDI messages through the MIDI Out port. Therefore, the In cable of the Sound Blaster MIDI interface connects to the Out port of the synthesizer, keyboard, or other MIDI device.

- The MIDI Thru connection allows you to daisy-chain devices. When a device is connected to the Thru connection, it sends its messages into the device without interruption as though they were In messages.

The MIDI Thru Port

To understand how the MIDI Thru port works, consider the following example. Suppose you are playing a synthesizer and you want to play two drum machines as well. The synthesizer only has one MIDI Out port to connect the drums to. Therefore, you can connect the first drum to the MIDI Out port and the second drum machine to the first drum's MIDI Thru port. The MIDI Thru port retransmits all MIDI data received at the MIDI In port without changing the data.

In theory, the number of MIDI instruments that can be connected with Thru ports is unlimited. In practice, however, you cannot make unlimited connections this way because signals weaken as they travel through cable. For example, the eighth instrument connected by MIDI Thru ports will no longer be able to read the data or will translate the data incorrectly. Moreover, a signal requires a number (however small) of milliseconds to get from point A to B in a cable. When a large number of instruments are connected, a small delay will occur.

A handy device to solve these problems is the Output Selector, or MIDI Thru Box. This box has one MIDI IN port and as many as sixteen MIDI Thru ports. With a

MIDI Thru box, as many as sixteen MIDI instruments can simultaneously receive data from the master (the instrument being played).

> **TIP**
>
> If you need to connect several MIDI devices with long cables, consider getting a MIDI amplifier. This device amplifies the incoming MIDI signal before it is retransmitted.

MIDI Instruments

There are already MIDI versions of a lot of acoustic instruments, including the accordion, saxophone, guitar, piano, and drums. These instruments create MIDI data by using pickups (microphones) to receive the sound and by using some type of intelligent circuitry to convert the sound information into MIDI messages. Besides acoustic instruments, a number of digital instruments are available, with synthesizers and keyboards being the most important.

Besides creating sounds, you can make use of MIDI for presentations. For example, if you wanted to accompany a holiday video with sounds, you could use a MIDI synchronizer to make a certain musical composition begin at the same time as a certain scene.

Sequencers The nice thing about word processing is that when you make corrections, you don't have to type the whole document all over again. The same goes for composing with MIDI. Formerly, notes had to be written down, and if a big revision had to be made everything had to be recopied from scratch. With the MIDI sequencer, this is no longer true.

A *sequencer* is a device that stores and sometimes lets you edit the MIDI data created by other MIDI instruments. Software sequencers are computer sequencers. They usually allow you a great deal of flexibility in editing MIDI data. The MIDI sequencer is linked to the master and the slave(s). The MIDI sequencer stores all MIDI data supplied by the master. A MIDI sequencer is equipped with a disk drive for storing the MIDI data. This way, you always have the data at your disposal. It is also possible to play the received data with the sequencer. The MIDI data can even be manipulated to a certain extent. You can, for example, change incorrect notes.

MIDI Software

As programmers, the biggest advantage of MIDI is the fact that MIDI instruments can be connected directly to the computer. By linking MIDI to the computer, we can access the MIDI system by means of the MIDI language. By programming with the computer, you can replace devices such as MIDI sequencers with software. Moreover, a software sequencer is much more flexible and cheaper than a "sequencer in a box."

Most software programs concerning MIDI are sequencers. The biggest advantage of the software sequencer is that it is always up to date with the latest MIDI developments. Other advantages of a software MIDI sequencer are:

- Data can be presented visually on the screen.
- The cut and paste functions allow you to edit data directly on the screen.
- The software can be extended at all times.
- A software sequencer can contain many more functions because a computer is an open, interactive system.
- The software sequencer is more user-friendly.
- The user has more control over the sequencer.

What You Can Do with Sound Blaster and MIDI

A standard card, the MPU-401 plug-in board manufactured by Roland, has been developed for the MIDI connection between MIDI instruments and personal computers.

Many sequencers make use of this card. Unfortunately, however, the Sound Blaster MIDI interface is not compatible with the MPU-401. They are not compatible because the MPU-401 may not be duplicated—or, to be exact, the MPU-401 includes a chip containing specific software. Sequencers that use the MPU-401 software are strictly forbidden from using the software in combination with the Sound Blaster.

A second problem is that the ports to which the MIDI data have to be sent are not the same on the Sound Blaster as they are on the MPU-401. Nevertheless, the Sound

Blaster is fully compatible with the MIDI protocol the way it is specified by the MIDI Association. The annoying thing is that the software has to be rewritten to be compatible with the Sound Blaster.

The first company that has done this is Voyetra. This company has released three sequencers, varying from simple to very comprehensive, that all take advantage of the MIDI possibilities the Sound Blaster offers. To give you an idea of how a sequencer functions, Chapter 3 contains a description of the Voyetra Sequencer Junior.

There is one other problem associated with the Sound Blaster and its support of the MIDI standard: the Sound Blaster MIDI is half-duplex, which means that you can either send or receive data, but not do both at the same time. Therefore, when the Sound Blaster sends MIDI data to the master, the Sound Blaster can't at the same time receive MIDI data you create while playing the master. This shortcoming has been repaired with the introduction of the Sound Blaster Pro. The Sound Blaster Pro is a full-duplex card.

The Sound Blaster Pro is equipped with the MIDI time-stamp protocol. This protocol is used to synchronize MIDI devices. Every MIDI signal is assigned a time code. This way, you can determine exactly at what moment a MIDI code is received.

All Sound Blasters keep a 64-byte buffer for storing MIDI data. The buffer is filled and emptied according to the FIFO (first in, first out) system, which means that the first byte to enter the buffer is also the first byte to leave the buffer.

The Sound Blaster MIDI Interface meets the requirements of the International MIDI Association. You can connect all MIDI devices to Sound Blaster's MIDI interface. As far as the Sound Blaster 1.0 and 1.5 are concerned, you have to make sure the devices do not depend on a full-complex MIDI connection.

PART II

Programming the Sound Blaster

CHAPTER

SIX

Programming the Timer Chip

- How the timer chip operates

- Programming a timer chip through the channel ports

- How counters and the timer chip work together

- Setting a frequency for a timer channel

The timer chip is like a clock in your computer. Various software programs and drivers use the chip. The frequencies of the timer chip can be programmed for various purposes. Because certain types of sound require specific timing, you must have a clock running to make sure that the music is played at a steady, constant rate. This is what the timer chip is for.

PC-XTs use the timer chip 8253 and PC-ATs use the 8254. All timer chips have the same functioning modes and work the same way. Modern chips all duplicate the 8254 chip. So the information offered here applies to 486 and 386 machines as well as XTs and ATs.

How the Timer Chip Works

The timer works with a frequency of 1.19318 mHz and possesses three independent timer channels. Each channel can operate in six different modes. In effect, the 8253 and 8254 chips are three 16-bit timers in one. You interact with the timers by reading and writing to the register I/O port addresses 040h through 043h. Port 043h is used to program the timers. There are six different modes that each timer can operate in. Addresses 040h through 042h are used to read and write 16-bit values for the three times (numbered 0, 1, and 2).

For every timer channel, a 16-bit counter is set. The counter is increased by 1 at a fixed frequency of 1.19318 mHz. Interrupts are generated at constant intervals. The 16-bit counter ranges from 0 to 65535. The value 0 is equal to the value 65536.

Timer Channels

Each timer Channel 0 generates an IRQ 0—that is, INT 8—through the interrupt controller 8259. Channel 0 checks how the motors of the floppy drives are functioning.

Channel 1 is used for DMA memory refresh operations. The purpose of these operations is to constantly refresh all information in memory. The initial value for the counter is 18, so the frequency of the memory refresh is

$$1193180 / 18 = 66,287.78 \text{ Hz}$$

Channel 2 is free for general use. This channel is often used in combination with the speaker to create a beep of a particular pitch.

For the purposes of this book, only Channel 0 is of importance, because Channel 0 generates the interrupts at the processor. That's why the programmer only has to write his or her own interrupt routine for INT 8, which processes the music. This way, music can be played at a constant speed and the main program doesn't have to monitor or deal with it in any way. Of course, the main program has to start playing the music.

Usually, INT 8 is called 18.2 times a second. This rate is far to slow for playing music and samples. In this chapter, you'll see how you can set this value to a higher frequency.

Ports for the Timer Chip

The timer chip can be programmed through ports 40H to 43H. Ports 40H to 42H can be written as well as read to, but port 43H can only be written to. Ports 40H, 41H, and 42H are allocated to timer channels 0, 1, and 2 respectively. Through these ports the initial value of the counter can be set.

Port 43H is the general setting port. You can program a timer channel through one of the channel ports and through port 43H. Table 6.1 shows the functions of the different bits for port 43H.

One timer channel can be programmed through port 43H. You select this channel with bit 7 and 6, as shown in Table 6.2.

TABLE 6.1: Functions of Bits for Port 43H

Bits	Function
7, 6	Selects one of the three counters
5, 4	Sets the counter that was selected by 7, 6
3, 2, 1	Sets the operation mode of the counter
0	Selects either normal or BCD code

TABLE 6.2: The Timer Channel Selection

Bits 7 and 6	Channel
00b	0
01b	1
10b	2

Through ports 40H, 41H, or 42H, one of the timer channels is set with the 16-bit initial value. Since the ports themselves are only 8 bits large, putting a 16-bit value into the timer presents a problem. To place a 16-bit value into the timer, you use bits 5 and 4. Table 6.3 shows the bits that control the read-load format.

TABLE 6.3: Read-Load Bit Settings

Bits 5 and 4	Mode
00b	Read the current counter value directly
01b	Read and write only the most significant byte (MSB)
10b	Read and write only the least significant byte (LSB)
11b	Read or write the least significant byte (LSB) first, and then read or write the most significant byte (MSB)

The last three modes—bits 3 through 1—are the modes for selecting the mode the timer will operate in. If the first mode is selected, the current value of the counter can be read. The counter cannot be set.

Bits 3 to 1 determine the operation mode of the timer channel, as shown in Table 6.4.

Channel 0 operates in mode 3, which means that this timer channel works with a square wave. The last bit determines the internal functioning of the counter, as shown in Table 6.5.

TABLE 6.4: The Various Modes

Bits 3, 2, 1	Mode
000b	0
001b	1
010b	2
011b	3
100b	4
101b	5

TABLE 6.5: The Counter Modes

Bit 0	Counter
0b	Binary counter mode
1b	BCD counter mode

Counters and the Timer Chip

If the counter is set with an initial value, the decimal value has to be converted to a 16-bit binary number. Each time the binary counter decreases this binary number by one (111b, 110b, 101b,...). However, it is also possible to pass on the initial value according to the BCD coding and to use a BCD counter. With this technique, the BCD format is used for counting and that the counter passes from BCD number 10 to BCD number 9. The value 00010000b (= 10 BCD = 16 decimal) isn't followed by 00001111b (= 15 decimal) but by 00001001b (= 9 BCD = 9 decimal).

If a BCD counter is used, the 16-bit counter can be set with a maximum value of 10000. This way the range is much smaller. Setting a BCD number, however, is much easier than setting an ordinary binary number.

For Channel 0, the normal binary counter is used.

NOTE

When they create code, compilers and assemblers convert decimal numbers to their binary equivalents. Therefore, the BCD counter will not be used in this book and we will always use the normal binary counter.

TIP

After setting port 43H, an initial value has to be assigned to the selected timer channel. The timer chip will not process anything until the base value is set. In other words, as long as you've only written to port 43H and the initial value for the counters has not been set, no interrupt takes place.

To set a particular frequency for timer Channel 0, follow these steps:

1. Divide 1,193,180 by the frequency to calculate the initial value.
2. Write the value 00110110b to port 43H (channel 0 + *first LSB*; then *MSB* + mode 3 + binary counter).
3. Write the eight least significant bits to port 40H.
4. Write the eight most significant bits to port 40H.

INT 8 will now be called at the *indicated frequency*. Now you can set up your own interrupt routine. This routine has to call the old interrupt routine 18.2 times a second at regular intervals. It is necessary to call the old routine, especially if your program is memory-resident or works with time-sensitive parts.

Because the interrupt is passed on through chip 8259, you have to tell this chip that it may generate other interrupts on the processor. If you don't do this, no other IRQ takes place.

By writing the value 20H to port 20H, you indicate that the 8259 can process the next interrupt and pass it on to the processor. You don't have to do this if the old routine is called, because this routine passes the interrupt itself.

If your routine is slower than the speed at which it is called, you have to keep a flag that indicates whether the routine is already busy. If you don't, the routine will be processed again and again, even when it is still busy. However, don't forget to call the old interrupt routine at regular intervals.

The three listings that comprise the rest of this chapter contain code examples that represent a stopwatch. Listing 6.1 is an example in Pascal, Listing 6.2 is an example in C, and Listing 6.3 is an example in Assembly. In the listings, Timer Channel 0 is set at a frequency of 100 Hz. A counter keeps track of the exact time in hundredths of a second.

In the Pascal and C listings (Listing 6.1 and 6.2), the old interrupt routine is set at another free interrupt, so the old interrupt is called in a simple way. In the Assembly listing, a FAR JMP is used. You can also use a FAR CALL, but don't forget to put the flags in the stack with PUSHF before this FAR CALL takes place, because the routine ends with a IRET.

NOTE See "A Word about the Program Listings" in the Introduction of this book for advice about reading and copying listings.

Listing 6.1: Pascal Example of the Use of the Timer

```
/*Program TimerTest*/

/*Uses Dos, Crt*/

Const
  OldTimerInt = 103;    { old timer interrupt }

Var
  Counter : Word;       { counter for the old interrupt }
  HSec    : LongInt;    { number of hundredth of a second }
  Ch      : Char;       { for key press }

Procedure SetTimer(Rout : Pointer; Freq : Word);
{ Set timer interrupt, Rout is called Freq times a second. }

Var
  ICnt: Word;
  OldV: Pointer;
```

```
Begin
  Inline($FA);                    { CLI, interrupts off }
  ICnt:=1193180 Div Freq;         { calculate basic counter }
  Port[$43]:=$36;                 { set mode }
  Port[$40]:=Lo(ICnt);            { write LSB }
  Port[$40]:=Hi(ICnt);            { write MSB }
  GetIntVec(8,OldV);              { old int vector }
  SetIntVec(OldTimerInt,OldV);    { int 8 now Int OldT }
  SetIntVec(8,Rout);              { new int handler }
  Inline($FB);                    { STI, interrupts on }
End;

Procedure RestoreTimer;

Var
  OldV : Pointer;

Begin
  Inline($FA);                    { CLI, interrupts off }
  Port[$43]:=$36;                 { set frequency }
  Port[$40]:=0;                   { of 18.2 Hz }
  Port[$40]:=0;
  GetIntVec(OldTimerInt,OldV);    { restore INT vector }
  SetIntVec(8,OldV);
    Inline($FB);                  { STI, interrupts on }
End;

Procedure NewTimer; Interrupt;
{ The new timer interrupt }

Var
  R : Registers;    { Dummy needed for Intr }

Begin
  Dec(Counter);                   { decrease counter }
  If Counter = 0 Then Begin       { call old INT ? }
    Intr(OldTimerInt,R);          { yes }
    Counter:=100 DIV 18;          { restore counter }
  End
  Else                            { no }
    Port[$20]:=$20;               { int. is handled }
  Inc(HSec);                      { increase interrupt }
End;
```

```
Begin
  Counter:=1;                   { Initialize counter }
  SetTimer(@NewTimer,100);  { set int at 100 Hz }
  WriteLn;
  WriteLn('Stop watch , press a key ...');
  WriteLn;
  Ch:=ReadKey;                  { wait for key press}
  HSec:=0;                      { set Hund. Sec to 0 }
  Repeat
    GotoXY(1,WhereY);         { show time }
    Write((HSec Div 360000):2,':',
          (HSec Div 6000 Mod 60):2,':',
          (HSec Div 100 mod 60):2,'.',
          (Hsec Mod 100):2);
  Until KeyPressed;           { stop at key press }
  Ch:=ReadKey;                  { read key }
  RestoreTimer;                 { restore timer }
  WriteLn;
End.
```

Listing 6.2: C Example of the Use of the Timer

```c
/* Timer test program */
#pragma inline             /* use assembler */
#include <stdio.h>
#include <dos.h>
#include <conio.h>
#define OldTimerInt 103     /* old timer interrupt */

unsigned Counter;        /* counter for old interrupt */
long unsigned HSec;     /* number of hundredth of a second */

void SetTimer(void interrupt (*Rout) (), unsigned Freq)
/* Set timer interrupt, Rout is called Freq times a second. */
{
  int ICnt;
  asm cli;                  /* CLI, interrupts off */
  ICnt = 1193180 / Freq;    /* calculate basic counter */
  outportb(0x43,0x36);      /* set mode */
  outportb(0x40,ICnt & 255);/* write LSB */
  outportb(0x40,ICnt > 8); /* write MSB */
  setvect(OldTimerInt,getvect(8)); /* copy int 8 */
  setvect(8,Rout);          /* new int handler */
  asm sti;                  /* STI, interrupts on */
```

```
}

void RestoreTimer()
{
  asm cli;                   /* CLI, interrupts off */
  outportb(0x43,0x36);       /* set frequency */
  outportb(0x40,0);          /* of 18.2 Hz */
  outportb(0x40,0);
  setvect(8,getvect(OldTimerInt)); /* restore int 8 */
  asm sti;                   /* STI, interrupts on */
}

void interrupt NewTimer()
/* The new timer interrupt */
{
  struct REGPACK R;          /* dummy needed for intr */
  --Counter;                 /* decrease counter */
  ++HSec;
  if (Counter == 0) {        /* call old INT ? */
    intr(OldTimerInt,&R);    /* yes */
    Counter = 100 / 18;      /* restore counter */
  }
  else    /* no */

    outportb(0x20,0x20);     /* int. is handled */
}

void main()
{
  char Ch;
  int U,M,S,H;

  Counter = 1;               /* Initialize counter */
  SetTimer(NewTimer,100);    /* int at 100 Hz */
  printf("\n");
  printf("Stop watch , press a key...\n");
  printf("\n");
  Ch = getch();              /* wait for key press */
  HSec = 0;                  /* set Hund. Sec at 0 */
  do {
    gotoxy(1,wherey());      /* show time */
    H = HSec % 100;          /* hundredth of a second */
    S = (HSec / 100) % 60;   /* seconds */
    M = (HSec / 6000) % 60;  /* minutes */
    U = HSec / 360000;       /* hour */
```

```
    printf( "%2d:%2d:%2d.%2d",U,M,S,H);
}  while (!kbhit());           /* stop at key press */
Ch = getch();                  /* read key */
RestoreTimer();                /* restore timer */
printf("\n");
}
```

NOTE

Two machine code instructions are used by the ASM command. However, it turned out that the program also works without these instructions. They are included here for safety reasons only. If desired, you can leave out the lines with the ASM command so the program can be tested in the Turbo C editor. Don't forget to remove the first line containing #pragma inline.

Listing 6.3: Assembly Example of the Use of the Timer

```
        .MODEL TINY
        .CODE
        ORG 100H

cr = 13
lf = 10

Start PROC NEAR
        mov dx,offset IntroText         ; welcome
        mov ah,9                        ; message
        int 21H
        mov dx,offset NewTimer          ; routine
        mov ax,100                      ; frequency
        call SetTimer
        mov ah,0                        ; wait for
        int 16H                         ; key
        mov [WORD PTR Counter+0],0      ; start at 0
        mov [WORD PTR Counter+2],0
ShowCounter:
        mov ax,[WORD PTR Counter+0]     ; retrieve value
        mov dx,[WORD PTR Counter+2]
        mov di,offset HexText
        call ConvertHex                 ; to hexad.
```

```
            call ShowHex                    ; print
            mov ah,1                        ; test for
            int 16H                         ; key press
            jz ShowCounter                  ; a key ?
            mov ah,0                        ; yes, read
            int 16H                         ; from buffer
            call RestoreTimer
            mov dx,offset EndOfText         ; end
            mov ah,9                        ; message
            int 21H
            mov ax,4c00H                    ; return to
            int 21H                         ; DOS
ENDP

IntroText       DB cr,lf,"Press a key ...",cr,lf
                DB cr,lf,"$"
InfoText        DB "Counter : "
HexText         DB "00000000H.$"
EndText         DB cr,lf,cr,lf,"End ...",cr,lf,"$"
OldVector       DD 0                ; old timer handler
Counter         DD 0                ; the ticks counter

HelpCounter     DW 1                ; old handler call

; Show InfoText at same line.
ShowHex PROC NEAR
            mov ah,3                ; determine cursor position
            mov bh,0                ; at page 0
            int 10H
            xor dl,dl               ; go to beginning of
            mov ah,2                ; line
            int 10H
            mov dx,offset InfoText ; print info text
            mov ah,9
            int 21H
            ret
ENDP

; Set timer with the new frequency AX and set
; interrupt 8 with the new interrupt routine CS:DX.
SetTimer PROC NEAR
            cli                     ; interrupts off
            push es
            push ax                 ; store frequency
            mov ax,0                ; set vector segm.
```

```
          mov es,ax
          mov ax,cs
          xchg dx,[WORD PTR es:8*4+0]    ; change offset
          xchg ax,[WORD PTR es:8*4+2]    ; change segment
          mov [WORD PTR OldVector+0],dx ; and store
          mov [WORD PTR OldVector+2],ax ; them
          pop bx                    ; restore frequency
          pop es                    ; restore ES
          mov al,00110110b          ; chan. 0+L/M+mode 3+Bi
          out 43H,al
          mov dx,1193180 SHR 16     ; determine counter
          mov ax,1193180 AND 65535
          div bx
          out 40H,al                ; first LSB
          mov al,ah
          out 40H,al                ; and then MSB
          sti                       ; interr. on
          ret
ENDP

; Restore timer interrupt, so the old handler
; is called 18.2 times a second.
RestoreTimer PROC NEAR
          cli
          mov al,00110110b          ; chan. 0+L/M+mode 3+Bi
          out 43H,al
          mov al,0                  ; set frequency
          out 40H,al                ; at 18.2 Hz
          out 40H,al
          push ds                   ; reset int. vector
          lds dx,[OldVector]
          mov ax,2508H
          int 21H
          pop ds
          sti                       ; interr. on
          ret
ENDP

; The new timer interrupt, increase counter and call
; the old handler, if necessary.
NewTimer PROC FAR
          add [WORD PTR cs:Counter+0],1  ; increase
          adc [WORD PTR cs:Counter+2],0  ; counter
          dec [cs:HelpCounter]    ; decrease help counter
          jz OldInterrupt         ; old call ?
```

```
        push ax                 ; no, store AX
        mov al,20H              ; pass on that int.
        out 20H,al             ; is received
        pop ax                  ; restore AX
        iret
OldInterrupt:
        mov [cs:HelpCounter],100 / 18 ; restore help c.
        jmp dword ptr [cs:OldVector]  ; old handler
ENDP

; Convert DX:AX to a hexadecimal representation
; starting at ES:DI.
ConvertHex  PROC NEAR
        push ax                 ; store AX
        mov ax,dx               ; first process DX
        call HexWord
        pop ax                  ; restore AX
HexWord:
        push ax                 ; restore AX (AL)
        mov al,ah               ; first process AH
        call HexByte
        pop ax                  ; restore AL
HexByte:
        push ax                 ; store AX (AL)
        shr al,1                ; first process the
        shr al,1                ; most significant
        shr al,1                ; nibble (4 bits)
        shr al,1
        call HexNibble
        pop ax                  ; restore AX (AL)
        and al,15               ; least sig. nibble
HexNibble:
        add al,"0"              ; add '0' to AL
        cmp al,"9"              ; AL > 9
        jbe NoAsciiConversion
        add al,"A"-"9"-1        ; AL between 'A' and 'F'
NoAsciiConversion:
        stosb                   ; store AL
        ret
ENDP

END Start
```

CHAPTER

SEVEN

Programming the FM Chip

- Additive and frequency modulation synthesis

- How instrument and bank files work

- Playing music with the CMS format

- Playing music with a CMS file, with AdLib, and with the Sound driver

- Setting and changing the ports of an operator

- FM chip register settings

In this chapter you will learn how to program the FM chip to create sound and play back music. In order to create sound and play music, you can use a driver or program the FM chip. The FM chip is fully compatible with the AdLib card. Therefore, all AdLib software functions with the Sound Blaster card. However, not all Sound Blaster software works with AdLib. This isn't due to the FM chip but rather to the structure of the Sound Blaster (a subject explained later in this chapter).

How the FM Chip Creates Sound

You can create sound with various settings of the FM chip. In this section, we describe these settings and show you how to experiment with them.

Operators   The heart of the FM chip is the *operator*. The FM chip possesses eighteen operators. An operator consists of three parts:

- the oscillator
- the envelope generator
- the level controller

As shown in Figure 7.1, the *oscillator* generates a (transformed) sine wave, and this wave is in turn edited by the *envelope generator*. Next, the *level controller* determines the intensity of the wave. The final output is a signal that creates a sound.

NOTE   Later in this section we explain how each part of an operator can be set and changed.

FIGURE 7.1:

How an operator works

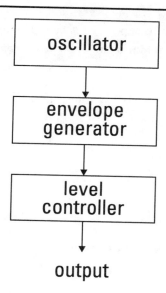

FM Chip Modes for Creating Sound   The FM chip offers three modes for creating sound:

- *Melody mode.* In this mode you can use nine instruments.

- *Rhythm mode.* In this mode, six normal instruments and five rhythm instruments are available. The five rhythm instruments are: the bass drum, high hat, tom-tom, snare drum, and top cymbal. As far as the rhythm instruments in this mode are concerned, you can only change the pitch of the bass drum and the tom-tom.

- *Composite voice synthesis mode.* In this mode, several voices can be switched on and off simultaneously. By using different pitches and volumes, and by rendering them at the same time, you can generate speech. Although generating speech is an interesting option, neither the AdLib nor the Sound Blaster documentation elaborate on it.

Additive and Frequency Modulation Synthesis   The FM chip offers two methods for creating sound for normal instruments and for the bass drum: additive synthesis and frequency modulation (FM) synthesis. Both additive synthesis and frequency modulation synthesis require two operators.

NOTE
The bass drum is the only rhythm instrument that uses two operators. The high hat, tom-tom, snare drum, and cymbal use only one operator.

As shown in Figure 7.2, additive synthesis uses the two operators in a parallel way: the output consists of the sum of the operators. Consider the following simplified formula:

```
F(t) = Op1(t) + Op2(t)
Op(t) = E(t) * sin(wt+Ω)
```

where

- F(t) is the output,

- Op1 and Op2 represent the operators, and

- E(t) and Ω differ for each operator.

This way of creating sound is very limited; only organ-like sounds can be produced.

FIGURE 7.2:

Additive synthesis

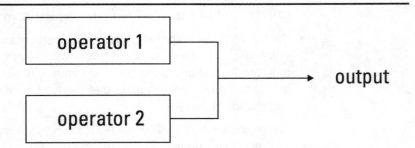

As shown in Figure 7.3, the second method, frequency modulation synthesis, lets you create more varied sounds. With this method, the two operators are used in a series. The first operator, the *modulator*, acts upon the second operator, the *carrier*. Consider the following formula:

```
Fm(t) = Em(t) * sin(wt+β*Fm(t))
Fc(t) = Ec(t) * sin(wt+Fm(t))
```

Here, the parameter w in the first formula can differ from the w in the second formula and the modulator can use its own output again as input. This is what is known as the *feedback principle*. The value of β can be changed so as to modify the intensity of the feedback.

The sound created by one of the two syntheses can be rendered for a certain time at a particular frequency. The tone (the sound rendered at a certain frequency) can be enabled and disabled in time. The sound continues or stops in accordance with the settings of the operators.

FIGURE 7.3:
Frequency modulation synthesis

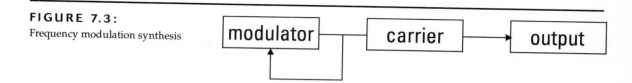

The Three Parts of an Operator

As you already know, the three parts of an operator are the oscillator, the envelope generator, and the level controller. The following section describes each in detail.

The Oscillator

The oscillator contains four adjustable settings:

- The *frequency multiplier* (MULTI) multiplies the frequency of the generated signal by a certain number. Because the final signal is determined by two operators, this setting allows you to create a signal consisting of two harmonic signals.

- The *frequency vibrato* (VIB), when selected, creates a small fluctuation in the frequency of the signal. In other words, it creates a vibrato effect.

- The *modulation feedback* (FB) allows you to set the intensity of this input signal. As mentioned earlier, the modulator can use its own output signal again as input.

- The *wave signal* (WS) lets you use a sine wave, as well as use a wave derived from a sine. Figure 7.4 shows the four possible waveforms.

FIGURE 7.4:

The four possible waveforms

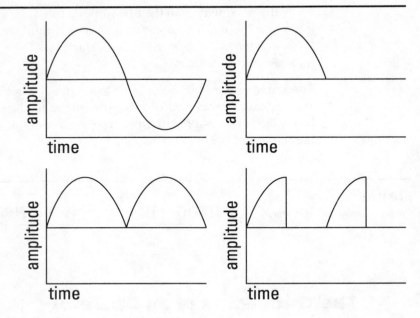

The Envelope Generator

As shown in Figure 7.5, the envelope generator has six settings. The six settings, along with the sustain level and maximum level, are:

Setting	Explanation
AR	*The attack rate.* The input signal begins at level 0 (complete silence). Next, the signal rises to its maximum level at a certain rate. This is the option you use to set the rate.
DR	*The decay rate.* After the signal reaches the maximum level, it drops to the sustain level at the rate you set with this option.

Setting	Explanation
SL	*The sustain level.* After the signal reaches the maximum level, it drops at the set decay rate to the sustain level. This level can be equal to the maximum level, so the established decay rate has little effect. As long as the note is selected, the signal stays at this level. When the note is no longer enabled, the signal drops to 0 at a certain speed. To accomplish this, the sustain sound has to be selected. If this is not the case, the signal drops to 0 at that speed after it reaches the sustain level.
RR	*The release rate.* This is the above-mentioned speed at which the signal drops from the sustain level to 0.
EG-TYP	*The sustain sound.* This option determines whether the sound has to stop at the sustain level as long as the note is selected.
KSR	*The length scale.* When this option is selected, the duration of a tone becomes dependent on the pitch of the tone. The higher tones of a piano, for instance, do not last as long as the lower tones. This option allows you to simulate this effect (the higher the tone the shorter its length).

FIGURE 7.5:

The envelope generator with and without sustaining sound

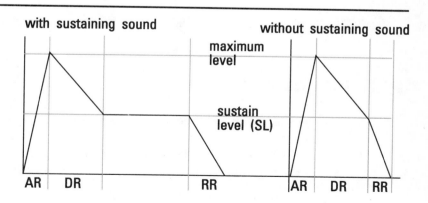

107

The Level Controller

The level controller contains three settings:

Setting	Explanation
TL	*The total level.* This is the final volume of the signal of the operator. With additive synthesis, both TL settings of the operators determine the volume of the final signal. With frequency modulation synthesis, the volume of the final signal is determined by the carrier.
KSL	*The intensity scale.* This option has the same kind of effect as the length scale of the envelope generator. For example, the low tones on a piano are not only longer, they are also louder than the high tones. You can obtain this effect with this option (the higher the tone the quieter the sound).
AM	*The amplitude vibrato.* Just like the frequency vibrato, this option causes a small fluctuation, except this time a fluctuation in the intensity of the signal is created.

NOTE   See "How the Registers Work in the FM Chip " later in this chapter for a discussion of the maximum and minimum values of these settings and how to make the settings themselves.

First we discuss how the settings are stored and how they can be used.

Instrument Formats

Depending on whether an instrument is normal or rhythmic, it has one or two operators. The settings for each instrument are stored in an *instrument file*, also called a *bank file*. There are a large number of instruments, and this produces a large number of small instrument files. These files can be difficult to manage.

To make instrument files easier to manage, Sound Blaster lets you work with instrument banks. An *instrument bank* contains the data for several instruments so you only have to work with one file instead of several. (Most AdLib software only works with instrument banks.) Both instrument files and instrument banks exist for the AdLib as well as the Sound Blaster. However, the structure of these files differs. The formats are discussed in the next four sections.

The SBI Format

SBI is the instrument format provided with the Sound Blaster. The instrument files have the extension .SBI. The file has the following structure:

00H–03H	*The file ID*. Here you find the text SBI, followed by the EOF sign 1AH. With this part you verify whether a file is an instrument file.
04H–23H	*The instrument name*. This name has to end with a zero byte. For example: Piano,0. As it will turn out later on, this field has little effect and you won't find it in the bank file.

The next sixteen bytes contain the same information for the modulator as for the carrier. The even bytes (24H, 26H, 28H, 2AH, and 2CH) contain the information for the modulator, and the odd bytes (25H, 27H, 29H, 2BH, and 2DH) contain the information for the carrier. After this comes an additional byte with data for the modulator.

The structure of these sixteen bytes is also used in the other file formats that are provided with the Sound Blaster. Table 7.1 shows the structure of the SBI format.

The INS Format

INS is the instrument format provided with the AdLib card. The instrument files have the extension .INS. As Table 7.2 shows, the structure of this format is very different from the SBI format.

TABLE 7.1: Structure of the SBI Format

Byte 24H and 25H: The audio settings

Bit	Setting
7	Frequency vibrato (VIB)
6	Amplitude vibrato (AM)
5	Sustain sound (EG-TYP)
4	Length scale (KSR)
3–0	Frequency multiplier (MULTI)

Byte 26H and 27H: The intensity scale and the volume of the signal

Bit	Setting
7–6	Intensity scale setting (KSL)
5–0	Signal (TL)

Byte 28H and 29H: The attack and decay rates

Bit	Setting
7–4	Attack rate (AR)
3–0	Decay rate (DR)

Byte 2AH and 2BH: The sustain level and the release rate

Bit	Setting
7–4	Sustain level (SL)
3–0	Release rate (RR)

Byte 2CH and 2DH: The type of sound wave

Bit	Setting
7–2	0
1–0	Wave type (WS)

TABLE 7.1: Structure of the SBI Format (continued)

Byte 2EH: Additional information about the feedback and the used synthesis

Bit	Setting
7–4	0
3–1	Feedback (FB)
0	Synthesis type (FM)

Byte 2FH–33H: Reserved for future extensions

TABLE 7.2: Structure of the INS Format

Byte	Setting
00H	Instrument type. If this byte contains the value 0, a normal instrument is involved; the value 1 indicates a rhythm instrument.
01H	If a rhythm instrument is involved, this byte contains an instrument number for the instrument type. This field has no function for a normal instrument.

The following bytes are for the modulator:

Byte	Setting
02H–03H	Intensity scale (KSL)
04H–05H	Frequency multiplier (MULTI)
06H–07H	Feedback setting (FB)
08H–09H	Attack rate (AR)
0AH–0BH	Sustain level (SL)
0CH–0DH	Sustain sound setting (EG-TYP)
0EH–0FH	Decay rate (DR)
10H–11H	Release rate (RR)
12H–13H	Volume level (TL)
14H–15H	Frequency vibrato setting (VIB)

TABLE 7.2: Structure of the INS Format (continued)

The following bytes are for the modulator:

Byte	Setting
16H–17H	Amplitude vibrato setting (AM)
18H–19H	Length scale setting (KSR)
1AH–1BH	Type of synthesis. This byte contains the value 1 if the frequency modulation synthesis has to be applied, and 0 if the additive synthesis is used. Note: This is the opposite of the settings used for the FM chip and the SBI.

The settings for the carrier are:

Byte	Setting
1CH–1DH	Intensity scale setting (KSL)
1EH–1FH	Frequency multiplier (MULTI)
20H–21H	Not used
22H–23H	Attack rate (AR)
24H–25H	Sustain level (SL)
26H–27H	Sustain sound (EG-TYP)
28H–29H	Decay rate (DR)
2AH–2BH	Release rate (RR)
2CH–2DH	Volume level (TL)
2EH–2FH	Frequency vibrato (VIB)
30H–31H	Amplitude vibrato (AM)
32H–33H	Length scale (KSR)
34H–35H	Not used

INS vs. SBI   There are distinct differences between the SBI and INS instrument files. Although the data of the SBI format occupies fewer bytes, a lot of information has been added to this format, so the files are almost the same size. In the INS format you can add some information about the type of instrument, whereas this is not possible in the SBI format. On the other hand, you can indicate the waveform in the SBI format. This is also possible for the instrument bank file in the INS format.

The IBK Format

IBK is the instrument bank format provided with the Sound Blaster. The files have the extension .IBK. An IBK file contains 128 instruments and has the structure shown in Table 7.3.

TABLE 7.3: Structure of the IBK Format

Byte	Setting
000H–003H	The file ID, followed by the EOF byte 1AH.
004H–803H	The instrument parameters. For each instrument, sixteen bytes have been reserved. The structure of these sixteen bytes is identical to the SBI format starting at offset 24H (see Table 7.1).
804H–C83H	The corresponding names of the 128 instruments. For each name, nine bytes have been reserved. The name has to end with a zero byte, so the maximum size of the name is eight bytes. For example: Harp,0.

The BNK Format

BNK is the format used with AdLib. A BNK file can contain up to 65,535 instruments. As already mentioned, the BNK format for retrieving and saving instrument data is supported by most new AdLib software. If no bank file is indicated, the STANDARD.BNK file is used.

The bank file consists of three parts:

- The first part is the header with general information.
- The second part consists of one or more records with instrument names.
- The third part contains one or more records with the instrument settings.

The size of the last two parts can vary.

The Header   The header has the following structure:

Byte	Setting
00H–01H	The file version. The first byte is the most significant part (in front of the point), the second byte is the least significant (after the point).
02H–07H	The file ID. Contains the text AdLib and allows you to verify whether the file is indeed an instrument bank.
08H–09H	The number of instrument data used.
0AH–0BH	The total number of instrument data present. This value is equal to or more than the number of instrument data used.
0CH–0FH	The absolute start of the list of instrument names. By setting the file pointer with this value, it will point to the first instrument name.
10H–13H	The absolute start of the instrument data list. The same applies here as for the previous field.
14H–1BH	Not used. All have the value 0.

The list of instrument names consists of two or more successive records. The number of records is indicated in the header.

The Record   A record has the following structure:

Byte	Setting
00H–01H	The data offset index. This value determines the start of the data according to the following calculation:

```
start = abs_data_start + size instrument setting * this value
```

Byte	Setting
02H	Indicates whether this record is used (value 1) or not (value 0).
03H–0BH	The instrument name, ending with a zero byte. The maximum size of the name (excluding the zero byte) is eight bytes.

The Data Record   The instrument data list also consists of one or more successive records. There are as many data records as instrument names. A data record has the following structure:

Byte	Setting
00H	Instrument type: 0 = normal; 1 = rhythm.
01H	The instrument number if a rhythm instrument is involved.
02H–1EH	Modulator settings.
1FH–2BH	Carrier settings.
2CH	Sine wave type for the modulator.
2DH	Sine wave type for the carrier.

The modulator and carrier settings are the same as the settings in the INS format, only this time every setting takes one byte instead of two. This doesn't matter because the largest possible value is 63.

The list of names has to be in alphabetical order and it may not contain unused names. Unused names have to come after the last name used. Since the list of instrument names is bound by these rules, you can use searching methods that are faster than the linear method (in which case you start at the first name and search down until you find a matching name). Because the names are accompanied by an index number, the data list doesn't have to be in the same order as the list of names and the instrument data don't have to follow each other directly.

Because the total amount and the number of data used are provided separately, you can reserve space in a bank file for any new instruments. That's why the complete file doesn't have to be read and written. Modifications can be placed directly into the file. This takes considerably less time than reading the whole file.

BNK vs. IBK   It is evident that the BNK format is more flexible than the IBK format, although IBK is more compact when a bank contains a large number of instruments. The IBK format, however, can contain 128 instruments at most. If you have more instruments you will have to use several IBK files. As you can see, every format has its advantages and disadvantages.

Programs for SBI, INS, IBK, and BNK

This section offers some programs that make managing the different formats easier. Listing 7.1 is a general library containing various functions for reading, editing, and writing the four formats. Several conversion routines are included. The INS and SBI formats are used internally (the reason for this will be made clear later on) and a *bank type* is created. A bank type is a linked list of several instruments. The library doesn't contain any extensive checking routines; it's up to you to make sure everything is done right. Of course, you can add your own checking routines to the library.

NOTE   The library is also used in the play routines and other programs.

Listing 7.1: Pascal Unit for Reading and Writing the Four Formats

```
Unit Instr;
{ Unit for keeping up instruments and banks }
Interface

Const
  SBIPt = 0;
  INSPt = 1;

Type
  { Define used types }
  INSOp     = Record
                KSL, MULTI, FB,
                AR, SL, EG_TYP,
                DR, RR, TL, AM,
                VIB, KSR, FM    : Word;
              End;
  INSFormat = Record
```

```
                    Mode,
                    Number    : Byte;
                    Modulator,
                    Carrier   : INSOp;
                    MWafeSel,
                    CWafeSel  : Word;
                  End;
    SBIFormat = Record
                    Snd, KSLTL,
                    ARDR, SLRR,
                    WS, FBFM   : Array [0..1] Of Byte;
                    Dummy      : Array [0..3] Of Byte;
                  End;
    SBIFormatP = ^SBIFormat;
    INSFormatP = ^INSFormat;
    InsName    = Array [0..8] Of Char;
    InsTp      = Record
                    Sort : Byte;
                    Case Boolean Of
                      True  : (INS : INSFormatP);
                      False : (SBI : SBIFormatP);
                  End;
    BnkTp      = ^BnkRc;
    BnkRc      = Record
                    Name : InsName;
                    Ins  : InsTp;
                    Next : BnkTp;
                  End;

{ Load instrument }
Procedure LoadINS(N : String; Var I : InsTp);
Procedure LoadSBI(N : String; Var I : InsTp);
{ Load bank file }
Procedure LoadBNK(N : String; Var B : BnkTp);
Procedure LoadIBK(N : String; Var B : BnkTp);
{ Save one instrument }
Procedure SaveINS(N : String; I : InsTp);
Procedure SaveSBI(N : String; I : InsTp);
{ Save bank }
Procedure SaveBNK(N : String; B : BnkTp);
Procedure SaveIBK(N : String; B : BnkTp);
{ Remove one instrument or whole bank from memory. }
```

```
Procedure RemoveIns(Var I : InsTp);
Procedure RemoveBnk(Var B : BnkTp);
{ Some routines for maintaining a bank }
Procedure FindIns(N : InsName; B : BnkTp;
                  Var F : BnkTp);
Procedure DelIns(N : InsName; Var B : BnkTp);
Procedure AddIns(N : InsName; Var B : BnkTp;
                 I : InsTp);
Function NumberOfIns(B : BnkTp) : Word;
Procedure CopyIns(S : InsTp; Var T : InsTp);
Procedure GoodInsName(Var N : InsName);
{ Conversion routines }
Procedure SBIToINS(Var I : InsTp);
Procedure INSToSBI(Var I : InsTp);
Procedure StrToName(S : String; Var N : InsName);

Implementation

Type
  ByteArray  = Array [0..52] Of Byte; { help types   }
  WordArray  = Array [0..52] Of Word; { at conversion }
  { AdLib file formats }
  BNKHeader  = Record
                 Version   : Word;
                 ID        : Array [0..5] Of Char;
                 NoUsed,
                 NoTotal   : Word;
                 NameStart,
                 DataStart : LongInt;
                 Dummy     : Array [0..7] Of Byte;
               End;
  BNKInsName = Record
                 IndexNo   : Word;
                 Used      : Byte;
                 Name      : InsName;
               End;
  BNKOp      = Record
                 KSL, MULTI, FB,
                 AR, SL, EG_TYP,
                 DR, RR, TL, AM,
                 VIB, KSR, FM   : Byte;
               End;
  BNKInsData = Record
```

```
                    Mode,
                    Number      : Byte;
                    Modulator,
                    Carrier     : BNKOp;
                    MWS,
                    CWS         : Byte;
              End;
   { Sound Blaster file formats }
   SBIFile    = Record
                    ID          : Array [0..3] Of Char;
                    Name        : Array [0..31] Of Char;
                    Operators   : SBIFormat;
              End;
   IBKFile    = Record
                    ID   : Array [0..3] Of Char;
                    Data : Array [0..127] Of SBIFormat;
                    Name : Array [0..127] Of InsName;
              End;

Procedure SBI2INSOp(Var O : INSOp; H : SBIFormat;
                    T : Byte);
{ Converts SBI operator to INS operator. }
Begin
  With H Do Begin
    O.AM:=(Snd[T] AND 128) SHR 7;
    O.VIB:=(Snd[T] AND 64) SHR 6;
    O.EG_TYP:=(Snd[T] AND 32) SHR 5;
    O.KSR:=(Snd[T] AND 16) SHR 4;
    O.MULTI:=Snd[T] AND 15;
    O.KSL:=(KSLTL[T] AND 192) SHR 6;
    O.TL:=KSLTL[T] AND 63;
    O.AR:=(ARDR[T] AND 240) SHR 4;
    O.DR:=ARDR[T] AND 15;
    O.SL:=(SLRR[T] AND 240) SHR 4;
    O.RR:=SLRR[T] AND 15;
    O.FB:=(FBFM[T] AND 14) SHR 1;
    O.FM:=(FBFM[T] AND 1) XOR 1;
  End;
End;

Procedure INS2SBIOp(Var H : SBIFormat; O : INSOp;
                    T : Byte);
{ Converts INS operator to SBI operator. }
```

```
Begin
  With O Do Begin
    H.Snd[T]:=(AM SHL 7) OR (VIB SHL 6) OR
              (EG_TYP SHL 5) OR (KSR SHL 4) OR
              MULTI;
    H.KSLTL[T]:=(KSL SHL 6) OR TL;
    H.ARDR[T]:=(AR SHL 4) OR DR;
    H.SLRR[T]:=(SL SHL 4) OR RR;
    H.FBFM[T]:=(FB SHL 1) OR (FM XOR 1);
  End
End;

Procedure ByteToWord(Var I : INSOp; O : BNKOp);
{ Converts 8 bits to 16 bits }
Var
  P : ^ByteArray;
  Q : ^WordArray;
  T : Byte;
Begin
  Q:=Addr(I); P:=Addr(O);
  For T:=0 To 13 Do
    Q^[T]:=P^[T];
End;

Procedure WordToByte(Var O : BNKOp; I : INSOp);
{ Converts 16 bits settings to 8 bits }
Var
  P : ^ByteArray;
  Q : ^WordArray;
  T : Byte;
 Begin
  Q:=Addr(I); P:=Addr(O);   { copy from Q to P }
  For T:=0 To 13 Do
    P^[T]:=Lo(Q^[T]);       { uses the LSB }
End;

Procedure SBIToINS(Var I : InsTp);
{ Converts bit settings of SBI to bytes for INS. }
Var
  S : INSFormatP;
Begin
  If I.Sort<>INSPt Then Begin
    New(S);
    SBI2INSOp(S^.Modulator,I.SBI^,0);
    SBI2INSOp(S^.Carrier,I.SBI^,1);
```

```
        S^.MWafeSel:=I.SBI^.WS[O] AND 3;
        S^.CWafeSel:=I.SBI^.WS[1] AND 3;
        S^.Mode:=O;
        S^.Number:=O;
        Dispose(I.SBI);
        I.INS:=S;
        I.Sort:=INSPt;
    End;
End;

Procedure INSToSBI(Var I : InsTp);
{ Same story but this time the other way round. }
Var
    S : SBIFormatP;
Begin
    If I.Sort<>SBIPt Then Begin
        New(S);
        INS2SBIOp(S^,I.INS^.Modulator,O);
        INS2SBIOp(S^,I.INS^.Carrier,1);
        S^.WS[O]:=I.INS^.MWafeSel;
        S^.WS[1]:=I.INS^.CWafeSel;
        Dispose(I.INS);
        I.SBI:=S;
        I.Sort:=SBIPt;
    End;
End;

Procedure CopyIns(S : InsTp; Var T : InsTp);
Begin
    If S.Sort=InsPt Then Begin
        New(T.INS);
        T.INS^:=S.INS^;
        T.Sort:=InsPt;
    End
    Else Begin
        New(T.SBI);
        T.SBI^:=S.SBI^;
        T.Sort:=SBIPt;
      End
End;

Procedure LoadINS(N : String; Var I : InsTp);
Var
    F : File;
```

```pascal
Begin
  I.Sort:=INSPt;
  New(I.INS);
  Assign(F,N); Reset(F,1);
  BlockRead(F,I.INS^,SizeOf(I.INS^));
  Close(F);
  I.INS^.MWafeSel:=0; I.INS^.CWafeSel:=0;
End;

Procedure LoadSBI(N : String; Var I : InsTp);
Var
  H : SBIFile;
  F : File;
Begin
  Assign(F,N); Reset(F,1);
  BlockRead(F,H,SizeOf(H));
  If H.Id='SBI'+#$1A Then Begin
    New(I.SBI);
    I.SBI^:=H.Operators;
    I.Sort:=SBIpt;
  End;
  Close(F);
End;

Procedure LoadBNK(N : String; Var B : BnkTp);
Var
  Header  : BNKHeader;
  Name    : BNKInsName;
  Data    : BNKInsData;
  NamePos : LongInt;
  I       : InsTp;
  F       : File;
Begin
  B:=Nil;
  I.Sort:=INSPt;
  New(I.INS);
  Assign(F,N); Reset(F,1);
  BlockRead(F,Header,SizeOf(Header));
  If Header.ID='ADLIB-' Then Begin
    NamePos:=Header.NameStart;        { first name }
    While Header.NoUsed>0 Do Begin
      Seek(F,NamePos);                { go to name }
      BlockRead(F,Name,SizeOf(Name));
```

```
        NamePos:=FilePos(F);              { next name }
        If Name.Used<>0 Then Begin
          Seek(F,Header.DataStart+     { go to data }
               Name.IndexNo*SizeOf(Data));
          BlockRead(F,Data,SizeOf(Data));
          I.INS^.Mode:=Data.Mode;
          I.INS^.Number:=Data.Number;
          ByteToWord(I.INS^.Modulator,Data.Modulator);
          ByteToWord(I.INS^.Carrier,Data.Carrier);
          I.INS^.MWafeSel:=Data.MWS;
          I.INS^.CWafeSel:=Data.CWS;
          AddIns(Name.Name,B,I);
        End;
        Dec(Header.NoUsed)              { number of instr. }
      End
    End;
  Close(F);
  Dispose(I.INS);
End;

Procedure LoadIBK(N : String; Var B : BnkTp);
Var
  F   : File;
  IBK : IBKFile;
  I   : InsTp;
  T   : Word;
Begin
  B:=Nil; I.Sort:=SBIPt;
  New(I.SBI);
  Assign(F,N); Reset(F,1);
  BlockRead(F,IBK,SizeOf(IBK));  { reads all }
  Close(F);
  If IBK.ID='IBK'+#$1A Then
    For T:=0 To 127 Do             { 128 instr. }
      If IBK.Name[T][0]<>#0 Then Begin
        I.SBI^:=IBK.Data[T];
        AddIns(IBK.Name[T],B,I);
      End;
  Dispose(I.SBI);
End;

Procedure SaveINS(N : String; I : InsTp);
Var
  F  : File;
  C  : InsTp;
```

```
Begin
  CopyIns(I,C);
  SBIToINS(I);
  Assign(F,N); ReWrite(F,1);
  BlockWrite(F,I.INS^,SizeOf(I.INS^)-2);
  Close(F);
  RemoveIns(C);
End;

Procedure SaveSBI(N : String; I : InsTp);
Var
  D : SBIFile;
  F : File;
  C : InsTp;
Begin
  D.Id[0]:='S'; D.Id[1]:='B'; D.Id[2]:='I';
  D.Id[3]:=#$1A;
  CopyIns(I,C);
  INSToSBI(C);
  Assign(F,N); ReWrite(F,1);
  D.Operators:=C.SBI^;
  BlockWrite(F,C.INS^,SizeOf(C.INS^)-2);
  Close(F);
  RemoveIns(C);
End;

Procedure SaveBNK(N : String; B : BnkTp);
Var
  F        : File;
  Header   : BNKHeader;
  Name     : BNKInsName;
  Data     : BNKInsData;
  NumberOf : Word;
  H        : BnkTp;
  C        : InsTp;
Begin
  Assign(F,N); ReWrite(F,1);
  NumberOf:=NumberOfIns(B);  { determine number of instr. }
  Header.Version:=1;         { set header }
  Header.ID:='ADLIB-';
  Header.NoUsed:=NumberOf;
  Header.NoTotal:=NumberOf;
  Header.NameStart:=SizeOf(Header);
```

```
      Header.DataStart:=SizeOf(Header)+
                      NumberOf*SizeOf(Name);
      BlockWrite(F,Header,SizeOf(Header));
      H:=B;
      Name.IndexNo:=0;                     { start at index 0 }
      Name.Used:=1;                        { all samples are used }
      While H<>Nil Do Begin                { process names }
        Name.Name:=H^.Name;
        BlockWrite(F,Name,SizeOf(Name));
        Inc(Name.IndexNo);
        H:=H^.Next;
      End;
      H:=B;
      While H<>Nil Do Begin                { process data }
        CopyIns(H^.Ins,C);
        SBIToINS(C);
        Data.Mode:=C.INS^.Mode;
        Data.Number:=C.INS^.Number;
        WordToByte(Data.Modulator,C.INS^.Modulator);
        WordToByte(Data.Carrier,C.INS^.Carrier);
        Data.MWS:=C.INS^.MWafeSel;
        Data.CWS:=C.INS^.CWafeSel;
        BlockWrite(F,Data,SizeOf(Data));
        H:=H^.Next;
        RemoveIns(C);
      End;
      Close(F);
    End;

    Procedure SaveIBK(N : String; B : BnkTp);
    Var
      F   : File;
      IBK : IBKFile;
      Ins : InsTp;
      T   : Word;
      C   : InsTp;
    Begin
      IBK.Id[0]:='I'; IBK.Id[1]:='B'; IBK.Id[2]:='K';
      IBK.Id[3]:=#$1A;
      T:=0;
      While (T<128) AND (B<>Nil) Do Begin    { 128 instr }
        CopyIns(B^.Ins,C);
        INSToSBI(C);
        IBK.Name[T]:=B^.Name;
        IBK.Data[T]:=C.SBI^;
```

```
    Inc(T);
    B:=B^.Next;
    RemoveIns(C);
  End;
  While (T<128) Do Begin     { fill remaining instr. }
    IBK.Name[T][0]:=#0;       { with #0 }
    Inc(T);
  End;
  Assign(F,N); ReWrite(F,1); { save IBK }
  BlockWrite(F,IBK,SizeOf(IBKFile));
  Close(F);
End;

Procedure RemoveIns(Var I : InsTp);
Begin
  If I.Sort=InsPt Then
    Dispose(I.INS)
  Else
    Dispose(I.SBI)
End;

Procedure RemoveBnk(Var B : BnkTp);
Var
  H : BnkTp;
Begin
  While B<> Nil Do Begin
    H:=B^.Next;
    RemoveIns(B^.Ins);               { process instr. }
    Dispose(B);                 { remove bank record }
    B:=H;
  End;
 End;

Procedure FindIns(N : InsName; B : BnkTp;
                  Var F : BnkTp);
Begin
  GoodInsName(N);            { all capitals }
  F:=B;
  While (F<>Nil) And (N<>F^.Name) Do
    F:=F^.Next;
End;
```

```
Procedure DelIns(N : InsName; Var B : BnkTp);
Var
  H,
  V  : BnkTp;
Begin
  V:=Nil;                          { previous bank record }
  H:=B;                            { works with H instead of B }
  GoodInsName(N);
  While (H<>Nil) And (N<>H^.Name) Do Begin
    V:=H;                          { save previous record }
    H:=H^.Next;
  End;
  If H<>Nil Then Begin             { H<>Nil then found }
    RemoveIns(H^.Ins);
    If V<>Nil Then
      V^.Next:=H^.Next     { link previous record }
    Else
      B:=H^.Next;      { V=Nil then first record }
    Dispose(H);                { remove found record }
  End
End;

Procedure AddIns(N : InsName; Var B : BnkTp;
                    I : InsTp);
Var
  H,
  Q,
  V  : BnkTp;
Begin
  V:=Nil;
  H:=B;
  GoodInsName(N);
  New(Q);
  CopyIns(I,Q^.Ins);
  Q^.Name:=N;
  While (H<>Nil) And (N>H^.Name) Do Begin
    V:=H;                    { maintain alphabetic }
    H:=H^.Next;              { order }
  End;
  If (H=Nil) Or (N<>H^.Name) Then Begin
    Q^.Next:=H;                 { insert new record }
    If V<>Nil Then
      V^.Next:=Q
```

```
    Else
      B:=Q
  End
End;

Function NumberOfIns(B : BnkTp) : Word;
Var
  I : Word;
Begin
  I:=0;
  While B<>Nil Do Begin
    Inc(I);
    B:=B^.Next;
  End;
  NumberOfIns:=I;
End;

Procedure GoodInsName(Var N : InsName);
Var
  I : Byte;
Begin
  I:=0;
  While (I<9) And (N[I]<>#0) Do Begin
    N[I]:=UpCase(N[I]);
    Inc(I)
  End;
  While (I<9) Do Begin
    N[I]:=#0;
    Inc(I)
  End
End;

Procedure StrToName(S : String; Var N : InsName);
Var
  T : Byte;
Begin
  T:=0;
  While (T<8) AND (T<Length(S)) Do Begin
    N[T]:=UpCase(S[T+1]);
    Inc(T)
  End;
  While (T<9) Do Begin
```

```
      N[T]:=#0;
      Inc(T);
    End;
  End;
End.
```

Listing 7.2: Pascal Program for Converting a BNK File to an IBK File

The next listing uses the library to convert a BNK file to an IBK file. This is only one example—it can be extended with many extra options, depending on what you need to do. Using this program, you can build your own instrument bank manager.

```
Program BNKtoIBK;
Uses Instr;

Var
  Bank : BNKTp;

Begin
  WriteLn;
  If ParamCount <> 2 Then Begin
    WriteLn('Use BNK2IBK name.BNK name.IBK .');
    WriteLn;
    Halt(1);
  End;
  WriteLn('Reading: ',ParamStr(1),'.');
  { reads one format }
  LoadBNK(ParamStr(1),Bank);
  WriteLn('Writing: ',ParamStr(2),'.');
  { writes other format }
  SaveIBK(ParamStr(2),Bank);
  WriteLn;
  RemoveBnk(Bank);
End.
```

Playing Music

This section discusses the music formats for the Sound Blaster and the AdLib. The drivers SBFMDRV.COM (Sound Blaster) and SOUND.COM (AdLib) are used to play music. Both drivers make use of the timer interrupt so you don't have to pay attention to the music playing itself and can run your own programs.

Playing Music with the CMF Format

The CMF format is the music format provided with the Sound Blaster. Music files have the extension .CMF. In this section, the structure of CMF files is discussed first. Next comes a look at the functions of the driver, and then a lesson on how to play the music by means of the driver.

A CMF file consists of three parts:

- The header
- An instrument definition block
- The actual music data

NOTE The CMF format described below is Version 1.10.

The Header The header contains general information, some of which is used while playing. The header has the following structure:

Byte	Setting
00H–03H	The file ID. Contains the text CTMF (and not the EOF byte 1AH).
04H–05H	Format version. The first byte contains the number in front of the point and the second byte contains the number after the point. For Version 1.10, these two bytes have the values 01H and 0AH.
06H–07H	The absolute start of the instrument definitions from the beginning of the file.
08H–09H	The absolute start of the music data.

Byte	Setting
0AH–0BH	The number of clock ticks for a quarter note. Refer to the next field for an explanation of clock ticks. Suppose there are 96 ticks per second and the tempo is 120 (quarter notes per minute). In this case, this field has a value of 48, which means that a quarter note lasts half a second, which, by the way, is the default value.
0CH–0DH	The number of clock ticks per second. The value determines how often the timer interrupt takes place. If this field contains the value 96, this means that an interrupt takes place 96 times a second. A higher value results in better precision while playing. However, you have to adjust the piece of music to the new rate yourself.
0EH–0FH	The absolute start of the music title; has to end with a zero byte. If the word has the value zero, there is no title.
10H–11H	The absolute start of the name of the composer. Here the same rules apply as to the title (see above).
12H–13H	The absolute start of the comment; again the same rules apply as to the title.

NOTE We advise *not* using more than 32 characters (including the zero byte) for the title, the name, and the comment. This way, you avoid problems with the supporting software.

Byte	Setting
14H–23H	Voice data table. The SBFMDRV driver supports sixteen voices. In this table you can indicate whether a voice is used. If so, the byte has the value 1; otherwise it has the value 0.
24H–25H	The number of instruments used; a CMF file contains information about the instruments used. This field indicates the number of instruments used.

| 26H–27H | The basic tempo: this is the general tempo. |
| 28H–??? | Here the various texts (title, composer, comment) can be placed. |

The Instrument Block   After the header comes the instrument block with the correct data for each instrument. The data consist of sixteen bytes having the same structure as the sixteen bytes in the IBK and SBI formats (starting at offset 24H). The header contains the number of defined instruments and the start of the block. The size of the block is sixteen times the number of instruments used.

The Music Block   Finally comes the music block with the actual song data. This block has the MIDI format described in Chapter 8. In this format, three types of events are defined: a MIDI event, a system exclusive event, and a meta event. An *event* is an action that takes place at a certain time. The CMF format only supports the first two events, MIDI and system exclusive.

Defined MIDI Events

The following additional MIDI events are also defined:

Event	Use
66H, M	The parameter M contains a value between 1 and 127. The value of M is assigned to the status byte. (Using the status byte will be discussed later in this section.)
67H, M	The parameter M determines the play mode. If this parameter has the value 0, the melody mode is used. In this mode, nine instruments are available and are distributed over the sixteen MIDI channels. The rhythmic mode is used if M has the value 1. In this mode, six normal and five rhythm instruments are available. These five rhythm instruments are located on the MIDI channels shown in Table 7.4.

TABLE 7.4: The Five Rhythm Instruments

Channel	Instrument Type
12	Bass drum
13	Snare drum
14	Tom-tom
15	Cymbal
16	High-hat

As of Version 2.0, the SBFMDRV driver also supports the following two events:

Event	Use
68H, M	Raises the pitch of all following notes by $M/128$ of a semitone. After this event, all notes sound a little higher.
69H, M	Has the same effect as the previous event, but this time all notes are lowered by $M/128$.

TIP   The size of this block is equal to the size of the CMF file minus the start of the music block.

The SBFMDRV Driver

The SBFMDRV driver plays the CMF format described above using the timer. The driver is programmed through an interrupt and has to be loaded beforehand by launching the SBFMDRV.COM program. This program installs the driver on a free interrupt between vectors 128 and 191. The text FMDRV is located at offset 259 or 103H in the segment of the selected interrupt vector. This can be used to find the correct interrupt of the driver.

NOTE   See Listing 7.3 for an example of how FMDRV can be used to find the correct interrupt.

The following routines are defined in Pascal:

```
Procedure CallFMDRV(BX: Word; Var AX,CX,DX,DI: Word)
```

where

- Variables AX, BX, CX, DX, and DI represent the corresponding registers mentioned.
- Variable BX determines the selected function and, depending on this function, one or more registers are used.

NOTE   Only function 14 (supported by Version 1.21) uses the register DI. In case you do not use this function, you can adjust the above-mentioned functions so that they expect AX, BX, CX, and DX only as input.

All registers and flags in the Assembly programmer are stored. The registers AX and DX are the only ones to be changed and usually contain a certain outcome.

Sound Blaster Pro Driver   The Sound Blaster Pro is accompanied by a new version of the driver. This version contains two extra functions and plays the music through the FM chips, so some instruments can be heard on the left and others on the right. The driver also works with the standard Sound Blaster. The driver that accompanies the Sound Blaster is Version 1.02. The driver provided with the Sound Blaster Pro is Version 1.21.

NOTE   In the following descriptions of the functions, the input and the output are indicated by means of registers. These registers correspond to the variables defined in Pascal.

Function 0, Driver Version

Input: BX = 0

Output: AX = Version

This function returns the driver version in AX. The most significant byte (AH) contains the value in front of the point; the least significant byte (AL) contains the value after the point.

Function 1, Set Status Byte Address

Input: BX   = 1

                DX:AX = Segment:status byte offset

Output: None

The status byte indicates what the driver is doing. If this byte contains the value 0, the driver is doing nothing and so nothing is played. When a piece of music is played, the status byte contains the value 255 or FFH, even when the music has paused. With the marker event this byte can be loaded with its own value. This way you can keep track of the course of the playing and the correct actions can be performed at the right moment. This function also allows you to set the address of the status byte.

Function 2, Set Instrument Table

Input: BX   = 2

                CX   = Number of instruments

                DX:AX = Segment:data table offset

Output: None

You use this function to set an address to the instrument data. These instrument data are used to program the FM chip.

The structure of this table is identical to the instrument table in the CMF format: sixteen bytes per instrument. If the function is called, the MIDI channels are set with the first sixteen instruments of this table. If there are less than sixteen instruments, the last instrument is followed by the data of the first instrument to set the next MIDI channel. The driver has its own internal table with instrument data. This table is used if this function has not been called. The number of instruments may not exceed 128.

Function 3, Set Clock Frequency

Input:	BX = 3
	AX = 1193180/frequency (in Hz)
Output:	None

If the driver is not playing music, the timer interrupt is called the number of times a second that is set with this function. Usually this number is 18.2. To set this value you can assign the value 65535 or FFFFH to AX. Suppose you want the timer interrupt to be called 36 times a second. In this case, AX has the value 1193180/36 = 33144.

WARNING We advise you not to use Function 3 because it can change the functioning of the clock and cause unforeseen results.

Function 4, Set Frequency while Playing

Input:	BX = 4
	AX = 1193180/frequency (in Hz)
Output:	None

When the driver plays a piece of music, the timer interrupt is used in order to get a constant interval without the programmer having to take care of this task. With this function you can determine how many times a second the timer has to be called. The value you have to set here can be determined with the information at offset 0CH in the CMF file.

For example, if the value 96H is at offset 0CH-0DH, then AX has the value 1193180/12428, or 308CH.

You can use this function to change the playing rate by adjusting the frequency.

Function 5, Transpose the Music

Input: BX = 5

                AX = number of semitones

Output: None

You can use this function to transpose the music a number of semitones up or down. AX contains the number of semitones to transpose. Use a negative value to transpose to a lower clef or a positive value to transpose to a higher clef. In Pascal, however, AX has the type Word. To set a negative value you can use the formula $65535 - X$. The result represents the negative X.

Function 6, Play Music

Input: BX   = 6

                DX:AX = Segment:music data offset

Output: AX   = 0, music is played; 1, at this moment
                         another piece is played

Before this function is used, you can change several settings with the previous functions. The music data consists of the CMF format music block. If this function is successfully executed, AX has the value 0 and the status byte has the value 255.

Function 7, Stop Playing

Input: BX = 7

Output: AX = 0, music has stopped; 1, no music was played

This function allows you to stop the music that is played. AX contains the return code; after this function the status byte has the value 0.

Function 8, Reset Driver

Input: BX = 8

Output: AX = 0, no errors; 1, music is played

This function sets the volume of the FM chip at 0 and sets the internal instrument table. If a piece of music is being played, the previous function has to be called first. This function has to be called before you quit the program and return to DOS.

Function 9, Pause Playing

Input: BX = 9

Output: AX = 0, the music is paused; 1, no music is played

This function allows you to pause the music. It doesn't change the status byte. After this function you can use the next function to continue playing or you can use Function 7 to stop playing.

Function 10, Continue Playing

Input: BX = 10

Output: AX = 0, the music is continued; 1, no pause

The piece of music continues.

Function 11, Set User Routine

Input: BX   = 11

          DX:AX = segment:routine offset

Output: None

The user routine is called when the driver comes across a system exclusive event. At this call, ES:BX points at the byte following this event. The routine itself has to save all used registers and return to the driver with a RETF. After that, the driver will skip this event and continue playing. If you want to disable the user routine, DX and AX have to contain the value 0.

Function 12, Determine Address of MIDI Channel Settings

Input: BX = 12

Output: DX:AX = segment:MIDI channel settings offset

This function is supported as of Version 1.10. It returns the start address of the MIDI channel settings. After this function is called, DX:AX points at a list of sixteen bytes, where every byte belongs to the corresponding MIDI channel. The byte indicates whether the MIDI channel has to be audible. If the byte has the value 0, this MIDI channel is mute. If the byte contains the value 1, all notes are played. You can write to this list to enable or disable particular channels. This way you can, for instance, only listen to the rhythm section. If the driver is reset, all bytes are again loaded with the value 1, so all MIDI channels are reproduced.

Function 13, Ask for Current Address in Music Block

Input: BX = 13

Output: DX:AX = Segment:offset current address in music block

This function is supported as of Version 1.10. If a music block is processed, this function allows you to keep track of the driver, because it returns the address in the music block where the current playing routine is located. DX:AX points at the next MIDI event. This function indicates, for example, the progress of the playing.

Function 14, Set a Fade Effect

Input: BX = 14

AX = Start volume as a percentage

DX = End volume as a percentage

CX = Change intensity

DI = Step size

Output: None

This function is supported as of Version 1.21. With this function you can set a *fade*. A fade is when the volume gets louder or quieter at a constant speed. This way you can, for example, create a *fade-out*: at the end of the piece the music slowly fades away and is not cut off. You often find this kind of effect in everyday music (on the radio or on a CD). The opposite effect is called a *fade-in* and can be used at the beginning of a piece of music. With a fade-in, the sound gradually becomes audible.

The variables (registers) AX and DX both contain a value between 0 and 100. AX and DX represent a percentage that determines the final volume. Zero percent is the minimum volume (silence) and 100 percent is the maximum volume setting. The variable CX contains the value of the percentage with which AX increases or decreases until it is equal to the percentage in DX. The value of the variable DI indicates the interval in clock ticks. Suppose, for example, that the playing frequency is set at 110 Hz (110 times a second). If DI has the value 110, each second the percentage is increased or decreased by CX (until it is equal to DX).

For example, to create a fade-out you could set the variables as follows:

AX = 100, start at the current standard setting

DX = 0, fade to silence

CX = 5, by decreasing the percentage by 5 points

DI = 10, do this every ten clock ticks so the music is quiet and can be stopped after (100/5=20)*10 / playing frequency.

To obtain a fade-in, swap the values for AX and DX.

Function 15, Set the Number of Repetitions

Input:	BX = 15
	AX = Number of repetitions of the music
Output:	AX = Old setting

This function is supported as of Version 1.21. It allows you to play back a piece of music several times in succession. AX contains the number of repetitions (0 = no repetition). If AX has the value 65535 or 0FFFFH, the music is repeated endlessly until it is stopped by the program. After calling Function 8, the repetition is set at 0.

Playing Music

Playing CMF Music

This section describes how you can play a CMF file. Included here is a Pascal listing containing the playing unit.

To play a CMF file the driver has to be found first. To find the driver, search between interrupts 128 and 191. If the text FMDRV is located at offset 259 (103H), you have found the right interrupt.

Next the CMF file can be processed and played. Read the file as follows:

1. Open the file.
2. Read the header and extract the right data.
3. Move the file pointer to the instrument block.
4. Read the instrument block.
5. Move the file pointer to the music block.
6. Read the music block.
7. Close the file.

Now you can start playing the music by following these steps:

1. Reset the driver.
2. Set the status byte address.
3. Set the instrument table.
4. Set the playing frequency.
5. Set the music table and start playing.

If necessary, you can use the fade function (14) and the repeat function (15).

Playing a CMF file is easy. While playing, all instruments are found in the table. If you change an instrument in the table, you will hear the results in the music. However, hearing the change in instruments can take a while because the FM chip first has to be programmed with the instrument data and this doesn't happen until the driver comes across the right MIDI event.

141

> **TIP**
>
> If you modify the instrument table before you start playing, the changed instruments are used immediately.

Listing 7.3 contains a library that searches for the driver and then reads and plays a CMF file. Furthermore, the library contains functions to work with the INSTR library given earlier. The CallFMDRV function has already defined a couple of driver functions. You can add your own function to these functions. For example, you could add functions for pausing and continuing play.

> **NOTE**
>
> See "A Word about the Program Listings" in the Introduction for advice about using the program listings in this book.

Listing 7.3: Pascal Unit to Play a CMF File and Change Instruments

```
Unit PlayCmf;
{ Unit supporting the CMF format }

Interface
Uses Instr;
Type
  CMFTp = Record       { contains the required information }
            NumberOfIns,
            MusSize,
            ClockFreq  : Word;
            InsTable,
            MusTable   : Pointer;
          End;
Var
  StatusByte : Byte;

{ find the driver and set the status word address }
Function InitFMDriver : Boolean;
{ interface routine }
Procedure CallFMDRV(BX : Word; Var AX,CX,DX,DI : Word);
{ load .CMF file }
Procedure LoadCMF(N : String; Var C : CMFTp);
{ remove .CMF type from memory }
Procedure RemoveCMF(Var C : CMFTp);
```

```
{ play a loaded .CMF file }
Procedure PlayCMF(C : CMFTp);
{ stop playing }
Procedure StopCMF;
{ Replace instrument data with I, T is the instrument number }
Procedure ReplaceIns(T : Word; I : InsTp; C : CMFTp);
{ Copy all instrument data to a bank }
Procedure InsTabToBnk(C : CMFTp; Var B : BnkTp);

Implementation
Uses Dos;

Type
   CMFHeader = Record     { for the file }
                   ID           : Array [0..3] Of Char;
                   Version,
                   InsStart,
                   MusStart,
                   QuarterNote,
                   Frequency,
                   TitStart,
                   CompStart,
                   CommStart  : Word;
                   ChannelG   : Array [1..16] Of Byte;
                   NumberOfIns,
                   BasicTempo : Word;
               End;
   SBIList  = Array [1..128] Of SBIFormat;

Var
   FMIntr : Byte;          { the interrupt found }
Function InitFMDriver : Boolean;
Type
   HelpRc = Record
               Filling : Array [0..2] Of Byte;
               ID      : Array [0..4] Of Char;
           End;
Var
   I            : Byte;
   V            : ^HelpRc;
   H            : Pointer;
   F            : Boolean;
   AX,CX,DX,DI : Word;
Begin
   I:=128; F:=False;               { start at int 128 }
```

```
    Repeat
      GetIntVec(I,H);              { H contains vector }
      V:=Ptr(Seg(H^),$100);        { V points at COM }
      If V^.ID='FMDRV' Then        { testing for text }
        F:=True                    { found }
      Else
        Inc(I);                    { next interrupt }
    Until (I>191) OR F;
    FMIntr:=I;                     { store interrupt }
    If F Then Begin                { if found, set }
      AX:=Ofs(StatusByte);         { status byte }
      DX:=Seg(StatusByte);
      CallFMDRV(1,AX,CX,DX,DI);
    End;
    InitFMDriver:=F;               { return flag }
End;

Procedure CallFMDRV(BX : Word; Var AX,CX,DX,DI : Word);
Var
  R : Registers;
Begin
  R.AX:=AX; R.BX:=BX; R.CX:=CX;          { set reg. }
  R.DX:=DX; R.DI:=DI;
  Intr(FMIntr,R);                        { call driver }
  AX:=R.AX; CX:=R.CX;            { set reg. with new }
  DX:=R.DX; DI:=R.DI;            { values }
End;

Procedure LoadCMF(N : String; Var C : CMFTp);
Var
  Header : CMFHeader;
  F      : File;
Begin
  Assign(F,N); Reset(F,1);
  BlockRead(F,Header,SizeOf(Header));
  If Header.ID='CTMF' Then Begin
    C.NumberOfIns:=Header.NumberOfIns;  { only the }
    C.ClockFreq:=Header.Frequency;  { data required }
    C.MusSize:=FileSize(F)Header.MusStart;
    GetMem(C.InsTable,C.NumberOfIns*16);
    GetMem(C.MusTable,C.MusSize);
    Seek(F,Header.InsStart);        { read tables    }
    BlockRead(F,C.InsTable^,C.NumberOfIns*16);
    Seek(F,Header.MusStart);
    BlockRead(F,C.MusTable^,C.MusSize);
```

```
    End;
    Close(F);
  End;

  Procedure RemoveCMF(Var C : CMFTp);
  Begin
    FreeMem(C.InsTable,C.NumberOfIns*16);
    FreeMem(C.MusTable,C.MusSize);
  End;

  Procedure PlayCMF(C : CMFTp);
  Var
    AX,CX,DX,DI : Word;
  Begin
    CX:=C.NumberOfIns;                { set ins table      }
    AX:=Ofs(C.InsTable^);
    DX:=Seg(C.InsTable^);
    CallFMDRV(2,AX,CX,DX,DI);
    AX:=Trunc(1193180/C.ClockFreq);   { frequency   }
    CallFMDRV(4,AX,CX,DX,DI);
    AX:=Ofs(C.MusTable^);             { start music }
    DX:=Seg(C.MusTable^);
    CallFMDRV(6,AX,CX,DX,DI);
  End;

  Procedure StopCMF;
  Var
    AX,CX,DX,DI : Word;
  Begin
    CallFMDRV(7,AX,CX,DX,DI);   { stop music }
  End;

  Procedure ReplaceIns(T : Word; I : InsTp; C : CMFTp);
  Var
    K : InsTp;
    L : ^SBIList;
  Begin
    CopyIns(I,K);                  { make safety copy }
    INSToSBI(K);
    L:=C.InsTable;                 { copy data }
    L^[T]:=K.SBI^;                 { to table }
    RemoveIns(K);                  { remove copy }
  End;

  Procedure InsTabToBnk(C : CMFTp; Var B : BnkTp);
```

```
Var
  I : InsTp;
  T : Word;
  S : String;
  N : InsName;
  L : ^SBIList;
Begin
  B:=Nil;
  I.Sort:=SBIPt; New(I.SBI);      { create instrument }
  L:=C.InsTable;
  For T:=1 To C.NumberOfIns Do Begin
    Str(T,S);                       { use dummy name }
    StrToName('INS '+S,N);
    I.SBI^:=L^[T];
    AddIns(N,B,I);
  End;
End;
End.
```

Listing 7.4: Pascal Example of the Use of the Unit PLAYCMF

The next listing contains a program that loads and plays a CMF file. If the driver allows it, the program indicates how far the playing is advanced.

```
Program CMFTest;
Uses PlayCmf, CRT;

Var
  Song        : CMFTp;    { CMF music }
  Version,
  AX,CX,DX,DI : Word;
  Ch          : Char;     { key press }
  StartAddr,              { for function 13 }
  RelatAddr   : LongInt;
  Done        : Real;

Begin
  WriteLn;
  If ParamCount < 1 Then Begin        { no name }
    WriteLn('Error : use CMFTest file.ext !');
    WriteLn;
    Halt(1)
  End;
  If Not InitFMDriver Then Begin        { no driver }
    WriteLn('Error : CMF driver not found !');
```

```
    WriteLn;
    Halt(1)
  End;
  CallFMDRV(O,Version,CX,DX,DI);      { determine version }
  LoadCMF(ParamStr(1),Song);          { load file }
  WriteLn('Playing ',ParamStr(1),'..');
  If Version>9 Then
    WriteLn;
  StartAddr:=LongInt(16*Seg(Song.MusTable^))+
            Ofs(Song.MusTable^);  { start music }
  PlayCMF(Song);
   Repeat
    If Lo(Version)>9 Then Begin      { function 13 }
      CallFMDRV(13,AX,CX,DX,DI);       { allowed }
      RelatAddr:=LongInt(DX*16)+AX-StartAddr;
      Done:=100*RelatAddr/Song.MusSize;
      GotoXY(1,WhereY);                { print % }
      Write('Done : ',Done:7:2,' %.');
    End;
  Until (StatusByte=0) Or KeyPressed;
  If KeyPressed Then                 { key pressed }
    Ch:=ReadKey;
  WriteLn; WriteLn;
  StopCMF;                           { stop playing and }
  CallFMDRV(8,AX,CX,DX,DI);          { reset driver }
End.
```

Playing Music with the ROL Format

The ROL format is the music format provided with the AdLib. In AdLib, music files have the .ROL extension. This section describes the structure of a ROL file, explores the functions of the SOUND.COM driver, and explains how to produce music with this driver.

The Structure of the ROL Format

The structure of a ROL file is more complex than that of a CMF file. The ROL file starts with a header containing general information. Here you find the information used by the Visual Composer, the music editor provided with the AdLib. The header is followed by information about the music. In this book, we describe format Version 0.4. A ROL file also contains several floating-point numbers that are coded according to the IEEE format. This format corresponds to the single type in Pascal.

The Header   The header has the following structure:

Byte	Setting
00H–01H	The format version. The number in front of the point has the value 0 for Version 0.4.
02H–03H	The format version. The number after the point has the value 4 for Version 0.4.
04H–2BH	Not used.
2CH–2DH	The number of ticks per second.
2EH–2FH	The number of quarter notes per measure; this function exists for the Visual Composer.
30H–31H	The Y-axis scale; used by Visual Composer.
32H–33H	The X-axis scale; used by Visual Composer.
34H	Not used; has to be 0.
35H	The play mode. If this byte has the value 0, the music is written in the rhythmic mode. If this byte contains the value 1, the piece is written in the melody mode. For the first mode, eleven voices are defined; for the second mode, nine voices.
36H–C4H	Not used; the first 90 bytes have to be 0.
C5H–C8H	The basic tempo. The four bytes contain a floating-point number.

The Music Data   Next come the data for the music. These data also consist of several parts containing information about events (changes that occur at a certain moment). First come the tempo events:

Byte	Setting
00H–01H	This value indicates the number of events and the numbers of repetitions of the two following fields.
02H–03H	Time of the tempo event in the number of ticks.

Byte	Setting
04H–07H	The tempo multiplier. Used to calculate the new tempo. The new tempo is equal to this number multiplied by the basic tempo. The number in the four bytes is a floating-point number with a value between 0.01 and 10.00.
08H–…	Any number of tempo events.

Instrument Data   Next comes the same information for every instrument voice on the FM chip. There are nine or eleven voices, depending on the play mode. For each voice the ROL format contains the fields mentioned below. First come all fields for the first voice, next the fields for the second voice, etc. The first part contains information about the notes to be played:

Byte	Setting
00H–0EH	Not used.
0FH–10H	The sum of the duration of all notes indicated as the number of ticks increased by 1. This field has to be used to read the two following fields. If this field has the value 0, the next two fields do not exist and this voice will not be played.
11H–12H	The note value. If it contains the value 0, this means there is a silence. Otherwise, this field has to contain a value between 12 and 107. A value of 60 represents middle C. A higher or lower value represents a semitone higher (C sharp) or a semitone lower (B).
13H–14H	The duration of the note in the number of clock ticks.
15H–…	Any repetitions of the two previous fields, as long as the sum of the duration of the notes is less than the total sum (that is given at offset 0FH).

After this comes information about the instruments used in this voice:

Byte	Setting
00H–0EH	Not used.

Byte	Setting
0FH–10H	The number of pitch events. This 16-bit value contains the number of repetitions of the next two fields.
11H–12H	The time of the pitch event as the number of ticks.
13H–16H	The pitch variation. These four bytes contain a floating-point number with a value between 0.0 and 2.0. This value sets the change of the pitch. The functioning is demonstrated with the following formula:

```
New pitch = pitch + 0.5 * (value - 1)
```

	By pitch we mean a note on the staff. This note can be raised or lowered by a semitone at most (D becomes D sharp or C sharp). The pitch increases when the value of these four bytes is bigger than 1.0. If the value is less than 1.0, the pitch decreases.
17H–…	Any repetitions of the two previous fields.

ROL vs. CMF   It is clear that the ROL format is more complex than the CMF format (even though we didn't describe the structure of the music block of the CMF format). The major difference is that a CMF file contains information about the various instruments, and CMF also uses two play modes (rhythmic and melody) at the same time. In a ROL file, only the names of the instruments can be used and the play mode is known beforehand.

The advantage of using the instrument names is that the instruments can be adjusted without changing the ROL file. Furthermore, the format of the instrument data can be changed without affecting the ROL format. The disadvantage of using the names is that, besides a ROL file, there also has to be an instrument bank or several instrument files if you want to play the ROL file. This makes it difficult to exchange ROL files. Especially if you use self-defined instruments, this can lead to sizable instrument bank files.

Playing Music with the Sound Driver

The Sound driver has to be present in memory beforehand in order for you to use it. To place it in memory, launch SOUND.COM. SOUND.COM loads itself so that it is resident in memory. You can program the driver with an interrupt—that is, with interrupt 101 or 65H. Just like the SBFMDRV driver, you can check whether the driver is present. The offset of the interrupt routine is preceded by the text SOUND-DRIVER-ADLIB, followed by three bytes having no function. This text is preceded by two bytes containing the version of the driver. Both numbers are structured according to the BCD code.

> **NOTE** See Listing 7.5 for an example of a function that checks the text and returns the version of the driver.

The driver needs two pieces of data as input: the function number and a pointer to the address of the rest of the data that can differ from call to call. The function number is located in register SI, and ES:BX points at the remaining input data. These data consist of one or more integers, so ES:BX is pointing at an array of one or more integers. There is a maximum of five integers, so the next function can be used in Pascal:

```
Procedure CallSound(F,P0,P1,P2,P3,P4: Integer)
```

After calling this function, it sometimes returns a result. This result is located in register AX and is placed in the SNDIOResult variable.

The driver has a buffer (whose size can be changed while loading) in which the various operations are stored until they have to be processed. The advantage of this method is that an entire piece of music can be passed on to the driver in one go and that the driver plays this music without you having to interfere.

Following is a discussion of the Sound Driver's 23 functions.

> **NOTE** Several versions of the Sound driver are available. In this book we describe Version 1.51.

Function 0, Initialize Driver and FM Chip

Input: None

Output: None

This function initializes the driver. The relative volume is set at 100 percent so everything sounds at maximum volume. Furthermore, the FM chip is set in melody mode and all nine instruments are set with the data for the electric piano. The buffer is emptied and the tempo is set at 90 quarter notes per minute. Finally, the use of the wave type is disabled and the difference in pitch is set at one semitone (these two functions are explained later).

Function 1, Unknown

The AdLib documentation doesn't provide information about this function. It is probably an internal function.

Function 2, Set Start of Music

Input: P0 = numerator of the start

                P1 = denominator of the start

Output: None

The fraction P0/P1 determines the start of the music, and all times indicated with the other functions will take place with reference to this time. In other words, the fraction P0/P1 is added to the given times. This way playing can begin at a particular moment. To start playing immediately, P0 and P1 must have the value 0 and 1 respectively.

NOTE   Obviously the numerator P0 may not contain the value 0. This also applies to the other numerators.

Function 3, Start or Stop Playing

Input: P0 = action

Output: None

You call this function to start the driver. If P0 has the value 1, the driver starts processing the actions in the buffer. If P0 has the value 0, processing is stopped. Thus, this function can also be used to pause and continue playing. During playing, the processed actions are removed from the buffer so new functions can be added to the buffer.

Function 4, Ask Current Driver Status

Input: None

Output: SNDIOResult = current activity

This function determines whether the driver is processing the buffer. If this is the case, the variable SNDIOResult contains the value 1. Otherwise, it contains the value 0. This function also allows you to determine whether the driver has played everything and has reached the end of the music.

Function 5, Clear Buffer

Input: None

Output: None

This function instructs the driver to disable all voices and to clear the buffer. After this, you can start playing back again.

Function 6, Set Play Mode

Input: P0 = play mode

Output: None

This function selects the melody or the rhythmic mode. Melody mode is selected when P0 has the value 0; rhythmic mode is selected with the value 1. After this function is called the relative volume is set again at 100 percent and all voices are set at the default piano. The pitch (see below) is set again at one semitone. Consequently, this function has to be called before the other functions.

NOTE The value P0 is the opposite of the value in the ROL format!

Function 7, Ask Current Mode

Input:	None
Output:	SNDIOResult = current play mode

This function returns the mode that was set with the previous function. After calling this function, SNDIOResult contains the current setting: 0 for the melody mode or 1 for the rhythmic mode.

Function 8, Set Relative Volume Event

Input:	P0 = numerator of the relative volume
	P1 = denominator of the relative volume
	P2 = numerator of the time
	P3 = denominator of the time
Output:	SNDIOResult = buffer result

With this function you set a volume event for the currently selected voice. The time is determined by the division P2/P3, and the relative volume is set with the value P0/P1. The value P0/P1 may not exceed 1. The established intensity of an instrument is multiplied by this volume. The value that is determined by this function serves as a kind of general volume setting. Just as with the other functions that set an event, SNDIOResult has a value unequal to 0 if the event has been successfully placed in the buffer. However, if SNDIOResult contains the value 0, the buffer is full. If the driver is not processing the buffer, you have to give it an instruction to do so (with function 3). During the processing of the actions stored in the buffer, room for new actions will be made available and the call can be successfully repeated.

Function 9, Set Tempo Event

Input: P0 = tempo

                P1 = numerator of the time

                P2 = denominator of the time

Output: SNDIOResult = buffer result

This function allows you to set a tempo event. This is a general event that affects all voices. Once more P1/P2 constitutes the time and the value SNDIOResult has the same meaning as for the previous functions.

Function 10, Transpose Music

Input: P0 = transposing value

Output: None

Just as with the CMF driver, the music can be transposed a number of semitones up or down. If P0 has a positive value, the music is transposed up. If it contains a negative value, the music is transposed down. This function can be represented in the following formula:

```
Note to play = real value + P0
```

Function 11, Ask Transposing Value

Input: None

Output: SNDIOResult = transposing value

This function allows you to ask for the current value.

Function 12, Select Active Voice

Input: P0 = active voice

Output: None

Most events can be set separately for each voice. You use this function to select a voice. If the driver is set at the melody mode, the value of P0 has to lie between 0 and 8. For the rhythmic mode, the value has to be between 0 and 10. After this function, the events for the voice can be set. The numbers for the rhythmic instruments are defined in Table 7.5. In the melody mode, voices 0 through 8 are available for the normal instruments.

TABLE 7.5: Numbers for Rhythm Instruments

Voice	Type of Instrument
0...5	Normal instruments
6	Bass drum
7	Snare drum
8	Tom-tom
9	Cymbal
10	High-hat

Function 13, Return Active Voice

Input: None

Output: SNDIOResult = active voice

This function allows you to return the active voice.

Function 14, Set a Note Event with a Playing Time

Input: P0 = pitch

                P1 = numerator of the playing time

P2 = denominator of the playing time

P3 = numerator of the total time

P4 = denominator of the total time

Output: SNDIOResult = buffer result

This function adds a note event for the active voice to the buffer. The note is played with a pitch of P0. The playing time is determined by the division P1/P2 and the total time is set with the division P3/P4. If the total time is larger than the playing time, there is a silence if the playing stops. The note is played when the total time of the previous note has passed. The variable SNDIOResult contains the result mentioned above. The value of P2 and P4 may be between 1 and 255. The pitch (P0) contains a value between –48 and 47, where 0 is the middle C of a piano. Table 7.6 shows the note values.

TABLE 7.6: Note Values

Note	Values							
C	–48	–36	–24	–12	0	12	24	36
C#	–47	–35	–23	–11	1	13	25	37
D	–46	–34	–22	–10	2	14	26	38
D#	–45	–33	–21	–9	3	15	27	39
E	–44	–32	–20	–8	4	16	28	40
F	–43	–31	–19	–7	5	17	29	41
F#	–42	–30	–18	–6	6	18	30	42
G	–41	–29	–17	–5	7	19	31	43
G#	–40	–28	–16	–4	8	20	32	44
A	–39	–27	–15	–3	9	21	33	45
A#	–38	–26	–14	–2	10	22	34	46
B	–37	–25	–13	–1	11	23	35	47

NOTE   The note values in the ROL file have to be decreased by 60 before they can be passed on to the driver.

Function 15, Set a Note Event

Input: P0 = pitch

P1 = numerator of the duration

P2 = denominator of the duration

Output: SNDIOResult = buffer result

When the total time is equal to the playing time, you can use this function. It works the same as the previous function. When you use it, the total time and the playing time are set to the same value (duration).

Function 16, Set an Instrument Event

Input: P0 = offset of the instrument data

P1 = segment of the instrument data

P2 = numerator of the time

P3 = denominator of the time

Output: SNDIOResult = buffer result

With this function you set an event that sets a particular instrument for the active voice. P1:P2 points at a buffer of integers that contains the information for the modulator and the carrier. The buffer contains 26 or 28 integers, depending on function 23. Its structure is the same as the structure used in the INS format. The 26 integers can be followed by another two integers with information about the waveform for the modulator and the carrier, respectively. The division P2/P3 determines the time of the event. The buffer with the instrument data has to contain the right data until after the event; then the buffer can be modified.

Function 17, Set a Tone Change Event

Input:	P0 = octave difference (has to be zero)
	P1 = numerator of the change
	P2 = denominator of the change
	P3 = numerator of the time
	P4 = denominator of the time
Output:	SNDIOResult = buffer result

This function allows you to adjust the frequency of the notes. It sets an event for the active voice at the time P3/P4. After this event is processed, P1/P2 part of a semitone is added to or subtracted from the notes (depending on the sign of P1). After this, the frequency is being calculated. This way every tone sounds a little higher or lower. With function 22 you can set a bigger range and use a particular part of two tones, for example, instead of a particular part of a semitone. This way, the note sounds one note lower instead of a quarter note lower. The value of P1 has to lie between –100 and 100; the value of P2 has to be between 1 and 100.

Function 18, Set the Number of Ticks Per Quarter Note

Input:	P0 = number of ticks
Output:	None

With this function you set the smallest part of the quarter note. All note events have to be set at a multiple of 1/P0. The rate of the timer is also changed with this function, and the value of P0 therefore has to satisfy the following condition:

```
18.2 <= (P0 * Tempo/60) that is P0 >= 1092/Tempo
```

The number of clock interrupts (ticks) per second is

```
Ticks = 60 or P0 (if this one is larger than 60) * Tempo/60
```

Function 19, Play a Note Immediately

Input: P0 = voice

P1 = pitch

Output: None

This function plays immediately—and with the current settings—a note on the selected voice. The function switches the note on (with function 20 you can switch this note off). This is useful when a certain action suddenly occurs (such as explosions). By setting the data for a particular voice beforehand, this particular voice can be played at any time. With this function and the next two functions you can also directly play a piece of music. Be careful, however, to get the timing right.

Function 20, Stop Playing

Input: P0 = voice

Output: None

With this function you can switch off the note started with the previous function.

Function 21, Directly Set an Instrument

Input: P0 = voice

P1 = offset of the instrument data

P2 = segment of the instrument data

Output: None

This function works the same as function 16, but here the instrument is set directly. After this function you can immediately change the instrument data because the FM chip is directly programmed with this data.

WARNING   Functions 22 and 23 are only supported as of Version 1.03.

Function 22, Set the Range of the Pitch Change

Input: P0 = number of semitones

Output: None

This function allows you to change the range of function 17 and can be set with a number of semitones. After calling function 0, the value is set at 1 in order to stay compatible with older versions. If necessary, this function has to be called after function 0.

Function 23, Set Wave Information Flag

Input: P0 = use of wave information

Output: None

Functions 16 and 21 both set instruments, but older versions lack data about the used sine wave. This function indicates that this information is present and can be used. If you set P0 to the value 1, functions 16 and 21 will accept two additional integers after the 26 integers containing information about the wave types. If P0 has the value 0, the default sine wave is used. This option is also set after calling function 0, once again to guarantee compatibility with older versions. If necessary, this function has to be called after function 0.

Sound Driver vs. CMF   The Sound driver offers a more extended choice of functions than the CMF Driver, which can only play CMF music. The Sound driver allows you to play various formats.

Playing ROL Music

Playing a ROL file is more difficult than playing a CMF file. Since all kinds of addresses have to be kept up to date, it takes longer to read ROL files. And playing the file itself is also more complex because the buffer size of the Sound driver can vary, so it can take a while before the entire piece of music is sent to the Sound driver. This can lead to all kinds of delays.

LoadROL Function   Before a ROL file can be played, it has to be read. The LoadROL function provides an example of how ROL files are read. LoadROL works as follows:

1. The function opens the file.

2. It reads the header and extracts the required information.

3. It reads the tempo events.

4. It reads the total duration of the notes for the first voice.

5. It determines the number of note events.

6. It reads these events.

7. It reads the instrument events for the first voice.

8. It reads the volume and pitch events.

9. LoadROL repeats steps 4 through 8 for the remaining voices.

10. It closes the file.

Before the file can be played, a bank file has to be loaded. Playing the file is accomplished as follows:

1. The driver is reset.

2. The correct values—the tempo, extra information, etc.—are set.

3. A determination is made to see if all event pointers point to the first event.

4. The next event that has to take place is found.

5. The next event is sent to the driver.

6. If everything works out, a search is made for the next event and step 5 is repeated until all events are processed. However, if the next event is not found, the buffer is full and has to be processed. To do this the driver starts processing the buffer.

7. A search is made for the next event.

8. The next event is sent to the driver.

9. Step 8 is repeated until the event has successfully been added to the buffer.

10. The next event is found and step 8 is repeated until all events are processed.

NOTE In step 5 and 6, a certain number of events can be processed instead of filling the buffer so that the music can be started earlier. This method is also used in the next listing.

Listing 7.5 provides a library for loading and playing a ROL file. As with the CMF library, a few functions are defined with the function CallSound, and you can add your own functions to the library (for example, pause and continue). The library is designed to play a ROL format, not to change it. The various types have to be adjusted if you want to be able to change, remove, and add events. This way you can write your own ROL editor.

NOTE In Listing 7.5, a type is defined that uses an array containing one element. Further on in the listing, however, elements with a higher index are used. This is possible because a certain amount of memory for this array is reserved beforehand, so several elements can be accessed. To access these elements without an error occurring, the Range Checking has to be switched off ($R–). Moreover, Pascal only supports the single type if the co-processor option is enabled ($N+). Since most users do not have a co-processor, the emulator has to be used ($E+). These options cause the program in the example to be quite large after it is compiled.

Listing 7.5: Pascal Unit for Loading and Playing a ROL File

```
Unit PlayRol;
{ Unit to load and play .ROL files. }
{$N+E+R}

Interface
```

```
Uses Instr;

Const
  ProcessEvents = 100;

Type
  { the different events }
  InsEvRc  = Record
               Time  : Word;
               Ins   : InsName;
               Dummy : Array [0..2] Of Byte;
             End;
  MultEvRc = Record
               Time : Word;
               Mult : Single;
             End;
  NoteEvRc = Record
               Tone    : Integer;
               Time    : Word;
             End;
  NoteEvs  = Record
               Number : Word;
               E      : Array [1..1] Of NoteEvRc;
             End;
  InsEvs   = Record
               Number : Word;
               E      : Array [1..1] Of InsEvRc;
             End;
  MultEvs  = Record
               Number : Word;
               E      : Array [1..1] Of MultEvRc;
             End;
  NoteEvPt = ^NoteEvs;
  MultEvPt = ^MultEvs;
  InsEvPt  = ^InsEvs;
  { each voice has the same events }
  VoiceRc = Record
               Used   : Boolean;
               NoteT,              { are used }
               NoteO,              { while playing }
               InsO,               { idem }
               VolO,               { idem }
               PitchO : Word; { idem }
               NoteEv : NoteEvPt;
               InsEv  : InsEvPt;
```

```
                    VolEv,
                    PitchEv : MultEvPt;
                  End;
     RolTp     = Record
                    BasicTempo    : Single;
                    Mode,
                    NoOfVoices,
                    TickBeat,
                    TempoO    : Word;  { to play }
                    TempoEv   : MultEvPt;
                    Voice     : Array [0..10] Of ^VoiceRc;
                  End;

Var
  SNDIOResult : Word;

{ Test whether the Sound driver is present, SNDIOResult
  then contains the version. }
Function TestForSNDDriver : Boolean;
{ Load a .ROL file }
Procedure LoadRol(N : String; Var R : RolTp);
{ Remove ROL data from memory }
Procedure RemoveRol(Var R : RolTp);
{ Play music, use bank B }
Procedure PlayRol(Var R : RolTp; B : BnkTp);
{ Reset driver }
Procedure ResetSoundDrv;
{ General interface routine }
Procedure CallSound(F,P0,P1,P2,P3,P4 : Integer);

Implementation
Uses Dos;

Const
  SNDIntr     = 101;

Type
  EventList = (TempoEve, VolEve, InsEve,
               NoteEve, PitchEve, NoEve);
  RolHeader  = Record
                  MajVersion,
                  MinVersion  : Word;
                  Dummy0       : Array [0..39] Of Char;
                  TickBeat,
                  BeatSecond,
```

```
                    YScale,
                    XScale      : Word;
                    Dummy1      : Byte;
                    PlayMode    : Byte;
                    Dummy2      : Array [0..142] Of Byte;
                    BasicTempo  : Single;
                  End;
      TestHeader = Record
                     Version : Word;
                     ID      : Array [0..18] Of Char;
                     Dummy   : Array [0..2] Of Byte;
                   End;
Var
  SDiv   : Word;
  Bank   : BnkTp;

Function TestForSNDDriver : Boolean;
Var
  P : ^TestHeader;
  Q : Pointer;
Begin
  GetIntVec(SNDIntr,Q);              { driver address }
  P:=Ptr(Seg(Q^),Ofs(Q^)-SizeOf(TestHeader));
  SNDIOResult:=P^.Version;
  TestForSNDDriver:= P^.ID='SOUND-DRIVER-AD-LIB';
End;

Procedure CallSound(F,P0,P1,P2,P3,P4 : Integer);
Var
  R : Registers;
  A : Array [0..4] Of Integer;
Begin
  A[0]:=P0; A[1]:=P1; A[2]:=P2;  { copy data }
  A[3]:=P3; A[4]:=P4;
  R.SI:=F;                        { SI is function }
  R.ES:=Seg(A);                   { ES:BX points at }
  R.BX:=Ofs(A);                   { data list }
  Intr(SNDIntr,R);
  SNDIOResult:=R.AL;
End;

Procedure LoadRol(N : String; Var R : RolTp);
Var
  F : File;
  Procedure ReadMultEvents(Var N : MultEvPt);
```

```
Var
  S,
  Number : Word;
Begin
  S:=SizeOf(MultEvRc);
  BlockRead(F,Number,2);
  GetMem(N,2+Number*S);
  N^.Number:=Number;
  BlockRead(F,N^.E,Number*S);
End;

Procedure ReadInsEvents(Var N : InsEvPt);
Var
  S,
  Number : Word;
Begin
  S:=SizeOf(InsEvRc);
  BlockRead(F,Number,2);
  GetMem(N,2+Number*S);
  N^.Number:=Number;
  BlockRead(F,N^.E,Number*S);
End;

Procedure ReadNoteEvents(Var N : NoteEvPt);
Var
  S,
  Total,
  Sum,
  Duration,
  Number   : Word;
  Start    : LongInt;
Begin
  S:=SizeOf(NoteEvRc);
  BlockRead(F,Total,2);
  Start:=FilePos(F);
  Sum:=0;                          { determine number }
  Number:=0;                       { of notes }
  While Sum<Total Do Begin
    Seek(F,FilePos(F)+2);
    BlockRead(F,Duration,2);
    Sum:=Sum+Duration;
    Inc(Number);
  End;
  Seek(F,Start);                   { read notes }
  GetMem(N,2+Number*S);
```

```
      N^.Number:=Number;
      BlockRead(F,N^.E,Number*S);
    End;

Var
  Header     : RolHeader;
  Number     : Word;
  MaxVoice   : Byte;
  V          : Byte;
Begin
  Assign(F,N); Reset(F,1);
  BlockRead(F,Header,SizeOf(Header));
  R.BasicTempo:=Header.BasicTempo;   { process header }
  R.Mode:=Header.PlayMode;
  R.TickBeat:=Header.TickBeat;
  If R.Mode=1 Then
    R.NoOfVoices:=8
  Else
    R.NoOfVoices:=10;
  ReadMultEvents(R.TempoEv);              { read tempo ev. }
  For V:=0 To R.NoOfVoices Do Begin
    New(R.Voice[V]);
    With R.Voice[V]^ Do Begin
      Seek(F,FilePos(F)+15);
      ReadNoteEvents(NoteEv);
      Seek(F,FilePos(F)+15);
      ReadInsEvents(InsEv);
      Seek(F,FilePos(F)+15);
      ReadMultEvents(VolEv);          { read volume ev. }
      Seek(F,FilePos(F)+15);
      ReadMultEvents(PitchEv);     { read pitch ev. }
      Used:=NoteEv^.Number > 0;
    End;
  End;
  Close(F);
End;

Procedure RemoveRol(Var R : RolTp);
Var
  V : Byte;
Begin
  For V:=0 To R.NoOfVoices Do Begin
    With R.Voice[V]^ Do Begin
      FreeMem(NoteEv,
              2+NoteEv^.Number*SizeOf(NoteEvRc));
```

```
      FreeMem(InsEv,
             2+InsEv^.Number*SizeOf(InsEvRc));
      FreeMem(PitchEv,
             2+PitchEv^.Number*SizeOf(MultEvRc));
      FreeMem(VolEv,
             2+VolEv^.Number*SizeOf(MultEvRc));
    End;
    Dispose(R.Voice[V]);
  End;
  FreeMem(R.TempoEv,
         2+R.TempoEv^.Number*SizeOf(MultEvRc));
End;

Procedure ToneEvent(V,T,S,H : Integer);
Begin
  CallSound(12,V,0,0,0,0);          { select voice }
  If H<>0 Then
    If S<>0 Then                    { silence after note ? }
      CallSound(14,H60,T,SDiv,T+S,SDiv)     { yes }
    Else
      CallSound(15,H60,T,SDiv,0,0)          { no }
  Else
    CallSound(14,H60,0,SDiv,T,SDiv);   { no note }
End;

Procedure VolEvent(V,T : Word; F : Single);
Begin
  CallSound(12,V,0,0,0,0);          { select voice }
  CallSound(8,Trunc(F*255),255,T,SDiv,0)
End;

Procedure PitchEvent(V,T : Word; F : Single);
Begin
  CallSound(12,V,0,0,0,0);          { select voice }
  CallSound(17,0,Trunc(F*255),255,T,SDiv);
End;

Procedure InsEvent(V,T : Word; I : InsName);
Var
  B : BnkTp;
Begin
  GoodInsName(I);
  FindIns(I,Bank,B);                { find data }
  If B <> Nil Then Begin            { found ? }
    SBIToIns(B^.Ins);               { for safety reasons }
```

```
      CallSound(12,V,0,0,0, 0);      { select voice }
      CallSound(16, Ofs(B^.Ins.INS^.Modulator),
                    Seg(B^.Ins.INS^.Modulator),T,SDiv,0);
   End
End;

Procedure TempoEvent(T : Word; B,F : Single);
Begin
   CallSound(9,Trunc(B*F),T,SDiv,0,0);
End;

Procedure ResetRol(Var R : RolTp);
Var
   V : Byte;
Begin
   For V:=0 To R.NoOfVoices Do       { go along all voices }
      With R.Voice[V]^ Do Begin
         NoteT:=0;                    { total duration 0 }
         NoteO:=1;                    { first note event }
         InsO:=1;                     { idem for instr. }
         VolO:=1;                     { idem for volume }
         PitchO:=1;                   { idem for pitch }
      End;
      R.TempoO:=1;                    { idem for tempo }
End;

Function GiveEv(Var R : RolTp; V : Byte;
                   E : EventList) : Word;
Var
   H : Word;

Begin
   H:= $FFFF;
   If E <> TempoEve Then
      With R.Voice[V]^ Do
         Case E Of
            VolEve    : If VolO<=VolEv^.Number Then
                           H:=VolEv^.E[VolO].Time;
            InsEve    : If InsO<=InsEv^.Number Then
                           H:=InsEv^.E[InsO].Time;
            PitchEve  : If PitchO<=PitchEv^.Number Then
                           H:=PitchEv^.E[PitchO].Time;
            NoteEve   : If NoteO<=NoteEv^.Number Then
                           H:=NoteT;
         End
```

```
      Else
        If R.TempoO <= R.TempoEv^.Number Then
           H:=R.TempoEv^.E[R.TempoO].Time;
      GiveEv:=H;              { give time for next event }
End;


Procedure FindNextEv(Var R : RolTp; Var V : Byte;
                       Var E : EventList);
Var
  T : Byte;
  H : EventList;
  G : Word;
Begin
  E:=NoEve;                     { nothing found }
  G:=GiveEv(R,0,TempoEve);      { next tempo event }
  If G <> $ffff Then            { does event exist ? }
    E:=TempoEve;                { yes, choose this one }
  For T:=0 To R.NoOfVoices Do { go along all voices }
    If R.Voice[T]^.Used Then
      For H:=VolEve To PitchEve Do { and all events }
        If G > GiveEv(R,T,H) Then Begin
          G:=GiveEv(R,T,H);   { copy lowest time }
          E:=H;               { accompanying event }
          V:=T;               { and voice }
        End;
End;


Procedure SetEvent(Var R : RolTp; V : Byte;
                     E : EventList);
Begin
  If E <> TempoEve Then        { does voice count ? }
    With R.Voice[V]^ Do        { yes }
      Case E Of
        VolEve     : With VolEv^.E[VolO] Do
                       VolEvent(V,Time,Mult);
        InsEve     : With InsEv^.E[InsO] Do
                       InsEvent(V,Time,Ins);
        NoteEve    : With NoteEv^ Do
                       If E[NoteO+1].Tone <> 0 Then
                         With E[NoteO] Do
                           ToneEvent(V,Time,0,Tone)
                       Else
                         With NoteEv^ Do
                           ToneEvent(V,E[NoteO].Time,
                                     E[NoteO+1].Time,
```

```
                                        E[NoteO].Tone);
          PitchEve : With PitchEv^.E[PitchO] Do
                        PitchEvent(V,Time,Mult);
        End
    Else
    With R.TempoEv^.E[R.TempoO] Do
        TempoEvent(Time,R.BasicTempo,Mult);
End;

Procedure IncreaseEv(Var R : RolTp; V : Byte;
                        E : EventList);
Begin
    If E <> TempoEve Then        { does voice count ? }
        With R.Voice[V]^ Do        { yes, choose voice }
            Case E Of                { increase event }
                VolEve    : Inc(VolO);
                InsEve    : Inc(InsO);
                NoteEve   : With NoteEv^ Do Begin
                               Inc(NoteT,E[NoteO].Time);
                               Inc(NoteO);
                               If E[NoteO].Tone=0 Then
                               Begin           { process silence }
                                   Inc(NoteT,E[NoteO].Time);
                                   Inc(NoteO);
                               End
                            End;
                PitchEve : Inc(PitchO);
            End
    Else
        Inc(R.TempoO);                { increase event }
End;

Procedure PlayRol(Var R : RolTp; B : BnkTp);
 Var
    Event   : EventList;
    Voice   : Byte;
    Counter : Word;
Begin
    Bank:=B;                           { set instr. bank }
    CallSound(2,0,1,0,0,0);            { start at begin }
    CallSound(5,0,0,0,0,0);            { delete all buffers }
    CallSound(6,R.Mode XOR 1,0,0,0,0); { set mode }
    CallSound(18,R.TickBeat,0,0,0,0);  { set ticks }
    SDiv:=R.TickBeat;                  { for timing }
    ResetRol(R);                       { restore data }
```

```
       Counter:=0;
       Repeat                          { fill buffer }
         FindNextEv(R,Voice,Event);
         SetEvent(R,Voice,Event);
         If SNDIOResult<>0 Then
           IncreaseEv(R,Voice,Event);
         Inc(Counter);
       Until (SNDIOResult=0) Or (Event=NoEve) OR
             (Counter>ProcessEvents);
       CallSound(3,1,0,0,0,0);         { start playing }
       While Event<>NoEve Do Begin
         Repeat                        { place in buffer }
           SetEvent(R,Voice,Event)
         Until SNDIOResult<>0;         { successful ? }
         IncreaseEv(R,Voice,Event);    { yes, next event }
         FindNextEv(R,Voice,Event);
       End;
     End;

Procedure ResetSoundDrv;
Begin
  CallSound(0,0,0,0,0,0);
End;
End
```

Listing 7.6: Pascal Example of the Use of the Unit PlayRol

Listing 7.6 contains an example of a program that loads and plays a ROL file.

```
Program RolTest;
Uses PlayRol,Crt,Instr;

Var
  Song    : RolTp;      { Rol music }
  Ch      : Char;       { key }
  Bank    : BnkTp;      { instrument bank }
  BnkFile : String;     { file used }

Function BCD(I : Byte) : Byte;
{ Convert BCD to decimal }
Begin
  BCD:=10*(I div 16) + I mod 16;
End;

Begin
```

```
    WriteLn;
    If ParamCount<1 Then Begin    { 1 or 2 parameters ? }
      WriteLn('Use ROLTEST name.rol [name.bnk] !');
      WriteLn;
      Halt(1)
    End;
    If Not TestForSNDDriver Then Begin { Sound drv. ? }
      WriteLn('Error : Sound driver not found !');
      WriteLn;
      Halt(1)
    End;
    If ParamCount=1 Then          { bank file ? }
      BnkFile:='Standard.Bnk'     { no, 'STANDARD.BNK' }
    Else
      BnkFile:=ParamStr(2);       { yes, use it }
    WriteLn('Sound version : ',BCD(Hi(SNDIoResult)),'.',
            BCD(Lo(SNDIOResult)));
    ResetSoundDrv;
    WriteLn('Loading : ',ParamStr(1));
    LoadRol(ParamStr(1),Song);
    WriteLn('Loading : ',BnkFile);
    LoadBnk(BnkFile,Bank);
    WriteLn; WriteLn('Playing ...');
    PlayRol(Song,Bank);
    Repeat
      CallSound(4,0,0,0,0,0); { playing stopped ? }
    Until (SNDIOResult=0) Or KeyPressed; { yes or key }
    If KeyPressed Then Begin
      Ch:=ReadKey;                { read key }
      ResetSoundDrv;              { and stop playing }
    End;
    WriteLn;
End.
```

Programming the FM Chip

Although you can use the drivers we have described thus far to play music with the FM chip, they are useless if you want to apply direct effects. If you use your own music format, the CMF driver is eliminated, because this driver only supports the

CMF format. The Sound driver is more flexible. However, the Sound driver has one disadvantage: when playing large pieces of music, the program must wait for free space in the buffer—free space that often doesn't become available fast enough. For such instances, it is useful to have your own playing routine.

Another reason for having your own playing routine is so you can add sounds to your program, as you might do, for example, if you wanted to mark error messages with sounds. In this case, it is far easier and more efficient to incorporate a few simple routines in a program than it is to use the Sound driver. With your own routines, memory is used more optimally and more free memory is available for the program itself. This section describes the parts of the FM chip and tells you how to program the FM chip yourself.

The previous sections described the settings for the operator, but they didn't mention the possible values. The values are discussed in this section. Even if you do not intend to program the FM chip yourself, consider reading this section if only to get a better understanding of the functioning of the FM chip.

Before explaining what the FM chip can do, this section first describes how to program the FM chip.

How the FM Chip Works

In the FM chip, all settings are stored internally in variables. These variables are called *registers*. The FM chip is programmed using an index and a data port. A particular number is sent to the index port. This number represents the selection of a certain register. Next, the register can be set with new data through the data port.

Following is an example in "pseudo code":

```
[1] OUT Index,11
[2] OUT Data,123
[3] OUT Index,13
[4] OUT Data,24
[5] OUT Data,210
```

The above code means the following, referred to by line:

Line	Meaning
1	Register 11 is selected.
2	The value 123 is assigned to register 11.

Line	Meaning
3	Register 13 is selected.
4	The value 24 is assigned to register 13.
5	The value 210 is added to register 13 and the previous value (24) is overwritten.

In our example code, line 4 is of little use because register 13 gets a new value in line 5.

AdLib Ports

The AdLib card has the following ports:

388H	Index and status port (read and write)
389H	Data port (write only)

Sound Blaster Ports

The Sound Blaster supports the following ports (notice that the first two are the same as the ports supported by the AdLib—up to this point Sound Blaster is compatible with AdLib):

388H	Index and status port (read and write)
389H	Data port (write only)
2X8H	Index and status port (read and write)
2X9H	Data port (write only)

With the Sound Blaster, X is the chosen base port. For this reason, not all software (for the FM chip) that works on the Sound Blaster automatically works on the AdLib. Obviously, we advise you to use the ports 388H and 389H, if only because this way you do not have to detect the base port of the Sound Blaster.

New Ports   In addition to the four ports mentioned above, the Sound Blaster has four new ports, two for the left channel (the first chip) and two for the right channel (the second chip). The ports for the left channel (the first chip) are:

2X0H	Index and status port (read and write)
2X1H	Data port (write only)

The ports for the right channel (the second chip) are:

2X2H	Index and status port (read and write)
2X3H	Data port (write only)

If you use ports 388H and 389H or 2X8H and 2X9H, both the left and the right channels are edited (ports 2X0H and 2X1H as well as the ports 2X2H and 2X3H are written with data).

To set an instrument at both chips, for example, you can program the two FM chips through ports 2X8H and 2X9H. Next, reproduce the instrument over the left channel through ports 2X0 and 2X1 and over the right channel through ports 2X2 and 2X3.

NOTE	See Listing 7.10 at the end of this chapter for an example of reproducing instruments.

As mentioned earlier, the data port is write-only. The status register can also be read through the index port. This register is discussed later.

After setting the index port, the program has to wait 3.3 microseconds before the register can be written. Then the program has to wait at least 23.3 microseconds before a new register can be selected through the index port.

FM Chip Register Settings

The FM chip doesn't use all 256 registers. Table 7.7 shows the FM chips register settings. This distribution is the same for every register group. Among the different register groups (that is, operator settings), 20 registers (0 .. 15H) are for 18 operators. The registers 6, 7, EH, and FH are not used. Table 7.8 shows the distribution of the operators among the registers. This distribution is the same for every register group.

TABLE 7.7: FM Chip Register Settings

Register	Bit 7	Bit 6	Bit 5	Bit 4	Bit 3	Bit 2	Bit 1	Bit 0
01H	Test							
02H	Fast Counter							
03H	Slow Counter							
04H	IRQ	Mask st Cnt	SI Cnt				Start/Stop SI Cnt	Fst Cnt
08H	CSM	SEL						
20H–35H	AM	VIB	EG-TYP	KSR	MULTI			
40H–55H	KSL		Total Level (TL)					
60H–75H	ATTACK RATE (AR)				DECAY RATE (DR)			
80H–95H	SUSTAIN LEVEL (SL)				RELEASE RATE (RR)			
A0H–A8H	F-NUMBER							
B0H–B8H			KEY	BLOCK			F-NUMBER	
BDH	Intensity AM VIB		Rhythm	BASS	SNARE	TOM	TOP CYMBAL	HI HAT
C0H–C8H					FEEDBACK			FM
E0H–F5H							WS	

The FM chip has two standard play modes, the melody mode and the rhythmic mode. In the melody mode, each instrument (or voice) has two operators (as is indicated in Table 7.8). In the rhythmic mode, there are four instruments that consist of only one operator.

The distribution of the operators among the first six instruments is equal in the melody mode. Table 7.9 shows the distribution for the five rhythmic instruments. The bass drum is considered a normal instrument.

TABLE 7.8: FM Chip Register Settings

Operator	1	2	3	4	5	6	7	8	9
Voice	1	2	3	1	2	3	4	5	6
Type	Modulator			Carrier			Modulator		
Register	00H	01H	02H	03H	04H	05H	08H	09H	0AH
Operator	10	11	12	13	14	15	16	17	18
Voice	4	5	6	7	8	9	7	8	9
Type	Carrier			Modulator			Carrier		
Register	0BH	0CH	0DH	10H	11H	12H	13H	14H	15H

TABLE 7.9: Arrangement of the Five Rhythm Instruments

Instrument	Operator(s)
Bass drum	13 and 16
Snare drum	17
Tom-tom	15
Top cymbal	18
High-hat	14

How the Registers Work in the FM Chip

You can use the registers to program the FM chip. You can set the oscillator, the envelope generator, and the level controller. In the discussion of the registers, often more than one or a few bits are treated, where b7 is the most significant bit (value 128) and b0 is the least significant bit (value 1). The bits that are not mentioned have no value and have to be set to 0.

Following is a look at each register.

Register 1, Test Register

Before you can program the FM chip, this register must have the value 0.

Register 2, the Fast Counter

The FM chip has two counters. They are eight bits large and count from 0 to 255. The default value for the fast counter can be written to register 2. If the counter is started, the FM chip sets the counter with the value that is indicated here. Next, the counter is increased by 1 every 80 microseconds (0.00008 seconds). If an overflow occurs (from 255 to 0, so carry = 1), the counter is set again at the indicated value. You calculate the duration of every overflow with the following formula:

```
T = (256 - the default value) * 0.08 milliseconds
```

Suppose the register is loaded with the value 140. In this case it would take 9.28 (256 − 140 = 116, 116*0.08 = 9.28) milliseconds before an overflow would take place. The status register allows you to check whether an overflow has occurred. This is discussed later in this chapter.

This counter is also used in the composite voice synthesis mode. If an overflow takes place, all instrument voices are switched on and immediately switched off, so all voices reproduce a sound at the same time.

Register 3, the Slow Counter

With this register you set the default value for the other counter. The difference is that this time the counter is increased every 320th microsecond. So this counter is four times as slow. Here the following formula applies:

```
T = (256 - the default value) * 0.32 milliseconds
```

If this register is loaded with the value 140, it takes 37.12 milliseconds before an overflow takes place. With the status register you can check whether an overflow has occurred.

Register 4, the Counter Controller

This register checks the two previous counters:

Bit 7   If this bit gets the value 1, the flags are loaded in the status register with the value 0. After that, the bit again has the value 0.

Bit 6   If this bit is 1, the overflow of the fast counter is not indicated in the status register.

Bit 5   If this bit is 1, the overflow of the slow counter is not indicated in the status register.

Bit 1   If this bit has the value 1, the slow counter is loaded with the indicated default value and the counter is increased. If this bit has the value 0, the slow counter stops and doesn't work.

Bit 0   If this bit has the value 1, the fast counter is loaded with the indicated default value and the counter is increased. If this bit has the value 0, the fast counter stops and doesn't work.

The Status Register

Before we continue with the discussion of the remaining registers, we need to look at the status register. The value of this register can be read by means of the index register (388H, 2X8H, 2X0H, or 2X2H). Only the three most significant bits have a function:

Bit 7   If this bit has the value 1, one of the other two bits also has the value 1.

Bit 6   This is the flag for the fast counter; this bit contains the value 1 if an overflow has taken place.

Bit 5   This bit has the same function as Bit 6 but for the slow counter.

After an overflow has taken place, the corresponding bit stays set. By loading bit 7 of register 4 with 1, all bits are set again at 0. With this register and the registers 2, 3, and 4, a constant timing can be applied without using the timer. First, a counter with a default value has to be loaded; next, register 4 has to start this counter. Simultaneously, the status register can be set with the value 0. Next, a waiting period occurs until an overflow happens, which is indicated in the status register. The status register has to be set again at the value 0 before a particular action can be executed. By checking the status register once again, a constant period of time is created. If you do not intend to do this, you can use this register in combination with the previous three registers to test whether an FM chip is present, as shown in Listing 7.7. Of course, for the Sound Blaster there are other ways to detect this chip, but for the Ad-Lib card this is the only way.

Listing 7.7: Pascal Example Testing for the Presence of the FM Chip

```
Function TestFMChip : Boolean;
Var
  S1, S2, T : Byte;
Begin
  WriteFM(1,0);      { delete test register }
  WriteFM(4,$60);    { disable connection/stop counters }
  WriteFM(4,$80);    { delete status register  }
  S1 := ReadFM;      { read status }
  WriteFM(2,$ff);    { set counter 1 at 255 }
  WriteFM(4,$21);    { connection on + start counter 1 }
  For T:=0 To 200 Do { wait a while }
    S2 := ReadFM;
  S2 := ReadFM;          { read status }
  WriteFM(4,$60);    { disable connection/stop counters }
  WriteFM(4,$80);
  TestFMChip:=((S1 AND $E0)=0) AND ((S2 AND $E0)=$C0);
End;
```

Register 8, General Control Register

Bit 7   With this bit you select the normal synthesis mode or the composite voice synthesis mode. If this bit is reset (=0), normal synthesis is selected. If, however, the bit is set (=1), the second mode is selected. If this bit is set, all instruments have to be switched off (later we describe how to do this).

Bit 6   This bit determines the split point of the notes to be played. If this bit is reset, bit 8 of the frequency setting determines the split point. If this bit is set, bit 9 of the frequency setting determines the split point. See Table 7.10.

TABLE 7.10: Note Selection

SEL = 0																
Octave	0		1		2		3		4		5		6		7	
F-number b9	1		1		1		1		1		1		1		1	
F-number b8	0	1	0	1	0	1	0	1	0	1	0	1	0	1	0	1
Split point	0	1	2	3	4	5	6	7	8	9	10	11	12	13	14	15
SEL = 1																
Octave	0		1		2		3		4		5		6		7	
F-number b9	0	1	0	1	0	1	0	1	0	1	0	1	0	1	0	1
F-number b8	X		X		X		X		X		X		X		X	
Split point	0	1	2	3	4	5	6	7	8	9	10	11	12	13	14	15

Registers 20H-35H, AM/VIB/EG-TYP/KSR/ MULTI Settings for the Operators

Bit 7: AM	This bit determines whether there is a fluctuation in the intensity of the operator signal. As soon as this bit is set, the option is selected. When the bit is reset, no fluctuation takes place. The frequency of the fluctuation is 3.7 Hz. There are two possibilities for setting the intensity of the fluctuation; this option is described at register BDH.
Bit 6: VIB	This bit has the same function as bit 7, only this time a fluctuation in pitch is selected. This happens with a frequency of 6.4 Hz. To set the size of the difference, there are two possibilities; this option is also discussed at register BDH.
Bit 5: EG-TYP	This bit indicates whether the envelope generator has to stay at the sustain level as long as the voice is enabled (set) or whether it has to go directly (reset) to 0 at the release rate (see Figure 7.5 at the beginning of this chapter).

Bit 4: KSR	You use this bit to make higher tones sound shorter. This happens by increasing the values for the attack, decay, and the release rate, as well as the sustain level. This way the note is processed faster and sounds shorter. This takes place when the bit is set. The option is disabled when resetting.
Bit 3...0: MULTI	The value set here selects the factor by which the established frequency is multiplied. Since this factor can be set separately for every operator, harmonic signals can be created. Table 8.6 shows all possible MULTI settings and the corresponding multiplication factors.

TABLE 7.11: The MULTI Settings

MULTI	Multiplication Factor
0	0.5
1	1
2	2
3	3
4	4
5	5
6	6
7	7
8	8
9	9
10	10
11	11
12	12
13	13
14	14
15	15

Registers 40H–55H, KSL/TL Settings for the Operators

Bit 7 and 6: KSL	With these bits you make sure the higher tones don't sound as loud. Table 7.12 shows the extent of the intensity decrease.
Bit 5...0: TL	These six bits set the level of the signal created by the operator. Zero is the maximum level and 63 is the minimum level. The level of the signal is represented by the following formula:

$$Level = (63 - TL) * 0.75 \text{ dB}$$

TABLE 7.12: Sound Decrease at KSL

KSL	Volume Decrease Per Octave
0	0 dB
1	3 dB
2	1.5 dB
3	6 dB

Registers 60H–75H, AR/DR Settings for the Operators

Bit 7...4: AR	The value of the attack rate. Zero is the lowest rate (actually it is not a rate at all, since you hear no tone) and 15 the highest rate.
Bit 3...0: DR	The value of the decay rate. The same values go for the decay rate as for the attack rate.

If the value 0 is set here, the sustain level is never reached and the signal continues at the maximum level until this voice is switched off and the tone drops at the release rate to level 0.

Registers 80H–95H, SL/RR Settings for the Operators

Bit 7...4: SL   The value for the sustain level. This register group can also be set at a value between 0 and 15. In this case, 0 represents the maximum level and 15 the minimum level (silence).

Bit 3...0: RR   The value for the release rate (between 0 and 15, with 0 being the lowest rate and 15 the highest). If RR has the value 0, the tone continues forever, even after the voice is switched off. The only way to stop it is to change the release rate or to set the TL at 63.

Registers E0H–15H, WS Settings for the Operators

Bit 1 and 0: WS   The value of these two bits selects one of the (adjusted) sine waves.

Registers C0H–C8H, FB/FM Settings for the Modulator Operators

This register group allows you to set the feedback and the kind of synthesis for each of the nine modulators. You have to use the register belonging to the modulator. The number of this register corresponds to the voice belonging to the modulator.

Bit 3...1: FB   The value set here determines the feedback intensity of the modulator. Table 7.13 indicates the factor by which the modulator signal is multiplied before it is used again as input. If the established value is 0, there is no feedback (as 0 multiplied by 0 is 0).

Bit 0: FM   This bit indicates whether the instrument is determined by additive synthesis (set) or frequency modulation synthesis (reset). Refer to the beginning of this chapter for the difference between these syntheses.

TABLE 7.13: The Various Feedback Amplifications

Feedback	0	1	2	3	4	5	6	7
Factor	0	$\pi/16$	$\pi/8$	$\pi/4$	$\pi/2$	π	$\pi\times2$	$\pi\times4$

The next two register groups set the frequency of the sound for each voice. In the melody mode, each voice corresponds with the same port. In the rhythmic mode, this also goes for the six normal instruments. The bass drum can be programmed through the seventh port and the tom-tom through the ninth port. The three remaining instruments cannot change pitch, so they don't have to be set. Thus, the eighth port has no function when the rhythmic mode is selected.

Registers A0H–A8H, the Frequency Settings for the Nine Voices

Bit 7...0:
F-NUMBER

These bits contain the eight least significant bits of the 10-bit value of the frequency setting for a particular voice. This is discussed in detail in the following register description.

Registers B0H–B8H, the Voice Selection and the Frequency Settings

Bit 5: KEY

When the voice is switched on, the operators established for this voice are used to create sound.

If bit EG-TYP is set, the sound will remain at the sustain level until this KEY bit is reset and the voice is switched off. This doesn't mean that the sound is immediately stopped. After resetting the KEY bit, the sound will drop to 0 at the release rate. If the EG-TYP is reset, this will happen immediately after the sustain level is reached, whether the KEY bit is reset again or not.

If the FM chip is set at this time, it will start generating the sound again, even if the previous note is still sounding and has to be cut off.

In the rhythmic mode, the bit has to be set when the bass drum is played and stay reset for the tom-tom (further on we describe how these instruments are switched on and off).

Bit 4...2:
BLOCK
The value that is set by these three bits determines the number of times the frequency is doubled. In other words, with this value you determine the octave in which the note is played.

Bit 1 and 0:
F-NUMBER
These are the two most significant bits of the frequency setting that make up ten bits together with the previous register group. The relationship between F-NUMBER, BLOCK, and the actual frequency is represented by the following formula:

```
Frequency = 50,000 * F-NUMBER * 2 ^ (BLOCK - 20)
```

Table 7.14 shows the frequencies of the notes in a particular octave. The value for BLOCK in this octave is 4. By using the values calculated for F-NUMBER, you only have to change the value of BLOCK if you want to use another octave.

Register BDH, the Vibrato Intensities and the Rhythmic Settings

Bit 7
Determines the intensity of the fluctuation in the signal intensity of the operators. If the bit is set, the maximum value of the fluctuation is 4.8 dB; if the bit is reset, the maximum value is 1 dB.

Bit 6
This bit has the same function as bit 7, but now the intensity of the fluctuation in frequency is determined. If the bit is set, the maximum fluctuation is 14 percent; if the bit is reset, it is 7 percent.

TABLE 7.14: Frequencies and F-NUMBER in an Octave

Note	Frequency	F-NUMBER
C	261.63	343
C#	277.18	363
D	293.66	385
D#	311.13	408
E	329.63	432
F	349.23	458
F#	369.99	485
G	392.00	514
G#	415.30	544
A	440.00	577
A#	466.16	611
B	493.88	647

The two bits described above set the same fluctuation for all operators. Consequently, it is not possible to set different fluctuations. The bits only affect the operators that use one or both settings.

Bit 5	This bit sets the mode. If this bit is reset, the FM chip uses the melody mode with nine instruments. If the bit is set, the FM chip uses the rhythmic mode with eleven instruments.
Bit 4…0	These bits have the same function as the KEY bit. They switch a rhythmic instrument on or off and they only function if bit 5 is set. An instrument is switched on when the corresponding bit is set. By resetting the bit, the instrument is switched off. As for the effect of the release rate and the sustain level, the same applies to these bits as to the KEY bit. Table 7.15 shows the instruments that correspond to each bit.

TABLE 7.15: The Rhythm Instruments in Register BDH

Bit	Instrument
4	Bass drum
3	Snare drum
2	Tom-tom
1	Top cymbal
0	High-hat

TIP To play the bass drum you have to set not only the bit for the bass drum, but also the KEY bit for the seventh voice (A6H and B6H). This does not apply to the tom-tom.

A Library for Programming the FM Chip

This section contains a library you can use to program the FM chip directly. In the library, the programming is divided into three parts:

1. Setting the instrument data.
2. Setting or changing the volume.
3. Playing a voice at a certain frequency.

The first two points can be combined if the volume does not have to be adjusted. You can easily change this in the library. Of course, all three points can be combined if you want to generate one particular sound only once.

When you are setting the instrument, the port groups 20H, 40H, 60H, 80H, E0H, and sometimes C0H (for the modulator) have to be programmed. The most appropriate format is the SBI format, because the 16-bit format corresponds to the settings of the registers and the library also makes use of this (using the previous INSTR library).

The registers can only be written with data. It is not possible to read the current settings of a particular register (except for the status register). If the program wants to change certain data in a register and will leave the other settings intact, it has to memorize the current settings of the register in a variable. A good example of this is register BDH. The program has to remember itself which rhythm instruments are on and which are off, because when a particular rhythm instrument is switched on the others can not be switched on or off just like that.

When setting the volume, the library retains a copy of the volume. If a new instrument is set, it uses the data of this copy. However, don't forget that besides the TL setting, the KSL setting is also located in register group 40H. The latter first has to be removed with AND and OR commands, after which it has to be added again (see the library listing for the implementation).

TIP

In the FM synthesis, the modulator serves as an entry for the carrier. Only the volume of the carrier has to be changed, because this one takes care of the final signal. In the additive synthesis, the two operators are used parallel to each other and the volume of both operators has to be changed.

Of course, you can also indicate the instrument each time you set the volume. By using internal variables, the used solution is more abstract: setting the volume is independent of the chosen instrument setting.

After an instrument is set it can be played. To do so, you first have to determine the play mode (in the rhythmic mode instrument 9 is a different instrument than in the melody mode). The normal instruments are set through register groups A0H and B0H. For a rhythm instrument, register BDH also has to be used. As we've mentioned before, the other two register groups only have to be set for the bass drum and the tom-tom. Since every rhythm instrument has to be switched on and off separately, a copy of the current settings is used here.

Listing 7.8 is a Pascal unit for directly programming the FM chip.

Listing 7.8: Pascal Unit for Directly Programming the FM Chip

```pascal
Unit FMDirect;

Interface
Uses Instr;

Const
  Melody       = True;        { the two play modes }
  Rhythmic     = False;
  { the frequencies for the var. notes }
  FrLst : Array [0..11] Of Word = (343, 363, 385, 408,
                                   432, 458, 485, 514,
                                   544, 577, 611, 647);

  BassDrum  =  7;
  SnareDrum =  8;
  TomTom    =  9;
  TopCymbal = 10;
  HiHat     = 11;

Var
  Port  : Word;
{ set register }
Procedure WriteFM(I,D : Byte);
{ read status register }
Function ReadFM : Byte;
{ execute timer test }
Function TestFMChip : Boolean;
{ set play mode }
Procedure PlayMode(M : Boolean);
{ set volume for a particular voice }
Procedure Volume(N : Byte; V : Real);
{ ask voice volume }
Function GiveVolume(N : Byte) : Real;
{ play a note on a particular voice }
Procedure PlayNote(N : Byte; T : Word);
{ switch off voice }
Procedure SwitchOffNote(N : Byte);
{ set instrument }
Procedure SetIns(N : Byte; I : InsTp);

Implementation

Const
  { the 18 operator offsets }
```

```
    OpAd  : Array [1..18] Of Byte = (00,01,02,03,04,05,
                                     08,09,10,11,12,13,
                                     16,17,18,19,20,21);
    { the modulator operator offsets }
    Ins9  : Array [1..9] Of Byte  = (01,02,03,07,08,09,
                                     13,14,15);
    { the modulator + rhythm. ins operator offsets }
    Ins11 : Array [1..11] Of Byte = (01,02,03,07,08,09,
                                     13,17,15,18,14);
Type
   VolumeRc = Record   { for the volume setting }
                  KSLTL : Array [0..1] Of Byte;
                  Sort  : Byte;
                  Value : Real;
              End;
   VolumeAr = Array [1..11] Of VolumeRc;
   Ar       = Array [1..11] Of Byte;   { help array }
   ArPt     = ^Ar;
Var
   Volumes     : VolumeAr;  { volume settings }
   MelodyMode  : Boolean;   { play mode }
   BasicIns    : ArPt;      { ins. table to be used }
   PortBD      : Byte;      { for the rhythm. ins. }
Procedure WriteFM(I,D : Byte);
Var
  K,S : Word;
Begin
  Port[Port]:=I;                     { select register }
  For K:=0 To 28 Do S:=K;            { wait 3.3 microsec }
  Port[Port+1]:=D;                   { set register }
  For K:=0 To 68 Do S:=K;            { wait 23.3 microsec }
End;

Function ReadFM : Byte;
Begin
  ReadFM:=Port[Port];                { read data }
End;

Function TestFMChip : Boolean;
Var
  S1, S2, T : Byte;
Begin
  WriteFM(1,0);     { delete test register }
  WriteFM(4,$60);   { disable connection/stop counters }
```

```
  WriteFM(4,$80);   { delete status register  }
  S1 := ReadFM;     { read status }
  WriteFM(2,$ff);   { set counter 1 at 255 }
  WriteFM(4,$21);   { connection on + start counter 1 }
  For T:=0 To 200 Do { wait a while }
    S2 := ReadFM;
  S2 := ReadFM;     { read status }
  WriteFM(4,$60);   { disable connection/stop counters }
  WriteFM(4,$80);
  TestFMChip:=((S1 AND $E0)=0) AND ((S2 AND $E0)=$C0);
End;

Procedure PlayMode(M : Boolean);
Begin
  MelodyMode:=M;    { set mode }
  WriteFM(8,0);     { set CSM & SEL at 0 }
  If MelodyMode Then Begin
    BasicIns:=Addr(Ins9);          { use 9 ins. }
    PortBD:=PortBD And (Not 32); { rhythm. mode off }
  End
  Else Begin
    BasicIns:=Addr(Ins11);         { use 11 ins. }
    PortBD:=PortBD Or 32;          { rhythm. mode on }
  End;
End;

Function GiveRBit(N : Byte) : Byte;
{ give the bit belonging to the rhythmic instrument }
Begin
  Case N Of
    BassDrum  : GiveRBit:=16;   { bit 4 }
    SnareDrum : GiveRBit:=8;    { bit 3 }
    TomTom    : GiveRBit:=4;    { bit 2 }
    TopCymbal : GiveRBit:=2;    { bit 1 }
    HiHat     : GiveRBit:=1;    { bit 0 }
  Else
    GiveRBit:=0;                { no bit }
  End;
End;

Procedure SetOperator(N,M : Byte; I : SBIFormat);
{ set modulator or carrier at voice N }
Var
  H : Byte;
```

```
Begin
  H:=OpAd[BasicIns^[N]+3*M];   { determine oper. port }
  WriteFM(H+$20,I.Snd[M]);      { set AM/VIB/... }
  WriteFM(H+$60,I.ARDR[M]);     { set AR + DR }
  WriteFM(H+$80,I.SLRR[M]);     { set SL + RR }
  WriteFM(H+$E0,I.WS[M]);       { set WS }
  Volumes[N].KSLTL[M]:=I.KSLTL[M]; { copy volume }
  If (M=0) And (MelodyMode OR (N<8)) Then Begin
    WriteFM(N-1+$C0,I.FBFM[0]);      { set FM + FB }
    Volumes[N].Sort:=I.FBFM[0] AND 1;  { synth. type }
  End;
End;

Procedure Volume(N : Byte; V : Real);
Var
  KSL,
  TL,
  B    : Byte;
Begin
  If MelodyMode Or (N<8) Then Begin { carrier }
    B:=BasicIns^[N];                { determine oper. offset }
    KSL:= Volumes[N].KSLTL[1] And 192; { copy KSL }
    TL:=(Volumes[N].KSLTL[1] And 63) Xor 63;
    TL:=Round(V*TL);                { new volume }
    If TL>63 Then TL:=63;           { too large ? }
    WriteFM($40+OpAd[B+3],KSL OR (TL XOR 63));
  End;
  If (Volumes[N].Sort=1) Or       { addit. synthesis ? }
     (Not MelodyMode And (N>7)) Then Begin   { rhythm. ? }
    KSL:=Volumes[N].KSLTL[0] And 192;         { yes }
    TL:=(Volumes[N].KSLTL[0] And 63) Xor 63;
    TL:=Trunc(V*TL);      { set modulator or rhythm. }
    If TL>63 Then TL:=63;
    WriteFM($40+OpAd[B],KSL OR (TL XOR 63));
  End
  Else
    WriteFM($40+OpAd[B],Volumes[N].KSLTL[0]);
  Volumes[N].Value:=V;
End;

Function GiveVolume(N : Byte) : Real;
Begin
  GiveVolume:=Volumes[N].Value;
End;
```

```
Procedure SetIns(N : Byte; I : InsTp);
Var
  C : InsTp;
  P : ArPt;
  V : Real;
Begin
  CopyIns(I,C);                { use copy }
  INSToSBI(C);                 { use SBI format }
  V := GiveVolume(N);          { set volume temporarily }
  Volume(N,0.0);               { at 0 }
  SetOperator(N,0,C.SBI^);     { process modulator }
  If MelodyMode Or (N<8) Then
    SetOperator(N,1,C.SBI^);   { and if needed carrier }
  Volume(N,V);                 { restore volume }
  RemoveIns(C);                { remove copy }
End;

Procedure PlayNote(N : Byte; T : Word);
Var
  FNr : Word;
  Blk : Byte;
Begin
  FNr := FrLst[T Mod 12];              { determine frequency }
  Blk := ((T Div 12) And 7) Shl 2;    { and octave }
  If MelodyMode Or (N<8) Then Begin { set + switch }
    WriteFM($A0+N-1,FNr and 255);      { on note }
    WriteFM($B0+N-1,(FNr Shr 8) Or Blk Or 32);
  End;
  If Not MelodyMode And (N=TomTom) Then Begin
    WriteFM($A8,FNr And 255);      { only setting }
    WriteFM($B8,(FNr Shr 8) Or Blk);
  End;
  If Not MelodyMode And (N>6) Then Begin
    PortBD:=PortBD Or GiveRBit(N); { process rhythm. }
    WriteFM($BD,PortBD)            { instrument }
  End;
End;

Procedure SwitchOffNote(N : Byte);
Begin
  If MelodyMode Or (N<8) Then
    WriteFM($B0+N-1,0);
  If Not MelodyMode And (N>6) Then Begin
    PortBD := PortBD And (Not GiveRBit(N));
    WriteFM($BD,PortBD);
```

```
   End;
End;

Var
   K : Byte;
Begin
  Port:=$388;
  PortBD:=0;
  For K:=1 To 11 Do
    Volumes[K].Value:=0;
End.
```

Listing 7.9 shows the use of the various functions of the library. First the instrument bank STANDARD.BNK is read. Next the instrument PIANO1 is set. The settings are also represented (where the TL and SL settings are the opposite of the actual value). You can now play the notes yourself using the two bottom rows of keys. With the square brackets ([and]) you can decrease or increase the octave, and with the curly brackets ({ and }) you can change the volume. As soon as you press the spacebar the tone stops. You can set a new instrument with the *I* key, and with Esc you quit the program.

You can extend this program with, for example, an editor for the various instrument settings and create your own instrument editor. Refer to the comments in the listing for further information.

Listing 7.9: Pascal Listing of a Keyboard Example

```
Program KeyBoard;

Uses FMDirect, Instr, Crt;
{ A simple keyboard that programs the FM chip directly. }

Const
  { define piano keys }
  KeyB  : String[12] = 'ZSXDCVGBHNJM';
  { and the corresponding notes }
  NoteT : String[12] = 'C#D#EF#G#A#B';
Var
  Instru  : InsTp;      { instrument to be played }
  Bank    : BnkTp;      { used instrument bank }
  Name    : InsName;    { instrument to be found }
  Counter,              { for finding the note }
  Octave,               { current octave }
  Voice   : Byte;       { for rhythmic instruments }
```

```
  Note    : Word;       { note played }
  Key     : Char;       { read key press }
  Vol     : Real;       { current volume }
Procedure OperatorInfo(K : Byte; I : InsOp);
{ give information about the modulator or carrier }
Var
  C : Byte;
Begin
  If K>1 Then Begin
    For C:=3 To 13 Do Begin
      GotoXY(58,C); Write('   -   ');
    End;
    GotoXY(54,14);Write('   -   ');
    GotoXY(54,15);Write('   -   ')
  End
  Else Begin
    C:=K*5+53;
    GotoXY(C, 3);Write(I.KSL:4);
    GotoXY(C, 4);Write(I.MULTI:4);
    GotoXY(C, 5);Write(I.AR:4);
    GotoXY(C, 6);Write((I.SL XOR 15):4);
    GotoXY(C, 7);Write(I.EG_TYP:4);
    GotoXY(C, 8);Write(I.DR:4);
    GotoXY(C, 9);Write(I.RR:4);
    GotoXY(C,10);Write((I.TL XOR 63):4);
    GotoXY(C,11);Write(I.AM:4);
    GotoXY(C,12);Write(I.VIB:4);
    GotoXY(C,13);Write(I.KSR:4);
    If K=0 Then Begin
      GotoXY(C,14);Write(I.FM:4);
      GotoXY(C,15);Write(I.FB:4)
    End;
  End;
End;

Procedure NewIns(S : String);
{ Find new instrument and set it }
Var
  N : InsName;
  H : BnkTp;
Begin
  StrToName(S,N);              { convert to name }
  FindIns(N,Bank,H);           { find instrument }
  If H<>Nil Then Begin    { found ? }
    RemoveIns(Instru);         { remove old inst. }
```

```
      Copy Ins(H^.Ins,Instru);{ copy from bank }
      SBIToINS(Instru);          { use INS format }
      SwitchOffNote(Voice);
      Volume(Voice,0);
      If Instru.Ins^.Mode = 1 Then
        Voice:=Instru.Ins^.Nummer+1    { rhythmic }
      Else
        Voice:=1;                        { melody }
      SetIns(Voice,Instru);
      Volume(Voice,Vol);
      Name:=N;                    { copy name }
      OperatorInfo(0,Instru.Ins^.Modulator);
      If (Instru.Ins^.Mode=1) And
         (Instru.Ins^.Number>6) Then  { no carrier ? }
        OperatorInfo(2,Instru.Ins^.Carrier)   { yes }
      Else
        OperatorInfo(1,Instru.Ins^.Carrier);  { no }
  End;
End;

Procedure Initialization;
{ set screen and the variables needed }
Begin
  If Not TestFMChip Then Begin
    WriteLn;
    WriteLn('Error, no FM chip present !');
    WriteLn;
    Halt(1);
  End;
  WriteLn;
  WriteLn('Reading bank file ...');
  LoadBnk('Default.Bnk',Bank);
  CopyIns(Bank^.Ins,Instru);  { Instru must be an INS }
  ClrScr;
  Octave:=3;                     { begin in octave 3 }
  Vol:=1.0;                      { maximum volume }
  Note:=$ffff;                   { no note }
  PlayMode(Rhythmic);            { for rhythm. ins. }
  GotoXY( 1, 1);Write('Instrument :');
  GotoXY( 1, 3);Write('Volume     :');
  GotoXY( 1, 5);Write('Octave     :');
  GotoXY( 1, 7);Write('Voice      :');
  GotoXY( 1, 9);Write('Note       :');
  GotoXY( 1,11);Write('Keyboard');
  GotoXY( 1,12);Write(' S D   G H J ');
```

```
   GotoXY( 1,13);Write('Z X C V B N M');
   GotoXY(40, 1);Write('Setting    Mod. Car.');
   GotoXY(40, 2);Write('--------------------');
   GotoXY(40, 3);Write('KSL              ');
   GotoXY(40, 4);Write('Freq mult        ');
   GotoXY(40, 5);Write('Attack rate      ');
   GotoXY(40, 6);Write('Sustain level    ');
   GotoXY(40, 7);Write('Sustaining       ');
   GotoXY(40, 8);Write('Decay rate       ');
   GotoXY(40, 9);Write('Release rate     ');
   GotoXY(40,10);Write('Total level      ');
   GotoXY(40,11);Write('AM               ');
   GotoXY(40,12);Write('VIB              ');
   GotoXY(40,13);Write('KSR              ');
   GotoXY(40,14);Write('Freq synthesis ');
   GotoXY(40,15);Write('Feedback         ');
   NewIns('Piano1');
End;

Procedure PrintAll;
{ print information about note, volume, voice,
  octave en ins. name }
Var
   C : Char;
Begin
   GotoXY(14,1); Write(Name:2);
   GotoXY(14,3); Write(Vol:4:2);
   GotoXY(14,5); Write(Octave:2);
   GotoXY(14,7); Write(Voice:2);
   GotoXY(14,9);
   If Note <> $ffff Then Begin
     C:=NoteT[1+(Note Mod 12)];
     If C='#' Then              { black key ? }
       Write(NoteT[Note Mod 12],C)   { yes }
     Else
       Write(C,' ');
   End;                                  { no }
End;

Procedure AskNewIns;
{ ask for a new ins. name and set it }
Var
   S : String;
Begin
   GotoXY(1,17); Write('New name (max 9 char.) : ');
```

```
      ReadLn(S);
      If S<>'' Then
        NewIns(S);
      GotoXY(1,17);   { delete question }
      Write('                                          ');
    End;

    Begin { main }
      Initialization;
      Repeat
        PrintAll;
        Note:=$ffff;                { no note }
        Key:=UpCase(ReadKey);    { determine key press }
        Case Key Of
          '[' : If Octave>0 Then Dec(Octave);
          ']' : If Octave<7 Then Inc(Octave);
          '{' : If Vol>0 Then Vol:=Vol-0.01;
          '}' : If Vol<1 Then Vol:=Vol+0.01;
          'I' : AskNewIns;
          ' ' : SwitchOffNote(Voice);
        Else
          For Counter:=1 To 12 Do        { one of the }
            If KeyB[Counter]=Key Then    { piano keys ?}
              Note:=Octave*12+Counter-1; { yes }
        End; {Case}
        If Note<>$ffff Then Begin    { play note ? }
          SwitchOffNote(Voice);      { yes, switch off previous }
          PlayNote(Voice,Note);      { play new }
        End;
        Volume(Voice,Vol);          { set volume }
      Until Key=#27;                { ESC is end }
      SwitchOffNote(Voice);         { end of the note }
      Volume(Voice,0);              { set volume at 0 }
      GotoXY(1,17);                 { give end message }
      WriteLn('See you ...');
      WriteLn;
    End.
```

The two FM chips of the Sound Blaster Pro can be set separately. Listing 7.10 sets an instrument by writing to ports 2X8H and 2X9H. Next, the instrument is reproduced from left to right using ports 2X0H, 2X1H, 2X2H, and 2X3H, and vice versa until a key is pressed. Of course, there are many other possibilities.

You can extend the last library with a number of functions for the Pro. Using the information provided in Chapter 11 you can, for instance, reproduce everything through the left or the right channel. This way you can use fifteen normal and five rhythm instruments by setting one FM chip in the melody mode and the other FM chip in the rhythmic mode.

Listing 7.10: Pascal Listing of an Example for the Sound Blaster Pro

```pascal
Program SBProTest;

Uses Instr, FMDirect, CRT;

Const
  Rate = 0.001;    { size of the decrease }
  I : InsFormat = (Mode:0;Number:0;    { a hum }
                   Modulator :
                   (KSL:1;MULTI:1;FB:3;AR:15;SL:0;
                    EG_TYP:1;DR:0;RR:2;TL:0;AM:1;
                    VIB:1;KSR:0;FM:1);
                   Carrier :
                   (KSL:0;MULTI:1;FB:0;AR:15;SL:0;
                    EG_TYP:1;DR:0;RR:2;TL:0;AM:1;
                    VIB:1;KSR:0;FM:0);
                   MWafeSel:0;CWafeSel:0);
  Ins : InsTp    = (Sort : INSPt; INS : @I);

Var
  Ch      : Char;            { key press }
  Cnt,                       { counter }
  Vol     : Real;            { volume }
  PCopy   : Word;            { SBPro port }

Begin
  Port:=$220;                { test left chip }
  If Not TestFMChip Then     { test OK ? }
    Port:=$240;              { no, other base port }
  PCopy:=Port;
  Port:=PCopy+8;             { directly through SBPro }
  If TestFMChip Then Begin
    PlayMode(Melody);
    SetIns(1,Ins);           { set to both chips }
    Volume(1,0);             { reproduce nothing }
    PlayNote(1,48);          { switch on tone }
    Vol:=1;                  { left at maximum }
```

```
      Cnt:-Rate;                  { decrease VOL each time }
      Repeat
        Port:=PCopy;              { left port at 0 }
        Volume(1,Vol);            { set volume VOL }
        Port:=PCopy+2;            { right port at 2 }
        Volume(1,1.0-Vol);        { set opposite VOL }
        Vol:=Vol+Cnt;             { decrease/increase VOL }
        If (Vol>1.0) Or (Vol<0.0) Then Begin
           Vol:=Vol-Cnt;          { one step back }
           Cnt:-Cnt;              { opposite sign }
        End;
      Until KeyPressed;           { repeat until key pressed }
      Ch:=ReadKey;                { read }
       Port:=PCopy+8;              { both FM chips }
      SwitchOffNote(1);
   End;
End.
```

CHAPTER

EIGHT

Programming CMS Chips

- How the CMS driver works and is installed

- CMS chip functions

- Creating sounds with CMS chips

- Generating noises with CMS chips

- Programming tone, pitch, and note duration

CMS chips have always been the least appreciated part of the Sound Blaster. Only Versions 1.0 to 2.0 of the Sound Blaster support CMS chips. This chapter is written for owners of the Sound Blaster who have Versions 1.0 to 2.0. If you do not have the CMS stereo chips, you can use the Phillips SAA 1099 chips instead.

CMS chips have their own functionality. They are the only part of the standard Sound Blaster that can reproduce stereo sounds. This fact alone makes them worth examining.

> **NOTE** See "CMS Stereo Chips" in Chapter 2 if you need background information about what these chips can and can't do. Information about installing CMS chips and about the Phillips SAA 1099 chip, a chip equivalent to the CMS, can be found in Chapter 4.

The CMS Driver

CMS chips differ in many respects from the FM chip. The addresses that have to be written to send data are different, as are the functions of the addresses themselves. Fortunately, all the functions needed to play a CMS song are supplied by the CMS driver, CMSDRV.COM.

CMS songs have the extension .CMS. You can create CMS songs with the CDMS Composer from Creative Labs. The CDMS composer was provided with the Game Blaster, the predecessor to the Sound Blaster. If you do not have the Game Blaster card you can always try to download the CDMS composer from a bulletin board.

> **NOTE** See "CDMS Composer" in Chapter 3 for a detailed discussion of what the CDMS Composer is capable of.

Installing the CMS Driver To install CMSDRV.COM, simply run the program. The driver will stay resident in memory. It can be accessed through an interrupt. When executed, the program tries to take over interrupt 80H, but if interrupt

80H is already used by another program the driver searches for the next highest free interrupt. To find out whether an interrupt is free, the driver checks whether the interrupt points at 0:0.

The CMSDRV Interrupt   The driver will take over the free interrupt and make the interrupt vectors point at itself (the copy of CMSDRV in memory). Now the question is, how can you tell which interrupt the driver has taken over?

To find out, the following method is used to look for the text "CMSDRV" in memory: the interrupt vectors are read, beginning at address 80H (the memory address at which the text CMSDRV has to begin) and adding 0104H. If you go over the interrupt numbers beginning at 80H and compare the accompanying vectors (increased by 0104H) to CMSDRV, you will find the right interrupt number.

Loading CMS Song Files in Memory   Once the driver is installed, you can load a CMS song file. You can load a CMS file at any free memory location, provided that the offset is in segment 0. The reason you can load a CMS file at any free memory location is that a memory address can be represented as a segment:offset:

- The segment comprises two bytes that can address 1024KB.

- The offset contains two bytes taking care of a total of 64KB.

With this system, addresses can be written in different ways. The address 66096, for example, can be written as 1010H:0130H or 1023H:0000H. This system makes it possible to load a CMS file every 16 bytes, since the first three digits of the offset number can be added to the last three digits of the segment.

TIP   The maximum size of a CMS file that can be loaded is 64 KB.

CMS Driver Functions

Now that the driver is present in memory, it can execute a number of functions. Of course, which functions it executes has a lot to do with the CMS song. Following is an examination of the six CMSDRV.COM driver functions.

Function 0

Function 0 returns the version number of the driver. The version number is represented by two numbers separated by a period.

Input:	ah	= 0
Output:	ah	= Number in front of the point
	al	= Number after the point

Function 1

Function 1 plays the CMS song. The driver has to know which segment contains the song (the offset is not necessary because it is always equal to 0).

The driver uses a *play flag* that contains the status of the driver. The play flag is a memory byte you select. If the contents of the play flag are equal to 255, the driver is busy playing a CMS song. If the contents are equal to 0, the driver is inactive.

Input:	ah	= 1
	al	= The number of times a CMS song has to be played. This number can vary from 1 to 255; 0 indicates that the song has to be played non-stop.
	es	= The segment address of the play flag.
	bx	= The offset address of the play flag.
	cx	= The segment address of the CMS song.
Output:	ax	= 0 means that everything has gone well. The music is now playing.
	ax	= 1 means that the indicated CMS song contains errors or it is not a CMS song.
	ax	= 2 means that the CMS song is created with a composer version that the driver doesn't support.

Function 2

Function 2 pauses the music.

Input:	ah	= 2
Output:	ax	= 0 means that the action has succeeded and the music has been paused.
	ax	= 1 means that no music was playing so therefore it can't be paused.

Function 3

Function 3 ends the pause and makes sure the music continues playing. This function is only effective if the music is paused.

Input:	ah	= 3
Output:	ax	= 0 means that the action has succeeded and the music continues playing.
	ax	= 1 means that no music was paused.

Function 4

Function 4 stops the CMS song.

Input:	ah	= 4
Output:	None	

Function 5

Function 5 disables the Ctrl+keypad 5 capability. The driver can also be controlled with the computer keyboard, using the following key presses (all numbers are on the numeric keypad):

Key Press	Use
Ctrl+5 three times	Stops the song.
Ctrl+5 twice	Pauses the song.
Ctrl+5 once	Starts the song.

Function 5 disables the keyboard capabilities listed above.

Input: ah   = 5

Output: None

Playing CMS Songs

How the driver is used becomes much clearer once you study an example. The sample program in this section plays a CMS song by executing the following steps:

1. It checks whether the CMSDRV.COM is present and finds the interrupt number.

2. It loads the CMS file on a segment with offset 0.

3. It reserves a play flag.

4. It instructs the driver to play the CMS song.

5. If the output is unequal to 0, it leaves the program and shows an error message.

6. It waits for user input. Four defined keys execute the play, pause, continue, and stop functions.

7. It quits the program if the user presses the stop key.

Notice that the Ctrl+keypad 5 function is not disabled. Instead of using the four defined keys, you can also use the Ctrl+5 function to stop, start, and pause the song.

NOTE See "A Word about the Program Listings" in the Introduction for advice about reading and using the listings in this book.

Listing 8.1: Pascal Unit to Play CMS Songs

```
{ **********************************************
**   Unit CMS supporting PLAYCMS.PAS         **
**   Turbo Pascal 4.0                         **
********************************************** }

Unit CMS;

INTERFACE

Uses Crt,Dos;
var Play_flag:byte;
    songseg:word;
    intno:byte;

Function CheckDrv:byte;
Function PlaySong:boolean;
Function Pause:boolean;
Function Continue:boolean;
Procedure stop;
Procedure unlock_key;

IMPLEMENTATION

Function CheckDrv:byte;              { see if the driver }
const header:string[6]='CMSDRV'; { is present in memory }

var vect:byte;                       { by searching for the }
    found:boolean;                   { identification string }
    regs:Registers;
    temp:string[6];

begin
  vect:=$80;
  found:=false;
  while not found and (vect<>0) do
  begin
    regs.ah:=53;          { function 53 of int 21H }
    regs.al:=vect;        { reads a vector }
    intr($21,regs);

    Move(mem[regs.es:$104],temp[1],6); temp[0]:=#6;
                          { copy to a buffer }
        if temp=header then   { set length at 6 }
```

```
        found:=true
      else
        Inc(vect);
  end;
  checkdrv:=vect;
end;

Function PlaySong:boolean;    { start playing }
var regs:registers;

begin
  regs.ah:=1;
  regs.al:=1;
  regs.es:=Seg(Play_flag);
  regs.bx:=Ofs(Play_flag);
  regs.cx:=songseg;
  intr(intno,regs);
  if (regs.ax<>0)
  then
    playsong:=true
  else
    playsong:=false;
end;

Function Pause:boolean;    { pause the song }
var regs:registers;
begin
  regs.ah:=2;
  intr(intno,regs);
  if (regs.ax<>0)
  then
    pause:=true
  else
    pause:=false;
end;

Function Continue:boolean;  { end pause }
var regs:registers;
begin
  regs.ah:=3;
  intr(intno,regs);
  if regs.ax<>0
  then
    continue:=true
  else
```

```
        continue:=false;
end;

Procedure stop;        { stop playing }
var regs:registers;

begin
  regs.ah:=4;
  intr(intno,regs);
end;

Procedure unlock_key;  { unlock numeric keypad }
var regs:registers;
begin
  regs.ah:=5;
  intr(intno,regs);
end;

begin
end.
```

Listing 8.2: Pascal Example Playing CMS Songs

```
{ ***********************************************
** PLAYCMS.PAS                                 **
** Turbo Pascal 4.0                            **
*********************************************** }

Program PlayCMS;

uses Crt,Dos,Cms;

var mempos:pointer;
    size:word;
    key:char;
    result:integer;

Function loadfile(filename:string):byte; { load a }
var handle:file;               { file at the beginning }
    regs:registers;            { of a segment }

begin
  {$I-}
  Assign(handle,filename);
  Reset(handle,1);
```

```
  size:=filesize(handle);
  GetMem(mempos,(size+15) AND $FFF0);
  songseg:=Seg(mempos^);
  BlockRead(handle,mem[songseg:0],size);
  close(handle);
  {$I+}
  If ioresult<>0 then loadfile:=1 else loadfile:=0;
end;

Procedure choice;
begin
  Write('Press P-pause, U-unpause, S-stop ');
  Writeln('or M-music maestro!');
end;

begin                          { main program }
  if paramcount<>1 then
  begin
    Writeln('Use: playcms < cms-file >');
    halt(1);
  end;

  intno:=checkdrv;
  if intno=0 then
  begin
    Writeln('CMSDRV.COM not loaded.');

    halt(2);
  end
  else
    Writeln('CMSDRV.COM found, interrupt : ',intno);

  result:=loadfile(paramstr(1));
  if result<>0 then
  begin
    if result=2 then
      writeln('Not enough memory available.')
    else
      writeln('Loading error ',paramstr(1));
    halt(3);
  end;

  choice;

  Repeat
```

```
      If Keypressed then
        key:=Upcase(readkey)
      else
        key:=#0;
      case key of              { process choice }

        'M':if playsong then
              writeln('Song starting error..')
            else
              choice;

        'P':if pause then
              writeln('No music is playing.')
            else
              choice;

        'U':if continue then
              writeln('Nothing paused.')
            else
              choice;
      end;
  Until (key='S');
  stop;
  unlock_key;
  freemem(mempos,(size+15) AND $FFF0);
end.
```

Listing 8.3: C Unit to Play CMS Songs

```
/* **********************************************
** Include file CMS.H in PLAYCMS.C           **
** Turbo C++ 2.0                             **
**********************************************/

typedef unsigned char byte;
typedef unsigned int  word;

word Play_flag;
word segm;          /* song segment */
byte intno;         /* interrupt number of the driver */

checkdrv()
{
  byte vect=0x80;    /* start searching at int. 80H */
  byte found=0;
```

```
    int number=0;
    char chr[6]="CMSDRV";              /* the identification */
    union REGS inregs,outregs;
    struct SREGS segregs;
    byte far *oldvect;  /* pointer to old vector */

    while (!found && vect!=0)
    {
       inregs.h.ah=53;      /* function 53 of int 21H */
       inregs.h.al=vect;    /* asks for the vector of an int.*/
       int86x(0x21,&inregs,&outregs,&segregs);
       outregs.x.bx=0x0104;        /* es:bx returns the vector */
                                   /* set bx at 0104H */

       oldvect=MK_FP(segregs.es,outregs.x.bx);
       for(number=0;oldvect[number]==chr[number];number++);

       if (number==7)        /* compare this vector to */
         found=1;                 /* the identification */
       else
         vect++;   /* if unequal-> next vector */
    }

    return(vect);    /* return number found */
}

playsong()
{
    union REGS inregs,outregs;
    struct SREGS segregs;

    inregs.h.ah=1;            /* function 1 of the CMSDRV */
    inregs.h.al=1;
    segregs.es=FP_SEG(Play_flag);
    inregs.x.bx=FP_OFF(Play_flag);
    inregs.x.cx=segm;
    int86x(intno,&inregs,&outregs,&segregs);
    if (outregs.x.ax!=0) return(1);
    return(0);
}

pause()

{
    union REGS inregs,outregs;
```

```
    inregs.h.ah=2;              /* function 2 of the CMSDRV */
    int86(intno,&inregs,&outregs);
    if (outregs.x.ax!=0) return(1);
    return(0);
}

continue()
{
  union REGS inregs,outregs;

    inregs.h.ah=3;              /* function 3 of the CMSDRV */
    int86(intno,&inregs,&outregs);
    if (outregs.x.ax!=0) return(1);
    return(0);
}

void stop()
{
  union REGS inregs,outregs;
    inregs.h.ah=4;              /* function 4 of the CMSDRV */
    int86(intno,&inregs,&outregs);
}

void unlock_key()
{
  union REGS inregs,outregs;
    inregs.h.ah=5;              /* function 5 of the CMSDRV */
    int86(intno,&inregs,&outregs);
}
```

Listing 8.4: C Example to play CMS Songs

```
/* ********************************************
**    PLAYCMS.C                              **
**    Turbo C++ 2.0                          **
******************************************** */

#include <dos.h>
#include <fcntl.h>
#include "cms.h"

extern word Play_flag;
extern word segm;
extern byte intno;
```

```
loadfile( char *filename ) /* read file at the */
{                          /* beginning of a segment */
  int handle;
  long filesize;
  struct REGPACK reg;

  if ( (handle=open(filename,O_RDONLY | O_BINARY))==1)
    return(1);
  filesize = filelength(handle);
  if (allocmem(((filesize+16)>4), &segm) !=1)
    return(2);
  reg.r_ax=0x3f00;
  reg.r_bx=handle;
  reg.r_cx=filesize;      /* function 3fh of int 21H */
  reg.r_dx=0;             /* reads a file at an */
  reg.r_ds=segm;          /* absolute address */
  intr(0x21,&reg);
  if (reg.r_flags & 1 )
  {
    freemem(segm);
    return(1);
  }
  close(handle);
  return(0);
}

void choice()
{
  printf("\nPress p-pause, u-unpause, s-stop ");
  printf("of m-music maestro!\n");
}

main ( int argc, char *argv[])
{
  chr key;
  int result;

  if ( !(argc==2) )
  {
    printf("Use: playcms < cms-file > \n");
    return(-1);
  }

  if ( (intno=checkdrv())==0 )
  {
```

```
        printf("CMSDRV.COM not loaded.. \n");
        return(-2);
    }

    if (!((result=loadfile(argv[1]))==0 ))
    {

      if (result==2)
        printf("Not enough memory available.\n");
      else
        printf("Loading error %s.\n",argv[1]);
      return(-3);
    }
    choice();
    while ((key=toupper((key=getch())))!='S')
    {
      switch(key)            /* process choice */
      {
        case 'M':
            if (playsong()==1)
            {
              printf("Song starting error..\n");
              break;
            }
            choice();
            break;
        case 'P':
            if (pause()==1)
            {
              printf("No music is playing.\n");
              break;
            }
            choice();
            break;
        case 'U':
            if (continue()==1)
            {
              printf("Nothing paused.\n");
              break;
            }
            choice();
            break;
        default:
            break;
      }
```

```
}

stop();
unlock_key();
freemem(segm);
return(0);
}
```

How to Create Sound with the CMS Chips

Since two stereo chips are present, you would think that one chip takes care of the sound from the left channels and the other takes care of sound from the right channels. But this is not the case. Even with one chip removed, you can still have stereo control over some of the voices.

Each CMS chip has six independent voices at its disposal. The two CMS chips do not conflict because each has its own control port:

- The first CMS chip controls voices 0 through 5 and uses ports 2X1H and 2X0H.

- The second chip controls voices 6 through 11 and uses ports 2X3H and 2X2H. The X in the hexadecimal numbers refers to the I/O jumper setting. The default setting of the Sound Blaster I/O jumper is 220H, with the 2 replacing the X in this case.

Indexing Registers   To control the six voices, every CMS chip has 32 internal registers that describe the ups and downs of the six voices. These registers are write-only; they can only be written.

Because it would require too many memory addresses for each register on the card to have its own port, you must index them. To do this, you send the number of the register you want to change to one port, and then you send the information you want to write to that register to another port. One port tells the board where to put the information, and the other contains the information itself.

For the sake of convenience, we assume that the I/O jumper is at 220H. Port 221H of the first CMS chip and port 223H of the second CMS chip point to the register addresses. The numbers that are sent to these ports have to be between 0 and 31.

Ports 220H and 222H of the first and the second CMS chip respectively contain the values that have to be written to the register addresses.

Suppose value 32 has to be written to register 3 of the second CMS chip (in order to control one of the voices between 6 and 11), and the second chip has the address port 223H and the data port 222H. First, the value 3 is sent to address port 223 so the chip knows that the next value that is sent to the data port has to be written to register 3. Then the value 32 is sent to data port 222H.

As we mentioned before, the 32 registers contain the information needed to generate sound on the six voices. The timbre of a tone on each voice is determined by the frequency, the octave, the amplitude, and the envelope of that tone.

Controlling the Octave, Amplitude, and Envelope of a Tone

The following sections explains how to control the tone frequency. How to control the octave, amplitude, and envelope of a tone are discussed as well.

Controlling Tone Frequency

Each CMS chip has six frequency generators at its disposal.

In one CMS chip, six registers are reserved for the tone numbers of each frequency generator. The tone number register is eight bits large, so it can contain values between 0 and 255. The pitch and frequency of a tone are one and the same. The frequency is always measured in Hz. The following formula is used to calculate the frequency of a tone:

$$\text{frequency (in Hz)} = (15625 * (2^{\wedge}\text{octave number})) / (511 - \text{tone number})$$

Controlling the Octave of a Tone

Because tone numbers from 0 to 255 are insufficient to represent the many existing pitches, the pitches are divided into eight octaves. Every octave has its own frequency range. Table 8.1 shows the eight octaves and their frequency ranges.

TABLE 8.1: The Eight Octaves and their Frequency Ranges

Octave	Range
0	31 Hz to 61 Hz
1	61 Hz to 122 Hz
2	122 Hz to 244 Hz
3	244 Hz to 488 Hz
4	489 Hz to 977 Hz
5	978 Hz to 1.95 kHz
6	1.96 kHz to 3.91 kHz
7	3.91 kHz to 7.81 kHz

Exactly three bits are needed to represent 8 octaves, so 2 octave numbers fit into one byte. That is why only three registers have been reserved for the octave numbers of the six frequency generators.

Controlling the Amplitude of the Tone

The amplitude corresponds to the sound intensity of the tone. This sound intensity can be set separately for each voice. The stereo part is involved when establishing the amplitude because the amplitude can be set for both the left and right channels.

There are six registers, one for every voice. The four highest bits determine the amplitude for the right channel and the four lowest bits determine the amplitude for the left channel. You can adjust the volume for both the left and the right output in sixteen steps.

Controlling the Envelope of the Tone

Two envelope generators are available for indicating a tone's direction of amplitude. The generators can assume the following waveforms:

Waveform Type	Description
Zero amplitude	No volume.
Maximum Amplitude	Maximum volume.

Waveform Type	Description
Single decay	A single linear decrease in the volume.
Repetitive decay	Repetitive linear decreases in the volume. Repetitive-decay waveforms are shown in Figure 8.1.
Single triangular	A linear increase, followed by a linear decrease in the volume.
Repetitive triangular	Repetitive linear increases, followed by linear decreases in the volume.
Single attack	A single linear increase in the volume.
Repetitive attack	Repetitive linear increases in the volume.

When the maximum volume is reached for attack and decay, the volume immediately drops to zero. When the envelope generators are used, the maximum volume is brought back to $7/8$ of the maximum value of the amplitude register.

There are two envelope registers, one for frequency generators 0 through 2 and one for frequency generators 3 through 5. Three bits each are required for the eight envelopes. Table 8.2 shows how the envelope byte is completed.

When the octaves 5, 6, and 7 are reached, the frequency steps get larger, so a 4-bit number has to be used.

The External and Internal Clocks   To determine whether a repetitive envelope has to start with an attack or a decay, the envelope generator uses an internal or an external clock. When the internal clock is used, frequency generator 1 (for the first envelope generator) or frequency generator 4 (for the second envelope generator) is used. In this case, you can no longer use these frequency generators.

You yourself are, in effect, the external clock. By writing to the corresponding envelope generator register, you start a new attack or decay according to the established envelope.

FIGURE 8.1:

The different waveforms

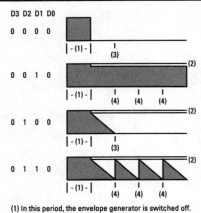

(1) In this period, the envelope generator is switched off.
(2) When the envelope generator is on, the maximum volume is 7/8 of the maximum amplitude value.
(3) From this point on, a new cycle can start by writing a value to the envelope generator register.
(4) At this point, a new type of cycle starts like the value of the envelope register.

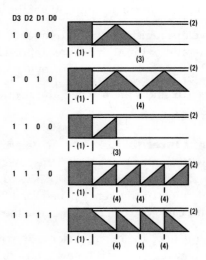

Generating Noises

A sound chip has to be able to do more than just reproduce notes, as notes alone are not enough to produce the wide range of sound effects currently required by many games. Therefore, a noise generator is available to create various sound effects.

TABLE 8.2: The Envelope Generator

Bit Number	Status (0=off, 1=on)	Description
bit 0	0	The same envelopes apply to both the left and the right output.
	1	The envelopes for the left and the right output are opposites.
bit 3,2,1	0 0 0	No amplitude.
	0 0 1	Maximum amplitude.
	0 1 0	Single decay.
	0 1 1	Repetitive decay.
	1 0 0	Single attack + decay (= triangular).
	1 0 1	Repetitive triangular.
	1 1 0	Single attack.
	1 1 1	Repetitive attack.
bit 4	0	4-bit envelope resolution.
	1	3-bit envelope resolution.
bit 5	0	Internal envelope clock; frequency generator 1 or 4.
	1	External envelope clock; by writing to this register byte.
bit 6	0,1	Has no function.
bit 7	0	Envelope generator off.
	1	Envelope generator on.

Whereas the frequency generator uses sine waves to reproduce tones, the noise generator uses random numbers. These random numbers constitute a kind of noise. The sound a noise generator produces is often referred to as *white noise*.

Each CMS chip has two noise generators. The pitch of the noise—that is, the speed at which new random numbers are chosen—depends on two bits in the noise generator register. The noise generator register contains two bits for noise generator 0 and two bits for noise generator 2. The values of these bits determine the frequency of the noise. The possible values are:

Bit 0	Bit 1	Frequency Value
0	0	31.25 kHz
0	1	15.6 kHz
1	0	7.8 kHz
1	1	Between 61 Hz and 15.6 kHz

When both bits are 1, the value in the frequency generator registers 0 and 3 determines the frequency value of the noise generators 0 and 1, respectively.

Mixing Tones and Noise

The CMS chip has six mixers, one for each voice. With the mixers you can mix tones and noise.

Two internal registers are reserved for telling the mixers which of the two (noise or tones) they have to let through. In both registers, six bits are prescribed for indicating a corresponding voice. The first register indicates whether the tones are to be let through. When the bit is set (=1), the tone generated by the frequency generator may pass. The second register determines whether the sound of the noise generator is to be let through. Table 8.3 shows the rest of the combinations.

Figure 8.2 shows how the different parts of the CMS chip are connected. This figure should give you a better understanding of the structure of a CMS chip.

Internal Register Addresses   Registers have been discussed on the previous pages of this chapter, but we have yet to show you what the address of each generator is. Tables 8.4 and 8.5 show all internal registers and their addresses and data bits. Table 8.4 concerns the first CMS chip, and Table 8.5 the second. In the tables, all numbers are represented in hexadecimal notation. The Xs indicate bits that are not used. The first CMS chip has the register address port 2X1H and the data port 2X0H, where X stands for the value 1, 2, 3, 4, 5, or 6, according to the I/O jumper setting. The second CMS chip has the register address port 2X3H and the data port 2X2H, where X stands for the values 1, 2, 3, 4, 5, or 6 according to the I/O jumper setting.

TABLE 8.3: Bits for Mixing Tones

Frequency-Enable Register	Noise-Enable Register	Description
0	0	Neither the tones nor the noise are let through.
0	1	Only the noise passes.
1	0	Only the tones pass.
1	1	Both the noise and the tones pass.

FIGURE 8.2:

The structure of the CMS chip

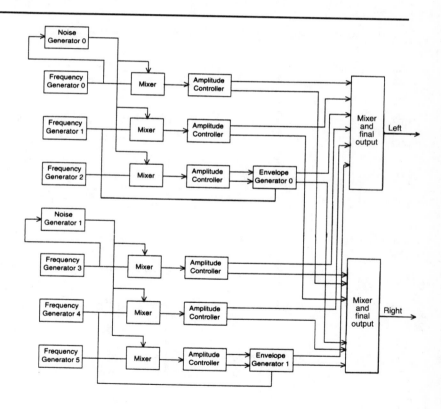

TABLE 8.4: The First CMS Chip

Regular Address	Databus Input								Function Description
	Bit 7	Bit 6	Bit 5	Bit 4	Bit 3	Bit 2	Bit 1	Bit 0	
00	AmR3	AmR2	AmR1	AmR0	AmL3	AmL2	AmL1	AmL0	Amplitude values right and left for voice 0
01	AmR3	AmR2	AmR1	AmR0	AmL3	AmL2	AmL1	AmL0	Amplitude values right and left for voice 1
02	AmR3	AmR2	AmR1	AmR0	AmL3	AmL2	AmL1	AmL0	Amplitude values right and left for voice 2
03	AmR3	AmR2	AmR1	AmR0	AmL3	AmL2	AmL1	AmL0	Amplitude values right and left for voice 3
04	AmR3	AmR2	AmR1	AmR0	AmL3	AmL2	AmL1	AmL0	Amplitude values right and left for voice 4
05	AmR3	AmR2	AmR1	AmR0	AmL3	AmL2	AmL1	AmL0	Amplitude values right and left for voice 5
06	X	X	X	X	X	X	X	X	Reserved for extension
07	X	X	X	X	X	X	X	X	Reserved for extension
08	Tn7	Tn6	Tn5	Tn4	Tn3	Tn2	Tn1	Tn0	Tone number for frequency generator 0
09	Tn7	Tn6	Tn5	Tn4	Tn3	Tn2	Tn1	Tn0	Tone number for frequency generator 1
0A	Tn7	Tn6	Tn5	Tn4	Tn3	Tn2	Tn1	Tn0	Tone number for frequency generator 2
0B	Tn7	Tn6	Tn5	Tn4	Tn3	Tn2	Tn1	Tn0	Tone number for frequency generator 3
0C	Tn7	Tn6	Tn5	Tn4	Tn3	Tn2	Tn1	Tn0	Tone number for frequency generator 4
0D	Tn7	Tn6	Tn5	Tn4	Tn3	Tn2	Tn1	Tn0	Tone number for frequency generator 5
0E	X	X	X	X	X	X	X	X	Reserved for extension
0F	X	X	X	X	X	X	X	X	Reserved for extension
10	X	K1On2	K1On1	K1On0	X	K0On2	K0On1	K0On0	Octave number of frequency generator 1 (bits 4–6) and of frequency generator 0 (bits 0–2)

TABLE 8.4: The First CMS Chip (continued)

Regular Address	Databus Input								Function Description
	Bit 7	Bit 6	Bit 5	Bit 4	Bit 3	Bit 2	Bit 1	Bit 0	
11	X	K3On2	K3On1	K3On0	X	K2On2	K2On1	K2On0	Octave Number of frequency generator 3 (bits 4–6) and of frequency generator 2 (bits 0–2)
12	X	K5On2	K5On1	K5On0	X	K4On2	K4On1	K4On0	Octave number of frequency generator 5 (bits 4–6) and of frequency generator4 (bits 0–2)
13	X	X	X	X	X	X	X	X	Reserved for extension
14	X	X	K5	K4	K3	K2	K1	K0	Frequency enable for every voice
15	X	X	K5	K4	K3	K2	K1	K0	Noise enable for every voice
16	X	X	G1Cf1	G1Cf0	X	X	G0Cf1	G0Cf0	Noise generator clock frequency
17	X	X	X	X	X	X	X	X	Reserved for extension
18	G0E7	X	G0E5	G0E4	G0E3	G0E2	G0E1	G0E0	Envelope generator 0
19	G1E7	X	G1E5	G1E4	G1E3	G1E2	G1E1	G1E0	Envelope generator 1
1A	X	X	X	X	X	X	X	X	Reserved for extension
1B	X	X	X	X	X	X	X	X	Reserved for extension
1C	X	X	X	X	X	X	RST	SE	Reset/Sound enable all voices (0 through 5)
1D	X	X	X	X	X	X	X	X	Reserved for extension
1E	X	X	X	X	X	X	X	X	Reserved for extension
1F	X	X	X	X	X	X	X	X	Reserved for extension

TABLE 8.5: The Second CMS Chip

Regular Address	Databus Input								Function Description
	Bit 7	Bit 6	Bit 5	Bit 4	Bit 3	Bit 2	Bit 1	Bit 0	
00	AmR3	AmR2	AmR1	AmR0	AmL3	AmL2	AmL1	AmL0	Amplitude values right and left for voice 6
01	AmR3	AmR2	AmR1	AmR0	AmL3	AmL2	AmL1	AmL0	Amplitude values right and left for voice 7
02	AmR3	AmR2	AmR1	AmR0	AmL3	AmL2	AmL1	AmL0	Amplitude values right and left for voice 8
03	AmR3	AmR2	AmR1	AmR0	AmL3	AmL2	AmL1	AmL0	Amplitude values right and left for voice 9
04	AmR3	AmR2	AmR1	AmR0	AmL3	AmL2	AmL1	AmL0	Amplitude values right and left for voice 10
05	AmR3	AmR2	AmR1	AmR0	AmL3	AmL2	AmL1	AmL0	Amplitude values right and left for voice 11
06	X	X	X	X	X	X	X	X	Reserved for extension
07	X	X	X	X	X	X	X	X	Reserved for extension
08	Tn7	Tn6	Tn5	Tn4	Tn3	Tn2	Tn1	Tn0	Tone number for frequency generator 6
09	Tn7	Tn6	Tn5	Tn4	Tn3	Tn2	Tn1	Tn0	Tone number for frequency generator 7
0A	Tn7	Tn6	Tn5	Tn4	Tn3	Tn2	Tn1	Tn0	Tone number for frequency generator 8
0B	Tn7	Tn6	Tn5	Tn4	Tn3	Tn2	Tn1	Tn0	Tone number for frequency generator 9
0C	Tn7	Tn6	Tn5	Tn4	Tn3	Tn2	Tn1	Tn0	Tone number for frequency generator 10
0D	Tn7	Tn6	Tn5	Tn4	Tn3	Tn2	Tn1	Tn0	Tone number for frequency generator 11
0E	X	X	X	X	X	X	X	X	Reserved for extension
0F	X	X	X	X	X	X	X	X	Reserved for extension
10	X	K7On2	K7On1	K7On0	X	K6On2	K6On1	K6On0	Octave number of frequency generator 7 (bits 4–6) and of frequency generator 6 (bits 0–2)

TABLE 8.5: The Second CMS Chip (continued)

Regular Address	Databus Input								Function Description
	Bit 7	Bit 6	Bit 5	Bit 4	Bit 3	Bit 2	Bit 1	Bit 0	
11	X	K9On2	K9On1	K9On0	X	K8On2	K8On1	K8On0	Octave number of frequency generator 9 (bits 4–6) and of frequency generator 8 (bits 0–2)
12	X	K11On2	K11On1	K11On0	X	K10On2	K10On1	K10On0	Octave number of frequency generator 11 (bits 4–6) and of frequency generator 10 (bits 0–2)
13	X	X	X	X	X	X	X	X	Reserved for extension
14	X	X	V11	V10	V9	V8	V7	V6	Frequency enable for every voice
15	X	X	V11	V10	V9	V8	V7	V6	Noise enable for every voice
16	X	X	G3Cf1	G3Cf0	X	X	G1Cf1	G1Cf0	Noise generator clock frequency
17	X	X	X	X	X	X	X	X	Reserved for extension
18	G2E7	X	G2E5	G2E4	G2E3	G2E2	G2E1	G2E0	Envelope generator 2
19	G3E7	X	G3E5	G3E4	G3E3	G3E2	G3E1	G3E0	Envelope generator 3
1A	X	X	X	X	X	X	X	X	Reserved for extension
1B	X	X	X	X	X	X	X	X	Reserved for extension
1C	X	X	X	X	X	X	RST	SE	Reset/Sound enable all voices (6 through 11)
1D	X	X	X	X	X	X	X	X	Reserved for extension
1E	X	X	X	X	X	X	X	X	Reserved for extension
1F	X	X	X	X	X	X	X	X	Reserved for extension

Determining the Length of a Tone

One problem with CMS chips is that they have no internal clock for specifying or measuring the length of a note. The chips cannot terminate the tones they generate—it's up to the programmer to do that.

There are two ways to determine the length of a tone, with the internal clock and with timer interrupts:

- If you use the clock to determine how much time has passed since the beginning of a note, make sure that your application is occupied with controlling the CMS chips only. For example, an application occupied with calculating fractal images or with another intensive operation can throw off the clock by a few hundredths of a second during a time reading.

- With the timer interrupt method, you increase the number of times the timer interrupt is called and use a counter to determine the exact duration of a note.

The advantage of using the timer is that the application can continue executing other instructions. The interrupt program takes care of the processing of the tones and the sound effects.

Notes and Their Octave Frequencies

Table 8.6 shows all the notes with their octaves and frequencies. By using this table you can determine the octave and the frequency of every note.

Thief: An Example Application

In this section we'll examine how the CMS chips and their registers are used in a practical application.

Our example application is a little game in which the CMS chips are used to determine the player's direction. In the game, which is called Thief, a robber walks around in a 16 by 16 field carrying the loot from his latest heist, a bag with money inside it. Besides money, the bag holds a transmitter that produces a stereo signal every half second. When this signal is, for example, stronger on the left than on the right, the villain is to your left. As you approach the robber, the frequency of the signal gets higher. Your job is to catch the robber within one minute.

The screen shows the field with the walls as well as you, the detective. You can't see the robber, except when he appears every ten seconds.

TABLE 8.6: Notes and their Octave and Frequency Values

Note	Octave Number	Frequency Value	Note	Octave Number	Frequency Value	Note	Octave Number	Frequency Value
A	0	3	A	3	3	A	6	3
A#	0	31	A#	3	31	A#	6	31
B	0	58	B	3	58	B	6	58
C	0	83	C	3	83	C	6	83
C#	0	107	C#	3	107	C#	6	107
D	0	130	D	3	130	D	6	130
D#	0	151	D#	3	151	D#	6	151
E	0	172	E	3	172	E	6	172
F	0	191	F	3	191	F	6	191
F#	0	209	F#	3	209	F#	6	209
G	0	226	G	3	226	G	6	226
G#	0	242	G#	3	242	G#	6	242
A	1	3	A	4	3	A	7	3
A#	1	31	A#	4	31	A#	7	31
B	1	58	B	4	58	B	7	58
C	1	83	C	4	83	C	7	83
C#	1	107	C#	4	107	C#	7	107
D	1	130	D	4	130	D	7	130
D#	1	151	D#	4	151	D#	7	151
E	1	172	E	4	172	E	7	172
F	1	191	F	4	191	F	7	191
F#	1	209	F#	4	209	F#	7	209
G	1	226	G	4	226	G	7	226
G#	1	242	G#	4	242	G#	7	242
A	2	3	A	5	3			
A#	2	31	A#	5	31			
B	2	58	B	5	58			
C	2	83	C	5	83			
C#	2	107	C#	5	107			

TABLE 8.6: Notes and their Octave and Frequency Values (continued)

Note	Octave Number	Frequency Value	Note	Octave Number	Frequency Value	Note	Octave Number	Frequency Value
D	2	130	D	5	130			
D#	2	151	D#	5	151			
E	2	172	E	5	172			
F	2	191	F	5	191			
F#	2	209	F#	5	209			
G	2	226	G	5	226			
G#	2	242	G#	5	242			

Listing 8.5: Pascal Unit Supporting the Thief Game

```
{ *******************************************
** Unit CMSNOTE supporting THIEF.PAS      **
** Turbo Pascal 4.0                       **
******************************************* }

Unit CmsNote;

INTERFACE

Uses Crt,Dos;

const baseport=$220;        { selected port }
      OldTimV=103;          { old timer interrupt }
var newtimepointer:pointer;

Procedure settimer(Freq : word; Rout : pointer);
Procedure resettimer;
Procedure PlayNote(voice,ampl,tone,octave,
                   sort,noiseclock,envelope:byte;
                   duration:integer);

Procedure ResetCms;
Procedure InitCms;

IMPLEMENTATION
```

```
var timevoice:array[0..11] of integer;   { buffers }
    cmsonfreq:array[0..11] of byte;
    cmsonnoise:array[0..11] of byte;
    counter:byte;
    freqtot:byte;
    noisetot:byte;

procedure settimspeed(Freq : word);   { calculate the }
var                                    { number of clock ticks and }
  ICnt : longint;      { pass this to the timer chip }
begin
        inline($FA);
     ICnt:= 1193180 div Freq;
     port[$43]:=$36;
     port[$40]:=lo(ICnt);
     port[$40]:=hi(ICnt);
        inline($FB);
end;

procedure settimer(Freq : word; Rout : pointer);
var
  OldV : pointer;                { take over timer }
begin
        inline($FA);
        getintvec(8,OldV);
        setintvec(OldtimV,Oldv);
     setintvec(8,Rout);
     settimspeed(Freq);
        inline($FB);
end;

procedure resettimer;
Var
  OldV : pointer; { reset vector and speed }
begin
        inline($FA);
     port[$43]:=$36;
     port[$40]:=$0;
     port[$40]:=$0;
        getintvec(OldtimV,Oldv);
     setintvec(8,Oldv);
        inline($FB);
end;
```

```
Procedure PlayNote(voice,ampl,tone,octave,
                   sort,noiseclock,envelope:byte;
                   duration:integer);

var cmsvoice,cmsport:integer;  { initialize all }
    i,j,k,l:byte;    { registers and set flags }

begin
  cmsport:=baseport;
  cmsvoice:=voice;
  if (voice>=6) then   { bigger than 5; other chip }
  begin
    Dec(voice,6);
    Inc(cmsport,2);
  end;
  port[cmsport+1]:=voice;
  port[cmsport]:=ampl;              { amplitude }
  port[cmsport+1]:=8+voice;
  port[cmsport]:=tone;              { frequency }
  port[cmsport+1]:=$10+(voice DIV 2);

  j:=octave SHL ((voice AND 1)*4);
  port[cmsport]:=j;                 { octave }
  port[cmsport+1]:=$16;

  k:=noiseclock SHL (((voice DIV 3) AND 1)*4);
  port[cmsport]:=k;                   { noise frequency }
  port[cmsport+1]:=$18+(voice DIV 3);
  port[cmsport]:=envelope;          { envelope }

  if (sort AND 2)=2 then
    cmsonfreq[cmsvoice]:=1;   { frequency voice }
  if (sort AND 1)=1 then
    cmsonnoise[cmsvoice]:=1;  { noise voice }

  timevoice[cmsvoice]:=duration; { and the length of the note }
end;

Procedure NewTimer; INTERRUPT;  { decrease the duration of }
var freq,noise:byte;                  { all voices and pass }
    i,j:integer;               { the total of playing }
    cmsport:word;            { voices on to the chips }
```

```
      Regs:registers;
begin
 For i:=0 to 11 do
  begin
    if ((cmsonfreq[i]=1) OR (cmsonnoise[i]=1)) then
    begin
      if (timevoice[i]>0) then
        Dec(timevoice[i])
      else
        begin
          cmsonnoise[i]:=0;
          cmsonfreq[i]:=0;
        end;
    end;
  end;
 freqtot:=0;
 noisetot:=0;
 cmsport:=baseport;

For i:=0 to 5 do
 begin
   if (cmsonfreq[i]=1)  then Inc(freqtot,(1 SHL i));
   if (cmsonnoise[i]=1) then Inc(noisetot,(1 SHL i));
 end;
 port[cmsport+1]:=$14;
 port[cmsport]:=freqtot;
 port[cmsport+1]:=$15;
 port[cmsport]:=noisetot;

 freqtot:=0;
 noisetot:=0;

 for i:=6 to 11 do
 begin
   if (cmsonfreq[i]=1)  then Inc(freqtot,(1 SHL (i-6)));
   if (cmsonnoise[i]=1) then Inc(noisetot,(1 SHL (i-6)));
 end;
 port[cmsport+3]:=$14;
 port[cmsport+2]:=freqtot;

 port[cmsport+3]:=$15;
 port[cmsport+2]:=noisetot;

 Inc(counter);
```

```
      Intr(oldtimV,Regs);        { old timer interrupt }

end;

Procedure ResetCms;            { set the reset register }
begin
  port[baseport+1]:=$1c;
  port[baseport]:=2;
  port[baseport+3]:=$1c;
  port[baseport+2]:=2;
end;

Procedure InitCms;
var cnt:integer;

begin
  resetcms;
  port[baseport+1]:=$1c;        { enable sound }
  port[baseport]:=1;
  port[baseport+3]:=$1c;
  port[baseport+2]:=1;
  For cnt:=0 to 11 do
  begin                     { initialize all registers }
    timevoice[cnt]:=0;
    cmsonfreq[cnt]:=0;
    cmsonnoise[cnt]:=0;
    playnote(cnt,0,0,0,0,0,0,0);
  end;

  port[baseport+1]:=$14;
  port[baseport]:=255;
  port[baseport+3]:=$14;
  port[baseport+2]:=255;
  port[baseport+1]:=$15;
  port[baseport]:=0;
  port[baseport+3]:=$15;
  port[baseport+2]:=0;
end;

begin                      { initialize timer pointer }
  newtimepointer:=@newtimer;
end.
```

Listing 8.6: Pascal Listing of the Thief Program

```
{ ****************************************
** THIEF.PAS                            **
** Turbo Pascal 4.0                      **
**************************************** }

Program Thief;

Uses Crt,Dos,Cmsnote;

type screentype=array[0..1999] of byte;

var screen:screentype absolute $b800:0;
    cur_screen:word;
    xthief,ythief,xagent,yagent:byte;
    beepcount:integer;
    banditcount:integer;
    oldtimer:pointer;
    oldnum:byte;
    xmin:byte;
    ymin:byte;
    amplit:byte;
    oct:byte;
    stereo:byte;
    stop:byte;
    a,i,j:integer;
    ch:char;

Procedure SetScreen; { build a square on the screen }
var i:integer;
    regs:registers;

begin
  clrscr;
  cur_screen:=22;
  screen[0]:=218;
  i:=2;
  Repeat
    screen[i]:=196;
    inc(i,2);
  Until (i>=34);
  screen[34]:=191;
```

```
    i:=80;
    Repeat
      screen[i]:=179;
      screen[i+34]:=179;
      inc(i,80);
    Until (i>=80*17);
    screen[80*17]:=192;
    i:=80*17+2;
    Repeat
      screen[i]:=196;
      inc(i,2);
    Until (i>=(80*17+34));
    screen[80*17+34]:=217;

    regs.ax:=$0100;
    regs.cx:=$2000;
    Intr(16,regs);          { put the cursor far away}
end;

Procedure Putdoll(x,y,chr:byte);   { put a character }
var total:word;                    { in the square }
begin
  total:=0;
  Inc(total,((x+1)*2)+((y+1)*80));
  screen[total]:=chr;
end;

Procedure intelthief;       { determine the new }
var xr,yr:byte;             { coordinates of the thief }

begin
  xr:=random(2);
  yr:=random(2);

  if ((xr=1) AND (xthief<15))
  then
    Inc(xthief)
  else
    if (xthief>0) then Dec(xthief);

  if ((yr=1) AND (ythief<15))
  then
    Inc(ythief)
  else
```

```
      if (ythief>0) then Dec(ythief);
end;

Procedure Newtimerint; INTERRUPT;  { give alternately }
var regs:registers;                { left and right a }
                             { beep using the coordinates }
begin                        { of agent and thief }
  Inc(beepcount);

  if (beepcount=9) then
  begin
    if (stereo=0) then
    begin
      if (xagent<=xthief) then
      begin
        xmin:=(xthief-xagent);
        amplit:=0;
        amplit:=((15-xmin) SHL 4);
      end
      else
        amplit:=0;
      port[baseport+1]:=0;
      port[baseport]:=amplit;
    end
    else
    begin
      if (xagent>=xthief) then
      begin
        xmin:=(xagentxthief);
        amplit:=15-xmin;
      end
      else
        amplit:=0;
      port[baseport+1]:=0;
      port[baseport]:=amplit;
    end;
    stereo:=stereo XOR 1;

    if (yagent<ythief) then
    begin
      ymin:=(7-(ythief-yagent) div 2);
      oct:=ymin;
      port[baseport+1]:=$10;
      port[baseport]:=oct;
    end
```

```
    else
    begin
      ymin:=(7-(yagent-ythief) div 2);
      oct:=ymin;
      port[baseport+1]:=$10;
      port[baseport]:=oct;
    end;
    beepcount:=0;
    port[baseport+1]:=$14;
    port[baseport]:=1;
  end;
  if (beepcount=5) then
  begin
    Port[baseport+1]:=$14;
    Port[baseport]:=0;
  end;

  if (banditcount=0) then putdoll(xthief,ythief,32);

  Inc(banditcount);
  if (banditcount=182) then
  begin
    putdoll(xthief,ythief,2);
    banditcount:=0;
  end;

  intr(oldtimv,Regs);
end;

begin
  beepcount:=0;
  banditcount:=0;
  xmin:=0;
  ymin:=0;
  oct:=0;
  amplit:=0;
  stereo:=0;
  stop:=0;

  clrscr;
  Writeln(' The black agent has to catch');
  Writeln(' the white thief.');
  Writeln(' Use cursor keys.');
  Writeln(' High tones mean that the thief is');
  Writeln(' very close, low tones mean the contrary.');
```

```
Writeln(' The stereo effect determines whether the thief');
Writeln(' is to your left or to your right.');
Writeln(' Press a key to start.');
ch:=Readkey;

textmode(C40);
port[baseport+1]:=0;          { set note }
port[baseport]:=$ff;

port[baseport+1]:=$14;
port[baseport]:=0;

port[baseport+1]:=$8;
port[baseport]:=64;

port[baseport+1]:=$10;
port[baseport]:=4;
port[baseport+1]:=$15;
port[baseport]:=0;

port[baseport+1]:=$1c;
port[baseport]:=1;

setscreen;
randomize;
xthief:=random(16);
ythief:=random(16);
xagent:=8;
yagent:=8;

getintvec(8,oldtimer);              { take over vectors }
setintvec(oldtimv,oldtimer);
setintvec(8,@newtimerint);

while (stop<>1) do
begin
  putdoll(xagent,yagent,1);
  ch:=readkey;
  if ch=#0 then ch:=readkey;
  putdoll(xagent,yagent,32);
  putdoll(xthief,ythief,32);          { delete }
  case ch of                          { cursor keys }
    #77:if (xagent<15) then Inc(xagent); { determine }
    #75:if (xagent>0) then Dec(xagent);  { new }
    #72:if (yagent>0) then Dec(yagent); { coordinates }
```

```
      #80:if (yagent<15) then Inc(yagent);
      #27:stop:=1;
    end;

  intelthief;
  if ((xthief=xagent) AND (ythief=yagent)) then stop:=1;
end;

Port[baseport+1]:=$1c;
Port[baseport]:=0;

setintvec(8,oldtimer);

TextMode(c80);
Writeln('Gotcha !!');
Writeln;

initcms;
settimer(100,newtimepointer);
If Keypressed then ch:=readkey;

while not Keypressed do    { and an effect afterward }
begin
  for i:=255 downto 0 do
    playnote(0,100,i,5,2,0,0,50);
  for i:=0 to 255 do
    playnote(0,100,i,5,2,0,0,50);
end;

ch:=readkey;
resettimer;
resetcms;

end.
```

Listing 8.7: C Unit Supporting the Thief Game

```
/* *******************************************
**   Include file CMSNote.H in THIEF.C       **
**   Turbo C++ 2.0                           **
********************************************/

#define baseport 0x220    /* default port */

typedef unsigned char byte;
```

```
unsigned timevoice[12];   /* time for each voice */
byte cmsonfreq[12];    /* which freq voice is on? */
byte cmsonnoise[12];   /* and which noise voice ? */
byte counter;
byte freqtot,noisetot;   /* totals */
void playnote(byte voice,byte ampl,byte tone,
    byte octave,byte sort,byte noiseclock,
    byte envelope,unsigned duration)

{
  unsigned int cmsvoice,cmsport;
byte i,j,k,l;

  cmsport=baseport;
  cmsvoice=voice;
  if (voice>=6)      /* if the voice > 6, then */
  {                  /* the other CMS chip has to take over */
    voice-=6;
    cmsport+=2;
  }
  outp(cmsport+1,voice);
  outp(cmsport,ampl);                /* set amplitude */
  outp(cmsport+1,8+voice);
  outp(cmsport,tone);              /* set pitch */
  outp(cmsport+1,0x10+(voice/2));
  j=(octave<((voice&1)*4));
  outp(cmsport,j);                 /* set octave */
  outp(cmsport+1,0x16);
  k=(noiseclock < (((voice/3)&1)*4));
  outp(cmsport,k);                 /* the noise frequency */
  outp(cmsport+1,0x18+(voice/3));
  outp(cmsport,envelope);    /* and the envelope */
  if (sort&2)
    cmsonfreq[cmsvoice]=1; /* a frequency sound */
  if (sort&1)
    cmsonnoise[cmsvoice]=1;  /* or a noise sound */
  timevoice[cmsvoice]=duration;  /* and the duration of the note
*/
}

void interrupt (*oldtim)(void);    /* the old timer */

void interrupt newtim()          /* the new timer */
{
```

```
byte freq,noise;
int i,j;
unsigned int cmsport;

for(i=0;i<12;i++)        /* go along all voices */
 {
   if (cmsonfreq[i] || cmsonnoise[i] )
                         /* is the voice enabled? */
    {
   if (timevoice[i]>0)  /* decrease the duration of the */
     timevoice[i]--;    /* note if it is > 0 */
   else
       {                        /* if the duration is zero */
       cmsonnoise[i]=0;   /* disable voice */
       cmsonfreq[i]=0;
     }
     }
 }
freqtot=0;
noisetot=0;

cmsport=baseport;
for(i=0;i<6;i++)         /* calculate which voices */
{                        /* have to be switched on */
  if (cmsonfreq[i])  freqtot+=(1<i);
  if (cmsonnoise[i]) noisetot+=(1<i);
}
outp(cmsport+1,0x14);   /* set frequency */
outp(cmsport,freqtot);                 /* register */

outp(cmsport+1,0x15);   /* and noise register */
outp(cmsport,noisetot);

freqtot=0;
noisetot=0;

for(i=6;i<12;i++)   /* same for the voices */
{                                   /* 6 through 11 */
  if (cmsonfreq[i])  freqtot+=(1<<(i6));
  if (cmsonnoise[i]) noisetot+=(1<<--(i6));
}
outp(cmsport+3,0x14);
outp(cmsport+2,freqtot);

outp(cmsport+3,0x15);
```

```
    outp(cmsport+2,noisetot);

    counter++;              /* increment counter */
    oldtim();               /* call old timer */
}

void settimer(unsigned Freq,void interrupt (*newIRQ)())
{
    int ICnt;
    asm cli;
    ICnt = 1193180/Freq;    /* determine the number of clock */
    outp(0x43,0x36);        /* ticks of the timer and */
    outp(0x40,ICnt &255);   /* pass it on to the */
    outp(0x40,ICnt >8);     /* timer chip */
    oldtim=getvect(8);
    setvect(8,newIRQ);      /* take over timer interrupt */
    asm sti;
}

void resettimer()
{
    asm cli;
    outp(0x43,0x36);        /* reset clock ticks at */
    outp(0x40,0x0);         /* default position */
    outp(0x40,0x0);
    setvect(8,oldtim);      /* restore old timer */
    asm sti;
}

void resetcms()
{
    outp(baseport+1,0x1c); /* give reset command */
    outp(baseport,2);
    outp(baseport+3,0x1c);      /* for both chips */
    outp(baseport+2,2);
}

void initcms()
{
    int cnt;
    resetcms();
    outp(baseport+1,0x1c);      /* enable all sound */
    outp(baseport,1);
    outp(baseport+3,0x1c);
    outp(baseport+2,1);
```

```
  for (cnt=0;cnt<12;cnt++)
  {
    timevoice[cnt]=0;              /* initialize all */
    cmsonfreq[cnt]=0;            /* registers */
    cmsonnoise[cnt]=0;
    playnote(cnt,0,0,0,0,0,0,0);
  }

}
```

Listing 8.8: C Listing of the Thief Program

```
/* *********************************************
**   THIEF.C                                   **
**   Turbo C++ 2.0                             **
*********************************************/

#include <stdio.h>
#include <conio.h>
#include <stdlib.h>
#include <dos.h>
#include "cmsnote.h"

typedef unsigned int  word;
byte far *screen;          /* pointer to the screen */
byte xthief,ythief,xagent,yagent;  /* x/y coordinates */
                                /* of thief and agent */
void setscreen()
{
  int i;
  clrscr();
  screen=MK_FP(0xb800,22);  /* create a pointer to */
                                /* the screen */
  screen[0]=218;                    /* draw a square */
  for (i=2;i<34;i+=2) screen[i]=196;
  screen[34]=191;
  for (i=80;i<80*17;i+=80)
  {
    screen[i]=179;
    screen[i+34]=179;
  }
  screen[80*17]=192;
  for (i=(80*17)+2;i<(80*17)+34;i+=2) screen[i]=196;
  screen[(80*17)+34]=217;
```

```
    _setcursortype(_NOCURSOR);        /* remove cursor */
}

void putdoll( byte x, byte y, byte chr )
{
  word total=0;                       /* calculate location */
  total+=((++x)*2)+((++y)*80);  /* in screen */
  screen[total]=chr;                  /* place the character */
                                      /* on the screen */
}
void intelthief()
{
  byte xr,yr;              /* determine new x and y */
  xr=random(2);            /* coordinates of the thief */
  yr=random(2);
  if ((xr==1) && (xthief<15)) xthief++;
  else if (xthief>0) xthief--;
  if ((yr==1) && (ythief<15)) ythief++;
  else if (ythief>0) ythief--;

}

void interrupt (*oldtim)(void);    /* old timer int. */

  int beepcount=0;
  int banditcount=0;
  byte xmin=0,ymin=0;
  byte amplit=0,oct=0;
  byte stereo=0;

void interrupt newtimerint(void)  /* new timer */
{                                 /* takes care of the increment */
  beepcount++;          /* of the counters and sends a */
  if (beepcount==9)     /* beep based on the difference */
  {                     /* between the coordinates */
    if (stereo==0)
    {
      if (xagent<=xthief)
      {
        xmin=(xthief-xagent);
        amplit=0;
        amplit=((15-xmin)<<4);
      }
      else
        amplit=0;
```

```
    outp(baseport+1,0);
    outp(baseport,amplit);
  }
  else
  {
    if (xagent>=xthief)
    {
      xmin=(xagent-xthief);
      amplit=15x-min;
    }
    else
      amplit=0;
    outp(baseport+1,0);
    outp(baseport,amplit);
  }
  stereo=stereo^1;     /* next time other side */
  if (yagent<ythief)
  {
    ymin=(7(ythiefyagent)/2);
    oct=ymin;
    outp(baseport+1,0x10);
    outp(baseport,oct);
  }
  else
  {
    ymin=(7-(yagent-ythief)/2);
    oct=ymin;
    outp(baseport+1,0x10);
    outp(baseport,oct);
  }
beepcount=0;
outp(baseport+1,0x14);
outp(baseport,1);
}
if (beepcount==5)
{
  outp(baseport+1,0x14);
  outp(baseport,0);
}
if (banditcount==0) putdoll(xthief,ythief,32);

banditcount++;
if (banditcount==182)
{
  putdoll(xthief,ythief,2);
```

```
      banditcount=0;
    }

    oldtim();
}

void main()
{
    int a,i,j;
    int stop=0;
    clrscr();
    printf("\n\n\n  The black agent has to catch");
    printf(" the white thief. \n");
    printf("  Use cursor keys.\n");
    printf("  High tones mean that the thief is");
    printf(" very near, low tones mean the contrary.\n");
    printf("  The stereo effect determines whether the thief");
    printf(" is to your left or to your right.\n");
    printf("\n  Press a key to start.\n");
    getch();

    textmode(C40);
    outp(baseport+1,0);        /* set registers */
    outp(baseport,0xff);
    outp(baseport+1,0x14);
    outp(baseport,0);
    outp(baseport+1,0x8);
    outp(baseport,64);
    outp(baseport+1,0x10);
    outp(baseport,4);
    outp(baseport+1,0x15);
    outp(baseport,0);
    outp(baseport+1,0x1c);
    outp(baseport,1);

    setscreen();
    randomize();
    xthief=random(16);
    ythief=random(16);
    xagent=8;
    yagent=8;
    oldtim=getvect(8);
    setvect(8,newtimerint);
    while (!(stop))
    {
```

```
      putdoll(xagent,yagent,1);
       a=getch();
      if (!a) a=getch();
      putdoll(xagent,yagent,32);
      putdoll(xthief,ythief,32);
      switch (a)
      {
        case 77:                        /* cursor keys */
            if (xagent<15) xagent++;    /* determine new */
            break;                      /* coordinates */
        case 75:
            if (xagent>0) xagent--;
            break;
        case 72:
            if (yagent>0) yagent--;
            break;
        case 80:
            if (yagent<15) yagent++;
            break;
        case 27:
            stop=1;
            break;
        default:
            break;
      }
       intelthief();
       if ((xthief==xagent) && (ythief==yagent)) stop=1;
      }
     outp(baseport+1,0x1c);
     outp(baseport,0);
     setvect(8,oldtim);
     clrscr();
     _setcursortype(_NORMALCURSOR);
     textmode(C80);
     printf("\n    Gotcha !! \n\n");

     initcms();
     settimer(100,newtim);
     while (!kbhit())          /* an effect afterward */
     {
```

```
        for (i=255;i>0;i--)
        playnote(0,100,i,5,2,0,0,50);
        for (i=0;i<255;i++)
        playnote(0,100,i,5,2,0,0,50);
    }
    getch();
    resettimer();
    resetcms();

}
```

CHAPTER

NINE

Programming the Digital Sound Processor

- How samples are structured

- Recording and playing back samples

- The CT-VOICE driver functions

- The CT-TIMER, an alternative CT-VOICE driver

- Creating sound and sound effects, including echoes, and fade-ins and fade-outs

Chapter 2 explained the Sound Blaster's Digital Sound Processor (DSP) and how it records sound, plays back sound, and stores sound in memory. This chapter goes into more detail. It explains how samples are structured and how to program the DSP.

NOTE   Review "The Digital Sound Processor for Handling Digital Sound" in Chapter 3 if you are not familiar with what a sample and what a sampling rate are.

How Samples Are Structured

A sample consists of several bytes. The bytes in an 8-bit sample range from 0 to 255:

- 128 represents absolute silence.
- 0 and 255 represent the maximum values for, respectively, the negative and positive voltage that is sent to the speaker.

For stereo samples, the data for the left and the right channel are given alternately. Under this scheme, the data at the even addresses are destined for the left channel and the data at the odd addresses for the right channel.

The Sound Blaster lets you compress the data in a sample in order to preserve memory. For example, data consisting of 8-bit samples can be converted to 4-, 2.6-, or 2-bit samples. (To get a 2.6-bit sample, two values are converted into three bits and one value into two bits.) By converting data this way you can reduce the size of data in a sample by two, three, or four times. During the reproduction, the Sound Blaster card converts the data back to 8-bit samples.

Compressing sample data, while it saves memory, also reduces the quality of the sample. Consider what will be lost in sample data before you compress it. Some types of data are better candidates for compression than others. Voices, for example, do not require high-quality samples to be understood. The programs VEDIT and VOXKIT can convert 8-bit samples to 4-, 2.6-, or 2-bit samples.

Recording and Playing Back Samples

There are two ways to record and play back samples, directly and by using the DMA:

- Using the DMA (the direct memory access channel) takes very little processor time. By using the DMA, you'll make sure your other programs function at full speed.

- Recording and playing back samples directly gives you the opportunity to perform all kinds of editing, such as using echoes and filters and changing the pitch and the volume. Nevertheless, the direct method takes considerably more processor time. Other programs will function a lot more slowly when you use the direct method.

To play through the DMA, you use the CT-VOICE.DRV driver provided with the Sound Blaster. This driver, which is found in the VOXKIT directory or in the DRV directory, lets you record and play back samples in VOC format. Before we describe this driver, let's look at the VOC format. This format's version number is 1.10. It is used with both the Sound Blaster and the Sound Blaster Pro.

How the VOC Format Handles Samples

A VOC file consists of a header and a data block. The data block comprises the actual VOC format.

The Header

The header contains general information. This information is not used by the CT-VOICE driver. The header has to be skipped when you only want to use the data. The header has the following structure:

Byte	Setting
00H–13H	The file type description. These 19 bytes contain the following text: Creative Voice File, followed by the EOF byte 1AH.

Byte	Setting
14H–15H	The start of the file data block. This word (= 2 bytes) is defined because, in future versions, the size of the header might change. Usually these bytes contain the value 001AH.
16H–17H	The file version. The first byte contains the value after the point; the second byte contains the value in front of the point. For version 1.10 the first byte has the value 0AH (=10) and the second byte has the value 1.
18H–19H	The identification code. With this code you can verify whether the file is a real VOC file. The value is the complement of the file version in 16H and 17H, to which 1234H is added. For example, in version 1.10 the complement of 010AH is the value FEF5H (010AH XOR FFFFH); FEF5H + 1234H = 1129H.

The Data Block

The data block consists of one or more subblocks. Each subblock can contain a sample or other information. This way, you can store several samples made with different sampling rates in one file.

All subblocks consist of a small header and the correct data. The header contains information about the block type, the length of the block, and any additional information. The first four bytes are the same for every block:

- The first byte defines the block type.
- The next three bytes indicate the block length (the size of the data after these four bytes).

You don't have to know anything about the block type to be able to skip a block.

After the first four bytes, several different block types are possible. They are explained below.

Block Type 0, End of Data Block

Type 0 is the only block type without data indicating its length.

This block marks the end of the subblocks. If the CT-VOICE driver comes across this block, it stops processing other subblocks.

TIP

Check whether this block type is located at the end of the part to be played. If it is not, add this block type because otherwise the CT-VOICE driver will interpret the next byte after the last block as a block type. This can result in unpredictable and not necessarily happy situations, from noise and crackling sounds to a program or computer hang-up. If this block is not present at the end of a data block, the driver will read the next byte in memory as a block type.

Block Type 1, New Sample Data

With this block, a new sample can be played. In addition to the sample data, this block also contains information about the speed and the used compression (or packing) method.

Fields Block length includes the SR and PACK fields, and thus is equal to the size of the DATA + 2. *SR* stands for sampling rate. The value is determined with the following formula:

$$SR = 256 - 1,000,000 \text{ / sampling rate}$$

For a sampling rate of 10,000 Hz, SR contains the value 156, because $1,000,000 \div 10,000 = 100$, and $256 - 100 = 156$.

The maximum sampling rate is 23,000 Hz for the Sound Blaster and 44,100 Hz for the Sound Blaster Pro.

PACK contains the packing method. The following values are possible:

0:	8 bits normal, unpacked samples
1:	4 bits packed

| 2: | 2.6 bits packed |
| 2: | 2 bits packed |

DATA contains the sample data. The size of the data is equal to the block length minus 2.

Block Type 2, Sample Data

If you want to play several samples at the same rate and with the same packing method, you can use this block type. The sample data for this block are played with the settings of the last sample data block (see the description of block type 1). This way, you only have to change the sampling rate for one block, and that block will affect all others.

Fields   Block length is now equal to the size of the data. DATA contains the sample data.

Block Type 3, Silence

This block allows you to silence the Sound Blaster for a certain period of time. It inserts a silence of a certain duration. By replacing all pauses in the sample data with this silence block, the data occupy less memory. The VEDIT program offers the opportunity to do this.

Fields   The block length has the value 3.

PERIOD contains a 16-bit value. This value, increased by 1, indicates the duration of the silence in the number of units of the sampling rate.

SR is the sampling rate (see the description of block type 1 for an explanation of the sampling rate).

Following is an example of a calculation. Suppose the sampling rate is 4000 Hz and a value is processed 4000 times a second. If the period has the value 8000, this represents a silence of exactly two seconds (8000/4000). In other words, a value is supposedly processed 8000 times. The value of PERIOD, however, is 8000 − 1, or 7,999. So the higher the sampling rate, the more exact the duration, but the smaller the maximum duration.

Block Type 4, Marker

With this block you can give the status word a new value (see the next section). This way you can let your program wait until a particular sample is played. You only have to check the status word.

Fields   Block length contains the value 2.

MARKER contains a value between 1 and 65534 (FFFEH). The values 0 and 65535 are assigned to the CT-VOICE driver itself and may not be used.

Block Type 5, ASCII Text

With this block you can add a comment to a VOC block. The text terminates with a zero byte.

Fields   Block length contains the length of the text including the zero.

TEXT contains the text, as in this example: Drum.,0.

Block Type 6, Start of a Repetition

Block type 6 indicates the start of a repetition. The CT-VOICE driver will repeat all blocks between this block and the block type "end of repetition" an indicated number of times.

Fields   Block length contains the value 2.

COUNTER indicates the number of repetitions. The following blocks will be repeated COUNTER + 1 times. If COUNTER has the value 65535 (FFFFH), the blocks are repeated infinitely. The next section describes a function that ends such a repetition.

Block Type 7, End of Repetition

Block type 7 specifies the end of the repeated blocks. All subblocks between this block and the previous block type are repeated the number of times indicated at the previous block type. Refer to block type 6 for a further explanation.

Fields   Block length has the value 0.

WARNING	Nested repetitive blocks are not supported and are not allowed.

Block Type 8, Additional Information

Block Type 8 is only supported by the new CT-VOICE driver that is provided with the Sound Blaster Pro. When this block is processed, the next new sample block (type 1) uses the settings in this block instead of its own settings. This works only once. If necessary, you have to add this subblock for every new sample block. This block allows you to pass on additional information concerning the Sound Blaster Pro's extended DSP.

Fields   Block length has the value 4. SR again contains the sampling rate; this time it is a 16-bit value that is more exact. The value of SR is determined by the following formula:

SR = 65,536 − 256,000,000 / sampling rate

The maximum sampling rate is still 44,100 Hz. If a stereo sound sample is involved, the sampling rate has to be doubled. If this is the case, the formula is:

SR = 65,536 − 256,000,000 / (sampling rate ∗ 2)

As an example, a mono sample with a sampling rate of 20,000 Hz results in SR = 52,736 (65,536 − 256,000,000 / 20,000). A stereo sample with a sampling rate of 20,000 Hz results in SR = 59,136 (65,536 − 256,000,000 / 40,000). PACK contains the compression method mentioned at block type 1. Usually PACK has the value 0. MODE indicates whether the sample has to be played mono or stereo. The first happens when the byte has the value 0, the latter when the byte has the value 1. When the sample is played stereo, PACK must have the value 0.

The CT-VOICE Driver

The CT-VOICE driver contains functions for initializing the Sound Blaster card and for recording and playing back samples in the VOC format. In order to do its job, the CT-VOICE.DRV first has to be loaded at offset 0 in a segment. Next, the driver is called by a FAR call to the offset 0 in this segment. All registers used are stored by the driver itself, so they do not change. Listings 9.2 and 9.4 (found after the function descriptions) contain interfaces for Pascal and C. Listings 9.1 and 9.3 contain a short Assembly program that is used by Pascal and C.

The Sound Blaster Pro comes with a more sophisticated CT-VOICE driver that includes fourteen additional functions to support all possibilities of the Sound Blaster Pro. The standard CT-VOICE described here is Version 2.10. However, the extended CT-VOICE is fully compatible with the standard CT-VOICE driver and can also be used in combination with the standard Sound Blaster.

This section discusses the functions. First the call specifications for, respectively, Pascal, C, and Assembly are listed. Some functions, however, are only listed in Assembly because they are applied differently in Pascal and C. When variables in Pascal and C are used as input and output, the names of these variables in the Assembly part are assigned to a register. This makes it easier to explain the functions of the different registers. Nevertheless, the registers have to be loaded with a normal 16-bit value. When a result is returned in Assembly, it is placed in the variable SBIOResult. The type of this variable is word or unsigned int.

NOTE   The driver has to be called first with function 3 (initialization) before higher functions can be used. The functions 0 to 2 and 10 (of the extended version), however, can be used.

Function 0, Get Version Number

```
Function CTVersion: Word
int CTVersion()
```

Input:	BX	= 0
Output:	AH	= number in front of the point
	AL	= number after the point

Function 0 returns the version of the driver. With this function a program can test if it supports this version.

Function 1, Set I/O Port

```
Procedure UsePort(Port: Word)
void UsePort(int Port)
```

Input:	BX	= 1
	AX	= port
Output:	None	

Function 1 sets the I/O port for the Sound Blaster. The possible choices are 210H, 220H, 230H, 240H, 250H, or 260H. Pro users have to consider the fact that it only supports ports 220H and 240H. Function 1 has to be called before the card is initialized with function 3. The factory default value is 220H.

Function 2, Set IRQ Number

```
Procedure UseIRQ(IRQ: Word)
void UseIRQ(int IRQ)
```

Input:	BX	= 2
	AR	= IRQ
Output:	None	

Function 2 sets the correct IRQ interrupt. This interrupt is called after the end of a DMA transfer. Possible choices are 2, 3, 5, or 7. For the Sound Blaster Pro, the choices are 2, 5, 7, or 10. Just like function 1, function 2 has to be called before the initialization.

NOTE   See Chapter 1 for information about the various IRQ interrupts.

Function 3, Initialize Driver

```
Procedure InitializeDriver
int InitializeDriver()
```

Input:	BX	= 3
Output:	AX	= result

Function 3 has to be called to initialize the driver and the DSP. Only functions 0, 1, 2, and 10 can be called before this function to change the default settings. Other functions cannot be used before this function is called successfully. Function 3 returns a code indicating whether this is the case. The possible values are:

Value	Meaning
0	Everything works properly and the driver is ready for use.
1	The card is not a Sound Blaster (Pro) card or not a known card.
2	I/O read and write failure (wrong port).
3	DMA interrupt fails (IRQ number or DMA channel is set incorrectly).

The variable SBIOResult contains (just like for the other functions) the return code in Pascal or C.

Function 4, Turn On or Off the Connection to the Speaker

```
Procedure Speaker(W: word)
void Speaker(int W)
```

Input:	BX	= 4
	AX	= W
Output:	None	

The following applies to the value W:

- equal to 0, don't pass the signal on to the speaker.
- unequal to 0, pass the signal on to the speaker.

The initialization function 3 turns on this connection.

TIP

The programmer has to turn off this connection if the program returns to DOS or if a sample is recorded. The sound that is recorded can be heard through the speaker and disturbs the recording. This doesn't apply to the Sound Blaster Pro, because sampling has been improved for this card.

Function 5, Set Status Word Offset

Input:	BX	= 5
	ES:DI	= segment:word offset
Output:	None	

The status word indicates whether the driver is busy playing or recording a sample. If it is, the status word has the value 65535 (=FFFFH) or the value indicated by a marker block (see the previous section). As soon as this process is terminated, the status word reassumes the rest value 0.

Function 5 is only relevant for the Assembly programmer; in Pascal and C the variable StatusWord is defined. The type of this variable is word or unsigned int.

Function 6, Start Playing a VOC Block

```
Procedure PlayBlock(Start: VocTp)
void PlayBlock(VocTp Start)
```

Input:	BX	= 6
	ES:DI	= start of VOC sub-blocks
Output:	None	

Function 6 will play back a block satisfying the VOC format (see the previous section) with the use of the DMA. This hardly takes any processor time and allows other programs to continue normally. The status word will contain 65535 or FFFFH until this value is changed by a marker block or when the end of the blocks is reached (block type 0). This results in the value 0. For Pascal and C, a record or a structure VocTp, respectively, is defined containing additional information.

It is not possible to play back another sample block at the same time. To do this you first have to stop the output with function 8. By using the status word and a marker block, you determine which sample is played back and whether the reproduction has ended. With this information the right action can be executed.

Function 7, Record a Sample

```
Procedure RecordSample(Length: LongInt; Rate: Word; Var V: VocTp)
void RecordSample(long Length, unsigned Rate, VocTp &V)
```

Input:	BX	= 7
	AX	= Rate
	DX:CX	= Length
	ES:DI	= Start
Output:	None	

You use function 7 to record sound. The sample begins at the address Start and has a size of Length bytes and a rate of Rate Hz. The value of Rate lies between 4000 and 12,000 Hz for the standard Sound Blaster and between 4000 and 44,100 Hz for the Sound Blaster Pro. If you record a stereo sample, however, the sampling rate has to lie between 4000 and 22,050 Hz; nevertheless, the actual value for Rate is twice the sampling rate (for example, at a sampling rate of 13,000 Hz the value of Rate is 26,000 and *not* 13,000). The driver itself converts the Rate to an 8-bit value.

During the recording, the status word has the value 65535; next it reassumes the value 0. The recording can be interrupted with function 8.

NOTE Refer to function 16 for recording stereo samples.

The sample has a calculated header that meets the VOC format. For a stereo sample, the additional information block (type 8) is put in front of this header. The Length is the total length of the block. The actual length of the recorded sound is 8 or 16 bytes smaller.

Function 8, Stop Recording or Playing a Sample Block

```
Procedure StopVProcess
void StopVProcess()
```

Input:	BX	= 8
Output:	None	

With this function the recording or playing is stopped. The status word again has the value 0. When recording, the created VOC header is brought up to date with the correct data.

Function 9, Terminate Driver

```
Procedure DriverOff
void DriverOff()
```

Input:	BX	= 9
Output:	None	

When the driver is busy playing or recording, this process is stopped and the connection to the speakers is turned off. Function 9 always has to be called before quitting the program and returning to DOS.

Function 10, Pause Playing

```
Procedure Pause
void Pause()
```

Input:	BX	= 10
Output:	AX	= 0, playing is paused
		= 1, no sample is being played

The driver pauses the reproduction of a sample. If this is impossible, the value 1 is returned. For Pascal and C the result once again is placed in the variable SBIO-Result. Use function 11 to continue playing.

Function 11, Continue Playing

```
Procedure ContinuePlaying
void ContinuePlaying()
```

Input:	BX	= 11
Output:	AX	= 0, playing continues
		= 1, playing wasn't paused

The driver continues playing back a sample block. If the driver wasn't paused, the function returns the value 1; otherwise it returns the value 0.

Function 12, Stop a Repetition and Continue after the Repetition

```
Procedure StopRepetition(I: Word)
void StopRepetition(int I)
```

Input:	BX	= 11
	AX	= I
Output:	AX	= 0, everything went well
		= 1, no sample was being played

Function 12 relates to the VOC format that enables you to repeat one or more samples several times (infinitely if you want to). After a repetition, the function jumps to the next subblock, which allows you to repeat a particular part of the sample as long as the same action takes place (as, for instance, footsteps, a helicopter, a car, etc.). As soon as you want a change you can jump to the next data block. The variable I determines the method: if it has the value 0, the blocks are repeated for the last time; if the variable has the value 1, repeating is stopped immediately and the subblock directly after the end of the repetition is processed.

Function 13, Set User Routine

```
Procedure UserRoutine(P: ^Procedure)
Procedure NoUserRoutine
void UserRoutine(void *P ())
void NoUserRoutine()
```

Input:	BX	= 13
	DX:AX	= user routine offset
Output:	None	

With function 13 the programmer can call his or her own routine at the beginning of each subblock in a data block. However, things work differently for the Assembly programmer than they do for the Pascal and C programmer.

For the Assembly Programmer... For the Assembly programmer, the user routine has to satisfy three conditions:

- Since a FAR CALL is involved, the routine has to terminate with a RETF.
- Except for the carry flag, all used registers have to be saved.
- If the next subblock has to be skipped, the carry flag has to be set (=1). To process the next block, the carry flag has to be reset (=0).

At every call, ES:BX points at the data block to be processed. The byte at ES:BX indicates the block type.

It goes without saying that the carry flag always has to be deleted at an end block. Otherwise this block is skipped (although the block has no length) and the next bytes are considered a new subblock.

To switch off the user routine, AX and DX must have the value 0.

For Pascal and C Programmers... For Pascal and C programmers, a number of variables have been defined:

```
Var
  BlockStart  :  Pointer;
  BlockLength :  LongInt;
  BlockType   :  Byte;
  Continue    :  Boolean;

void          *BlockStart;
long          BlockLength;
unsigned char BlockType;
char          Continue;
```

When this procedure is called, these variables contain the right values for the upcoming block. The variable Continue allows you to indicate whether the next block must (True, 1) or must not (False, 0) be played. The remaining variables can be changed to one's heart's desire—they don't affect the progress of the procedure.

It goes without saying that after an end block the routine always has to process the next block first. Otherwise the next bytes will be considered as a sample block.

To turn off the user routine, call NoUserRoutine.

NOTE   Functions 14 through 27 are only supported by the new CT-VOICE driver for the Sound Blaster Pro.

Function 14, Start Playing a VOC Block Stored in an Extended Memory Block

```
Procedure PlayEMBBlock(Handle: Word; Start: LongInt)
void PlayEMBBlock(unsigned Handle, long Start)
```

Input:	BX	= 14
	DX	= Handle
	DI:SI	= start in extended memory
Output:	AX	= 0, everything went well
		= 1, an error has occurred

Function 14 plays a number of subblocks that are located in an *extended memory block* (EMB). You have to install the HI-MEM.SYS driver yourself and use this driver to allocate an EMB and load it with the correct VOC data. The variable Handle is the handle that belongs to the allocated block.

You can now play large VOC blocks without having them occupy a part of the memory used by DOS. Of course, this only works if your computer has real extended memory. The function doesn't work with simulated EMBs (that are, for example, on the hard disk) because the reproduction takes place through the DMA.

Function 15, Record a Sample Using an EMB

```
Function RecordEMBSample(Handle, SR: Word; Start: LongInt):
                        Boolean;
int RecordEMBSample(unsigned Handle, unsigned SR, long Start);
```

Input:	BX	= 15
	AX	= SR, sampling rate
	DX	= Handle
	DI:SI	= start in extended memory
Output:	AX	= 0, everything went well
		= 1, an error has occurred

Function 15 records a sample in EMB. The Handle variable indicates the correct EMB. The size of the EMB is also the size of the sample to record. The same rules apply to this function as to the normal recording function 7.

Function 16, Set Recording Mode

```
Procedure StereoRecording(V: Word)
void StereoRecording(int V)
```

Input:	BX	= 16
	AX	= V
Output:	AX	= old value

With Function 16, you determine whether the next recording has to be a mono or a stereo sample. If V contains the value 0, a mono sample is recorded and no additional information block is created. If V has the value 0, a stereo sample is recorded and an additional information block for the new sample block is created.

Function 17, Determine Input

```
Procedure Input(V: Word)
void Input(int V)
```

Input:	BX	= 17
	AX	= V
Output:	AX	= old setting

The value V determines the input choice for recording a sample. The possible values are 0, 1, and 3 for the mic, line, or CD input respectively. If a sample is recorded with the functions 7 or 15, the selected entry is used as input. It is not possible to record more than one input at a time, though several inputs can be transmitted and heard through the output.

You can, however, connect the output to the mic input or the line input. By doing so you can record, for example, the CD and the line input in one sample.

Function 18, Set Recording Filter

```
Procedure RecordingFilter(V: Word)
void RecordingFilter(int V)
```

Input:	BX	= 18
	AX	= V
Output:	AX	= old value

If V contains the value 0, a low pass filter is used. If the value of V is 1, a high pass filter is used.

Function 19, Set DMA Channel

```
Procedure UseChannel(C:Word)
void UseChannel(int C)
```

Input:	BX	= 19
	AX	= C
Output:	AX	= 0, everything went all right
		= FFFFH, no correct value

The variable C contains the selection for the DMA channel that is set on the Sound Blaster Pro for the DSP. Possible values for C are 0, 1, and 3. Just like the functions 1 and 2, this function has to be called before the driver is initialized with function 3.

Function 20, Determine Type of Sound Blaster Card

```
Var CardType: Word
int CardType
```

Input:	BX	= 20
Output:	AX	= 1, standard Sound Blaster
		= 2, Sound Blaster Pro
		= 3, Sound Blaster 2.0

Function 20 returns information about the type of card in the computer.

NOTE Functions 21 through 25 all refer to the mixer chip. The settings are written to the mixer chip and stored in internal variables by the CT-VOICE driver. Chapter 11 discusses the functioning of this chip in detail.

Function 21, Set Volume

```
Procedure Volume(S,C,V: Word)
void Volume(int S, int C, int V)
```

Input:	BX	= 20
	AX	= S
	CX	= V
	DX	= C
Output:	AX	<> FFFFH, AX contains the old value
		= FFFFH, an error has occurred

With function 21, you can change the volume of one of the parts of the mixer chip. The variable S determines which part is involved. The possible choices for S are:

Value	Meaning
0	The volume of the output signal
1	The volume of the VOICE part
2	The volume of the MICrophone input
3	The volume of the CD-ROM
4	The volume of the stereo LINE input

As described earlier, the choices 0, 1, 3, and 4 are stereo. With the value of C you can determine whether the left or the right channel has to be changed. If C has the value 1, only the volume of the left channel is modified. To modify the volume of the right channel, C must have the value 2. However, this doesn't apply to the CD-ROM option.

You set both volumes through the left channel; in that case C must always have the value 1.

The variable C doesn't affect the volume setting of the MIC, because this channel is a mono channel that must have the value 1. The maximum value of volume V is 15 for the options 0, 1, 3, and 4, and 7 for option 2. If the value of V is larger than this value, the driver sets it at the maximum value. The returned value is the old value of the volume. If the volume is set for both channels, the returned value is the old value of the volume of the right channel.

Function 22, Set Filters

```
Procedure Filter(S,V: Word)
void Filter(int S, int V)
```

Input:	BX	= 22
	AX	= S
	CX	= V
Output:	AX	= (see previous function)

The variable S determines which filter is turned on or off. If S has the value 0, the output filter is edited; if S has the value 1, the input filter is edited.

If the variable V has the value 0, the selected filter is turned on. If V has the value 1, the filter is turned off.

The returned value is the old setting of the filter.

Function 23, Reset Mixer Chip

```
Procedure ResetMixer
void ResetMixer()
```

Input:	BX	= 23
Output:	None	

Function 23 sets all volume and filter settings to their default values. All previous settings are lost. Chapter 11 lists and explains these default values. Function 23 is only supported by the old version 1.21 of the extended driver.

Function 24, Determine All Volume Settings

```
Procedure ReadAllVolumes
void ReadAllVolumes()
```

Input:	BX	= 24
Output:	None	

When the mixer chip is programmed directly (a subject treated in Chapter 11), Function 24 brings the CT-VOICE up to date. All settings of the mixer chip are read and placed in the internal variables of the driver. The old volume settings are over-written. Next, the internal variables again are equal to the current settings on the mixer chip.

Function 25, Ask Volume Setting

```
Function ReturnVolume(S,C: Word): Word
int ReturnVolume(int S, int C)
```

Input:	BX	= 25
	AX	= S
	DX	= C

Input:	BX	= 25
Output:	AX	= ask value
		= FFFFH, an error has occurred

In function 25, the variables S and C have the same function as they do in function 21. The variable S selects the part of the chip and the variable C determines the channel of the volume value. C may not contain the value 0. The returned value originates from the internal variables used by the CT-VOICE driver. This value is not necessarily the current setting on the mixer chip. This setting can be reprogrammed by another program. If you're not sure about this, we advise using function 24.

Function 26, Determine Sampling Rates

```
Procedure AskRate(Var Max, Min: Word; M, R: Word)
int AskRate(int *Max, int *Min, int M, int R)
```

Input:	BX	= 26
	AX	= R
	DX	= M
Output:	AX	= minimum sampling rate (Min)
	DX	= maximum sampling rate (Max)

With function 26, you can return the minimum and maximum sampling rate of a particular mode. The variable R indicates whether recording (0) or playing (1) is concerned. If the sound card is a Sound Blaster Pro, the variable M indicates whether the sampling rate applies to mono (value 0) or stereo. For other sound cards, M always must have the value 0. This function is not supported by Version 1.21 of the extended CT-VOICE driver and has been replaced by function 27.

Function 27, Ask Filter Setting

```
Function ReturnFilter(S: Word): Word
int ReturnFilter(int S)
```

Input:	BX	= 27
	AX	= S
Output:	AX	= old setting (0 or 1)
		= FFFFH, an error has occurred

With function 27, the possibilities for the variable S are the same as in function 22. As to the way it works, this function is the same as the previous function, except that this time the filter setting is returned. The returned value comes from memory and doesn't necessarily have to be the same as the current setting on the mixer chip.

Listings for the Pascal and C Interfaces

Following are the listings for the Pascal and C interfaces, using a few machine code routines. Here are the listings with the numbers and titles:

Listing	Title
9.1	Assembly Interface for Turbo Pascal
9.2	Pascal Unit Supporting the CT-VOICE/CT-TIMER Driver
9.3	Assembly Interface for Turbo C
9.4	Header for the Interface of CT-INTER.OBJ with CTVOICE.C
9.5	Header of the C Library Supporting the CT-VOICE/CT-TIMER Driver
9.6	C Library Supporting the CT-VOICE/CT-TIMER Driver

Listing 9.1: Assembly Interface for Turbo Pascal

```
        .MODEL TPASCAL
        .CODE

; File name = CT-INTER.ASM
; Assembler file taking care of the interface
; between the CTVOICE driver and Turbo Pascal.
;
; Run TASM CTINTER to create CTINTER.OBJ.
```

```
; This object file is used in CTVOICE.PAS.
;
; Defined procedures
;   Procedure CallCTVoice(Var R : Registers);
;   Procedure CTVoiceAddress(P : Pointer);
;   Procedure Variables(StPt, BsPt, BlPt, BtPt,
;                       CoPt : Pointer);
;   Procedure UserRoutine(P : Pointer);
;     P points at an interrupt routine in Pascal.

PUBLIC CTVoiceAddress, CallCTVoice
PUBLIC Variables, UserRoutine

; Define a structure for the type of Registers
; that can serve for the offset calculation.

Registers STRUC
rAX     dw 0
rBX     dw 0
rCX     dw 0
rDX     dw 0
rBP     dw 0
rSI     dw 0
rDI     dw 0
rDS     dw 0
rES     dw 0
rFlags  dw 0
ENDS
; Define a frequently used routine :
; copying a DWORD

@CopyDword MACRO Dest,Source
        mov ax,WORD PTR Source+0
        mov WORD PTR Dest+0,ax
        mov ax,WORD PTR Source+2
        mov WORD PTR Dest+2,ax
ENDM


; The global variables

CTVoicePt       DD 0            ; CT-VOICE address
UserRoutAddress DD ?            ; user routine
BlockStart      DD ?            ; Pointer address
BlockLength     DD ?            ; LongInt address
```

```
BlockType       DD ?              ; Byte address
Continue        DD ?              ; Boolean address

; Procedure CTVoiceAddress(P : Pointer);
; Set the start address of the CT-VOICE driver.

CTVoiceAddress PROC FAR P:DWORD
        @CopyDword cs:CTVoicePt,P
        ret
ENDP


; Procedure CallCTVoice(Var R : Registers);
; Calls the CTVOICE driver.

CallCTVoice PROC FAR R : DWORD;
        push ds                   ; has to be saved
        lds si,[R]                ; DS:SI points at R
        mov ax,[si+rSI]           ; save used SI
        push ax
        mov ax,[si+rAX]           ; set all registers
        mov bx,[si+rBX]
        mov cx,[si+rCX]
        mov dx,[si+rDX]
        mov di,[si+rDI]
        mov es,[si+rES]
        mov ds,[si+rDS]
        pop si                    ; set SI
        call [DWORD PTR cs:CtVoicePt]
        push ds                   ; save DS
        push si                   ; save SI
        lds si,[R]                ; DS:SI points at R
        mov [si+rAX],ax           ; save all regs.
        mov [si+rBX],bx
        mov [si+rCX],cx
        mov [si+rDX],dx
        mov [si+rDI],di
        mov [si+rES],es
        pop ax                    ; AX=SI after call
        mov [si+rSI],ax
        pop ax                    ; AX=DS after call
        mov [si+rDS],ax
        pop ds                    ; restore used DS
        ret
ENDP
```

```
; Procedure Variables(StPt, BsPt, BlPt, BtPt,
;                      CoPt : Pointer);
; Set pointers to StatusWord, BlockStart,
; BlockLength, BlockType & Continue.

Variables PROC FAR
Stp:DWORD,Bsp:DWORD,BlP:DWORD,BtP:DWORD,CoP:DWORD
        @CopyDword cs:BlockStart,BsP
        @CopyDword cs:BlockLength,BlP
        @CopyDword cs:BlockType,BtP
        @CopyDword cs:Continue,CoP
        mov bx,5                  ; set pointer to
        les di,StP                ; Status Word
        call [DWORD PTR cs:CTVoicePt]
        ret
ENDP


; Procedure UserRoutine(P : Pointer);
; Set user interrupt.

UserRoutine PROC FAR P : DWORD
        mov ax,[WORD PTR P+0]
        mov [WORD PTR cs:UserRoutAddress+0],ax
        mov dx,[WORD PTR P+2]
        mov [WORD PTR cs:UserRoutAddress+2],dx
        or ax,dx                  ; P=0:0 ?
        jnz NewUserRoutine
        mov bx,13                 ; yes, turn off routine
        call [DWORD PTR cs:CTVoicePt]
        ret
NewUserRoutine:
        mov ax,offset UserInterFace
        mov dx,cs
        mov bx,13                 ; set interface
        call [DWORD PTR cs:CTVoicePt]
        ret
ENDP


; This routine takes care of the interface for the
; interrupt routine in Pascal. The routine
; sets the required variables and calls the Pascal
; routine. After the call, it checks whether
; the next block has to be played.
```

```
UserInterFace PROC FAR
        push ax                      ; save used
        push si                      ; registers
        push ds
        lds si,[cs:BlockStart]       ; set BlockStart
        mov [si],bx                  ; starting from
        mov [si+2],es                ; block to be played
        lds si,[cs:BlockLength]      ; set BlockLength
        mov ax,[es:bx+1]             ; with a 24-bit
        mov [si],ax                  ; length
        mov ax,[es:bx+3]
        xor ah,ah                    ; delete 25..32 bits
        mov [si+2],ax
        lds si,[cs:BlockType]        ; set BlockType
        mov al,[es:bx]
        mov [si],al
        lds si,[cs:Continue]         ; set boolean
        mov byte ptr [si],1          ; at default True
        pushf                        ; simulate Int
        call [DWORD PTR cs:UserRoutAddress]
        cmp byte ptr [si],0          ; Continue = False ?
        jne ClearCarryFlag           ; no, process block
        cmp byte ptr [es:bx],0       ; last block ?
        je ClearCarryFlag            ; yes, process this block
        pop ds                       ; restore used
        pop si                       ; registers
        pop ax
        stc                          ; don't process block
        retf                         ; return to CT-VOICE
ClearCarryFlag:
        pop ds                       ; restore used
        pop si                       ; registers
        pop ax
        clc                          ; process block
        retf                         ; return to CT-VOICE
ENDP
        END                          ; end of assembler file
```

Listing 9.2: Pascal Unit Supporting the CT-VOICE/CT-TIMER Driver

NOTE Listing 9.2 uses standard memory allocation routines. In Pascal, only VOC files with a maximum size of 65520 bytes can be used, because GetMem cannot reserve a larger memory block.

```pascal
Unit CTVOICE;

{ Unit supporting the CT-VOICE driver.     }

Interface

Const
{ Errors occurring during the initialization }
  CallOk       = 0;
  CardError    = 1;
  IOPortError  = 2;
  DMAError     = 3;
{ For the speaker control }
  SpOn         = 1;
  SpOff        = 0;
{ Various block (Bl) types in the VOC format }
  EndBl        = 0;
  NwSampleBl   = 1;
  SampleBl     = 2;
  SilenceBl    = 3;
  MarkerBl     = 4;
  TextBl       = 5;
  RepeatBl     = 6;
  RepeatEndBl  = 7;
  ExtraInfoBl  = 8; { Only for the Pro }
{ Possible Sound Blaster cards }
  SoundBlaster = 0;
  SoundBlPro   = 1;
  SoundBl20    = 2;
{ The three parts that can serve as input }
  MIC          = 0;
  CD_ROM       = 1;
  Line         = 3;
{ Volume choices }
  MainVl       = 0;
```

```
  VoiceVl          = 1;
  MICVl            = 2;
  CD_ROMVl         = 3;
  LineVl           = 4;
  Both             = 0;
  Left             = 1;
  Right            = 2;
{ Filter settings }
  LowFilter        = 0;
  HighFilter       = 1;
  OutputFilter     = 0;
  InputFilter      = 1;
{ Record mode }
  Stereo           = 1;
  Mono             = 0;
{ Normal on and off }
  On               = 0;
  Off              = 1;


Type
{ Dummy array of almost 64K }
  IntArType = Array [0..$fff0] of Byte;
{ Record to keep info about VOC }
  VocTp      = Record
    Start  : Pointer;
    Length : LongInt;
    Block  : ^IntArType;
  End;
{ Procedure for the user routine }
  Proc   = Procedure;
  ProcTp = ^Proc;


Var
{ The status word indicates whether the CT-VOICE is busy }
  StatusWord   : Word;
{ Points at the beginning of the sub-block }
  BlockStart   : ^IntArType;
{ The length of the sub-block }
  BlockLength  : LongInt;
{ The block type of the sub-block }
  BlockType    : Byte;
{ Indicates whether the next block has to be played }
  Continue     : Boolean;
{ Type of card }
  CardType     : Byte;
```

```
{ Result of procedures }
  SBIOResult    : Word;

{** Disk I/O  **}
{ Load CT-VOICE driver }
Procedure LoadCTDriver(N : String);
{ Check whether a file meets the VOC format }
Function CheckVOCFile(N : String) : Boolean;
{ Load VOC file }
Procedure LoadVOCFile(N : String; Var V : VocTp);
{ Write VOC block }
Procedure SaveVOCFile(N : String; V : VocTp);
{ Remove the VOC block from memory }
Procedure DisposeVOC(Var V : VocTp);

{** Initialization **}
{ Determine version }
Function  CTVersion : Word;
{ Set base port }
Procedure UsePort(P : Word);
{ Set IRQ number }
Procedure UseIRQ(I : Word);
{ Set DMA channel (for the PRO !) }
Procedure UseChannel(D : Word);
{ Initialize driver }
Procedure InitializeDriver;

{** Utilities **}
{ Turn speaker on or off }
Procedure Speaker(W : Word);
{ Stop recording or playing }
Procedure StopVProcess;
{ Terminate the driver }
Procedure DriverOff;
{ Set user routine }
Procedure UserRoutine(P : ProcTp);
{ Ask for minimum and maximum sampling rate }
Procedure AskRate(Var Max, Min : Word; M, K : Word);

{** Mixer chip for de PRO **}
{ Set stereo or mono record mode }
Procedure RecordMode(B : Word);
{ Set input }
Procedure Input(S : Word);
{ Turn the recording filter on or off }
```

```
Procedure RecordingFilter(B : Word);
{ Set volume }
Procedure Volume(S,C,V : Word);
{ Turn input or output filter on or off}
Procedure Filter(S,V : Word);
{ Reset mixer chip }
Procedure ResetMixer;
{ Read all volume settings }
Procedure ReadAllVolumes;
{ Ask the various volume and filter settings }
Function ReturnVolume(S,V : Word) : Word;
Function ReturnFilter(S : Word) : Word;

{** Playing **}
{ Pause playing }
Procedure Pause;
{ Continue playing }
Procedure ContinuePlaying;
{ Stop repetition }
Procedure StopRepetition(I : Word);
{ Play a VOC block }
Procedure PlayBlock(V : VocTp);
{ Play a VOC block in an EMB (for PRO !) }
Procedure PlayEMBBlock(H : Word; S : LongInt);

{** Recording **}
{ Record a sample }
Procedure RecordSample(L : LongInt;SR : Word;
                       Var V : VocTp);
{ Record a sample in an EMB (for PRO !) }
Procedure RecordEMBSample(SR : Word; H : Word; S : LongInt);

{** VOC utilities **}
{ Set VOC Block at the first sub-block }
Procedure FirstSubBlock(Var V : VocTp);
{ Set VOC Block at the next sub-block }
Procedure NextSubBlock(Var V : VocTp);

{** Functions for de CT-TIMER.DRV **}
{ Set volume table }
Procedure VolumeTable(V : Pointer; S : Byte);
{ Set echo buffer }
Procedure EchoBuffer(E : Pointer; S : Word);
{ Execute a command string }
```

```
Procedure Command(S : String);
{ Ask current volume }
Function CVolume : Byte;

Implementation

Uses DOS;

Var
  CTAddress : Pointer;
  CTSize    : LongInt;
  R         : Registers;
{ Load and define machine code routines }
{$L CTINTERF.OBJ}
{$F+}
Procedure CTVoiceAddress(P : Pointer); External;
Procedure CallCTVoice(Var R : Registers); External;
Procedure Variables(StPt, BsPt, BlPt, BtPt,
                    CoPt : Pointer); External;
Procedure UserRoutine(P : ProcTp); External;
{$F-}


{** Disk I/O **}

Procedure LoadCTDriver(N : String);
Var
  F       : File;
  S       : String[8];
  Off, Sg : Word;

Begin
  if N='' then N:='CT-VOICE.DRV';   { check for name }
  Assign(F,N); Reset(F,1);
  Seek(F,2); BlockRead(F,S,9);      { read ID }
  Seek(F,0);
  S[0]:=#8;                         { set length }
  If S='CT-VOICE' then Begin
    CTSize:=FileSize(F);            { determine size }
    GetMem(CTAddress,CTSize+16);
    Off:=Ofs(CTAddress^);           { Make sure }
    Sg:=Seg(CTAddress^);            { the CT-VOICE }
    Sg:=Sg+Off shr 4;               { is loaded at an offset 0 }
    Off:=Off and 15;
    If Off <> 0 Then Begin          { offset = 0 ? }
      Inc(Sg);                      { next segment }
```

```
      Off:=0;                          { offset now is 0 }
    End;
    CTAddress:=Ptr(Sg,Off);
    BlockRead(F,CTAddress^,CTSize);
    Close(F);
    CTVoiceAddress(CTAddress);
    SBIOResult:=0;
  End
  Else Begin
    Close(F);                         { no driver }
    SBIOResult:=1;
  End
End;

Function CheckVOCFile(N : String) : Boolean;

Var
  F    : File;
  S    : String[19];
  T1,T2 : Word;
  R    : Boolean;
Begin
  R:=False;                           { set result }
  Assign(F,N); Reset(F,1);
  BlockRead(F,S,19);                  { read header ID }
  S[0]:=#18;
  If S='Creative Voice File' Then Begin
    Seek(F,$16);                      { point at version }
    BlockRead(F,T1,2);
    BlockRead(F,T2,2);
    T1:=(T1 XOR $FFFF) + $1234;       { check calcul. }
    R:=T1=T2;                         { equal ? }
  End;
  Close(F);
  CheckVOCFile:=R;                     { return result }
End;
Procedure LoadVOCFile(N : String; Var V : VocTp);
Var
  F        : File;
  T        : Word;
  SgH, OfH : Word;
  SgE, OfE : Word;
  HS       : LongInt;
```

```
Begin
  Assign(F,N); Reset(F,1);
  Seek(F,$14);                          { read header size }
  BlockRead(F,T,2);
  Seek(F,T);                            { skip it }
  V.Length:=FileSize(F)-T;
  GetMem(V.Start,V.Length);
  BlockRead(F,V.Start^,V.Length);
  Close(F);
  V.Block:=V.Start;
End;

Procedure SaveVOCFile(N : String; V : VocTp);
Var
  F   : File;
  S   : String;
  T   : Word;

Begin
  Assign(F,N); ReWrite(F,1);
  S:='Creative Voice File'+#$1A;   { ID Text }
  BlockWrite(F,S,20);
  T:=$001A; BlockWrite(F,T,2);     { header size }
  T:=$010A; BlockWrite(F,T,2);     { version 1.10 }
  T:=(T-$1234) XOR $FFFF;          { check }
  BlockWrite(F,T,2);
  BlockWrite(F,V.Start^,V.Length); { sample data }
  Close(F);
End;
Procedure DisposeVOC(Var V : VocTp);
Begin
  FreeMem(V.Start,V.Length);
  V.Start:=Nil;
  V.Length:=0;
  V.Block:=Nil;
End;


{** Initialization **}

{ The next procedures and functions take care of the }
{ interface between the CT-VOICE driver and Pascal. }
{ The functioning is quite logical and simple: }
{ no further comment is provided. }
```

```
Function CTVersion : Word;

Begin
  R.BX:=0;
  CallCTVoice(R);
  CTVersion:=R.AX
End;

Procedure UsePort(P : Word);
Begin
  R.BX:=1;
  R.AX:=P;
  CallCTVoice(R);
  SBIOResult:=R.AX;
End;

Procedure UseIRQ(I : Word);
Begin
  R.BX:=2;
  R.AX:=I;
  CallCTVoice(R);
  SBIOResult:=R.AX;
End;

Procedure UseChannel(D : Word);
Begin
  R.BX:=19;
  R.AX:=D;
  CallCTVoice(R);
  SBIOResult:=R.AX;
End;

Procedure InitializeDriver;
Begin
  R.BX:=3;
  CallCTVoice(R);
  If R.AX=0 Then
    Variables(@StatusWord,@BlockStart,@BlockLength,
              @BlockType,@Continue);
  SBIOResult:=R.AX;
End;
```

```
{** Utilities **}

Procedure Speaker(W : Word);
Begin
  R.BX:=4;
  R.AX:=W;
  CallCTVoice(R);
End;

Procedure StopVProcess;
Begin
  R.BX:=8;
  CallCTVoice(R);
End;

Procedure DriverOff;
Begin
  R.BX:=9;
  CallCTVoice(R);
End;

Procedure UserRoutine(P : ProcTp);
Begin
  If P=Nil Then
    UserRoutine(Ptr(0,0))
  Else
    UserRoutine(P);
End;

Procedure AskRate(Var Max, Min : Word; M, K : Word);
Begin
  R.BX:=26;
  R.AX:=K;
  R.DX:=M;
  CallCTVoice(R);
  Max:=R.DX;
  Min:=R.AX;
End;

{** Mixer chip **}

Procedure RecordMode(B : Word);
Begin
  R.AX:=B;
  R.BX:=16;
```

```
  CallCtVoice(R);
  SBIOResult:=R.AX;
End;

Procedure Input(S : Word);
Begin
  R.AX:=S;
  R.BX:=17;
  CallCtVoice(R);
  SBIOResult:=R.AX;
End;

Procedure RecordingFilter(B : Word);
Begin
  R.AX:=B;
  R.BX:=18;
  CallCtVoice(R);
  SBIOResult:=R.AX;
End;

Procedure Volume(S,C,V : Word);
Begin
  If C=Both Then Begin
    Volume(S,Left,V);
    C:=Right;
  End;
  R.AX:=S;
  R.BX:=21;
  R.CX:=V;
  R.DX:=C;
  CallCtVoice(R);
  SBIOResult:=R.AX;
End;

Procedure Filter(S,V : Word);
Begin
  R.AX:=S;
  R.BX:=22;
  R.CX:=V;
  CallCtVoice(R);
  SBIOResult:=R.AX;
End;
Procedure ResetMixer;
Begin
  R.BX:=23;
```

```
    CallCtVoice(R);
End;

Procedure ReadAllVolumes;
Begin
  R.BX:=24;
  CallCtVoice(R);
End;

Function ReturnVolume(S,V : Word) : Word;

Begin
  R.AX:=S;
  R.BX:=25;
  R.DX:=V;
  CallCtVoice(R);
  ReturnVolume:=R.AX;
End;

Function ReturnFilter(S : Word) : Word;

Begin
  If CTVersion=$20A Then
    R.BX:=27
  Else
    R.BX:=26;
  R.AX:=S;
  CallCtVoice(R);
  ReturnFilter:=R.AX;
End;

{** Playing **}

Procedure Pause;
Begin
  R.BX:=10;
  CallCTVoice(R);
  SBIOResult:=R.AX;
End;

Procedure ContinuePlaying;
Begin
  R.BX:=11;
  CallCTVoice(R);
```

```
    SBIOResult:=R.AX;
End;

Procedure StopRepetition(I : Word);
Begin
  R.BX:=12;
  R.AX:=I;
  CallCTVoice(R);
  SBIOResult:=R.AX;
End;

Procedure PlayBlock(V : VocTp);
Begin
  R.BX:=6;
  R.DI:=Ofs(V.Start^);
  R.ES:=Seg(V.Start^);
  CallCTVoice(R);
End;

Procedure PlayEMBBlock(H : Word; S : LongInt);
Begin
  R.BX:=14;
  R.DX:=H;
  R.DI:=S Shr 16;
  R.SI:=S And $FFFF;
  CallCTVoice(R);
  SBIOResult:=R.AX;
End;

{** Recording **}

Procedure RecordSample(L : LongInt; SR : Word;
                       Var V : VocTp);
Begin
  GetMem(V.Start,L);
  V.Length:=L;
  R.BX:=7;
  R.AX:=SR;
  R.DX:=L shr 16;
  R.CX:=L and 65535;
  R.ES:=Seg(V.Start^);
  R.DI:=Ofs(V.Start^);
  CallCTVoice(R);
End;
```

```
Procedure RecordEMBSample(SR : Word; H : Word; S : LongInt);
Begin
  R.AX:=SR;
  R.BX:=15;
  R.DX:=H;
  R.DI:=S Shr 16;
  R.SI:=S And $FFFF;
  CallCTVoice(R);
  SBIOResult:=R.AX;
End;

{** VOC utilities **}

Procedure FirstSubBlock(Var V : VocTp);
Begin
  V.Block:=V.Start;
End;

Procedure NextSubBlock(Var V : VocTp);
Var
  A : LongInt;

Begin
{ Calculate 24-bit address }
  A:=16*LongInt(Seg(V.Block^))+LongInt(Ofs(V.Block^));
{ Add the following : 4 + block length }
  A:=A+4+V.Block^[1]+256*V.Block^[2]+256*256*V.Block^[3];
{ Set V.Block }
  V.Block:=Ptr(A shr 4, A and 15);
End;

{** Functions for the CT-TIMER.DRV **}
Procedure VolumeTable(V : Pointer; S : Byte);
Begin
  R.BX:=128;
  R.AX:=0;
  R.CL:=S;
  R.DI:=Ofs(V^);
  R.ES:=Seg(V^);
  CallCtVoice(R);
End;
```

```
Procedure EchoBuffer(E : Pointer; S : Word);
Begin
  R.BX:=128;
  R.AX:=1;
  R.CX:=S;
  R.DI:=Ofs(E^);
  R.ES:=Seg(E^);
  CallCtVoice(R);
End;

Procedure Command(S : String);
Begin
  S:=S+#0;
  R.BX:=129;
  R.DI:=Ofs(S[1]);
  R.ES:=Seg(S[1]);
  CallCtVoice(R);
End;

Function CVolume : Byte;

Begin
  R.BX:=130;
  CallCtVoice(R);
  CVolume:=R.AL;
End;

End.
```

Listing 9.3: Assembly Interface for Turbo C

```
        .MODEL SMALL
        .CODE

; File : CT-INTER.ASM
; Assembler file taking care of the interface
; between the CT-VOICE driver and Turbo C.
;
; Run TASM /MX CT-INTER to create CTINTER.OBJ.
; Next, link CT-INTER.OBJ to the remaining files.
;
; Defined functions :
; - void CallCTVoice(struct REGPACK far *R);
; - void CTVoiceAddress(char far *A, unsigned G);
; - void Variables(void far *StPt, void far *BsPt,
```

```
;                      void far *BlPt, void far *BtPt,
;                      void far *CoPt)
; - void UserRoutine(void interrupt *P);
PUBLIC _CTVoiceAddress, _CallCTVoice
PUBLIC _Variables, _UserRoutine

; Define a structure for the type REGPACK
; that can serve for the offset calculation.
Registers STRUC
rAX     dw 0
rBX     dw 0
rCX     dw 0
rDX     dw 0
rBP     dw 0
rSI     dw 0
rDI     dw 0
rDS     dw 0
rES     dw 0
rFlags  dw 0
ENDS

; Define a frequently used routine :
; copying a DWORD

@CopyDword MACRO Dest,Source
        mov ax,WORD PTR Source+0
        mov WORD PTR Dest+0,ax
        mov ax,WORD PTR Source+2
        mov WORD PTR Dest+2,ax
ENDM

; The global variables

CTVoicePt       DD 0            ; CT-VOICE address
UserRoutAddress DD 0            ; user routine
BlockStart      DD 0            ; Pointer address
BlockLength     DD 0            ; LongInt address
BlockType       DD 0            ; Byte address
Continue        DD 0            ; Boolean address

; void CTVoiceAddress(char far *A, unsigned P)
; Set the start address of the CT-VOICE driver.

_CTVoiceAddress PROC FAR
        ARG A:DWORD,G:WORD
```

```
        push bp
        mov bp,sp
        push ds
        lds si,[A]              ; DS:SI points
        mov dx,ds               ; at CT-VOICE
        mov ax,si               ; DX:AX=DS:SI
        add ax,15               ; minimize and
        shr ax,1                ; round up
        shr ax,1
        shr ax,1
        shr ax,1
        add dx,ax
        mov es,dx               ; ES:0 starts CT-VOICE
        mov cx,[G]              ; CX=driver size
        mov di,cx               ; start at the end
        add si,cx               ; of the driver
        inc cx                  ; one byte more
        std
        rep movsb               ; copy driver data
        cld
        mov [WORD PTR CTVoicePt+0],0
        mov [WORD PTR CTVoicePt+2],es
        pop ds
        pop bp
        ret
ENDP

; void CallCTVoice(struct REGPACK far *R);
; Calls the CT-VOICE driver.

_CallCTVoice PROC FAR
        ARG R : DWORD
        push bp
        mov bp,sp
        push ds                 ; has to be saved
        lds si,[R]              ; DS:SI points at R
        mov ax,[si+rSI]         ; save used SI
        push ax
        mov ax,[si+rAX]         ; set all registers
        mov bx,[si+rBX]
        mov cx,[si+rCX]
        mov dx,[si+rDX]
        mov di,[si+rDI]
        mov es,[si+rES]
        mov ds,[si+rDS]
```

```
            pop si                      ; set SI
            call [DWORD PTR cs:CtVoicePt]
            push ds                     ; save DS
            push si                     ; save SI
            lds si,[R]                  ; DS:SI points at R
            mov [si+rAX],ax             ; save all regs.
            mov [si+rBX],bx
            mov [si+rCX],cx
            mov [si+rDX],dx
            mov [si+rDI],di
            mov [si+rES],es
            pop ax                      ; AX=SI after call
            mov [si+rSI],ax
            pop ax                      ; AX=DS after call
            mov [si+rDS],ax
            pop ds                      ; restore used DS
            pop bp
            ret
ENDP


; void Variables(void far *StPt, void far *BsPt,
;                void far *BlPt, void far *BtPt,
;                void far *CoPt)
; Set the pointers to StatusWord, BlockStart,
; BlockLength, BlockType & Continue.

_Variables PROC FAR
        ARG Stp:DWORD,Bsp:DWORD,BlP:DWORD,BtP:DWORD,CoP:DWORD
        push bp
        mov bp,sp
        @CopyDword cs:BlockStart,BsP
        @CopyDword cs:BlockLength,BlP
        @CopyDword cs:BlockType,BtP
        @CopyDword cs:Continue,CoP
        mov bx,5                    ; set pointer to
        les di,StP                  ; StatusWord
        call [DWORD PTR cs:CTVoicePt]
        pop bp
        ret
ENDP
; void UserRoutine(void interrupt *P);
; Set user interrupt.

_UserRoutine PROC FAR
        ARG P : DWORD
```

```
        push bp
        mov bp,sp
        mov ax,[WORD PTR P+0]
        mov [WORD PTR cs:UserRoutAddress+0],ax
        mov dx,[WORD PTR P+2]
        mov [WORD PTR cs:UserRoutAddress+2],dx
        or ax,dx                ; P=0:0 ?
        jnz NewUserRoutine
        mov bx,13               ; yes, turn off routine
        call [DWORD PTR cs:CTVoicePt]
        pop bp
        ret
NewUserRoutine:
        mov ax,offset UserInterFace
        mov dx,cs
        mov bx,13               ; set interface
        call [DWORD PTR cs:CTVoicePt]
        pop bp
        ret
ENDP
; This routine takes care of the interface for the
; interrupt routine in C. The routine
; sets the required variables and calls the C
; routine. After the call, it checks whether
; the next block has to be played.

UserInterFace PROC FAR
        push ax                 ; save used
        push si                 ; registers
        push ds
        lds si,[cs:BlockStart]  ; set BlockStart
        mov [si],bx             ; starting from
        mov [si+2],es           ; block to be played
        lds si,[cs:BlockLength] ; set BlockLength
        mov ax,[es:bx+1]        ; with the de 24-bit
        mov [si],ax             ; length
        mov ax,[es:bx+3]
        xor ah,ah               ; delete 25..32 bits
        mov [si+2],ax
        lds si,[cs:BlockType]   ; set BlockType
        mov al,[es:bx]
        mov [si],al
        lds si,[cs:Continue]    ; set boolean
        mov byte ptr [si],-1    ; at default True
        pushf                   ; simulate Int
```

```
                call [DWORD PTR cs:UserRoutAddress]
                cmp byte ptr [si],0     ; Continue = False ?
                jne ClearCarryFlag      ; no, process block
                cmp byte ptr [es:bx],0  ; last block ?
                je ClearCarryFlag       ; yes, process this block
                pop ds                  ; restore used
                pop si                  ; registers
                pop ax
                stc                     ; don't process block
                retf                    ; return to CT-VOICE
ClearCarryFlag:
                pop ds                  ; restore used
                pop si                  ; registers
                pop ax
                clc                     ; process block
                retf                    ; return to CT-VOICE
        ENDP
                END                     ; end assembler file
```

Listing 9.4: Header for the Interface of CT-INTER.OBJ with CTVOICE.C

NOTE

Listing 9.4 uses standard memory allocation routines. In Pascal, only
VOC files with a maximum size of 65520 bytes can be used, because
GetMem cannot reserve a larger memory block.

```
/* File : CT-INTER.H */
/* Header for the interface with the machine code */

/* Define machine code interface routines */
extern void far CallCTVoice(struct REGPACK far *R);
extern void far UserRoutine(void interrupt far *P);
extern void far CTVoiceAddress(char far *P,unsigned S);
extern void far Variables(void far *StPt,
            void far *BsPt, void far *BlPt,
            void far *BtPt, void far *CoPt);
```

Listing 9.5: Header of the C Library Supporting the CT-VOICE/CT TIMER Driver

```
/* File : CTVOICE.H                                        */
/* Header for CTVOICE library.                             */

/* Errors occurring during initialization */
#define CallOk          0
#define CardError       1
#define IOPortError     2
#define DMAError        3
/* For speaker control */
#define SpOn            1
#define SpOff           0

/* Various block (Bl) types in VOC format */
#define EndBl           0
#define NwSampleBl      1
#define SampleBl        2
#define SilenceBl       3
#define MarkerBl        4
#define TextBl          5
#define RepeatBl        6
#define RepeatEndBl     7
#define ExtraInfoBl     8       /* Only for the Pro */

/* Possible Sound Blaster cards */
#define SoundBlaster  0
#define OldSBPro      1
#define NewSBPro      2

/* The three part that can serve as input */
#define MIC             0
#define CD_ROM          1
#define Line            3

/* Volume choices */
#define MainVl          0
#define VoiceVl         1
#define MICVl           2
#define CD_ROMVl        3
#define LineVl          4
#define Both            0
#define Left            1
#define Right           2
```

```
/* Filter settings */
#define LowFilter      0
#define HighFilter     1
#define OutputFilter   0
#define InputFilter    1

/* Different record modes */
#define Stereo         1
#define Mono           0

/* Normal on and off */
#define On             0
#define Off            1

/* Dummy array of almost 64K */
typedef unsigned char IntArType[0xfff0];
/* Record to keep info about VOC */
typedef struct {
  void *Start;
  long Length;
  IntArType far *Block;
} VocTp;

/* Global variables */
extern unsigned StatusWord;
extern IntArType *BlockStart;
extern long BlockLength;
extern unsigned char BlockType;
extern unsigned char Continue;
extern unsigned char CardType;
extern unsigned SBIOResult;

/* Procedure for the user routine */

/*** Disk I/O ***/
/* Load CT-VOICE driver */
extern void LoadCTDriver(char *N);
/* Does a file meet the VOC format ? */
extern char CheckVOCFile(char *N);
/* Load VOC file */
extern void LoadVOCFile(char *N, VocTp *V);
/* Write a VOC block */
extern void SaveVOCFile(char *N, VocTp V);
```

```c
/* Remove the VOC block from memory */
extern void DisposeVOC(VocTp *V);

/*** Initialization ***/
/* determine version  */
extern unsigned CTVersion();
/* Set base port */
extern void UsePort(unsigned P);
/* Set IRQ number */
extern void UseIRQ(unsigned I);
/* Set DMA channel (for the PRO !) */
extern void UseChannel(unsigned D);
/* Initialize driver */
extern void InitializeDriver();

/*** Utilities ***/
/* Turn speaker on or off */
extern void Speaker(unsigned W);
/* Stop recording or playing */
extern void StopVProcess();
/* Terminate driver */
extern void DriverOff();
/* Set user routine */
extern void UserRoutine(void interrupt far *P);
/* Ask maximum and minimum sampling rate */
void AskRate(unsigned *Max, unsigned *Min,
             unsigned M, unsigned K);

/*** Mixer chip, for the PRO ***/
/* Set stereo or mono mode for recording */
extern void RecordMode(unsigned B);
/* Determine input */
extern void Input(unsigned S);
/* Turn recording filter on or off */
extern void RecordingFilter(unsigned B);
/* Set volume */
extern void Volume(unsigned S, unsigned C, unsigned V);
/* Turn input or output filter on or off */
extern void Filter(unsigned S, unsigned V);
/* Reset mixer chip */
extern void ResetMixer();
/* Read all volume settings */
extern void ReadAllVolumes();
```

```
/* Ask various volume and filter settings */
extern unsigned ReturnVolume(unsigned S, unsigned V);
extern unsigned ReturnFilter(unsigned S);

/*** Playing ***/
/* Pause playing */
extern void Pause();
/* Continue playing*/
extern void ContinuePlaying();
/* Stop repetition */
extern void StopRepetition(unsigned I);
/* Play VOC block */
extern void PlayBlock(VocTp V);
/* Play VOC block in an EMB (for PRO !) */
extern void PlayEMBBlock(unsigned H, long S);
/*** Recording ***/
/* Record a sample */
extern void RecordSample(long L, unsigned SR,
                         VocTp *V);
/* Record a sample in an EMB (for PRO !) */
extern void RecordEMBSample(unsigned SR, unsigned H,
                            long S);

/***VOC utilities ***/
/* Set VOC.Block at first sub-block */
extern void FirstSubBlock(VocTp *V);
/* Set VOC.Block at next sub-block in */
extern void NextSubBlock(VocTp *V);

/*** Functions for CT-TIMER.DRV ***/
/* Set volume table */
extern void VolumeTable(void *V, unsigned char S);
/* Set echo buffer */
extern void EchoBuffer(void *E, unsigned S);
/* Execute command string */
extern void Command(char * S);
/* Ask current volume */
extern unsigned char CVolume();
```

Listing 9.6: C Library Supporting the CT-VOICE/CT-TIMER Driver

```
/* File : CTVOICE.C                         */
/* Library supporting the CT-VOICE driver */

#include <stdio.h>
```

```c
#include <dos.h>
#include <alloc.h>
#include "CT-INTER.H"
#define extern              /* define global */
#include "CTVOICE.H"
#undef extern
struct REGPACK R;
char *CTAddress;

/*** Disk I/O ***/

void LoadCTDriver(char *N)
{
  FILE *F;
  char S[9];
  unsigned CTSize;

  if (strcmp(N,"") == 0)
    F=fopen("CT-VOICE.DRV","rb");
  else
    F=fopen(N,"rb");
  fseek(F,3,SEEK_SET); fread(&S,9,1,F);   /* read ID */
  fseek(F,OL,SEEK_END);
  S[9] = 0;                               /* set length */
  if (strcmp(S,"CT-VOICE") == 0) {
    CTSize = ftell(F);            /* determine size */
    fseek(F,OL,SEEK_SET);
    CTAddress = malloc(CTSize + 16);
    fread(CTAdres,CTSize,1,F);
    fclose(F);
    CTVoiceAddress((char far *) CTAddress, CTSize);
    SBIOResult = 0;
  }
  else {
    fclose(F);                             /* no driver */
    SBIOResult = 1;
  }
}

char CheckVOCFile(char *N)
{
  FILE *F;
  char S[20];
  unsigned T1, T2;
  char R;
```

```
  R = 0;                                  /* set result */
  F=fopen(N,"rb");
  fread(S,19,1,F);                        /* read header ID */
  S[20] = 0;
  if (strcmp(S,"Creative Voice File") == 0) {
    fseek(F,0x16,SEEK_SET);      /* point at version */
    fread(&T1,2,1,F);
    fread(&T2,2,1,F);
    T1 = (T1 ^ 0xFFFF) + 0x1234; /* verify calc. */
    R = T1 == T2;                /* equal ? */
  }
  fclose(F);
  return R;                               /* return result */
}

void LoadVOCFile(char *N, VocTp *V)
{
  FILE *F;
  unsigned T;
  unsigned SgH, OfH;
  unsigned SgE, OfE;
  long HS;

  F=fopen(N,"rb");
  fseek(F,0x14,SEEK_SET);              /* read header size */
  fread(&T,2,1,F);
  fseek(F,0L,SEEK_END);                /* skip it */
  V->Length = ftell(F) - T;
  fseek(F,T,SEEK_SET);
  V->Start = malloc(V->Length);
  fread(V->Start,V->Length,1,F);
  fclose(F);
  V->Block = V->Start;
}

void SaveVOCFile(char *N, VocTp V)
{
  FILE *F;
  char S[21]="Creative Voice File\x1A";
  unsigned T;

  F = fopen(N,"wb");
  fwrite(S,20,1,F);
  T = 0x001A; fwrite(&T,2,1,F);  /* header size */
```

```
  T = 0x010A;  fwrite(&T,2,1,F);   /* version 1.10 */
  T = (T - 0x1234) ^ 0xFFFF;       /* check */
  fwrite(&T,2,1,F);
  fwrite(V.Start,V.Length,1,F);    /* sample data */
  fclose(F);
}

void DisposeVOC(VocTp * V)
{
  free(V->Start);
  V->Start = NULL;
  V->Length = 0;
  V->Block = NULL;
}


/*** Initialization ***/

/* The next procedures and functions take care of   */
/* the interface between the CT-VOICE driver and C. */
/* Their functioning is quite logical and simple:   */
/* no further comment is provided.                  */

unsigned CTVersion(void)
{
  R.r_bx = 0;
  CallCTVoice(&R);
  return R.r_ax;
}

void UsePort(unsigned P)
{
  R.r_bx = 1;
  R.r_ax = P;
  CallCTVoice(&R);
  SBIOResult = R.r_ax;
}

void UseIRQ(unsigned I)
{
  R.r_bx = 2;
  R.r_ax = I;
  CallCTVoice(&R);
  SBIOResult = R.r_ax;
}
```

```
void UseChannel(unsigned D)
{
  R.r_bx = 19;
  R.r_ax = D;
  CallCTVoice(&R);
  SBIOResult = R.r_ax;
}

void InitializeDriver(void)
{
  R.r_bx = 3;
  CallCTVoice(&R);
  Variables(&StatusWord,&BlockStart,&BlockLength,
            &BlockType,&Continue);
  SBIOResult = R.r_ax;
}

/*** Utilities ***/

void Speaker(unsigned W)
{
  R.r_bx = 4;
  R.r_ax = W;
  CallCTVoice(&R);
}

void StopVProcess(void)
{
  R.r_bx = 8;
  CallCTVoice(&R);
}

void DriverOff(void)
{
  R.r_bx = 9;
  CallCTVoice(&R);
}

void UserRoutine(void interrupt far *P)
{
  if (P == NULL)
    UserRoutine(MK_FP(0,0));
  else
    UserRoutine(P);
}
```

```
void AskRate(unsigned *Max, unsigned *Min,
             unsigned M, unsigned K)
{
  R.r_bx = 26;
  R.r_ax = K;
  R.r_dx = M;
  CallCTVoice(&R);
  *Max = R.r_dx;
  *Min = R.r_ax;
}

/*** Mixer chip ***/

void RecordMode(unsigned B)
{
  R.r_ax = B;
  R.r_bx = 16;
  CallCTVoice(&R);
  SBIOResult = R.r_ax;
}

void Input(unsigned S)
{
  R.r_ax = S;
  R.r_bx = 17;
  CallCTVoice(&R);
  SBIOResult = R.r_ax;
}

void RecordingFilter(unsigned B)
{
  R.r_ax = B;
  R.r_bx = 18;
  CallCTVoice(&R);
  SBIOResult = R.r_ax;
}

void Volume(unsigned S,
            unsigned C,
            unsigned V)
{
  if (C == Both) {
    Volume(S,Left,V);      /* first left */
    C = Right;             /* then right */
```

```
  }
  R.r_ax = S;
  R.r_bx = 21;
  R.r_cx = V;
  R.r_dx = C;
  CallCTVoice(&R);
  SBIOResult = R.r_ax;
}

void Filter(unsigned S,
        unsigned V)
{
  R.r_ax = S;
  R.r_bx = 22;
  R.r_cx = V;
  CallCTVoice(&R);
  SBIOResult = R.r_ax;
}

void ResetMixer(void)
{
  R.r_bx = 23;
  CallCTVoice(&R);
}

void ReadAllVolumes(void)
{
  R.r_bx = 24;
  CallCTVoice(&R);
}

unsigned ReturnVolume(unsigned S, unsigned V)
{
  R.r_ax = S;
  R.r_bx = 25;
  R.r_dx = V;
  CallCTVoice(&R);
  return R.r_ax;
}
unsigned ReturnFilter(unsigned S)
{
  if (CTVersion() >= 0x20A) /* as from 2.10 other */
    R.r_bx = 27;            /* function number */
  else
    R.r_bx = 26;
```

```
  R.r_ax = S;
  CallCTVoice(&R);
  return R.r_ax;
}

/*** Playing ***/

void Pause(void)
{
  R.r_bx = 10;
  CallCTVoice(&R);
  SBIOResult = R.r_ax;
}

void ContinuePlaying(void)
{
  R.r_bx = 11;
  CallCTVoice(&R);
  SBIOResult = R.r_ax;
}
void StopRepetition(unsigned I)
{
  R.r_bx = 12;
  R.r_ax = I;
  CallCTVoice(&R);
  SBIOResult = R.r_ax;
}

void PlayBlock(VocTp V)
{
  R.r_bx = 6;
  R.r_di = FP_OFF(V.Start);
  R.r_es = FP_SEG(V.Start);
  CallCTVoice(&R);
}

void PlayEMBBlock(unsigned H,long S)
{
  R.r_bx = 14;
  R.r_dx = H;
  R.r_di = S >> 16;
  R.r_si = S & 0xffff;
  CallCTVoice(&R);
  SBIOResult = R.r_ax;
}
```

```
/*** Recording ***/
void RecordSample(long L, unsigned SR, VocTp *V)
{
  V->Start = (char far *) malloc(L);
  V->Length = L;
  R.r_bx = 7;
  R.r_ax = SR;
  R.r_dx = L > 16;
  R.r_cx = L & 65535;
  R.r_es = FP_SEG(V->Start);
  R.r_di = FP_OFF(V->Start);
  CallCTVoice(&R);
}

void RecordEMBSample(unsigned SR,unsigned H,long S)
{
  R.r_ax = SR;
  R.r_bx = 15;
  R.r_dx = H;
  R.r_di = S > 16;
  R.r_si = S & 0xffff;
  CallCTVoice(&R);
  SBIOResult = R.r_ax;
}

/*** VOC utilities ***/
void FirstSubBlock(VocTp * V)
{
  V->Block = V->Start;
}

void NextSubBlock(VocTp * V)
{
  long A;

  /* Calculate 24-bit address  */
  A = 16 * (long) FP_SEG(*V->Block) + (long) FP_OFF(*V->Block);
  /* Add: 4 + block length */
  A = A + 4 + (*V->Block[1]) + (*V->Block[2]) < 8 +
(*V->Block[3]) < 16;
  /* Set V.Block*/
  V->Block = MK_FP(A > 4,A & 15);
}
```

```
/*** Functions for the CT-TIMER.DRV ***/

void VolumeTable(void *V, unsigned char S)
{
  void far *H = (void far *) V;

  R.r_bx = 128;
  R.r_ax = 0;
  R.r_cx = S;
  R.r_di = FP_OFF(H);
  R.r_es = FP_SEG(H);
  CallCTVoice(&R);
}

void EchoBuffer(void *E, unsigned S)
{
  void far *H = (void far *) E;

  R.r_bx = 128;
  R.r_ax = 1;
  R.r_cx = S;
  R.r_di = FP_OFF(H);
  R.r_es = FP_SEG(H);
  CallCTVoice(&R);
}

void Command(char * S)
{
  strcat(S,0);
  R.r_bx = 129;
  R.r_di = FP_OFF(S);
  R.r_es = FP_SEG(S);
  CallCTVoice(&R);
}

unsigned char CVolume(void)
{
  R.r_bx = 130;
  CallCTVoice(&R);
  return R.r_ax & 0xff;
}
```

Example Test Programs for CT-VOICE Drivers

Listings 7 through 10 are example programs that demonstrate recording and playing back samples using the library. The four listings in Pascal and C function in the same way. Listings 7 and 8 are intended for the standard Sound Blaster. Listings 9 and 10 are aimed at the Sound Blaster Pro and demonstrate the extensive possibilities of that card.

The listings are as follows:

Listing	Title
9.7	Pascal Test Program for the Standard CT-VOICE Driver
9.8	Test Program for the Standard CT-VOICE Driver
9.9	Pascal Test Program for the Extended CT-VOICE Driver
9.10	C Test Program for the Extended CT-VOICE Driver

Listing 9.7: Pascal Test Program for the Standard CT-VOICE Driver

```
Program CTTest;

{ Test program for the standard CT-VOICE driver.  }

Uses CTVoice, CRT;

Var
  Sample  : VocTp;    { sample }

Begin
  ClrScr;
  LoadCTDriver('');              { load driver }
  WriteLn(Hi(CTVersion),'.',Lo(CTVersion));
  UsePort($220);               { set port }
  UseIRQ(7);                   { set IRQ }
  UseChannel(1);
  InitializeDriver;
  If SBIOResult = CallOk Then Begin
    Speaker(SpOff);              { turn off connection }
    RecordSample(60000,9000,Sample);
    GotoXY(1,1); Write('Recording ...');
    Repeat                     { wait until the }
    Until StatusWord=0;        { sample is recorded }
```

```
      FirstSubBlock(Sample);
      NextSubBlock(Sample);
      Sample.Block^[0]:=0;        { add end block }
      Inc(Sample.Length);         { incl. end block }
      SaveVOCFile('Test.Voc',Sample); { write }
      DisposeVoc(Sample);         { from memory }
      LoadVOCFile('Test.Voc',Sample); { load sample }
      GotoXY(1,2);
      Write('Playing ...');
      Speaker(SpOn);              { turn on passage }
      PlayBlock(Sample);          { play back sample }
      Repeat
      Until StatusWord=0;         { wait till the end }
      DriverOff;                  { everything off }
      WriteLn;
    End
    Else
      WriteLn('Error code : ',SBIOResult);
End.
```

Listing 9.8: Test Program for the Standard CT-VOICE Driver

```c
/* Test program for the standard CT-VOICE driver.    */

#include <conio.h>
#include "ctvoice.h"

VocTp Sample;    /* sample */
void main()
{
  clrscr();
  LoadCTDriver("");             /* load de driver */
  printf("%d.%d\n",CTVersion() > 8,CTVersion() & 0xff);
  UsePort(0x240);               /* set port */
  UseIRQ(10);                   /* set IRQ */
  UseChannel(0);
  InitializeDriver();
  if (SBIOResult == CallOk) {
    Input(CD_ROM);
    Speaker(SpOff);           /* turn off connection */
    RecordSample(40000,9000,&Sample);
    gotoxy(1,1); printf("Recording ...");
    do {                        /* wait until the sample is recorded */
    }  while (!(StatusWord == 0));
    FirstSubBlock(&Sample);
```

```
      NextSubBlock(&Sample);
      *Sample.Block[0] = 0;    /* add end block */
      ++Sample.Length;         /* incl. end block */
      SaveVOCFile("Test.Voc",Sample);   /* write */
      DisposeVOC(&Sample);     /* remove from memory */
      LoadVOCFile("Test.Voc",&Sample);  /* load sample */
      gotoxy(1,2);
      printf("Playing ...");
      Speaker(SpOn);           /* turn on connection */
      PlayBlock(Sample);       /* play back sample */
      do {                     /* wait until the sample is played */
      }  while (!(StatusWord == 0));
      DriverOff();
      printf("\n");
   }
   else
      printf("Error code : %d\n",SBIOResult);
}
```

Listing 9.9: Pascal Test Program for the Extended CT-VOICE Driver

```
Program CTProTest;

{ Test program for the extended CT-VOICE driver }

Uses CTVoice, CRT;
Var
   Ch       : Char;      { key }
   Vol      : Byte;      { volume }
   Sample   : VocTp;     { sample }

Begin
   ClrScr;
   LoadCTDriver('');                { load driver }
   WriteLn(Hi(CTVersion),'.',Lo(CTVersion));
   UsePort($220);                   { set base port }
   UseIRQ(7);                       { set IRQ number }
   UseChannel(1);                   { set DMA channel }
   InitializeDriver;
   If SBIOResult = CallOk Then Begin
      Input(CD_ROM);                { Line sample }
      Volume(CD_ROMVl,Both,15);   { set volume }
      Volume(MainVl,Both,15);
      Filter(InputFilter,On);
      Speaker(SpOff);               { turn off connection }
```

```
RecordMode(Stereo);
RecordSample(64000,20000,Sample);
GotoXY(1,1); Write('Recording ...');
Repeat                          { Wait until the }
Until StatusWord=0;             { sample is recorded }
Volume(CD_ROMVl,Both,0);   { set volume }
Volume(VoiceVl,Both,15);
FirstSubBlock(Sample);
If Sample.Block^[0]=8 Then
  NextSubBlock(Sample);
NextSubBlock(Sample);
Sample.Block^[0]:=EndBl;   { add end block }
Inc(Sample.Length);        { incl. end block }
SaveVOCFile('Test.Voc',Sample); { write }
DisposeVoc(Sample);             { remove from memory }
LoadVOCFile('Test.Voc',Sample); { load sample }
GotoXY(1,2); Write('Playing ...');
Speaker(SpOn);                  { turn on connection }
Ch:=#0;                         { for safety reasons }
Vol:=15;                        { start volume }
Repeat
  If StatusWord=0 Then PlayBlock(Sample);
  GotoXY(1,3);                  { print volume }
  Write('Volume = ',ReturnVolume(MainVl,Left),' ');
  If KeyPressed Then Begin  { key pressed }
    Ch:=ReadKey;
    If Ch=#0 Then Ch:=ReadKey;
    Case Ch of
      #72 : If Vol<15 Then Begin  { cursor up }
              Inc(Vol);
              Volume(MainVl,Both,Vol);
            End;
      #80 : If Vol>0 Then Begin  { cursor down }
              Dec(Vol);
              Volume(MainVl,Both,Vol);
            End;
      #27 : {Dummy};                { escape }
      Else    Begin                 { pause }
              Pause;
              Ch:=ReadKey;          { wait for key }
              ContinuePlaying;
              End
    End {Case}
  End; {If}
Until Ch=#27;                       { escape stops }
```

318

```
      Volume(CD_ROMVl,Both,15);
      DriverOff;
      WriteLn;
    End
    Else
      WriteLn('Error code : ',SBIOResult);
End.
```

Listing 9.10: C Test Program for the Extended CT-VOICE Driver

```c
/* Test program for the extended CT-VOICE driver */

#include <conio.h>
#include "ctvoice.h"
char Ch  = 0;          /* key */
char Vol = 15;         /* volume */
VocTp Sample;          /* sample */

void main()
{
  clrscr();
  LoadCTDriver("");              /* load driver */
  printf("%d.%d\n",CTVersion() > 8,CTVersion() & 0xff);
  UsePort(0x240);                /* set base port */
  UseIRQ(10);                    /* set IRQ number */
  UseChannel(0);                 /* set DMA channel */
  InitializeDriver();
  if (SBIOResult == CallOk) {
    Input(CD_ROM);               /* Line sample */
    Volume(CD_ROMVl,Both,15); /* set volume */
    Volume(MainVl,Both,15);    /* listen in */
    Filter(InputFilter,On);
    Speaker(SpOff);              /* turn off connection */
    RecordMode(Stereo);          /* record stereo */
    RecordSample(40000,20000,&Sample);
    gotoxy(1,1); printf("Recording ...");
    do {                 /* Wait until the sample is recorded */
    } while (!(StatusWord == 0));
    Volume(CD_ROMVl,Both,0);   /* close line */
    Volume(VoiceVl,Both,15);
    FirstSubBlock(&Sample);
    if (*Sample.Block[0] == ExtraInfoBl) /* skip extra */
      NextSubBlock(&Sample);             /* block */
    NextSubBlock(&Sample);
    *Sample.Block[0] = EndBl;  /* add end block */
```

```
  ++Sample.Length;                  /* incl. end block */
  SaveVOCFile("Test.Voc",Sample);    /* write */
  DisposeVOC(&Sample);              /* remove from memory */
  LoadVOCFile("Test.Voc",&Sample);  /* load sample */
  gotoxy(1,2); printf("Playing ...");
  Speaker(SpOn);                    /* turn on connection */
  do {
    if (StatusWord == 0) PlayBlock(Sample);
    gotoxy(1,3);                    /* print volume */
    printf("Volume = %d ",ReturnVolume(MainVl,Left));
    if (kbhit()) {                  /* key pressed */
      Ch = getch();
      if (Ch == '\x00') Ch = getch();
      switch (Ch) {

        case 'H'  : if (Vol < 15) { /* cursor up */
                      ++Vol;
                      Volume(MainVl,Both,Vol);
                    }
                    break;
        case 'P'  : if (Vol > 0) { /* cursor down */
                      --Vol;
                      Volume(MainVl,Both,Vol);
                    }
                    break;
        case '\x1B': break;        /* escape */
        default    : Pause();  /* other key */
                     Ch = getch();
                     ContinuePlaying();
      }
    }
  } while (!(Ch == '\x1B'));        /* escape stops */
  Volume(CD_ROMVl,Both,15);
  DriverOff();
  printf("\n");
}
else
  printf("Error code : %d\n",SBIOResult);
}
```

Programming the DSP

This section describes how you can, without using CT-VOICE and the DMA, record and play back sound by programming the Digital Sound Processor. Before elaborating on this subject, however, you need to know why programming the DSP directly is often useful.

In a nutshell, the advantage of programming the DSP directly is that you can play sound effects and music at the same time. Moreover, you can add sound effects to the sample beforehand (although not all effects can be applied, including setting the volume while playing back a recording).

One disadvantage of editing a sample beforehand is that, if you want to keep the original data, you have to make a copy of the sample data before you edit it. Normally you can't undo operations made on a sample. Consequently, editing in advance requires a lot of memory space and editing time, which can cause problems with large samples.

The major disadvantage of playing back directly is that it requires a lot of processor time and will considerably slow down other programs. It can also be a disadvantage not to be able to use hardware compression methods. You have to consider the pros and cons as you decide whether to play samples directly or through the DMA.

I/O Ports

The DSP uses four I/O ports. Bit 7 is the most significant bit. Following is a list of the I/O ports. In the list below, X represents the selected base port.

I/O Port	Use
2X6H	The reset port. This port is write-only.
2XAH	The data input port. This port is read-only.
2XCH	The command/data port (write) and the buffer status port (read). You can write data or a command to the port and read the buffer status through this port. As far as the buffer status is concerned, it is possible to write data or a command to this port if bit 7 is reset (0).

I/O Port	Use
2XEH	Indicates whether data are present. Again, bit 7 is used. If data are present, bit 7 is set (1).

The reset port is used to initialize the DSP. In combination with port 22AH, you can check whether the port is the right one. By going along all possible port selections you can determine which port is the right one (see Listing 9.11 and 9.12).

Resetting the DSP

In order to reset the DSP:

1. Write a 1 to port 2X6H.

2. Wait three microseconds.

3. Write a 0 to port 2X6H.

4. Read port 2XEH and verify whether bit 7 is reset (=1). Repeat this check a couple of times (for example, 100). If the bit is still reset (=0), resetting the DSP has failed. See step 7 below for possible causes for this failure. You don't have to execute steps 5 and 6 if the DSP has failed.

5. Read a byte from port 2XAH.

6. The read byte must have the value AAH. If this is not the case, you have to repeat steps 4 and 5 a number of times (let's say about ten). If the byte does contain the value AAH, resetting has been successful and the DSP can be used.

If the byte is still unequal to AAH, resetting the DSP has failed; see step 7 for possible causes.

7. If resetting has failed, there are two likely causes: the base port is incorrect or an error has occurred. Try to reset again or select another base port.

Usually resetting the DSP takes about 100 microseconds.

Listing 9.11: Pascal Listing for Automatic Detection of the Sound Blaster Port

```pascal
Program AutoDetect;

Const
  NumberOfTimes1 = 10;      { reset }
  NumberOfTimes2 = 50;      { data present test }

Var
  Port     : Word;      { current port }
  Found    : Boolean;   { port is SB port }
  Counter1 : Word;      { number of times resetting }
  Counter2 : Word;      { number of times reading }
Begin
  Port:=$210;                { start at port 210H }
  Found:=False;              { nothing found yet }
  Counter1:=NumberOfTimes1;  { initialize counter }
  While (Port<=$260) And Not Found Do Begin
    Port[Port+$6]:=1;   { reset Sound Blaster }
    Port[Port+$6]:=0;
    Counter2:=NumberOfTimes2; { data test }
    While (Counter2>0) And (Port[Port+$E] < 128) Do
      Dec(Counter2);
    If (Counter2=0) Or (Port[Port+$A]<>$AA) Then Begin
      Dec(Counter1);          { port 2XAH <> AAH }
      If Counter1=0 Then Begin
        Counter1:=NumberOfTimes1; { resetting failed }
        Port:=Port+$10    { try next port }
      End { If }
    End { If }
    Else
      Found:=True        { resetting successful }
  End; { While }
  If Found Then          { show result }
    WriteLn('Port found at ',Port)
  Else
    WriteLn('No port found !')
End. { program }
```

Listing 9.12: C Listing for Automatic Detection of the Sound Blaster Port

```c
#include <stdio.h>
#include <dos.h>

#define NumberOfTimes1 10   /* resetting */
#define NumberOfTimes2 50   /* data present test */

unsigned Port = 0x210;   /* current port */
char Found = 0;          /* port is SB port */
unsigned Cnt1, Cnt2;     /* reset & wait */

void main()
{
  Cnt1 = NumberOfTimes1;       /* initialize counter */
  while ((Port <= 0x260) && !Found) {
    outportb(Port + 0x6,1);    /* reset Sound Blaster */
    outportb(Port + 0x6,0);
    Cnt2 = NumberOfTimes2;     /* data test */
    while ((Cnt2 > 0) && (inportb(Port + 0xE) < 128))
    --Cnt2;
    if ((Cnt2==0) || (inportb(Port + 0xA) != 0xAA)) {
    --Cnt1;                    /* port 2XAH <> AAH */
      if (Cnt1 == 0) {
        Cnt1 = NumberOfTimes1;  /* resetting failed */
        Port = Port + 0x10;     /* try next */
      }
    }
    else                        /* resetting successful */
      Found = 1;                /* port found */
  }
  if (Found)                    /* show result */
    printf("Base port found at %d\n",Port);
  else
    printf("No base port found !\n");
}
```

When the DSP has been reset, you can record or play back sound. You do this by first sending a command byte to the DSP and then reading or writing a byte.

Recording Sound

To record sound:

1. Send the command 20H to the command port 2XCH.

2. If you work in a fast language (like Assembly) or on a very fast computer, you must check with bit 7 of the data available port 2XEH to see whether the DSP can return a byte. The DSP can return a byte if bit 7 has the value 1 (is set).

3. Read a byte from data input port 2XAH.

4. At this point, wait so the sample is recorded at a constant rate (this is explained later). Return to step 1 until the end of the recording—that is, the end of the buffer—is reached.

If you sample with the CT-VOICE driver anyway, you can use the above-mentioned method to conduct a "silence test." To do this, you read a byte from, for example, a microphone input. If this byte has a value between 128+A and 128−A, no sound is recorded by the microphone. If the byte value is not within this range, the microphone receives sound and you can record a sample using the CT-VOICE driver. The constant A is necessary because the input is liable to experience interference such that the noise will never have the exact value 128 that indicates complete silence. The following listings, 9.13 and 9.14, contain examples of silence tests.

Listing 9.13: Pascal Example of a Silence Test

```
Const
  Threshold = 10;          { silence area }

Procedure WaitForSound(Port : Word);

Var
  H : Byte;                { sample byte }

Begin
  Repeat
    Port[Port+$C]:=$20;  { read byte }
    Repeat               { data present ? }
    Until Port[Port+$E]>=128;
    H:=Port[Port+$A];    { yes, read these data }
  Until (H<128-Threshold) OR (H>128+Threshold);
End;                     { H is not in silence area }
```

Listing 9.14: C Example of a Silence Test

```
#define Threshold 10      /* Limit : 128-Thr. en 128+Thr. */

void WaitForSound(unsigned Port)
{
 /* Wait until input is no longer between 128-Threshold
    and 128+Threshold. */
  unsigned short H;      /*  sample byte  */

  do {
    outportb(Port + 0xC,0x20);   /* read byte */
    do {                         /* data present ? */
    }  while (!(inportb(Port + 0xE) >= 128));
    H = inportb(Port + 0xA);     /* yes, read these data */
  }  while (!((H < 128 - Threshold) |
            (H > 128 + Threshold)));
}               /* H is not in silence area */
```

Playing Sound with the DSP

To play sound with the DSP:

1. Send the command 10H to the command port 2XCH.

2. If you work in a fast language (like Assembly) or on a very fast computer, you must check with bit 7 of the data status port 2XCH to see whether the DSP can receive a byte. It can receive a byte provided that bit 7 has the value 0 (is reset).

3. Send the data byte to data port 2XCH.

4. Wait to make sure the sample is played at a constant rate. Return to step 1 until the end of the sample is reached.

Both recording and sampling occur at a constant speed. This is done by recording and playing back the value at particular moments and at equal intervals. To achieve a constant speed, the timer has to be used. Especially in high-level languages, the code for recording and playing can differ considerably, so the duration for the codes also varies. If a waiting loop is used instead of the timer, playing can be much slower or faster than recording.

Of course, you can equalize the recording and playing rate by experimenting. However, if a particular part of a code is processed faster on some computers, recording and playing speeds can differ. Moreover, while recording, an interrupt might be generated that occupies a certain amount of time. Consider, for instance, a parking program for the hard disk on the timer. This interrupt can occur at a different moment when playing or maybe doesn't occur at all. In this case, the recording and the reproduction will differ.

The next section discusses an alternative driver that uses the timer to record and play back sound.

CT-TIMER, an Alternative CT-VOICE Driver

The alternative driver, CT-TIMER, is compatible with the "normal" CT-VOICE driver. Moreover, it possesses a number of additional functions. And by using it you can replace one driver with the other and still use the VOC format. To avoid confusion, we will call this second driver the CT-TIMER.

We chose the Assembly language to write the driver because this language (when assembled) results in a compact and fast code. Speed is very desirable because we speed up the timer interrupt.

Suppose you have a sampling rate of 10,000 Hz. At this rate, the timer interrupt is called 10,000 times a second. If the timer interrupt called a Pascal or C program, it would take more time to process the program code. If the call was made just once it wouldn't matter, but at 10,000 times a second you soon notice the program slowing down. Although we chose the fast Assembly code and tried to optimize it, you will notice that the computer works rather slowly anyway. Unfortunately, this is inevitable. A lower sampling rate, however, ensures that more time is available for the program. The computer works faster than it would at a higher sampling rate.

Although the driver accelerates the timer, it still calls the old timer program 18.2 times a second, so all time-sensitive functions work normally. If the timer interrupt is taken over by your own program while playing, this new routine is called at the speed of the current sampling rate. So you'd better avoid this.

CT-TIMER Functions

We have defined three new functions for this driver. They start at 128 so they don't overwrite the official functions.

Function 128, Set Buffer

```
Procedure VolumeTable(V: Pointer; C: Byte)
Procedure EchoBuffer(E: Pointer; C: Word)
void VolumeTable(void *V, unsigned char C)
void EchoBuffer(void *E, unsigned C)
```

Input:	BX	= 128
	AX	= 0, volume table
		= 1, echo buffer
	CX	= C
	ES:DI	= V or E
Output:	None	

Function 128 sets the two buffers used. The next section explains the use of these buffers. When setting the volume table, the variable C determines the number of steps with which the volume can be adjusted. The variables E and V have to point at an allocated memory block. The memory required for the volume table is 256 * (C + 1) (the volume can be set from 0 through C)! Usually the size of the echo buffer is equal to C. The driver itself creates the volume table of the allocated memory. Consequently, the memory indicated by the pointer V may not be modified.

Function 128 has to be called after initialization if you want to make use of the echo effect or the volume effect.

Function 129, Process Command String

```
Procedure Command(S: String)
void Command(char *S)
```

Input:	BX	= 129
	ES:DI	= segment:string offset
Output:	None	

Function 129 allows you to send a "command string" to the driver. This is also explained in the next section. In Assembly, the string has to terminate with a 0 byte; in Pascal and C, this is done automatically.

Function 130, Ask Current Volume

```
Function CVolume: Byte
int CVolume ()
```

| **Input:** | BX | = 130 |
| **Output:** | AX | = current volume setting |

For most effects, the volume is modified. With function 130 you can read the volume setting of the driver.

Creating Sound Effects

By applying various (mostly mathematical) operations to the sample data, you can obtain all kinds of sound effects. This chapter discusses some of them. Not all effects fully correspond to the physical and mathematical theory, but the effects that are implemented this way are simple and short.

Because most operations are of a mathematical nature, the values between -128 and 127 are used instead of 0 through 255. This means that first the value 128 is subtracted from the sample byte. Next the operation is executed and the value 128 is added again to the sample value, like so:

$$S = F(S - 128) + 128$$

In the formulas, the next variables are used:

| S | The old sample value (byte) |
| F(X) | The "mathematical" operation |

The Volume Effect

For the volume, each sample value increases or decreases by a certain percentage, like so:

$$F(S) = S * V / VO$$

The variable V represents the current volume, whereas VO represents the maximum volume. The sample has a lower volume when V is less than VO. If V is larger than VO, the sample is amplified. This can be useful to very soft samples.

With the volume effect you can create fade-ins and fade-outs:

- With a fade-in, a sample starts with the volume at zero, and subsequently the volume is raised at a constant rate until a certain value is reached.

- The fade-out effect works in the same way but this time the volume decreases at a constant rate until it reaches zero, and the sound slowly fades away. Fade-outs, as everyone knows, are often used in music to end songs.

The CT-TIMER uses a volume table with all calculated values for certain volume selections. It does this because dividing and multiplying take more time than looking up the volume in a table. With function 128 you can indicate the start of a free memory block where this information is stored.

Mixing Samples

It is quite easy to mix two samples. You add up the different sample values and divide them by the number of added values. The formula for mixing voice 0 and 1 is:

$$F (S0, S1) = (S0 + S1) / 2$$

When the number of samples consists of a power of two, the fast-shift routines can be used. You don't have to execute the division, but you do have to consider the maximum and minimum values. If one of these two values is overwritten, the sample value has to be equal to this value.

Creating an Echo

Echoes are commonly heard sound effects. By changing the parameters, you can obtain all kinds of echo effects, from a long echo to a robotic distortion. Calculating echo effects takes a lot of time, however. You can set two parameters for the echo:

- The time before the sound is heard again, and

- The rate at which it quiets down.

For example, suppose at time I the sample value P is reproduced. After an X number of bytes, this sample value is reproduced again together with the new sample value, but this time the sample value P is not as loud.

In the CT-TIMER, echo effects are realized by using a buffer. In this buffer, the played value is stored each time. The next time this value can be increased by a certain percentage and be mixed with the new value. The result replaces the old sample value.

Because this method uses integer calculations, sometimes a sample value doesn't reach the exact value of 128 and creates noise. When you create the echo sample beforehand in Pascal or in C, you would do better to use floating-point numbers. Another possibility is to take the original sample value after a few steps. This value has to be decreased by the correct percentage and then be subtracted from the current sample value.

To create a "robot" echo effect, take very small steps; for a more resounding echo effect, take larger steps.

Turning Sound Effects On and Off

The question remains: how do you turn sound effects on and off in the CT-TIMER driver? This could be done by using a new block type. However, because this type is probably not supported by other VOC editors, using a new block type is not an elegant solution. To set the effects you will have to use an existing block type. A marker block or a text block can be used. A text block is the best solution for the CT-TIMER because a text block doesn't affect other programs, whereas a marker block does.

Commands can be processed in the text. If the first character is a #, the CT-TIMER verifies whether the following characters constitute a command. If they do, the corresponding routine will be called. Commands can also be executed by using function 129.

Commands can be written in uppercase, lowercase, or a combination of the two. Each command must be followed by one or more numbers in the normal decimal format, like so: #Volume 123. Following is a look at the commands.

#Volume v   #Volume v sets the volume at value v. If v is larger than the maximum value allowed, it is set at the maximum value. This function automatically turns on the volume effect.

#VolumeOff   #VolumeOff turns off the volume effect.

#Fade s e p   With the #Fade s e p command you can set a fade:

- s is the start volume
- e is the end volume
- p represents the number of bytes that have to be processed each time before the volume is modified

For example, a fade-in is set with #Fade 0 x 200 and a fade-out is set with #Fade x 0 200, where x is the maximum volume value. This function also turns on the volume effect.

#FadeOff   #FadeOff stops the fade and turns off this sound effect. The volume effect, however, is not changed.

#Echo s p   In the #Echo s p command:

- s represents the number of steps in bytes before the value is repeated. This value has to be smaller than or equal to the size of the echo buffer!
- p represents the decrease percentage, which is equal to p/256.

Because a buffer is used, the echo continues when another sample or a silence block is played.

You can prevent this with the next command or by calling #Echo s p again. At the beginning of this command the buffer is cleared.

#EchoOff   #EchoOff stops the echo effect.

#EffectOff   #EffectOff turns off all sound effects.

When no effects are applied, playing takes less time.

The commands can be programmed in a VOC editor that is able to add and adjust text (like VEDIT). Listings 9.15 and 9.16 show an example using the additional functions.

The CT-TIMER uses two tables located in the files CONVTABL.INC and WAIT-TABL.INC. These files are generated by the GW-BASIC program found in Listings 9.17 and 9.18. Without these files, a "fatal" error occurs when assembling!

Listing 9.15: Example of a Pascal Program for the CT-TIMER Functions

```
Program CTTimerTest;

{ Test program for the CT-TIMER driver. }

Uses CTVoice, CRT;

Var
  Ch      : Char;     { key }
  Vol     : Byte;     { volume }
  Sample  : VocTp;    { sample }
  EBuffer,
  VBuffer : Pointer;  { echo + volume buffer }

{ Creates the function St, that has a number as
  input and converts is to a string. }
Function St(N : Word) : String;
Var
  S : String;
Begin
  Str(N,S); St:=S;
End;

Begin
  ClrScr;
  LoadCTDriver('CT-TIMER.DRV'); { load driver }
```

```
UsePort($220);                      { set port }
InitializeDriver;
If SBIOResult = CallOk Then Begin
   GetMem(VBuffer,129*256);    { reserve memory }
   VolumeTable(VBuffer,128);   { for the buffers }
   GetMem(EBuffer,4096);
   EchoBuffer(EBuffer,4096);
   Speaker(SpOff);                  { turn off connection }
   RecordSample(60000,8000,Sample);
   GotoXY(1,1); Write('Recording ...');
   Repeat                           { Wait until the }
   Until StatusWord=0;              { sample is recorded }
   GotoXY(1,2); Write('Playing ...');
   Speaker(SpOn);                   { turn on connection }
   Ch:=#0;                          { for safety reasons }
   Vol:=128;                        { start volume }
   Command('Fade 0 128 100');
   Command('Echo 2000 180');
   Repeat
      If StatusWord=0 Then          { play back sample }
        PlayBlock(Sample);          { again }
      GotoXY(1,3);                  { print volume }
      Write('Volume = ',CVolume,' ');
      If KeyPressed Then Begin   { key pressed }
        Ch:=ReadKey;
        If Ch=#0 Then Ch:=ReadKey;
        Case Ch of
          #72 : If Vol<128 Then Begin   { cursor up }
                   Inc(Vol);                { increase volume }
                   Command('Volume '+St(Vol));
                End;
          #80 : If Vol>0  Then Begin   { cursor down }
                   Dec(Vol);                { decrease volume }
                   Commando('Volume '+St(Vol));
                End;
          #27 : {Dummy};                       { escape }
          Else    Begin              { other key pauses }
                   Pause;
                   Repeat Until KeyPressed;
                   Ch:=ReadKey;         { wait for key }
                   ContinuePlaying;
                End
        End {Case}
      End; {If}
   Until Ch=#27;
```

```
    Command('FADE 128 0 100');
    Repeat                          { Wait until }
      GotoXy(1,3);                  { volume is 0. }
      Write('Volume = ',CVolume,' ');
      If StatusWord=0 Then PlayBlock(Sample);
    Until CVolume=0;
    DriverOff;
    WriteLn;
  End
  Else
    WriteLn('Error code : ',SBIOResult);
End.
```

Listing 9.16: Example of a C Program for the CT-TIMER Functions

```c
/* Test program for the CT-TIMER driver.           */
#include <conio.h>
#include "ctvoice.h"

char Ch = 0;                /* key */
unsigned char Vol = 32;     /* volume */
VocTp Sample;               /* sample */
void *EBuffer;              /* echo buffer */
void *VBuffer;              /* volume buffer */
char S[30];

void main()
{
  clrscr();
  LoadCTDriver("CT-TIMER.DRV");   /* load driver */
  UsePort(0x240);                 /* set port */
  InitializeDriver();
  if (SBIOResult == CallOk) {
    VBuffer = (void *) malloc(33*256); /* reserve */
    VolumeTable(VBuffer,32);           /* buffers */
    EBuffer = (void *) malloc(4096);
    EchoBuffer(EBuffer,4096);
    Speaker(SpOff);                 /* turn off connection */
    RecordSample(32000,8000,&Sample);
    gotoxy(1,1); printf("Recording ...");
    do {          /* Wait until the sample is recorded */
    } while (!(StatusWord == 0));
    printf("Playing ...");
    Speaker(SpOn);                  /* turn on connection */
    Command("Fade 0 32 400");   /* fade in sample */
```

```
      Command("Echo 100 180");     /* use echo */
      do {
        if (StatusWord == 0)        /* play back sample */
          PlayBlock(Sample);        /* again */
        gotoxy(1,3);                /* print volume */
        printf("Volume = %d ",CVolume());
        if (kbhit()) {              /* key pressed */
          Ch = getch();
          if (Ch == '\x00') Ch = getch();
          switch (Ch) {
            case 'H'   : if (Vol < 32) { /* cursor up */
                           ++Vol;         /* increase volume */
                           sprintf(S,"Volume %d",Vol);
                           Commando(S);
                         }
                         break;
            case 'P'   : if (Vol > 0) {  /* cursor down */
                           --Vol;         /* decrease volume */
                           sprintf(S,"Volume %d",Vol);
                           Command(S);
                         }
                         break;
            case '\x1B': break;

            default    : Pause();      /* other key */
                         Ch = getch();/* pauses */
                         ContinuePlaying();
          }
        }
      }  while (!(Ch == '\x1B'));
      Command("FADE 32 0 400");    /* fade out sample */
      do {                  /* Wait until volume is 0 */
        gotoxy(1,3);
        printf("Volume = %d ",CVolume());
        if (StatusWord == 0) PlayBlock(Sample);
      }  while (!(CVolume() == 0));
      DriverOff();
      printf("\n");
    }
    else
      printf("Error code : %d\n",SBIOResult);
}
```

Listing 9.17: The CT-TIMER Source in Assembly

```
        .MODEL TINY
        .CODE
        ORG 0h


; File name : CT-TIMER.ASM
; CT-TIMER.DRV, a CT-VOICE compatible driver,
; that, however, uses the timer instead of the
; DMA. This way all kinds of effects are possible.
;
; RUN : TASM CT-TIMER.ASM
;       TLINK /T CT-TIMER.OBJ, CT-TIMER.DRV
;
; Possible situations.
Nothing         = 0
Playing         = 1
Recording       = 2
Pausing         = 3
AnotherBlock    = 4


; Block types
EndBl           = 0
NewSampleBl     = 1
SampleBl        = 2
SilenceBl       = 3
MarkerBl        = 4
TextBl          = 5
RepeatStartBl   = 6
RepeatEndBl     = 7


Start:  jmp Control


IDText          DB "CT-VOICE"
;-------------------------------------------------------------
; Driver variables
;-------------------------------------------------------------

                ORG 30h      ; for compatibility
SBIOPort        DW 220h      ; base port
SBIRQNumber     DB 7         ; not used
InitiationFlag  DB 0         ; driver initialized ?
StatusPointer   DD 0         ; address (Status word)
OldTimerCounter DW 0         ; for the correct functioning
OldTimerICounter DW 0        ; of the old timer
```

```
OldTimerPointer    DD 0              ; routine
SilenceFlag        DB 0              ; silence of sample
BlockStart         DD 0              ; pointer at sub-block
RepeatStart        DD 0              ; to repeat
RepeatEnd          DD 0              ; one or more sub-blocks
RepeatCounter      DW 0
RepeatFlag         DB 0
PlayFlag           DB 0              ; busy playing ?
PlayBackup         DB 0              ; copy of PlayFlag
SamplePointer      DD 0              ; for the playing and
SampleLength       DD 0              ; recording routines
EffectsFlag        DB 0              ; effects of application
ActionFlag         DB Nothing       ; what is the current action
ActionBackup       DB 0              ; copy of ActionFlag
UserRoutePtr       DD 0              ; user routine
UserRouteFlag      DW 0              ; user routine ?
CommandString      DD 0              ; address(effect string)
VolumeTable        DD 0              ; address(Volume Table)
CurrentVolume      DB 0              ; goes without saying
MaximumVolume      DB 0              ; idem
EchoMulti          DB 0              ; settings for the
EchoBuffer         DD 0              ; echo effect
EchoEnd            DW 0              ; end of echo
BufferStart        DW 0              ; buffer start
BufferEnd          DW 0              ; actual buffer end
MultiTable         DB 256 dup (0)    ; help table for echo
FadeCounter        DW 0              ; settings for the
FadeInit           DW 0              ; fade effect
FadeVolume         DB 0
FadeAdd            DB 0


; The functions of the driver, effects, sub-blocks
FunctionTable      DW DetermineVersion,SetIOBase
                   DW SetIRQ,InitDriver,SetSpeaker
                   DW SetStatusAddr,PlayVOCBlock
                   DW RecordVOC,StopVOCProcess
                   DW DeInitDriver,Pause,Continue
                   DW QuitRepeat,UserRoute
ExtraFunctions     DW SetBuffer, ProcessCommandString
                   DW CurrentVolumeQ
EffectFunctions    DW Volume          ; last applied
                   DW Fade
                   DW Echo
                   DW 4 Dup (NoEffect)
                   DW NoEffect        ; first applied
```

```
BlockRoutines    DW REndBl,RNewSampleBl,RSampleBl
                 DW RSilenceBl,RMarkerBl,RTextBl
                 DW RRepeatStartBl,RRepeatEndBl

; Effect strings :
; DB comparison string, DW function.
CommandStrings   DB "ECHO",0
                 DW EchoEffect
                 DB "FADE",0
                 DW FadeEffect
                 DB "VOLUME",0
                 DW VolumeEffect
                 DB "ECHOOFF",0
                 DW EchoEffectOff
                 DB "FADEOFF",0
                 DW FadeEffectOff
                 DB "VOLUMEOFF",0
                 DW VolumeEffectOff
                 DB "EFFECTOFF",0
                 DW EffectsOff
                 DB 0

; The two tables calculated by CALCTABL.BAS
SRConvTable      LABEL WORD
INCLUDE CONVTABL.INC
WaitTable        LABEL WORD
INCLUDE WAITABL.INC


;-----------------------------------------------------------------
; Various effects
;-----------------------------------------------------------------
; At the call of each effect the sample value is in
; AL. After the call AL has to contain the
; processed value.
; The values of ES & DX are already saved, the
; other registers have to be saved.
; When DS is called, it has the same value as CS.

; Volume : process current volume, use
; previously calculated table.
Volume PROC NEAR
        push bx                     ; save BX
        les bx,[VolumeTable]        ; ES:BX = @VolumeTable
        add bh,[CurrentVolume]
        sub al,128
```

```
            xlat es:[bx]                ; replace AL
            add al,128
            pop bx                      ; restore BX
            ret
ENDP


; Fade effect : both the fade-in and the fade-out
; effect.
Fade PROC NEAR
            dec [FadeCounter]           ; volume change ?
            jnz EndFade
            mov dx,[FadeInit]           ; yes, restore counter
            mov [FadeCounter],dx
            mov dl,[CurrentVolume]      ; edit volume
            add dl,[FadeAdd]
            mov [CurrentVolume],dl
            cmp dl,[FadeVolume]         ; correct value reached
            jne EndFade
            and [EffectsFlag],not 2     ; yes, turn off effect
EndFade:
            ret
ENDP


; Echo effect, mix the samples but do not divide by two.
Echo PROC NEAR
            push bx                     ; save BX
            sub al,128
            cbw                         ; 8 bits -> 16 bits
            mov dx,ax                   ; DX = 16-bit value
            les bx,EchoBuffer           ; ES:BX = @EchoBuffer
            mov al,es:[bx]              ; AL = previous value
            cbw                         ; 8 bits -> 16 bits
            add ax,128
            add ax,dx
            or ah,ah                    ; 0 <= AX <= 255 ?
            jz NoOverflow
            mov al,ah                   ; no, AL = 0 or 255
            cbw                         ; determine on the basis of
            not ah                      ; sign
            mov al,ah
NoOverFlow:
            push ax                     ; save for later use
            mov dx,bx
            mov bx,offset MultiTable
            xlat
```

```
        mov bx,dx
        mov es:[bx],al          ; store value
        inc bx                  ; next byte
        cmp bx,[EchoEnd]        ; end ?
        jb EchoOk
        mov bx,[BufferStart]    ; yes, go to beginning
EchoOk:
        mov [Word ptr EchoBuffer],bx
        pop ax                  ; restore value
        pop bx                  ; and BX
        ret
ENDP


; No effect , dummy routine.
NoEffect PROC NEAR
        ret
ENDP


;------------------------------------------------------------------
; Various routines to set effects
;------------------------------------------------------------------
; These routines are called by RTextBl.
; The routines can use the routine
; ReturnParameter that returns the value of the parameter
; in AX. CF contains the Error Flag.

; Set volume, #VOLUME value.
VolumeEffect PROC NEAR
        call ReturnParameter    ; get value
        jc VolumeEError
        cmp al,[MaximumVolume]  ; bigger than maximum
        jb NoVolumeMax
        mov al,[MaximumVolume]  ; yes, then becomes maximum
NoVolumeMax:
        cmp [WORD PTR VolumeTable+2],0
        je VolumeEError         ; volume table ?
        mov [CurrentVolume],al  ; yes, change volume
        or [EffectsFlag],1      ; and turn on effect
VolumeEError:
        ret
ENDP


; Set fade, #FADE start,end,rate.
; Depending on start and end a fade-in
; or a fade-out effect is created.
```

```
FadeEffect PROC NEAR
        call ReturnParameter       ; get start
        jc FadeEError
        push ax
        call ReturnParameter       ; get end
        pop bx
        jc FadeEError
        push bx
        push ax
        call ReturnParameter       ; get rate
        pop cx
        pop bx
        jc FadeEError
        mov [FadeCounter],ax        ; set whatever is necessary
        mov [FadeInit],ax
        mov [FadeVolume],cl
        mov [CurrentVolume],bl
        mov al,1
        cmp bl,cl                   ; start < end ?
        jb PositiveFade
        neg al                      ; yes, AL=-AL
PositiveFade:
        mov [FadeAdd],al            ; store 1 or -1
        or [EffectsFlag],3          ; turn on effect
FadeEError:
        ret
ENDP

; Set echo, #ECHO step size, multiplier.
; Delete buffer and draw up a fade table.
EchoEffect PROC NEAR
        call ReturnParameter        ; get step size
        jc EchoEError
        push ax
        call ReturnParameter        ; multiplier
        pop bx
        jc EchoEError
        cmp [WORD PTR EchoBuffer+2],0
        je EchoEError               ; buffer set ?
        mov ch,al                   ; ch = multi value
        mov ax,cs                   ; yes, ES=CS
        mov es,ax
        mov di,offset MultiTable
        xor cl,cl                   ; calculate MultiTable
```

```
CalculateMult:
        mov al,cl
        sub al,128              ; decrease old value
        cbw                     ; calculation :
        mov dl,ch               ; xEchoMulti/256
        mov dh,0
        imul dx
        mov al,ah
        stosb                   ; store value
        inc cl                  ; after 255 comes 0
        jnz CalculateMult
        mov ax,[BufferStart]
        mov [WORD PTR EchoBuffer],ax
        add bx,ax
        cmp bx,[BufferEnd]      ; buffer overflow ?
        jb BufferSmaller
        mov bx,[BufferEnd]      ; yes
BufferSmaller:
        mov cx,bx               ; clear buffer
        sub cx,ax
        mov [EchoEnd],bx
        les di,EchoBuffer
        xor al,al
        rep stosb
        or [EffectsFlag],4      ; turn on effect
EchoEError:
        ret
ENDP

; Turn off volume effect.
VolumeEffectOff PROC NEAR
        and [EffectsFlag],not 4
        ret
ENDP
; Turn off fade effect.
FadeEffectOff PROC NEAR
        and [EffectsFlag],not 4
        ret
ENDP

; Turn off echo effect.
EchoEffectOff PROC NEAR
        and [EffectsFlag],not 4
        ret
ENDP
```

```
; Turn off all effects.
EffectsOff PROC NEAR
        mov [EffectsFlag],0
        ret
ENDP
;----------------------------------------------------------------
; Various routines used by the driver functions
;----------------------------------------------------------------

; Write a command, try this 200H times.
TestWriteSB PROC NEAR
        push cx                 ; save used CX
        mov cx,200h             ; try 200H times
        mov ah,al               ; AH=copy command
        mov dx,[SBIOPort]       ; DX=2X0
        add dx,0Ch              ; DX=2XC
TestWriteWait:
        in al,dx
        or al,al                ; test bit 7
        jns TestWriteOk         ; =0 ?
        loop TestWriteWait      ; no, once again
        stc                     ; failed
        pop cx
        ret
TestWriteOk:
        mov al,ah               ; successful
        out dx,al               ; write command
        clc
        pop cx
        ret
ENDP

; Read data. Try this 200H times.
TestReadSB PROC NEAR
        push cx                 ; save used CX
        mov dx,[SBIOPort]
        add dl,0Eh              ; DX=2XEH
        mov cx,200h
TestReadWait:
        in al,dx
        or al,al                ; test bit 7
        js TestReadOk           ; =1 ?
        loop TestReadWait       ; no, once again
        stc                     ; failed
```

```
        pop cx
        ret
TestReadOk:
        sub dl,04h              ; DX=2XAH
        in al,dx                ; read data
        clc                     ; successful
        pop cx
        ret
ENDP


; Write a command or data to the SB, wait
; if the SB can receive no command.
WriteSB PROC NEAR
        mov dx,[SBIOPort]       ; DX=2XCH
        add dx,0Ch
        mov ah,al               ; AH=copy AL
WriteWait:
        in al,dx
        or al,al
        js WriteWait            ; bit 7=1 ?
        mov al,ah               ; no, write data
        out dx,al               ; or command
        ret
ENDP


; Read SB data, check whether data is present.
; Wait as long as this is not the case.
ReadSB PROC NEAR
        mov dx,[SBIOPort]       ; DX=2XEH
        add dl,0Eh
        sub al,al
ReadWait:
        in al,dx
        or al,al
        jns ReadWait            ; bit 7=0 ?
        sub dl,4                ; no, read data from
        in al,dx                ; port 2XAH
        ret
ENDP


; Reset SB with the established IO port.
ResetSoundBl PROC NEAR
        mov dx,[SBIOPort]
        add dl,6                ; DX=2X6H
        mov al,1
```

```
        out dx,al                ; write 1
        in al,dx                 ; wait a moment
        in al,dx
        in al,dx
        in al,dx
        sub al,al
        out dx,al                ; write 0
        mov bl,10h               ; try 10H times
ResetTestLoop:
        call TestReadSB
        cmp al,0AAh              ; AL=AAH ??
        je ResetTestOk
        dec bl                   ; no, once again
        jnz ResetTestLoop
        stc                      ; reset failed
        ret
ResetTestOk:
        clc                      ; reset successful
        ret
ENDP

; Set timer interrupt.
SetTimerInt PROC NEAR
        pushf                    ; save flags
        push es
        cli                      ; interrupts off
        mov dx,0                 ; set interrupt
        mov es,dx
        mov dx,cs
        xchg ax,[WORD PTR es:8*4+0]
        xchg dx,[WORD PTR es:8*4+2]
        mov [WORD PTR OldTimerPointer+0],ax
        mov [WORD PTR OldTimerPointer+2],dx
        mov [OldTimerICounter],1 ; call the timer
        mov [OldTimerCounter],1  ; each time
        pop es
        popf                     ; restore I-flag
        ret
ENDP
; Restore timer interrupt and reset timer
; rate at 18.2 times a second.
RestoreTimerInt PROC NEAR
        pushf                    ; save flags
        push es
        cli                      ; interrupts off
```

```
        mov al,36h                  ; reset timer
        out 43h,al                  ; so it is called 18.2
        xor al,al                   ; times a second
        out 40h,al
        xor al,al
        out 40h,al
        xor ax,ax                   ; restore interrupt
        mov es,ax                   ; vector
        mov ax,[WORD PTR OldTimerPointer+0]
        mov dx,[WORD PTR OldTimerPointer+2]
        mov [WORD PTR es:8*4+0],ax
        mov [WORD PTR es:8*4+2],dx
        pop es
        popf                        ; restore I-flag
        ret
ENDP

; Set status word at a certain value.
SetStatusWord PROC NEAR
        push ds
        push si
        lds si,[StatusPointer]
        mov [si],ax                 ; set value
        pop si
        pop ds
        ret
ENDP

; Minimize segment:offset so offset is
; between 0 and 15.
Minimize PROC NEAR
        push ax                     ; save AX
        shr ax,1                    ; AX=AX/2
        shr ax,1                    ; idem
        shr ax,1                    ; idem
        shr ax,1                    ; AX=offset/16
        add dx,ax                   ; increase segment
        pop ax                      ; restore offset AX
        and ax,15                   ; AX between 0 and 15
        ret
ENDP
; Convert a segment:offset to a 20-bit address.
Calculate20Bits PROC NEAR
        push bx                     ; save BX
        xor bx,bx
```

```
        shl dx,1                ; DX=DX*2
        rcl bl,1                ; BL=bit of DX
        shl dx,1
        rcl bl,1
        shl dx,1
        rcl bl,1
        shl dx,1                ; DX=DX*2*2*2*2=DX*16
        rcl bl,1                ; BL=DX/4096
        add ax,dx               ; AX=offset+segment*16
        adc bl,0                ; process overflow
        mov dx,bx               ; DX=bits 20 .. 16
        pop bx
    ret
ENDP


; Go to next block.
NextBlock PROC NEAR
        les di,[BlockStart]     ; ES:DI=current start
        mov ax,[es:di+1]        ; BL,AH,AL = 20 bits
        mov bl,[es:di+3]        ; size
        xor bh,bh
        add di,4
        add ax,di               ; add offset DI to
        adc bx,0                ; BL,AH,AL
        and bx,0fh
        mov dx,es               ; calculate new ES
        ror bx,1
        ror bx,1
        ror bx,1
        ror bx,1                ; BX=BX*16*16*16
        add dx,bx               ; DX=new segment
        call Minimize
        mov [WORD PTR BlockStart+0],ax
        mov [WORD PTR BlockStart+2],dx
        ret
ENDP


; Skip a number of blocks until the indicated
; block is found.
FindBlock PROC NEAR
        les di,[BlockStart]     ; ES:DI=current start
        cmp al,[es:di]          ; compare block types
        je BlockFound           ; equal ?
        push ax                 ; no, save block type
        call NextBlock
```

```
        pop ax                          ; restore block type
        jmp FindBlock                   ; start again
BlockFound:
        ret                             ; block type found
ENDP


; Convert ASCII character to uppercase.
UpCase PROC NEAR
        cmp al,'a'
        jb NoLetter
        cmp al,'z'
        ja NoLetter
        sub al,'a'-'A'
NoLetter:
        ret
ENDP


; Determine the next number in a command string.
ReturnParameter PROC NEAR
        les di,[CommandString]  ; ES:DI
        cmp BYTE PTR [es:di],0   ; zero character ?
        je ReturnParameterError
        xor bh,bh               ; no, no end
SkipRest:
        mov bl,[es:di]          ; BL = character
        cmp bl,0                ; end string ?
        je ReturnParameterError
        inc di                  ; no, increase DI
        cmp bl,'9'              ; is BL a number ?
        ja SkipRest
        cmp bl,'0'
        jb SkipRest
        mov ax,bx               ; yes, AX=BX-'0'
        sub ax,'0'
DetermineNumber:
        mov bl,[es:di]          ; BL = character
        cmp bl,'9'              ; BL again a number ?
        ja EndNumber
        cmp bl,'0'
        jb EndNumber
        sub bx,'0'              ; yes, AX=AX*10+BX-'0'
        mov cx,10
        mul cx
        add ax,bx
```

```
        inc di                  ; next character
        jmp DetermineNumber
EndNumber:
        mov [WORD PTR CommandString],di ; store current
        clc                     ; pointer
        ret
ReturnParameterError:
        mov [WORD PTR CommandString],di
        stc
        ret
ENDP

; Verify whether a string contains a command. If necessary
; call the routine that corresponds to command.
CommandTest PROC NEAR
        les di,[CommandString]  ; ES:DI = start text
        mov si,offset CommandStrings
        xor bx,bx               ; start at DI+0
CompareCommand:
        lodsb                   ; character from table
        cmp al,0                ; end of string ?
        je EndCommand
        call Upcase             ; no
        mov ah,al               ; AH = Upcase(AL)
        mov al,[es:di+bx]       ; character from string
        call Upcase
        inc bx                  ; next character
        cmp al,ah               ; AL=AH ?
        je CompareCommand
        xor ah,ah               ; no, skip rest of the
SkipRestCom:                    ; command string
        lodsb
        or al,al                ; AL=0 ?
        jnz SkipRestCom         ; yes -> Z-flag = 1
SkipCall:
        add si,2                ; skip offset call
        xor bx,bx               ; start of text
        cmp [si],bl             ; end of table ?
        jne CompareCommand
        ret                     ; yes, no command !
EndCommand:
        mov al,[es:di+bx]       ; next character
        call UpCase
        cmp al,'A'              ; is this a letter ?
        jb ProcessCommand
```

```
                cmp al,'Z'
                jb SkipCall
        ProcessCommand:
                add di,bx                       ; no, text the same
                mov WORD PTR [CommandString+0],di
                call WORD PTR [si]
                ret
        ENDP


        ; Process the recorded sample. Bring
        ; VOC block header up to date.
        ProcessRecording PROC NEAR
                mov ax,[WORD PTR SamplePointer+0]
                mov dx,[WORD PTR SamplePointer+2]
                call Calculate20Bits
                mov bx,ax
                mov cx,dx
                mov ax,[WORD PTR BlockStart+0]
                mov dx,[WORD PTR BlockStart+2]
                call Calculate20Bits
                sub bx,ax               ; calculate sample
                sbb cx,dx               ; size
                sub bx,4                ; skip header and
                sbb cx,0                ; the last byte
                les di,[BlockStart]     ; store length in
                mov [es:di+1],bx        ; VOC header
                mov [es:di+3],cl
                les di,[SamplePointer]  ; put an EndBlock type
                mov BYTE PTR [es:di],0  ; at the end
                ret
        ENDP


        ;------------------------------------------------------------
        ; VOC sub-block routines
        ;------------------------------------------------------------


        ; Process a VOC sub-block.
        ProcessVOCBlock PROC NEAR
                cmp [UserRouteFlag],0   ; user routine ?
                je ProcessBlockType
                les bx,[BlockStart]     ; yes, call this routine
                call dword ptr [UserRoutePtr]
                jnc ProcessBlockType    ; process this block ?
```

```
        call NextBlock          ; no, next block
        jmp ProcessVOCBlock     ; start again
ProcessBlockType:
        les di,[BlockStart]     ; ES:DI=start block
        mov bl,[es:di]          ; BL=block type
        cmp bl,7                ; known type ?
        jbe ProcessThisBlock
        call NextBlock          ; no, next block
        jmp ProcessVOCBlock     ; start again
ProcessThisBlock:
        shl bl,1                ; call corresponding
        xor bh,bh               ; routine
        call [bx+offset BlockRoutines]
        call NextBlock          ; for next time
        cmp [ActionFlag],AnotherBlock
        je ProcessVOCBlock      ; or this time ?
        ret                     ; no, ready
ENDP


; The end block, stop playing.
REndBl PROC NEAR
        mov [PlayFlag],0        ; playing stopped
        call RestoreTimerInt    ; restore timer
        mov ax,0
        call SetStatusWord      ; StatusWord=0
        mov [ActionFlag],Nothing ; doing nothing
        ret
ENDP


; New sample + settings.
RNewSampleBl PROC NEAR
        mov [SilenceFlag],0     ; no silence
        mov [PlayFlag],0        ; stop playing
        mov bl,[es:di+4]        ; set the right values
        xor bh,bh               ; based on SR
        shl bx,1
        mov ax,[bx+WaitTable]
        mov [OldTimerICounter],ax
        mov [OldTimerCounter],ax
        mov ax,di               ; sample starts at
        add ax,6                ; offset 6
        mov [WORD PTR SamplePointer+0],ax
        mov [WORD PTR SamplePointer+2],es
        mov ax,[es:di+1]        ; copy length
        mov dl,[es:di+3]
```

```
        xor dh,dh                  ; after 2 bytes
        sub ax,2                   ; are skipped
        sbb dx,0
        mov [WORD PTR SampleLength+0],ax
        mov [WORD PTR SampleLength+2],dx
        mov al,0B6h                ; set sampling rate
        out 43h,al                 ; at timer
        mov ax,[bx+SRConvTable]
        out 40h,al
        mov al,ah
        out 40h,al
        mov [PlayFlag],1           ; start playing
        mov [ActionFlag],Playing
        ret
ENDP

; New sample.
RSampleBl PROC NEAR
        mov [SilenceFlag],0        ; no silence
        mov [PlayFlag],0           ; stop playing
        mov ax,di                  ; set start
        add ax,6                   ; of sample
        mov [WORD PTR SamplePointer+0],ax
        mov [WORD PTR SamplePointer+2],es
        mov ax,[es:di+1]           ; and copy its length
        mov [WORD PTR SampleLength+0],ax
        mov al,[es:di+3]
        xor ah,ah
        mov [WORD PTR SampleLength+2],ax
        mov [ActionFlag],Playing
        mov [PlayFlag],1           ; start playing
        ret
ENDP

; Silence block.
RSilenceBl PROC NEAR
        mov [PlayFlag],0           ; stop playing
        mov bl,[es:di+6]           ; set values based
        xor bh,bh                  ; on SR
        shl bx,1
        mov ax,[bx+WaitTable]
        mov [OldTimerICounter],ax
        mov [OldTimerCounter],ax
        mov ax,[es:di+4]           ; copy length
        mov [WORD PTR SampleLength+0],ax
```

```
        xor  ax,ax
        mov  [WORD PTR SampleLength+2],ax
        mov  al,0B6h              ; set sampling rate
        out  43h,al               ; at the timer
        mov  ax,[bx+SRConvTable]
        out  40h,al
        mov  al,ah
        out  40h,al
        mov  [SilenceFlag],1      ; play abs. silence
        mov  [PlayFlag],1         ; start playing
        mov  [ActionFlag],Playing
        ret
ENDP

; Set status word with new value.
RMarkerBl PROC NEAR
        mov  ax,[es:di+4]         ; get value and
        call SetStatusWord        ; set it
        mov  [ActionFlag],AnotherBlock
        ret
ENDP

; Process a text block. If the first character is #,
; check whether it is a command.
RTextBl PROC NEAR
        add  di,4
        cmp  BYTE PTR [es:di],'#' ; character = # ?
        jne  NoCommand
        inc  di                   ; yes, store start
        mov  [WORD PTR CommandString+0],di
        mov  [WORD PTR CommandString+2],es
        call CommandTest          ; process command
NoCommand:
        mov  [ActionFlag],AnotherBlock
        ret
ENDP

; Start the repetition. Set all right values.
RRepeatStartBl PROC NEAR
        mov  [WORD PTR RepeatStart+0],di
        mov  [WORD PTR RepeatStart+2],es
        mov  ax,[es:di+4]
        inc  ax
        mov  [RepeatCounter],ax
        mov  [RepeatFlag],1
```

```
            mov [ActionFlag],AnotherBlock
            ret
    ENDP


; End of the repetition, start again if necessary.
RRepeatEndBl PROC NEAR
            xor ax,ax                   ; AX=0
            cmp [RepeatFlag],1          ; repetition busy ?
            jne EndRepetition
            mov ax,[RepeatCounter]      ; yes, AX=number of times
            sub ax,1                    ; to come
            jc Infinite                 ; AX was 0 ?
            jz EndRepetition            ; no, ax is 0 ?
            mov [RepeatCounter],ax      ; no, store AX
    Infinite:
            mov ax,[WORD PTR RepeatStart+0]    ; copy
            mov [WORD PTR BlockStart+0],ax     ; start
            mov ax,[WORD PTR RepeatStart+2]    ; repetition
            mov [WORD PTR BlockStart+2],ax
            mov [ActionFlag],AnotherBlock
            ret
    EndRepetition:
            mov [RepeatCounter],ax      ; no further repetition
            mov [RepeatFlag],0
            mov [Actionflag],AnotherBlock
            ret
    ENDP


; The interrupt handler for playing.
PlayingHandler PROC FAR
            push ax                     ; save AX
            cmp [cs:PlayFlag],1         ; play back sample ?
            je YesPlaying
    PlOldTimer:
            dec [cs:OldTimerCounter]    ; no
            jnz NoOldPlCall             ; to old timer ?
            mov ax,[cs:OldTimerICounter] ; yes, restore
            mov [cs:OldTimerCounter],ax  ; counter
            pop ax                      ; restore AX
            jmp DWORD PTR [cs:OldTimerPointer]
    NoOldPlCall:
            mov al,20h                  ; pass on that
            out 20h,al                  ; the interrupt is
            pop ax                      ; received
            iret
```

```
YesPlaying:
        push dx                  ; play back a sample
        push ds
        mov ax,cs                ; DS=CS
        mov ds,ax
        mov al,10h               ; command 10H
        call WriteSB
        cld                      ; decrease length
        sub [WORD PTR SampleLength+0],1
        jnz NoPlEnd
        sub [WORD PTR SampleLength+2],1
        jns NoPlEnd
        mov [PlayFlag],0         ; end of sample
        mov al,20h               ; timer has to be
        out 20h,al               ; processed each time
        sti                      ; turn on interrupts
        push di                  ; save registers
        push es
        push bx
        push cx
        push si
        mov al,128               ; AL=absolute silence
        call WriteSB
        call ProcessVOCBlock
        pop si                   ; restore registers
        pop cx
        pop bx
        pop es
        pop di
        pop ds
        pop dx
        pop ax
        iret
NoPlEnd:
        push es
        push di
        mov al,128               ; AL=absolute silence
        cmp [SilenceFlag],1      ; play silence ?
        je ProcessEffects
PlayNoSilence:
        les di,[SamplePointer]   ; no
        mov al,[es:di]           ; AL=sample value
        add [WORD PTR SamplePointer+0],1
        jnc ProcessEffects
        add [WORD PTR SamplePointer+2],1000h
```

```
ProcessEffects:
        cmp [EffectsFlag],0     ; effect present ?
        jne YesEffects
        jmp NoEffects           ; no, skip it
YesEffects:
        mov dh,[EffectsFlag]    ; DI=effects flag
        mov di,dx
        xx=7*2                  ; TASM variable xx
        REPT 8                  ; repeat block 16 times
        LOCAL NoEditing
        rol di,1                ; apply effect ?
        jnc NoEditing
        call [EffectFunctions+xx] ; yes, call it
NoEditing:
        xx=xx-2
        ENDM                    ; end repeat block
NoEffects:
        pop di                  ; play back value
        pop es
        call WriteSB
        pop ds
        pop dx
        jmp PlOldTimer
ENDP

; The interrupt handler for recording.

RecordingHandler PROC FAR
        push ax                 ; save AX
        cmp [cs:PlayFlag],1     ; record sample ?
        je YesRecording
RecOldTimer:
        dec [cs:OldTimerCounter] ; no
        jnz NoOldRecCall         ; to old timer ?
        mov ax,[cs:OldTimerICounter] ; yes, restore
        mov [cs:OldTimerCounter],ax  ; counter
        pop ax                   ; restore AX
        jmp DWORD PTR [cs:OldTimerPointer]
NoOldRecCall:
        mov al,20h              ; pass on that
        out 20h,al              ; the interrupt is
        pop ax                  ; received
        iret
```

```
YesRecording:
        push dx                         ; record a sample
        push ds
        mov ax,cs                       ; DS=CS
        mov ds,ax
        mov al,20h                      ; command 20H
        call WriteSB
        cld                             ; decrease length
        sub [WORD PTR SampleLength+0],1
        jnz NoRecEnd
        sub [WORD PTR SampleLength+2],1
        jns NoRecEnd
        mov [PlayFlag],0                ; end of sample
        mov al,20h                      ; time has to be
        out 20h,al                      ; processed each time
        sti                             ; turn on interrupts
        push di                         ; save registers
        push es
        push bx
        push cx
        push si
        call ReadSB
        call ProcessRecording
        call REndBl                     ; restore driver
        pop si                          ; restore registers
        pop cx
        pop bx
        pop es
        pop di
        pop ds
        pop dx
        pop ax
        iret
NoRecEnd:
        push es
        push di
        les di,[SamplePointer]  ; no
        call ReadSb
        mov [es:di],al                  ; AL=sample value
        add [WORD PTR SamplePointer+0],1
        jnc NoSegmentOverflow
        add [WORD PTR SamplePointer+2],1000h
NoSegmentOverFlow:
        pop di                          ; play value
        pop es
```

```
        pop ds
        pop dx
        jmp RecOldTimer
ENDP


;--------------------------------------------------------------
; The driver functions
;--------------------------------------------------------------

; Return driver version. This driver
; corresponds with version 1.10.
DetermineVersion PROC NEAR
        mov ax,10Ah              ; AX=version 1.10
        ret
ENDP

; Set base port, first test for
; right port selection.
SetIOBase PROC NEAR
        test ax,0Fh              ; test first 4 bits
        jnz NoRightPort          ; all 0 ?
        cmp ax,210h              ; yes, AX >= 210H ?
        jb NoRightPort
        cmp ax,260h              ; yes, AX <= 260H ?
        ja NoRightPort
        mov [SBIOPort],ax        ; yes, new port
NoRightPort:
        ret
ENDP


; Set right IRQ; since no use is made of
; the DMA, this is a dummy function.
SetIRQ PROC NEAR
        ret
ENDP


; Initialize driver. Test whether the base port
; is correct.
InitDriver PROC NEAR
        call ResetSoundBl
        mov ax,2                 ; wrong port
        jc NoGoodReset
        dec al                   ; turn on speaker
        call SetSpeaker
        mov [InitiationFlag],1   ; initiation OK.
```

```
        mov [ActionFlag],Nothing
        xor ax,ax
NoGoodReset:
        ret
ENDP
; Set speaker position.
SetSpeaker PROC NEAR
        mov ah,0D1h                 ; AH=speaker on
        or al,al
        jnz SpeakerControl
        mov ah,0D3h                 ; AH=speaker off
SpeakerControl:
        mov al,ah                   ; set speaker
        call WriteSB
        ret
ENDP

; Set status word address.
SetStatusAddr PROC NEAR
        mov [WORD PTR StatusPointer+0],di
        mov [WORD PTR StatusPointer+2],es
        ret
ENDP

; Play VOC block.
PlayVocBlock PROC NEAR
        cmp [ActionFlag],Nothing ; not busy ?
        je PlayBlock
        mov ax,1                    ; no, busy !
        ret
PlayBlock:
        mov [OldTimerCounter],1 ; call old timer
        mov ax,di                   ; optimize
        mov dx,es                   ; sample start
        call Minimize
        mov [WORD PTR BlockStart+0],ax
        mov [WORD PTR BlockStart+2],dx
        mov [PlayFlag],0            ; play nothing
        mov ax,offset PlayingHandler
        call SetTimerInt            ; set timer-int.
        mov ax,0FFFFh
        call SetStatusWord          ; StatusWord=0FFFFH
        mov [ActionFlag],Playing
        call ProcessVOCBlock        ; start at first block
```

```
        xor ax,ax
        ret
ENDP

; Record a VOC block.
RecordVOC PROC NEAR
        sub cx,6
        sbb dx,0
        jnc EnoughMemory
        mov ax,2
        stc
        ret
EnoughMemory:
        mov [WORD PTR SampleLength+0],cx
        mov [WORD PTR SampleLength+2],dx
        mov cx,ax
        mov dx,000Fh
        mov ax,4240h
        div cx
        neg ax                  ; SR=256-1000000/rate
        push ax                 ; save for later use
        mov ax,di               ; Optimize ES:DI
        mov dx,es
        call Minimize
        mov di,ax
        mov es,dx
        pop bx                  ; BX=SR
        mov BYTE PTR [es:di],1  ; block type 1
        mov [es:di+4],bl        ; SR
        mov BYTE PTR [es:di+5],0 ; normal 8-bit sample
        mov [WORD PTR BlockStart+0],di
        mov [WORD PTR BlockStart+2],es
        add di,6                ; start of sample data
        mov [WORD PTR SamplePointer+0],di
        mov [WORD PTR SamplePointer+2],es
        xor bh,bh               ; set pointer
        shl bx,1
        push bx
        mov ax,offset RecordingHandler
        call SetTimerInt
        pop bx
        mov ax,[bx+WaitTable]   ; for the old timer
        mov [OldTimerICounter],ax ; call
        mov [OldTimerCounter],ax
        mov al,0B6h             ; set sampling rate
```

```
        out  43h,al                  ; at timer
        mov  ax,[bx+SRConvTable]
        out  40h,al
        mov  al,ah
        out  40h,al
        mov  [PlayFlag],1            ; start recording
        mov  ax,0FFFFh
        call SetStatusWord           ; StatusWord=0FFFFH
        mov  [ActionFlag],Recording
        ret
ENDP


; Stop recording or playing. Restore timer and if
; necessary process block length when recording.
StopVOCProcess PROC NEAR
        cmp  [ActionFlag],Playing ; busy ?
        je   StopPlaying
        cmp  [ActionFlag],Pausing
        je   StopPlaying
        cmp  [ActionFlag],Recording
        je   StopRecording
        mov  ax,1                    ; no !
        ret
StopPlaying:
        mov  [PlayFlag],0            ; stop playing
        call RestoreTimerInt         ; restore timer
        mov  ax,0
        call SetStatusWord           ; delete StatusWord
        mov  [ActionFlag],Nothing
        xor  ax,ax
        ret
StopRecording:
        mov  [PlayFlag],0
        call RestoreTimerInt
        call ProcessRecording
        mov  ax,0
        call SetStatusWord
        mov  [ActionFlag],Nothing
        xor  ax,ax
        ret
ENDP
```

```
; Turn off driver. Stop playing and turn off speaker.
DeInitDriver PROC NEAR
        mov al,0                  ; turn off speaker
        call SetSpeaker
        mov [InitiationFlag],0
        jmp StopVOCProcess
ENDP


; Pause playing.
Pause PROC NEAR
        cmp [ActionFlag],Playing ; busy playing
        je PauseOk
        mov ax,1                  ; no !
        ret
PauseOk:
        mov [ActionFlag],Pausing
        mov al,[PlayFlag]         ; store old flag
        mov [PlayFlag],0          ; stop timer
        mov [PlayBackup],al
        xor ax,ax
        ret
ENDP


; Continue previously paused block.
Continue PROC NEAR
        cmp [ActionFlag],Pausing ; busy pausing ?
        je ContinueOk
        mov ax,1                  ; no !
        ret
ContinueOk:
        mov [ActionFlag],Playing ; busy playing
        mov al,[PlayBackup]       ; set play flag
        mov [PlayFlag],al
        xor al,al
        ret
ENDP
; Leave a repeat loop.
QuitRepeat PROC NEAR
        cmp [RepeatFlag],1       ; busy repeating ?
        je QuitRepeatOk
        mov ax,1                  ; no !
        ret
```

```
QuitRepeatOk:
        mov [RepeatCounter],1  ; last repetition
        cmp ax,0               ; immediately ?
        jne Immediately
        mov ax,0               ; no
        ret
Immediately:
        mov al,RepeatEndBl     ; yes, continue immediately
        call FindBlock
        mov [RepeatCounter],1  ; at block after end
        mov [PlayFlag],0       ; repeat block
        call ProcessVOCBlock
        ret
ENDP

; Set user routine.
UserRoute PROC NEAR
        mov [WORD PTR UserRoutePtr+0],ax
        mov [WORD PTR UserRoutePtr+2],dx
        or ax,dx
        mov [UserRouteFlag],ax
        ret
ENDP

; Set buffer for echo effect and volume effect.
SetBuffer PROC NEAR
        cmp ax,0
        je VolumeBuffer
        mov [WORD PTR EchoBuffer+0],di
        mov [WORD PTR EchoBuffer+2],es
        mov [BufferStart],di
        add cx,di
        mov [BufferEnd],cx
        mov [EchoEnd],cx
        ret
VolumeBuffer:
        mov [WORD PTR VolumeTable+0],di
        mov [WORD PTR VolumeTable+2],es
        mov [MaximumVolume],cl
        mov dl,cl
        mov cl,0
CalcNextVolume:
        mov ch,0
```

```
        CalcSampleValue:
                mov al,ch
                imul cl
                idiv dl
                stosb
                inc ch
                jnz CalcSampleValue
                inc cl
                cmp cl,dl
                jbe CalcNextVolume
                ret
        ENDP

        ; Set an effect by processing a command string.
        ProcessCommandString PROC NEAR
                mov [WORD PTR CommandString+0],di
                mov [WORD PTR CommandString+2],es
                call CommandTest
                ret
        ENDP

        ; Ask current volume.
        CurrentVolumeQ PROC NEAR
                mov al,CurrentVolume
                xor ah,ah
                ret
        ENDP

        ;-------------------------------------------------------------
        ; The interface
        ;-------------------------------------------------------------
        ; This is where the call part starts.
        Control PROC FAR
                push bx                 ; save registers
                push cx
                push dx
                push bp
                push di
                push si
                push ds
                push es
                push cs
                pop ds                  ; DS=CS
                cld
                cmp bx,3                ; BX <= 3 ?
```

```
        jbe CallAllowed
        cmp [InitiationFlag],1   ; no
        je CallAllowed           ; driver init. ?
        mov ax,-1                ; no, wrong function
        jmp short NoCall
CallAllowed:
        cmp bx,13                ; function <= 13 ?
        jbe ProcessFunction
        cmp bx,128               ; no, function < 128 ?
        jae ExtraFunction
        mov ax,-2                ; yes, wrong function
        jmp NoCall
ExtraFunction:
        cmp bx,128+(EffectFunctionsExtraFunctions)/2
        jae NoCall
        sub bx,128-(ExtraFunctions-FunctionTable)/2
ProcessFunction:
        shl bx,1                 ; call function
        call [bx+OFFSET FunctionTable]
NoCall:
        pop es
        pop ds
        pop si
        pop di
        pop bp
        pop dx
        pop cx
        pop bx
        retf
ENDP

END Start
```

Listing 9.18: Basic Program Generating the Two Tables that Are Used in the CT-TIMER

```
100 ' Table creator for CT-TIMER.ASM
110 ' Open used files
120 OPEN "convtabl.inc" FOR OUTPUT AS #1
130 OPEN "waitabl.inc" FOR OUTPUT AS #2
140 ' Calculate for every SR the corresponding values
150 FOR SR!=0! TO 255!
160 ' Calculate the actual sampling rate
170 SAMPLINGRATE! = 1000000!/(256!-SR!)
180 ' Calculate the value for the timer
```

```
190 TIMERRATE = INT(1193280!/SAMPLINGRATE!)
200 ' Calculate the number of times to wait
210 WAITRATE = INT(SAMPLINGRATE!/18.2)
220 ' Write the values to the files
230 IF SR! MOD 6 = 0 THEN GOSUB 300 ELSE GOSUB 340
240 NEXT
250 ' Close files
260 CLOSE #1
270 CLOSE #2
280 END
290 ' Start at a new line
300 PRINT #1, : PRINT #1,CHR$(9);"dw";TIMERRATE;
310 PRINT #2, : PRINT #2,CHR$(9);"dw";WAITRATE;
320 RETURN
330 ' Write the data to the files
340 PRINT #1,",";TIMERRATE;
350 PRINT #2,",";WAITRATE;
360 RETURN
```

CHAPTER

TEN

Programming with MIDI

- Settings and modes for transmitting data with the MIDI protocol

- Reading MIDI implementation charts

- How status bytes work in MIDI

- Voice, Mode, System, and Real Time messages in MIDI

- The MIDI file format

- How MIDI works with the Sound Blaster

This chapter explains programming with MIDI. It alos looks at the various MIDI settings and modes and how they effect sound. It tells you how to read an implementation chart. Next, the chapter explains how status and data bytes work in MIDI, the MIDI file format, and the preculiarities of MIDI as it works with the Sound Blaster.

NOTE   Chapter 4 explains what MIDI is and takes a close look at connecting MIDI devices, at MIDI instruments, and at MIDI software.

MIDI: An Overview

The MIDI (Musical Instrument Digital Interface) protocol includes sixteen channels, each of which can send different data—that is, can send different notes. Because there are sixteen channels, you can play up to sixteen instruments at the same time under the MIDI protocol. One instrument is assigned to each channel.

Many MIDI instruments allow you to set the MIDI channel yourself. Both the master instrument and the slaves can use one MIDI channel. However, in order for, let's say, eight MIDI instruments daisy-chained on *different* channels to play different notes at the same time, you need a sequencer. Only with a sequencer can you transmit different data simultaneously through sixteen channels.

Settings and Modes for Transmitting Data

In the MIDI protocol, there are three settings for determining how MIDI instruments send and receive data. The three settings are Omni, Poly, and Mono.

Omni On and Omni Off   When a MIDI instrument can only send and receive one MIDI channel, this setting is called the Omni off. The Omni off setting is used mainly in MIDI setups that include a sequencer and in setups in which a number of MIDI instruments are interconnected.

With the Omni on setting, the slave can receive all sixteen MIDI channels at the same time. Use this setting when you want to play two or more MIDI instruments at the same time or when you want to play entire compositions on one MIDI instrument.

Mono and Poly   Under the Mono (monophonic) setting, one voice is played on each channel. Under the Poly (polyphonic) setting, more than one voice is played on each channel. The Mono setting is used mainly with MIDI guitars, where every string has its own MIDI channel. For keyboards and synthesizers, the Poly setting is usually used.

> **NOTE**   In electronic music, the term *voice* refers to the sound an instrument makes.

The Four MIDI Modes

To make it easier to choose between Omni, Poly, and Mono settings, the MIDI protocol lets you specify four modes with the Mode selector. These modes are described in Table 10.1.

TABLE 10.1: The Four MIDI Modes

Mode	Description
Mode 1	Omni on and Poly. All sixteen MIDI channels are received with several voices playing at once on every channel.
Mode 2	Omni on and Mono. All sixteen MIDI channels are received but only one voice is played at a time.
Mode 3	Omni off and Poly. Only the selected channel is received, but with several voices. This mode is used most often.
Mode 4	Omni off and Mono. Only the selected MIDI channel is received and, moreover, only one voice per channel is played. Mode 4 mainly applies to MIDI guitars.

Channel and System Messages

Two kinds of messages are exchanged between master and slave instruments: *Channel* messages and *System* messages.

- System messages address the MIDI system as a whole. They are used, for example, to synchronize a sequencer and a synthesizer. System messages can be sent through a random MIDI channel, because System messages are received by each instrument connected to the MIDI system.

- Channel messages concern the music being played. Channel messages are sent through one of the sixteen MIDI channels and can only be received by one MIDI instrument, the instrument that is set at the MIDI channel through which the messages are sent.

Channel Mode and Voice Messages   Channel messages come in two types, Mode messages and Voice messages. Mode messages describe the different modes (see Table 10.1). Voice messages can be divided into five categories:

- Note information. Note information includes instructions about notes, such as when to play a key and when to release it.

- Program changes. A program change is the way a new sound or instrument is selected. For example, if you send a stream of note information to a synthesizer module, the sound that comes out depends on the last program change. If the last program change set the instrument to a piano, it sounds like a piano. You can send program changes in the midst of music data to change instruments whenever you want, as often as you want.

- Control changes. Control change messages change the way an instrument sounds. Whereas program changes switch instruments, control changes modify the sound of the instrument itself.

- Aftertouch effects. Almost all synthesizers possess the Aftertouch effect for re-creating the tonal changes that a note undergoes as it is held. After you press and hold down a key, an Aftertouch message is sent that assigns vibrato or volume change to the note.

- Pitch Bender messages. The Pitch Bender is a small joystick next to the synthesizer keyboard. With this bender you can change the pitch of notes.

NOTE Only a few keyboards have a Pitch Bender or Aftertouch. Messages containing Pitch Bender or Aftertouch information are ignored when they are sent to a keyboard without these functions.

System Exclusive Messages   System messages are received and retransmitted by every connected MIDI instrument. They allow you, for example, to synchronize a sequencer and a synthesizer so they start playing at the same time.

One of the most common types of system messages is the *System Exclusive* (SysEx-System) message. These messages are meant for specific MIDI devices from particular manufacturers. System Exclusive messages allow you to change parameters that are not specified as defaults in the MIDI protocol, but that differ from manufacturer to manufacturer. With SysEx messages you can, for example, change the parameters of a sound to create a nondefined sound.

System exclusive messages always include an ID number that indicates the manufacturer of the device the System Exclusive message is meant for. When a slave receives System Exclusive messages with ID numbers that do not pertain to it, it ignores these messages.

Reading MIDI Implementation Charts

So you can find out what a particular MIDI instrument can do, every MIDI instrument has its own *MIDI implementation chart*. This chart tells exactly what messages the MIDI instrument can and cannot receive and transmit. MIDI implementation charts are standardized. Each chart, no matter who manufactured the MIDI instrument, has the same columns and rows. Only the contents are different.

Figure 10.1 shows a MIDI implementation chart for the MT-32. Figure 10.2 shows one for the DX7, a Yamaha Synthesizer. The MT-32 is a sound module from the Japanese manufacturer Roland. Because the MT-32 is a sound module, it doesn't have a keyboard and thus cannot send musical data. The only data the MT-32 can send is the System Exclusive message that is necessary to respond to System Exclusive messages that are sent to the MT-32. The DX7 has a keyboard, which makes its implementation chart quite different from that of the MT-32.

FIGURE 10.1:

Implementation chart for the MT-32

MULTI TIMBRE SOUND MODULE				
MODEL MT-32				Version: 1.02
MIDI Implementation Chart				
	Function...	Transmitted	Recognized	Remarks
Basic Chanel	Default		2-10	
	Changed		1-8, 10	
Mode	Default		Mode 3	
	Messages			
	Altered	•••••••••••••••		
Note Number		* 0-127	0-127	
	True Voice	•••••••••••••	12-108	
Velocity	Note ON	*	O v=1-127	
	Note OFF	*	X	
After Touch	Key's	*	X	
	Ch's	*	X	
Pitch Bender		*	O 0-24 semi	
Control Change	1	*	O	Modulation
	7	*	O	Part Volume
	10	*	O	Panpot
	11	*	O	Expression
	12			
	:	*	X	
	63			
	64	*	O	Hold 1
	65			
	:	*	X	
	120			
	121	*	O	Reset all controllers
Prog Change		*	O 0-127	
	True #		0-127	
System Exclusive	O	O		
System Common	Song Pos	X	X	
	Song Sel	X	X	
	Tune	X	X	
System Real Time	Clock	X	X	
	Commands	X	X	
Aux Message	Local ON/OFF	X	X	
	All Notes OFF	X	O (123-127)	
	Active Sense	X	O	
	Reset	X	X	
Notes		* in OVERFLOW MODE received message goes thru MIDI OUT.		

Mode 1: OMNI ON, POLY   Mode 2: OMNI ON, MONO
Mode 3: OMNI OFF, POL   Mode 4: OMNI OFF, MONO

FIGURE 10.2:

Implementation chart for the DX7

Yamaha digital programmable algorithm synthesizer
Model DX7

MIDI Implementation Chart

	Function...	Transmitted	Recognized	Remarks
Basic Chanel	Default	1	1	
	Changed	X	1-16	
Mode	Default	Mode 3	Mode 3	
	Messages	X	omni on, poly, mono	
	Altered			
Note Number		36-96	0-127	
	True Voice			
Velocity	Note ON	O	O	
	Note OFF	X (9n 0vh)	X	
After Touch	Key's	X	X	Older Dx7's used
	Ch's	O	O	control 3 for this message
Pitch Bender		O	O	
Control Change	1	O	O	Mod
	2	O	O	Breath
	4	O	O	Food Control
	6	O	O	Data entry
	64	O	O	Sustain
	65	O	O	Portamento
	96/97	O	O	+/-
Prog Change		0-63	0-127	
	True #		1-32	
System Exclusive		O	O	Data dumps, parameters
System Common	:Song Pos.	X	X	
	:Song Sel	X	X	
	:Tune	X	X	
System Real Time	:Clock	X	X	
	:Commands	X	X	
Aux Message	:Local ON/OFF	X	X	
	:All Notes OFF	X	O	
	:Active Sense	O	O	
	Reset	X	X	
Notes				

Mode 1: OMNI ON, POLY   Mode 2: OMNI ON, MONO
Mode 3: OMNI OFF, POL   Mode 4: OMNI OFF, MONO
O=Yes   X=No

A MIDI implementation chart has four columns titled Function, Transmitted, Recognized, and Remarks:

Column	Meaning
Function	Indicates the different parts that are of importance to linking MIDI instruments.
Transmitted	Indicates what functions can be transmitted by the MIDI instrument.
Recognized	Indicates what functions can be received by the MIDI instrument.
Remarks	Contains remarks concerning the different functions.

At the bottom of the chart, modes 1 to 4 are listed with their definitions and the symbols that define yes and no. On most charts, an *O* indicates the presence of a function and an *X* indicates the absence of a function.

Asterisks in a chart indicate that the corresponding function does not apply to the MIDI instrument. When a function is confirmed with a *O*, it is often accompanied by a couple of numbers. These numbers indicate the value range of the function.

Functions on MIDI Implementation Charts

To give you a better understanding of MIDI implementation charts, following is a detailed explanation of the functions:

Basic Channel

Default	These are the channels that are selected when the device is switched on.
Changed	These channels can be chosen by means of, for example, the MIDI Channel button on the synthesizer.

Mode

Default:	When the instrument is switched on, this is the active mode.

Messages:	Which Mode messages can be sent and received.
Altered:	Whether the modes are altered when a Mode message is transmitted.
Note Number	The total number of notes that can be sent or received.
True Voice:	Notes that are too high or too low will sometimes be played in a lower or higher octave. This row indicates which notes can be played without being modified.

Velocity

Note On	The values of the key-down velocity.
Note Off	The values of the key-up velocity.

Aftertouch — How the vibrato or volume change of notes are handled

Key's	Whether the MIDI instrument can handle polyphonic aftertouch (aftertouch for every note being played).
Channel's	Whether the MIDI instrument handle channel aftertouch.

Pitch Bender — Whether it is possible to process Pitch Bender information and, if so, what the value range of the Pitch Bender is.

Control Change — Indicates which Control Change messages the MIDI instrument can send or receive.

Program Change — Indicates which Program Change messages the MIDI instrument can send and receive.

True	This indicates whether numbers that are too high are referred back to other numbers.

System Exclusive	Whether the MIDI instrument can send or receive System Exclusive messages.

System Common

Song Position	Whether the MIDI instrument works with a MIDI Song Position Pointer in a MIDI-oriented environment so that the position in a piece of music can be passed on.
Song Select	If the instrument does work with a Position Pointer, whether the song can be selected.
Tune	Whether it is also possible to select an accompanying rhythm.

System Real Time

Clock	Whether the MIDI instrument can handle System Real Time Clock messages. (If it can, it can be synchronized with another instrument.)
Commands	Whether System Real Time commands also let the MIDI instrument know when to start and to stop.

Aux Message

Local ON/OFF	When Local is ON, the played notes will also be heard on the MIDI instrument (in contrast to Local OFF).
All Notes OFF	Whether all notes can be switched off at once.
Active Sense	Whether the MIDI instrument can receive messages or whether it sends messages itself to verify whether the MIDI instrument is still active.
Reset	Whether the MIDI instrument can be reset (in the same state the instrument is in when it is started).

Notes	This column usually contains supplements and exceptions to various rules.

MIDI Specifications

The default cables used for MIDI have 5-pin DIN plugs. The cables are shielded twisted-pair cables with the protection fixed onto pin 2 for both ends. The twisted pair is connected to pins 4 and 5. Pins 1 and 3 are not connected. We advise you not to use cables longer than fifty feet (fifteen meters).

The MIDI interface is an asynchronous serial interface with a baud rate of 31.25. In other words, 31,250 bits per second are transmitted. There are eight data bits, with one start bit and one stop bit.

Status Bytes and Data Bytes

The bytes that are sent can be subdivided into two groups, status bytes and data bytes:

- Status bytes are the actual commands. Status bytes can be recognized easily. The value of a status byte is always between 128 and 255 (because the most significant bit of the status byte always =0).

- Data bytes contain the corresponding information. The most significant bit of the data bytes is always =0, so data bytes have a value between 0 and 127. It is easy to see where a new command starts. You only have to wait for a byte with a value greater than or equal to 128.

The MIDI protocol is based on sixteen independent MIDI channels. The four lowest bits of the byte are used to choose the channel, as four bits are enough to represent the number 0 through 15.

A status byte can affect only one MIDI channel. To affect more MIDI channels, you have to send the same number of status bytes together with the accompanying data bytes to every channel. However, status bytes with a value from 240 to 255 apply to all channels and therefore have sixteen possible functions.

Figure 10.3 shows the structure of a status byte.

FIGURE 10.3:

The structure of a status byte

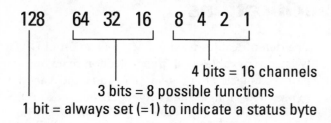

Status bytes with a value from 128–239 are called Voice messages because these messages are intended for only one voice. Status bytes in the range 250–255 are System messages. System messages relate to the MIDI system and therefore have to be sent through all channels.

> **NOTE**   See "Channel and System Messages" earlier in this chapter for an explanation of system messages.

Status bytes are classified as follows:

Status Bytes	Use
128–143	Indicate the Note Off data. This means that the struck note will be released. The status byte is followed by two data bytes, the first indicating the pitch and the second indicating the key-up velocity.
144–159	Indicate the Note On data. This message is generated when a note is struck. The status byte is followed by two bytes, the first indicating the note value and the second indicating the key-down velocity. Table 10.2 shows the note numbers with the corresponding octave numbers and notes.

Status Bytes	Use
160–175	Describe the Key Pressure. Key Pressure is the same as Polyphonic Aftertouch, which means that Aftertouch codes are generated for every note played. The status byte again is followed by two bytes, the first indicating the pitch and the second indicating the pressure value.
176–191	Are Parameter bytes that indicate the controller number and value. The first of the two bytes that follow indicates the controller number and the second indicates its value. Table 10.3 shows the controllers with their number, function, value, and use.
192–207	Indicate the Program Change. The status byte is followed by one byte indicating the number of the new sound.
208–223	Describe the Channel Pressure. In contrast to Key Pressure, this time the Aftertouch code per channel is passed on. The status byte is only accompanied by one byte and it indicates the value of the channel pressure.
224–239	Contain Pitch Wheel data. The Pitch Wheel allows you to easily change the pitch of the played note. The Pitch Wheel is similar to a small analog joystick that detects very small changes. That's why two bytes are added constituting a 14-bit number. A Pitch Wheel message has the following structure:

1110CCCC 0LLLLLLL 0HHHHHHH

where the Cs indicate the channels, the Ls represent the lowest 7-bit values, and the Hs represent the highest 7-bit values. |

TABLE 10.2: Note Numbers with their Octave Numbers and Notes

Octave Number												
	C	C#	D	D#	E	F	F#	G	G#	A	A#	B
0	0	1	2	3	4	5	6	7	8	9	10	11
1	12	13	14	15	16	17	18	19	20	21	22	23
2	24	25	26	27	28	29	30	31	32	33	34	35
3	36	37	38	39	40	41	42	43	44	45	46	47
4	48	49	50	51	52	53	54	55	56	57	58	59
5	60	61	62	63	64	65	66	67	68	69	70	71
6	72	73	74	75	76	77	78	79	80	81	82	83
7	84	85	86	87	88	89	90	91	92	93	94	95
8	96	97	98	99	100	101	102	103	104	105	106	107
9	108	109	110	111	112	113	114	115	116	117	118	119
10	120	121	122	123	124	125	126	127				

Voice, Mode, and System Messages

Following is a look at Voice, Mode, and System messages and how they are transmitted in MIDI.

Voice Messages

The rule of the "running status byte" applies to all Voice messages. In other words,, you don't have to send a status byte before every data byte, because when two or more Voice messages are generated consecutively on the same channel, the status byte may be left out. The data bytes are immediately followed by the data bytes of the next message of the same type. Because all data bytes are less than 128, a byte greater than 127 indicates a message of another type.

Velocity data bytes are represented according to a logarithmic scale. MIDI devices that cannot generate velocity always send a velocity value of 64.

TABLE 10.3: Controller Numbers

Number	Function	Value	Use
0	Continuous controller #0	0–127	MSB
1	Modulation Wheel	0–127	MSB
2	Breath Control	0–127	MSB
3	Continuous controller #3	0–127	MSB
4	Foot Controller	0–127	MSB
5	Portamento time	0–127	MSB
6	Data Entry	0–127	MSB
7	Main Volume	0–127	MSB
8	Continuous controller #8	0–127	MSB
9	Continuous controller #9	0–127	MSB
"	"	"	"
31	Continuous controller #31	0–127	MSB
32	Continuous controller #0	0–127	LSB
33	Modulation Wheel	0–127	LSB
34	Breath Control	0–127	LSB
35	Continuous controller #3	0–127	LSB
36	Foot controller	0–127	LSB
37	Portamento time	0–127	LSB
38	Data Entry	0–127	LSB
39	Main Volume	0–127	LSB
40	Continuous controller #8	0–127	LSB
41	Continuous controller #9	0–127	LSB

TABLE 10.3: Controller Numbers (continued)

Number	Function	Value	Use
"	"	"	"
63	Continuous controller #31	0–127	LSB
64	Damper pedal on/off (sustain)	0=off	127=on
65	Portamento on/off	0=off	127=on
66	Sostenuto on/off	0=off	127=on
67	Soft pedal on/off	0=off	127=on
68	Undefined on/off	0=off	127=on
69	Hold 2	0=off	127=on
70	Undefined on/off	0=off	127=on
"	"	"	"
80	General purpose controller #5	0–127	MSB
81	General purpose controller #6	0–127	MSB
82	General purpose controller #7	0–127	MSB
83	General purpose controller #8	0–127	MSB
84	Undefined on/off	0=off	127=on
85	Undefined on/off	0=off	127=on
86	General purpose controller #5	0–127	LSB
87	General purpose controller #6	0–127	LSB
88	General purpose controller #7	0–127	LSB
89	General purpose controller #8	0–127	LSB
90	Undefined on/off	0=off	127=on
91	Undefined on/off	0=off	127=on

TABLE 10.3: Controller Numbers (continued)

Number	Function	Value	Use
92	Tremolo Depth	0–127	
93	Chorus Depth	0–127	
94	Detune	0–127	
95	Phaser Depth	0–127	
96	Data Entry +1	127	
97	Data Entry −1	127	
98	Nonregistered parameter MSB		
99	Nonregistered parameter LSB		
100	Registered parameter MSB		
101	Registered parameter LSB		
102	Undefined	?	
"	"	"	"
121	Undefined	?	
122	Local Control on/off	0=off	127=on
123	All notes off	0	
124	Omni mode off (incl. all notes off)	0	
125	Omni mode on (incl. all notes off)	0	
126	Mono mode on (incl. all notes off)	*	
127	Poly mode on (incl. mono=off and all notes off)	0	

* This value is equal to the number of channels or equal to 0 when the number of channels is equal to the number of channels of the receiving device.

The value of the Pitch Wheel bytes ranges from 0 to 16383. When the Pitch Wheel is in rest position, the value is equal to 8192.

Mode Messages

Mode messages have a status byte that ranges from 176 to 191, and the first data byte has a value between 122 and 127. The Mode messages are as follows:

- Local Control. The first data byte has the value 122, and the second byte is 0 if local control is off and 127 if local control is on. When local control is on, all notes played on the keyboard are actually played on the MIDI instrument. If local control is off, the MIDI instrument doesn't play anything. In both cases, the data of the played notes are generated and sent to the MIDI Out port.

- All Notes Off. Here, the first data byte has the value 23 and the second has the value 0. This function disables all notes played on the MIDI channel indicated by the status byte.,

- Omni Mode Off. The first data byte has the value 24 and the second is 0. This function indicates that voice messages are only received on the base channel.

- Omni Mode On. This function indicates that all MIDI channels can receive voice messages. The first data byte is 125 and the second is 0.

- Monophonic Mode. Here, the first data byte has the value 126 and the second byte indicates the number of monophonic channels. If the second byte has the value 0, the number of channels is equal to the numbers of voices of the receiving device. This mode assigns exactly one voice to each channel.

- Polyphonic Mode. This function indicates that every channel can receive several voices. The first byte has the value 127 and the second byte is 0.

A combination of the last four Mode messages results in Modes 1 to 4 (see Table 10.1 earlier in this chapter). If a receiving MIDI device does not support a certain mode, it usually switches over to Mode 1.

System Messages

Messages with status byte numbers 240 to 247 are System messages. As explained earlier in this chapter, System messages are specific to the device and are always indicated in the MIDI implementation chart. System messages include the following status bytes:

Status Byte	Meaning
240	Indicates a System Exclusive (SysEx) command. Here the manufacturer can place all functions a MIDI instrument generates that are *not* specified by the MIDI protocol. A SysEx command contains a variable number of data bytes. The end of a System Exclusive command is indicated by status byte number 247, the Terminator message, or by a new status byte.
241	This byte is undefined.
242	Determines the Song Position. This is intended especially for MIDI sequencers. The Song Position allows sequencers to start at any point in a piece of music. The status byte is followed by two data bytes that constitute a 14-bit number; the seven lowest bits come first. The song position is indicated in beats, with one beat equal to six MIDI clock ticks.
243	Is defined to execute a Song Select. It is followed by one data byte indicating the number of the selected song.
244	This byte is undefined.
245	This byte is undefined.
246	Indicates a Tune Request. The Tune Request doesn't contain any data bytes. This command instructs analog synthesizers to tune their oscillators.
247	Is the status byte number of the End Of Exclusive (EOX), or Terminator, command. It contains no data bytes. The terminator is used to indicate the end of a System Exclusive block.

System Exclusive Blocks   A System Exclusive block may only contain data bytes. Using a Terminator message at the end of a SysEx block is optional. The first data byte of a SysEx block is always the MIDI ID number. This ID number is a unique number for manufacturers of MIDI devices, established by the MIDI Association. Numbers 1 to 31 are allocated to American manufacturers, numbers 32 to 63 to European manufacturers, and numbers between 64 to 95 to Japanese manufacturers.

The most important manufacturers as far as Sound Blaster is concerned are:

1 Sequential Circuits

2 Big Briar

3 Octave/Plateau

4 Moog

5 Passport Designs

32 Bon Tempi

33 S.I.E.L.

34 Ircam

35 SynthAxe

36 Hohner

64 Kawai

65 Roland

66 Korg

66 Yamaha

67 Casio

NOTE   Appendix F lists the codes for all MIDI instrument manufacturers.

Real Time Messages

The last group of messages are Real Time messages. The status bytes of these messages range from 248 to 255. Real Time messages can be inserted between the other messages and have the same size as the status bytes themselves; they don't contain any data bytes. Real Time messages depend on the device, so they are always indicated in the MIDI Implementation Chart. Real Time messages are as follows:

Message	Explanation
Timing Clock	Status byte 248. A timing clock message is sent every 24 clock ticks in a quarter note and is often used to synchronize MIDI instruments and drum machines.
Start	Status byte 250. This is the start command for sequencers and drum machines.
Continue	Status byte 251. This message instructs the device to continue playing on the next clock tick.
Stop	Status byte 252. Instructs the sequencer or drum machine to stop playing.
Active Sensing	Status byte 254. The active sensing byte is sent every 300 milliseconds. It allows the receiving devices to detect any disturbances and to switch over to another mode.
System Reset	Status byte 255. When a system reset message is sent, every receiving device returns to the state it was in when it was turned on. Think of this message as a kind of emergency brake.

To give you an idea of how these messages work, consider the following example. A keyboard is connected to the Sound Blaster through the MIDI Connector Box. MIDI channel 4 on the keyboard is selected. The implementation chart indicates that this keyboard generates a velocity 64 for Note On and a velocity 0 for Note Off. You play a note, and then you select another sound. You play another note and hold the key down, and you play another note and release the key you were holding down. The Sound Blaster receives the following bytes:

147 50 64 50 0 195 4 157 55 64 55 0 59 64 62 64 62 0 59 0

Byte 147 is a status byte that means Note On channel 4. It has to be followed by two data bytes indicating the pitch and the velocity of the note. A D in octave 4 is played at a velocity 64. The next byte is not a status byte. This means that another Note On message is sent on the same channel. The same note now has the velocity 0, which means that the key is released. The next byte is a status byte indicating a Program Change on Channel 4. The value of the selected sound is 4. Next comes a Note On status byte indicating the G in octave 4. This note is held down and released two bytes later. The bytes 59 and 64 result in a Note On message for the B in octave 4. While this note is pressed, the D in octave 5 is also pressed (62 64).

The only information missing at this moment is the time the messages are received, which means we don't know how long the different notes are held down. Fortunately, the computer has a solution for this problem, as the next section explains.

The MIDI File Format

MIDI data cannot be stored just like that. For a text file you only have to store the characters and codes of which the text is composed. In the MIDI format, on the other hand, the time at which the MIDI data have to be played is very important. Simply pasting the time before a MIDI message and writing it to a file would not suffice.

Delta Time Because status bytes are always greater than or equal to 80H and the values of data bytes are always less than 80H, it is easy to detect the start of a message. Processing the start time of a message is very important. The MIDI protocol specifies that the first message always start at time 0. The times of the following messages are calculated on the basis of the difference in time between a message and the preceding message. In the protocol this is called the *delta time* and you want to be sure to define this time correctly so the beginning of messages can be found.

The last byte of the delta time always has to be less than 128 (bit 7, the data byte, is reset), and the preceding bytes always have to be greater than or equal to 128 (bit 7, the status byte, is set). This way, you can easily locate the beginning of a message. However, calculating the delta time can be complicated.

Storing data this way is called *variable length* storage. The list below demonstrates that converting to variable length storage can lead to some confusion. The left column lists the variable length numbers and the right column shows their normal equivalents. Both sets of numbers are in hexadecimals.

Variable Length Numbers	Normal Equivalent Numbers
7FH	7FH
81H	80H
C000H	2000H
7FFFH	3FFFH
8180H	4000H
C08000H	100000H
FFFF7FH	1FFFFFH
81808000H	200000H
C0808000H	8000000H
FFFFFF7FH	FFFFFFFH

MIDI's Header and Track Block Structure

The MIDI file format consists of blocks. There are two types of blocks: header blocks and track blocks. Each file has one header block and can contain several track blocks:

- The header block contains information that is necessary for the MIDI file.
- The track blocks contain MIDI data streams with information about, at most, sixteen MIDI channels.

Header Blocks

A header block has the following structure:

    MThd < header data length > < header data >

The header data is divided into the following parts:

< format > < number of tracks > < division >

In detail, the header looks as follows:

- 4 bytes with the letters *MThd*
- 4 bytes indicating the header data length
- 2 bytes for the format
- 2 bytes for the number of tracks in the file
- 2 bytes for the division

The most significant byte comes first. In general, the length of the header data is equal to 00000006H.

The Two Format Bytes   The two format bytes indicate the file type of the MIDI file. There are three different file types: 0, 1, and 2:

File Type	Description
0	The MIDI file consists of one track containing the data of all sixteen MIDI channels.
1	The MIDI file consists of one or more synchronized tracks.
2	The MIDI file consists of one or more independent tracks.

The next two bytes contain the number of tracks the MIDI file is composed of. The last two bytes establish the division of a quarter note. The delta time depends on this division. A division of 1 means that a delta time of 2 is equal to the time of a half note. Sometimes these two bytes have a negative value. In that case, the time division is measured in seconds. This time is converted to the more common standards of time measurement, the SMPTE and MTC formats. The highest byte can have the value –24, –25, –29, or –30. These numbers come from the world of video and represent the number of frames per second. The second byte indicates the subdivision within one frame. This must be a positive number. The most common values are 4, 8, 10, 80, and 100.

Track Blocks

The track blocks are defined as follows:

> MTrk < track data length > < track data >

where:

< track data >	=	< MTrk event > *
		(* = repetition possible)
< MTrk event >	=	< delta time > < event >
< event >	=	< MIDI event > or
		< SysEx event > or
		< meta event >

The variable length method is used to store the delta time. A MIDI event includes all MIDI channel messages. The running status method also applies here. The first event in the track data, however, has to contain a status byte.

The MIDI File Format and SysEx Messages

System Exclusive messages constitute a problem within the MIDI file format. SysEx messages can terminate with the value F7H, a value greater than 128 that can easily be considered the first byte of a variable length value. To solve this problem, the SysEx *event* is created. There are two types of SysEx events:

> F0H < length > < bytes following the F0H byte >
>
> F7H < length > < all bytes that have to be sent >

The reason for having two SysEx events is that some manufacturers transmit their System Exclusive messages as packets.

The length is stored using the variable length method and indicates the number of bytes that follow. The first SysEx event is used to store entire System Exclusive messages. The second event handles the packets. The running status may not be used.

A SysEx event at the end of an F0H or at the end of the last packet of an F7H event always has to terminate with an F7H. When the master has not sent F7H, the program has to add this byte itself.

When packets are sent, the first packet is always sent together with an F0H event, but is not terminated by an F7H. The next packets are all sent together with an F7H event. The last packet has to end with F7H. The F7H event can also be used to send messages that in fact are of no importance. Real Time, Song Pointer, and MIDI Time Code messages can be stored in these messages but they have to be ignored. These F7H events don't have to end with an F7H.

Meta Events and the MIDI File Format

Meta events are events containing non-MIDI information that are useful to this file format. Meta events have the following syntax:

FFH < type > < length > < data bytes >

The type indicating the event number is a byte with a value less than 128. The length of the upcoming data bytes is calculated according to the variable length method. The data bytes contain the data that apply to the meta event. Just as with System Exclusive events, the running status method may not be used.

A message always has to contain a status byte. Meta events that cannot be recognized by a program have to be skipped. Following is a description of the meta events that have to be recognized.

FFH 00H 02H ss ss Sequence Number   When this event is used, it has to be placed at the beginning of a track, even before the delta time and the MIDI events. The sequence number assigns a certain value to the track so you can wind or rewind these numbers using a cue message.

Meta event numbers 1 through 0FH are allocated to the text that can be placed in a song.

FFH 01H Length Text Event   Text events are placed at the beginning of a track and can contain a variety of text.

FFH 02H Length Text Copyright Notice   This event, which must be the first event at time 0 in the first track block, has to contain the characters (C), the year of the copyright, and the owner.

FFH 03H Length Text Sequence/Track Name   When this event is present in a track of file format 0 or in the first track of file format 1, the name refers to the sequence name. In all other cases the name indicates the track name.

FFH 04H Length Text Instrument Name   This event gives a description of the instrument used in the track.

FFH 05H Length Text Lyric   Here you can indicate the lyrics of the song. Usually you split up the lyrics and place them as lyric events at the delta times where the words have to be sung.

FFH 06H Length Text Marker   Indicates the name of the position in the sequence. The marker event occurs in file format 0 or in the first track of format 1.

FFH 07H Length Text Cue Point   The Cue point event carries the text that is applicable at a particular moment. For instance, a collapsing building could be accompanied by music and the text "House Knocked Down."

FFH 2FH 00H End of Track   The End of track event is not optional like all the other meta events. It must be placed at the end of a track to indicate the exact end of the track.

FFH 51H 03H tt tt tt Set Tempo   The Set tempo event is measured in the number of microseconds per MIDI quarter note. This event results in a change of tempo.

FFH 54H 05H hr min sec Frames Fractional Frames SMPTE Offset
This event indicates the SMPTE time at which a track has to start. The format is in SMPTE time; fractional frames indicate the number of hundredths of a second within one frame.

In file format 1, this event has to be defined together with the set tempo event. The SMPTE event must always be placed at the beginning of a track, before the delta time and before any other MIDI events.

FFH 58H 04H nn dd cc bb Time Signature   The Time signature event sets the time units that are used in the MIDI format. The *nn* stands for the numerator and the *dd* for the denominator of the time signature. The denominator is described as the negative power of 2. The *cc* parameter indicates the number of MIDI clock ticks within one metronome click (beat). The *bb* parameter indicates how many thirty-second notes can take place within one MIDI quarter note.

For example, the event FFH 58H 04H 06H 03H 24H 08H indicates that the time is described as 6/8 (because 2 to the power of −3 equals 1/8), so that 32 MIDI clock ticks occur in one beat and that eight thirty-second notes take place within one MIDI quarter note.

FFH 59H 02H sf mi Key Signature   This event defines the number of flats, sharps, and keys. For instance, sf=−5 means five flats, sf=5 means five sharps, sf=−1 means one flat, sf=0 is the key of C, mi=0 is the major key, and mi=1 is the minor key.

FFH 7FH Length Data Sequencer Specific Meta Event   You'll often find this meta event in the appendix of sequencer manuals because every manufacturer has its own definition for this event. Anyhow, the first byte of the data values is the manufacturer's ID number.

Now that we have examined the entire MIDI file format, the time has come to give a practical example. Figure 10.4 shows a song from the popular Wing Commander game.

MIDI and the Sound Blaster's DSP Chip

The Sound Blaster's DSP chip processes the MIDI data. This chip stores the incoming MIDI data in a 64KB buffer and sends the outgoing MIDI data to the MIDI output.

Because the MIDI system's baud rate is 31,250 baud, the MIDI data have to be handled carefully and quickly. If, let's say, approximately 3906 bytes per second are received, the buffer will be full in almost 1/50 of a second and the old MIDI data will be overwritten.

FIGURE 10.4:

Song from the Wing Commander game

```
4D 54 68 64 00 00 00 06-00 01 00 0E 01 E0 4D 54    MThd..........MT
72 6B 00 00 05 DB 00 FF-03 1F 42 61 72 72 61 63    rk........Barrac
6B 73 2D 47 6F 20 54 6F-20 53 6C 65 65 70 20 59    ks-Go To Sleep Y
6F 75 20 50 69 6C 6F 74-73 00 FF 54 05 60 00 00    ou Pilots..T.`..
00 00 00 FF 58 04 04 02-18 08 00 FF 51 03 09 62    ....X.......Q..b
58 83 60 FF 51 03 08 E3-64 83 60 FF 51 03 08 95    X.`.Q...d.`.Q...
44 83 60 FF 51 03 08 50-E8 83 60 FF 51 03 08 50    D.`.Q...P..`.Q..P
E8 83 60 FF 51 03 08 A8-CC 83 60 FF 51 03 08 8B    ..`.Q.....`.Q...
80 83 60 FF 51 03 08 95-44 83 60 FF 51 03 08 F6    ..`.Q...D.`.Q...
EC 83 60 FF 51 03 08 B2-90 83 60 FF 51 03 09 3B    ..`.Q.....`.Q..;
48 83 60 FF 51 03 08 B2-90 83 60 FF 51 03 08 9F    H.`.Q.....`.Q...
08 83 60 FF 51 03 08 C6-18 83 60 FF 51 03 09 B0    ..`.Q.....`.Q...
78 83 60 FF 51 03 08 CF-DC 83 60 FF 51 03 09 58    x.`.Q.....`.Q..X
94 83 60 FF 51 03 07 D1-F4 83 60 FF 51 03 08 E3    ..`.Q.....`.Q...
64 83 60 FF 51 03 08 81-BC 83 60 FF 51 03 08 81    d.`.Q.....`.Q...
BC 83 60 FF 51 03 08 8B-80 83 60 FF 51 03 08 64    ..`.Q.....`.Q..d
70 83 60 FF 51 03 08 ED-28 83 60 FF 51 03 08 64    p.`.Q...(.`.Q..d
70 83 60 FF 51 03 09 14-38 83 60 FF 51 03 08 A8    p.`.Q...8.`.Q...
CC 83 60 FF 51 03 08 BC-54 83 60 FF 51 03 08 6E    ..`.Q...T.`.Q..n
34 83 60 FF 51 03 08 64-70 83 60 FF 51 03 08 A8    4.`.Q..dp.`.Q...
CC 83 60 FF 51 03 08 8B-80 83 60 FF 51 03 08 A8    ..`.Q.....`.Q...
CC 83 60 FF 51 03 08 47-24 83 60 FF 51 03 08 3D    ..`.Q..G$.`.Q..=
60 83 60 FF 51 03 08 D9-A0 83 60 FF 51 03 08 C6    `.`.Q.....`.Q...
18 83 60 FF 51 03 08 64-70 83 60 FF 51 03 08 ED    ..`.Q..dp.`.Q...
28 83 60 FF 51 03 07 EF-40 83 60 FF 51 03 08 C6    (.`.Q...@.`.Q...
18 83 60 FF 51 03 08 95-44 83 60 FF 51 03 08 ED    ..`.Q...D.`.Q...
28 83 60 FF 51 03 08 B2-90 83 60 FF 51 03 08 CF    (.`.Q.....`.Q...
DC 83 60 FF 51 03 08 BC-54 83 60 FF 51 03 09 9C    ..`.Q...T.`.Q...
F0 83 60 FF 51 03 08 5A-AC 83 60 FF 51 03 09 4E    ..`.Q..Z..`.Q..N
D0 83 60 FF 51 03 08 E3-64 83 60 FF 51 03 08 C6    ..`.Q...d.`.Q...
18 83 60 FF 51 03 08 ED-28 83 60 FF 51 03 09 27    ..`.Q...(.`.Q..'
C0 83 60 FF 51 03 08 C6-18 83 60 FF 51 03 08 CF    ..`.Q.....`.Q...
DC 83 60 FF 51 03 08 95-44 83 60 FF 51 03 08 B2    ..`.Q...D.`.Q...
90 83 60 FF 51 03 09 14-38 83 60 FF 51 03 08 CF    ..`.Q...8.`.Q...
DC 83 60 FF 51 03 08 D9-A0 83 60 FF 51 03 08 CF    ..`.Q.....`.Q...
DC 83 60 FF 51 03 09 14-38 83 60 FF 51 03 08 C6    ..`.Q...8.`.Q...
18 83 60 FF 51 03 08 D9-A0 83 60 FF 51 03 08 33    ..`.Q.....`.Q..3
9C 83 60 FF 51 03 07 0E-A4 83 60 FF 51 03 07 EF    ..`.Q.....`.Q...
40 83 60 FF 51 03 08 0C-8C 83 60 FF 51 03 07 AA    @.`.Q.....`.Q...
E4 83 60 FF 51 03 08 0C-8C 83 60 FF 51 03 07 E5    ..`.Q.....`.Q...
7C 83 60 FF 51 03 07 D1-F4 83 60 FF 51 03 07 53    |.`.Q.....`.Q..S
00 83 60 FF 51 03 08 6E-34 83 60 FF 51 03 08 D9    ..`.Q..n4.`.Q...
A0 83 60 FF 51 03 07 D1-F4 83 60 FF 51 03 08 3D    ..`.Q.....`.Q..=
60 83 60 FF 51 03 07 F9-04 83 60 FF 51 03 08 C6    `.`.Q.....`.Q...
18 83 60 FF 51 03 08 A8-CC 83 60 FF 51 03 07 E5    ..`.Q.....`.Q...
7C 83 60 FF 51 03 07 BE-6C 83 60 FF 51 03 08 81    |.`.Q...l.`.Q...
BC 83 60 FF 51 03 07 C8-30 83 60 FF 51 03 08 D9    ..`.Q...0.`.Q...
A0 83 60 FF 51 03 08 64-70 83 60 FF 51 03 08 5A    ..`.Q..dp.`.Q..Z
AC 83 60 FF 51 03 08 6E-34 83 60 FF 51 03 07 E5    ..`.Q..n4.`.Q...
7C 83 60 FF 51 03 08 29-D8 83 60 FF 51 03 07 F9    |.`.Q..)..`.Q...
04 83 60 FF 51 03 08 0C-8C 83 60 FF 51 03 08 02    ..`.Q.....`.Q...
C8 83 60 FF 51 03 08 95-44 83 60 FF 51 03 09 0A    ..`.Q...D.`.Q...
74 83 60 FF 51 03 09 C4-00 83 60 FF 51 03 08 B2    t.`.Q.....`.Q...
90 00 FF 58 04 04 02 18-08 83 60 FF 51 03 07 70    ...X......`.Q..p
4C 83 60 FF 51 03 08 0C-8C 83 60 FF 51 03 07 83    L.`.Q.....`.Q...
D4 83 60 FF 51 03 08 95-44 83 60 FF 51 03 07 E5    ..`.Q...D.`.Q...
```

FIGURE 10.4:

Song from the Wing Commander
game (continued)

```
7C 83 60 FF 51 03 08 02-C8 83 60 FF 51 03 08 20    |.'.Q.....'.Q..
14 83 60 FF 51 03 08 5A-AC 83 60 FF 51 03 08 16    ..'.Q..Z..'.Q...
50 83 60 FF 51 03 08 02-C8 83 60 FF 51 03 07 DB    P.'.Q.....'.Q...
B8 83 60 FF 51 03 08 3D-60 83 60 FF 51 03 08 ED    ..'.Q..='.'.Q...
28 83 60 FF 51 03 09 45-0C 83 60 FF 51 03 08 20    (.'.Q..E..'.Q...
14 83 60 FF 51 03 08 5A-AC 83 60 FF 51 03 08 33    ..'.Q..Z..'.Q..3
9C 83 60 FF 51 03 08 A8-CC 83 60 FF 51 03 08 8B    ..'.Q.....'.Q...
80 83 60 FF 51 03 08 5A-AC 83 60 FF 51 03 08 5A    ..'.Q..Z..'.Q..Z
AC 83 60 FF 51 03 08 95-44 83 60 FF 51 03 08 64    ..'.Q...D.'.Q..d
70 83 60 FF 51 03 08 77-F8 83 60 FF 51 03 08 E3    p.'.Q..w..'.Q...
64 83 60 FF 51 03 08 BC-54 83 60 FF 51 03 09 45    d.'.Q...T.'.Q..E
0C 83 60 FF 51 03 08 E3-64 83 60 FF 51 03 08 A8    ..'.Q...d.'.Q...
CC 83 60 FF 51 03 08 ED-28 83 60 FF 51 03 08 E3    ..'.Q...(.'.Q...
64 83 60 FF 51 03 09 45-0C F8 00 FF 51 03 0A F2    d.'.Q..E....Q...
BC 83 60 FF 51 03 0A E8-F8 83 60 FF 51 03 0B 19    ..'.Q.....'.Q...
CC 83 60 FF 51 03 0B 54-64 83 60 FF 51 03 0B 23    ..'.Q.Td.'.Q..#
90 83 60 FF 51 03 0B FA-68 83 60 FF 51 03 0B 54    ..'.Q...h.'.Q..T
64 83 60 FF 51 03 0B FA-68 83 60 FF 51 03 0A E8    d.'.Q...h.'.Q...
F8 83 60 FF 51 03 0B 85-38 83 60 FF 51 03 0A C1    ..'.Q...8.'.Q...
E8 83 60 FF 51 03 0C 04-2C 83 60 FF 51 03 0A C1    ..'.Q...,.'.Q...
E8 83 60 FF 51 03 0B 40-DC 83 60 FF 51 03 0B 4A    ..'.Q..@.'.Q..J
A0 83 60 FF 51 03 0B B6-0C 83 60 FF 51 03 0A A4    ..'.Q.....'.Q...
9C 83 60 FF 51 03 0B 54-64 83 60 FF 51 03 0A E8    ..'.Q.Td.'.Q...
F8 83 60 FF 51 03 0B 06-44 83 60 FF 51 03 0B 8E    ..'.Q...D.'.Q...
FC 83 60 FF 51 03 0C 79-5C 83 60 FF 51 03 0B 7B    ..'.Q..y\.'.Q..{
74 83 60 FF 51 03 0B 7B-74 83 60 FF 51 03 0A 87    t.'.Q..{t.'.Q...
50 83 60 FF 51 03 0A 7D-8C 83 60 FF 51 03 0A B8    P.'.Q..}..'.Q...
24 83 60 FF 51 03 0B 71-B0 83 60 FF 51 03 0A D5    $.'.Q..q..'.Q...
70 83 60 FF 51 03 0A D5-70 83 60 FF 51 03 0B BF    p.'.Q..p.'.Q...
D0 83 60 FF 51 03 0B 10-08 83 60 FF 51 03 0A 7D    ..'.Q.....'.Q..}
8C 83 60 FF 51 03 0B D3-58 83 60 FF 51 03 0A AE    ..'.Q...X.'.Q...
60 83 60 FF 51 03 0B 85-38 83 60 FF 51 03 0B 71    '.'.Q...8.'.Q..q
B0 83 60 FF 51 03 0B B6-0C 83 60 FF 51 03 0B 40    ..'.Q.....'.Q..@
DC 83 60 FF 51 03 0B B6-0C 83 60 FF 51 03 0B BF    ..'.Q.....'.Q...
D0 83 60 FF 51 03 0A 91-14 83 60 FF 51 03 0B A2    ..'.Q.....'.Q...
84 83 60 FF 51 03 0B 23-90 83 60 FF 51 03 0A DF    ..'.Q..#..'.Q...
34 83 60 FF 51 03 0A AE-60 83 60 FF 51 03 0B 37    4.'.Q...'.'.Q..7
18 83 60 FF 51 03 0B B6-0C 83 60 FE 00 02 C8 05    ..'.Q.....'....
00 FE 00 02 CE 05 00 FF-51 03 0A DF 34 00 FF 2F    ........Q...4../
00 4D 54 72 6B 00 00 00-B6 00 FF 03 05 43 72 61    .MTrk........Cra
73 68 00 B9 07 66 81 B7-60 99 31 08 3C 89 31 40    sh...f..'.1..1@
00 99 31 0C 3C 89 31 40-00 99 31 10 3C 89 31 40    ..1..1@..1..1@
00 99 31 18 3C 89 31 40-00 99 31 20 3C 89 31 40    ..1..1@..1 .1@
00 99 31 30 3C 89 31 40-00 99 31 50 3C 89 31 40    ..10.1@..1P.1@
00 99 31 70 3C 89 31 40-8B 20 99 31 0C 3C 89 31    ..1p.1@. .1..1
40 00 99 31 10 3C 89 31-40 00 99 31 18 3C 89 31    @..1..1@..1..1
40 00 99 31 20 3C 89 31-40 00 99 31 2C 3C 89 31    @..1 .1@..1,.1
40 00 99 31 38 3C 89 31-40 00 99 31 48 3C 89 31    @..18.1@..1H.1
40 00 99 31 78 3C 89 31-40 82 83 06 99 31 7C 82    @..1x.1@....1|.
33 89 31 40 8C 30 99 31-7F 71 89 31 40 82 AE 66    3.1@.0.1.q.1@..f
FE 00 02 AA 00 00 FE 00-02 B0 00 00 FF 2F 00 4D    ............./.M
54 72 6B 00 00 00 2F 00-FF 03 04 46 6F 6F 74 83    Trk.../....Foot.
CD 4B 99 24 6C 81 25 89-24 40 8D 15 99 24 66 81    .K.$1.%.$@...$f.
15 89 24 40 82 AE 66 FE-00 02 23 00 00 FE 00 02    ..$@..f...#.....
29 00 00 FF 2F 00 4D 54-72 6B 00 00 00 01 B1 00 FF    )...'.MTrk......
03 05 53 6E 61 72 65 83-A4 00 99 26 10 81 70 89    ..Snare....&..p.
```

The MIDI read function has two modes for reading MIDI data from the buffer: a *direct mode* and an *interrupt mode* (the MIDI write mode can only be controlled directly):

- With the direct mode, a running program has to retrieve and send MIDI data through the MIDI port. The program has to check continually whether the MIDI port is ready and whether MIDI data is available.

- With the interrupt mode, a hardware interrupt is generated as soon as new MIDI data is received. The interrupt breaks in on the running program, which allows the MIDI data to be read from the MIDI port. Next you return to the running program. You have to write the interrupt handler—the program that is called when MIDI data are received—yourself.

Writing and Reading to the DSP

The MIDI port can be read and written by means of the DSP functions 30H through 3FH. To write to the DSP or to read it, the following ports are of importance:

2x6H	DSP RESET (write-only)
2xAH	DSP READ DATA (read-only)
2xCH	DSP WRITE DATA or COMMAND (write-only)
2xCH	DSP WRITE BUFFER STATUS (read-only)
2xEH	DSP DATA AVAILABLE STATUS (read-only)

The *x* in the hexadecimal numbers represents a value between 1 and 6, depending on the I/O jumper position. The factory position of this jumper is 220H. If you are keeping the 220H jumper position, substitute a 2 for the *x*.

MIDI DSP Functions   The MIDI functions of the DSP are:

30H	MIDI READ mode (direct)
31H	MIDI READ mode (interrupt)
38H	MIDI WRITE mode (direct)

As mentioned earlier, MIDI data can only be written directly to the MIDI port. To do this you write the 38H command to the DSP COMMAND port (2xCH) and then the MIDI byte that has to be written to the DSP DATA port (this is the same port as the DSP COMMAND port).

Before these instructions can be sent to the DSP, however, you have to check whether the DSP is able to process the data or the commands. To run this check, the DSP WRITE BUFFER STATUS (again port 2xCH) has to be read. If bit 7 of the read byte is set (=1), the DSP cannot receive new data or commands.

Reading MIDI Data Directly   To directly read the MIDI data, the 30H command has to be sent to the DSP COMMAND port (2xCH). To verify whether MIDI data is available, the DSP DATA AVAILABLE port (2xEH) has to be read. If bit 7 of this byte is set, MIDI data are available in the buffer and you can read one MIDI byte by reading the DSP READ DATA port (2xAH).

Reading MIDI Data with an Interrupt Routine

The recommended method of reading MIDI data is to use an interrupt routine. The Sound Blaster card contains a jumper for indicating which IRQ is allocated to the Sound Blaster. You can choose between 2, 3, 5, and 7. The routine has to be written in accordance with this interrupt number.

NOTE   See Chapter 1 for instructions about setting the jumpers on the Sound Blaster card.

To inform the DSP that it has to work with an interrupt, the 31H command has to be sent to the DSP. When MIDI data is received, the processor is interrupted and the interrupt routine is executed. To clear the Interrupt Request, the DSP STATUS port (2xEH) has to be read once. When this is done, the MIDI data byte can be retrieved at the DSP READ DATA port (2xAH).

If you no longer need the interrupt routine because, for example, you want to return to DOS, send the 31H command to stop the interrupt service.

Sending and Reading Commands and Data Bytes

Every byte sent to or read from the DSP has to go through a procedure. But before sending or reading bytes, you have to verify whether the DSP is ready to process a command or a data byte.

To send a command or a data byte to the DSP, you follow these steps:

1. Read the DSP WRITE BUFFER STATUS port 2xCH.

2. Check whether bit 7 of the read byte is reset (=0). If bit 7 is set, you have to repeat step 1.

3. Write the command or the data byte to the DSP WRITE DATA or COMMAND port 2xCH.

To read a data byte from the DSP READ DATA port you have to carry out these steps:

1. Read the DSP DATA AVAILABLE STATUS port 2xEH.

2. Check whether bit 7 of the read byte is set (=1). If it is not set, you have to repeat step 1.

3. Read the data byte from the DSP READ DATA port 2xAH.

MIDI and the Sound Blaster Pro

With the development of the Sound Blaster Pro, a number of functions have been added to give the MIDI more capability. The Pro can operate in the *UART mode*. In this mode, you can read and write MIDI data at the same time. UART mode handles the Pro's full-duplex capabilities. For the Sound Blaster Pro, the following DSP MIDI functions were added:

```
34H: MIDI UART mode (polling)
35H: MIDI UART mode (interrupt)
```

UART mode assumes you are reading MIDI data. If you want to write MIDI data, write the MIDI data in question to the DSP WRITE DATA port (2xCH). In UART mode, the DSP thinks that all data sent to the DSP DATA port is MIDI data that has to be transmitted.

Use of the MIDI Time Stamp   The MIDI time stamp is used with the Sound Blaster Pro, and every incoming MIDI byte is preceded by three time-stamp bytes. The three time-stamp bytes indicate the time that has elapsed since the last DSP RESET. Two new modes are added to tell the DSP it has to pass on time-stamp codes:

```
33H: MIDI Time Stamp Code (interrupt non-UART)
37H: MIDI Time Stamp Code (interrupt UART)
```

Using the time-stamp codes has a number of consequences for working with Sound Blaster Pro:

- The size of the MIDI data buffer is considerably reduced. In normal mode, the buffer could contain 64 MIDI codes, but now it can hold only 16 MIDI codes. Be sure to remove the data from the MIDI buffer in time.

- It is a lot easier to create a sequencer. After all, you don't have to pay attention to the time or the differences in time. The DSP chip simply stores them along with the MIDI bytes.

- In order to support the old Sound Blaster, you have to check the Sound Blaster version.

Checking DSP Versions   To check the Sound Blaster version, get the version number of the DSP chip. In order to do this a function has been created. Call this function by using the following DSP command:

```
E1H: Version number DSP
```

The DSP will place two bytes in the MIDI DATA buffer:

- The first byte received after reading the READ DATA port is the number in front of the point of the version number.

- The second byte indicates the number after the point.

NOTE Sound Blasters 1.0, 1.5, 1.6, and MCV all have a DSP with a version number between 1.5 and 2.0. The DSP version number of Sound Blaster Pro is 2.0 or higher.

Sample Program: A Sequencer

In this section the different MIDI write and read modes are used to write a simple sequencer. The most important fact for a sequencer is the time. If MIDI data is received at time X and the next MIDI data arrives at time $X + 31$, the 31 difference also has to be represented when the MIDI data is played back. In short, the differences in time between the successive MIDI streams have to be determined exactly.

This is where the timer chip comes in. The timer chip can be activated many times per second. The timer chip is interrupt-based, which means that the chip has its own interrupt line (number) and that it is automatically called a certain number of times (usually 18.2) per second so it can, for example, keep the time. It is the programmer's decision to determine how often this timer interrupt has to be called.

The simple sequencer described in the following pages has these functions:

- Recording incoming MIDI data until a key is pressed.
- Playing back incoming MIDI data until a key is pressed.

The first four listings in this chapter are as follows:

Listing	Title
10.1	MIDILIB
10.2	SEQ.PAS
10.3	MIDI.H
10.4	SEQ.C

NOTE   See "A Word about the Program Listings" in the Introduction for advice about reading and using these listings.

Listing 10.1: MIDILIB

```
{ ************************************************
**   Unit MIDILIB supporting SEQ.PAS          **
**   and MIDICMF.PAS                           **
**   Turbo Pascal 4.0/6.0                       **
************************************************ }

Unit midilib;

Interface

Const
port      = $220;
reset     = port+$06;        { registers DSP }
readdata  = port+$0a;
writecom  = port+$0c;
writebuf  = port+$0c;
dataavail = port+$0e;
OldtimV   = 103;

type
version=record
    high : byte;
    low  : byte;
  end;

procedure resetDSP;
procedure writedat( n : byte );
function readdat : byte;
function polreaddat : byte;
procedure settimspeed( Freq : word );
procedure settimer( Freq : word; Rout : pointer );
procedure resettimer;
procedure get_version_number( var number : version );

implementation
uses dos,crt;
```

```pascal
procedure resetDSP;        { initializing DSP chip }
var
 b : word;
begin
  port[reset]:=1;
  for b:=3 downto 0 do;
  port[reset]:=0;
  while (port[dataavail] and 128)=0 do;
  while not(port[readdata]=$aa) do;
  writeln('Reset DSP OK. ');
end;

procedure writedat(n : byte); { write a data byte }
begin                         { or command to the DSP }
  while (port[writebuf] and 128)<>0 do;
  port[writecom]:=n;
end;

function readdat : byte;  { read a byte from the DSP }
begin                                     { buffer }
  while (port[dataavail] and 128)=0 do;
  readdat:=port[readdata];
end;

function polreaddat : byte; { in polling mode also pay }
begin                         { attention to key press }
  while (((port[dataavail] and 128)=0) and not
        keypressed) do;
  polreaddat:=port[readdata];
end;


procedure settimspeed(Freq : word); { calculate and pass }
var                                  { timer speed }
  ICnt : longint;                    { on to the timer chip }
begin
  inline($FA);
  ICnt:= 1193180 div Freq;
  port[$43]:=$36;
  port[$40]:=lo(ICnt);
  port[$40]:=hi(ICnt);
  inline($FB);
  writeln('Clock tick = ',Freq);
end;
```

```pascal
procedure settimer(Freq : word; Rout : pointer);
var
  OldV : pointer;
begin
        inline($FA);
        getintvec(8,OldV);        { take over timer interrupt }
        setintvec(OldtimV,Oldv);
  setintvec(8,Rout);
  settimspeed(Freq);
        inline($FB);
end;

procedure resettimer;  { restore all changes }
Var                            { to the timer }
  OldV : pointer;
begin
  inline($FA);
  port[$43]:=$36;
  port[$40]:=$0;
  port[$40]:=$0;
  getintvec(OldtimV,Oldv);
  setintvec(8,Oldv);
  inline($FB);
end;

procedure get_version_number( var number : version );
begin                        { return DSP version number }

  writedat($E1);             { command return_version }
  number.high:= readdat;
  number.low:= readdat;
end;

end.
```

Listing 10.2: SEQ.PAS

```pascal
{ **********************************************
**   SEQ.PAS                                  **
**   Turbo Pascal 6.0                         **
********************************************** }

program sequencer;
```

```pascal
Uses Dos,Crt,midilib;

Const
port= $220;        { jumper values }
IRQ = $5;

var
  read_write : boolean;
  counter : longint;
  i : word;
  midi_time : array [0..1000] of longint;
  midi_note : array [0..1000] of byte;

procedure newtim; interrupt;  { new timer interrupt }
var R : registers;
begin
  if read_write then inc(counter)
  else
    if (counter>0) then dec(counter);
  intr(OldtimV,R);
end;


procedure newIRQ; interrupt;  { interrupt for }
var dummy : byte;             { interrupt mode }
begin
  if (i<1000) then
    begin
      midi_note[i]:=readdat;
      midi_time[i]:=counter;
      inc(i);
      counter:=0;
    end;
  dummy:=port[dataavail];
  port[$20]:=$20;
end;


procedure uartIRQ; interrupt; { interrupt for }
var dummy : byte;             { UART mode }
begin
  if (i<1000) then
    begin
      midi_time[i]:=readdat;
      midi_time[i]:=midi_time[i]+readdat*256;
      midi_time[i]:=midi_time[i]+readdat*65536;
      midi_note[i]:=readdat;
```

```
      inc(i);
    end;
  dummy:=port[dataavail];
  port[$20]:=$20;
end;

var
 k : word;
 oldport : byte;
 choice,allowed,dummy  : char;
 number : version;

begin                              { main program }
  resetDSP;
  clrscr;
  allowed:='2';
  choice:='0';
  writeln('1. MIDI polling mode.');
  writeln('2. MIDI interrupt mode.');
  get_version_number(number);
  if (number.high>=2) then
    begin
    writeln('3. MIDI UART with Time Stamp.');
    allowed:='3';
    end;
  write('DSP version number ');
  writeln(number.high,'.',number.low);
  writeln('Select a mode : ');
  while ( (choice<'1') or (choice>allowed)) do
  choice:=readkey;
  writeln('Press a key to start.');
  dummy:=readkey;
  writeln('Go !');
  case choice of
  '1'  :   begin
    writedat($30);               { polling mode }
    settimer(100,@newtim);    { use timer }
    read_write:= true;
    while ((i<1000) and not keypressed) do
    begin
      midi_note[i]:=polreaddat;
      midi_time[i]:=counter;
```

```
      inc(i);
      counter:=0;
   end;
end;

'2'   :   begin
   setintvec(8+IRQ,@newIRQ);     { set new IRQ }
   oldport:=port[$21];
   port[$21]:=oldport and ($ff xor (1 shl IRQ));
   writedat($31);                { interrupt mode }
   read_write:= true;
   settimer(100,@newtim);
   while not keypressed do;
   writedat($31);
   port[$21]:=oldport;
   end;
'3'   :   begin
   setintvec(8+IRQ,@uartIRQ);  { set UART IRQ }
   oldport:=port[$21];
   port[$21]:=oldport and ($ff xor (1 shl IRQ));
   writedat($37);             { UART mode with MTC }
   while not keypressed do;
   port[$21]:=oldport;
   end;
end;
if keypressed then dummy:=readkey;
if (choice<'3') then
   begin
    resetDSP;
    read_write:=false;
   end
else
   begin
    settimer(1000,@newtim);  { timer in milliseconds }
    read_write:=true;
    counter:=0;
   end;
if (midi_note[0]<$80) then    { started with a }
begin                         { running status byte ? }
   if (choice<'3') then writedat($38);
   writedat($90);
end;
k:=0;
while ((k<i) and not keypressed) do
```

```
  begin
   if (choice<'3') then
   begin                      { and send the MIDI }
    counter:=midi_time[k];    { data back again }
    while (counter>0) do;
    writedat($38);
    writedat(midi_note[k]);
    inc(k);
   end
   else
   begin                      { for the UART mode }
    while (counter<midi_time[k]) do;
    writedat(midi_note[k]);
    inc(k);
   end;
  end;
 resettimer;
 writeln('Ready.');
 if (choice='3') then resetDSP;
end.
```

Listing 10.3: MIDI.H

```
/* *********************************************
**      Include file MIDI.H for MIDICMF.C and   **
**      SEQ.C                                    **
**      Turbo C++ 2.0                            **
********************************************* */

#include <dos.h>
#pragma inline
#define reset       port+0x06     /* definition of */
#define readdata    port+0x0a     /* all DSP ports */
#define writecom    port+0x0c     /* conc. MIDI */
#define writebuf    port+0x0c
#define dataavail   port+0x0e

struct version                    /* record for */
  {                               /* version number */
    unsigned char high;
    unsigned char low;
  };

void resetDSP()                   /* reset DSP chip */
{
```

```
      int b;
      outp(reset,1);
      for (b=3;b>0;b--);
      outp(reset,0);
      while (!(inp(dataavail)&128));
      while (inp(readdata) !=0xaa );
      printf("\nReset DSP OK. \n");
}

void writedat(n)          /* write a byte to */
int n;                    /* the DSP */
{
   while (inp(writebuf)&128);
   outp(writecom,n);
}

readdat()                 /* read a byte from the DSP */
{
   short int n;
   while (!(inp(dataavail)&128));
   n=(inp(readdata));
   return(n);
}

polreaddat()         /* in polling mode you stay in */
{                    /* a loop without kbhit() */
   short int n;
   while (!(inp(dataavail)&128) && !kbhit());
   n=(inp(readdata));
   return(n);
}


void interrupt ( *oldtim )(void); /* old timer int */

void settimspeed(unsigned Freq)
{
   int ICnt;
   asm cli;
   ICnt = 1193180/Freq;      /* calculate the number */
   outp(0x43,0x36);          /* of clock ticks and pass */
   outp(0x40,ICnt &255);     /* on this number */
   outp(0x40,ICnt >>8);
   asm sti;
```

```
  printf("\nClock tick = %d\n",Freq);
}

void settimer(unsigned Freq,void interrupt (*newIRQ)())
{
  oldtim = getvect(8);      /* take over timer and */
  setvect(8,newIRQ);
  settimspeed(Freq);        /* set speed */
}

void resettimer()
{
  asm cli;
  outp(0x43,0x36);          /* reset all timer */
  outp(0x40,0x0);           /* occupations */
  outp(0x40,0x0);
  setvect(8,oldtim);
  asm sti;
}

struct version get_version_number()
{
  struct version number;

  writedat(0xE1);      /* give DSP version num. command */
  number.high= readdat();  /* read the values from the */
  number.low= readdat();   /* DSP buffer */
  return(number);          /* return values */
}
```

Listing 10.4: SEQ.C

```
/* ********************************************
**    SEQ.C                                  **
**    Turbo C++ 2.0                          **
******************************************** */

#include <stdio.h>
#include <dos.h>

#define  port 0x220    /* selected port */
#define  IRQ  0x5      /* selected IRQ */

#include "midi.h"
```

```c
unsigned char read_write=0;
long counter=0;
int i=0;

long midi_time[1000];            /* buffers for */
unsigned char midi_note[1000];   /* time and note */

void interrupt newtim()          /* counters */
{
  if (read_write)
    counter++;
  else
    if (counter>0) counter--;
  oldtim();
}

void interrupt newIRQ()     /* for interrupt mode */
{
  if (i<1000)
    {
      midi_note[i]=readdat();   /* read midi byte */
      midi_time[i++]=counter;   /* write time */
      counter=0;
    }
  inp(dataavail);
  outp(0x20,0x20);
}

void interrupt uartIRQ()      /* for UART mode */
{
  if (i<1000)
    {
      midi_time[i]=readdat();       /* time stamp */
      midi_time[i]+=readdat()*256;
      midi_time[i]+=readdat()*65536;
      midi_note[i++]=readdat();   /* midi byte */
    }
  inp(dataavail);
  outp(0x20,0x20);
}


void main(void)
{
```

```
int k=0;
unsigned char oldport;
char keuze='0',allowed;
struct version number;

resetDSP();
clrscr();
allowed='2';
printf("\n\n\n\n\n\t\t1. MIDI polling mode.\n\n");
printf("\t\t2. MIDI interrupt mode.\n\n");
number=get_version_number();
if (number.high>=2)
  {
  printf("\t\t3. MIDI UART with Time Stamp.\n\n");
  allowed='3';
  }
printf("\t\tDSP version number ");
printf("%d.%d\n\n",number.high,number.low);
printf("\t\tSelect a mode : ");
while ( choice<'1' || choice>allowed)
choice=getch();
printf("\nPress a key to start.\n");
getch();
printf("Go !\n");
switch(choice) {
case '1'  :                    /* polling mode */
  writedat(0x30);
  settimer(100,newtim);
  read_write=1;
  while ((i<1000) && !kbhit())
  {
    midi_note[i]=polreaddat();  /* reading each time */
    midi_time[i++]=counter;
    counter=0;
  }
  break;
case '2'  :                    /* interrupt mode */
  setvect(8+IRQ,newIRQ);
  oldport=inp(0x21);
  outp(0x21,oldport&(0xff^(1<<IRQ)));  /* mask IRQ */
  writedat(0x31);
  settimer(100,newtim);
  read_write=1;
  while(!kbhit());             /* wait for a key */
  writedat(0x31);              /* return to normal */
```

```
      outp(0x21,oldport);
      break;
  case '3'   :                    /* UART mode */
      setvect(8+IRQ,uartIRQ);
      oldport=inp(0x21);
      outp(0x21,oldport&(0xff^(1<<IRQ)));
      writedat(0x37);             /* command UART MTC */
      while(!kbhit());
      outp(0x21,oldport);
      break;
  default  : break;
      }
  if (kbhit()) getch();
  if (choice<'3')                 /* play all */
    {
     resetDSP();
     read_write=0;
    }
  else
    {
     settimer(1000,newtim);
     read_write=1;
     counter=0;
    }
  if (midi_note[0]<0x80)    /* started with running */
  {                                 /* status byte ? */
    if (choice<'3') writedat(0x38);
    writedat(0x90);
  }
  while (k<i && !kbhit())
   {
    if (choice<'3')
    {
     counter=midi_time[k];   /* if counter is zero, */
     while (counter>0);      /* send the MIDI byte */
     writedat(0x38);
     writedat(midi_note[k++]);
    }
    else
    {
     while (counter<midi_time[k]);
     writedat(midi_note[k++]);
    }
   }
  resettimer();
```

```
        printf("Ready.\n");
        if (choice=='3') resetDSP();
}
```

Playing CMF Songs through MIDI

The CMF format partly consists of a number of parameters Creative Labs invented and partly of a real MIDI file. To be specific, in the CMF format the header and instrument blocks are followed by the music block, which is the same as MIDI file format 0.

Listings 10.5 and 10.6 show a program that loads and plays this CMF file. The program makes use of the MIDILIB Unit in Pascal (see Listing 10.1) and of the MIDI.H file in C (see Listing 10.3). Both programs are used together with the sequencer program.

Listing 10.5: CMF MIDI Player in Pascal

```
{ **************************************************
** MIDICMF.PAS                                   **
** Turbo Pascal 4.0                              **
************************************************** }

Program Midicmf;

Uses Dos,Crt,midilib;

Const port = $220;    { selected jumpers }
      IRQ = $7;

var nexttoken:byte;
    clocktick:word;
    stop:byte;
    counter:longint;
    mempos:pointer;
    size:word;
    number_of_bytes:integer;
    result:integer;
    formattype:integer;
```

```
      cnt:integer;
      curmempos:word;
      ch:char;


Function ReadPos(index:word):byte;
                  { reads an indexed byte }
begin
  readpos:=mem[Seg(mempos^):Ofs(mempos^)+index]
end;


Function LoadFile( filename : string): byte;
var fp : FILE;
begin                    { loads a file in memory }

      {$I-}
      Assign(fp,filename);
      if ( ioresult <> 0 ) then
      begin
        loadfile:=1;
        exit;
      end;
      System.Reset(fp,1);
      {$I+}
      if ( ioresult <> 0 ) then
      begin
        loadfile:=2;
        exit;
      end;
      If (filesize(fp)>$FFFF) then
      begin
        Writeln('File too large for buffer.');
        loadfile:=3;
      end;
      size:= filesize(fp);
      getmem(mempos,size);
      if ( mempos=nil ) then
      begin
        writeln('no memory');
        loadfile:=4;
        exit
      end;
      blockread(fp,mempos^,size,number_of_bytes);
      if ((ioresult<>0) or (number_of_bytes<>size)) then
```

```
                begin
                  loadfile:=3;
                  exit;
                end;
              close(fp);
              loadfile:=0;
end;


Function Check:byte;                  { is the loaded }
const midiheader:string[4]='MThd';   { file a MIDI }
      cmfheader:string[4]='CTMF';    { or a CMF file ? }

var j:byte;
    temp:string[4];

begin
  j:=Readpos(4);
  Move(mempos^,temp[1],4); temp[0]:=#4; { size of 4 bytes}

  if (temp=cmfheader) then
    check:=0
  else
  if (temp=midiheader) then
    check:=1
  else
    check:=255;

end;



Procedure Error;
begin
  writeln('What you say is nonsense...');
  writeln(nexttoken);
  halt(1);
end;



Procedure Send(token:byte);  { send a byte to }
begin                          { the DSP }
  writedat($38);
  writedat(token);
end;
```

```
Function Next:byte;          { read the next byte }
begin
  next:=ReadPos(curmempos);
  Inc(curmempos);
end;


Procedure SysExmsg;
begin
  send(nexttoken);
  nexttoken:=next;

  while (nexttoken>=$f8) do       { real-time messages }
  begin
    send(nexttoken);
    nexttoken:=next;
  end;
  if (nexttoken<$80) then         { data byte }
  begin
    send(nexttoken);
    nexttoken:=next;
  end
  else
    error;

  while not (nexttoken=$f7) do    { EOX }
  begin
    while (nexttoken>=$f8) do      { real-time messages }
    begin
      send(nexttoken);
      nexttoken:=next;
    end;

    while (nexttoken<$80) do       { data bytes }
    begin
      send(nexttoken);
      nexttoken:=next;
    end;

  end;
  send(nexttoken);
  nexttoken:=next;
end;
```

```
Procedure SysSelect;
begin
  send(nexttoken);
  nexttoken:=next;
  while (nexttoken>=$f8) do     { real-time messages }
  begin
    send(nexttoken);
    nexttoken:=next;
  end;

  if (nexttoken < $80) then     { data byte }
  begin
    send(nexttoken);
    nexttoken:=next;
  end
  else
    error;
end;


Procedure SysSongPos;
begin
  send(nexttoken);
  nexttoken:=next ;
  while (nexttoken>=$f8) do    { real-time messages }
  begin
    send(nexttoken);
    nexttoken:=next;
  end;

  if (nexttoken < $80) then    { data byte }
  begin
    send(nexttoken);
    nexttoken:=next ;
    while (nexttoken>=$f8) do  { real-time messages }
    begin
      send(nexttoken);
      nexttoken:=next ;
    end;
    if (nexttoken < $80) then  { data byte }
    begin
      send(nexttoken);
      nexttoken:=next;
    end
```

```
      else
        error;
    end
  else
    error;

end;


procedure SysCommonMsg;
begin
  if (nexttoken=$f6) then
  begin
    send(nexttoken);
    nexttoken:=next;
  end
  else
    if (nexttoken=$f2) then
      syssongpos
    else
      if (nexttoken=$f3) then
        sysselect
      else
        error;
end;


Procedure Metaevent;          { handle the different }
var length:byte;              { meta events }
    i:integer;
    tempo:longint;
begin
  nexttoken:=next;
  Case nexttoken of

  3:begin                          { title }
      length:=next;
      for i:=0 to length-1 do Write(Chr(next));
      Writeln;
      nexttoken:=next;
    end;
$2f:begin                          { end of track }
      nexttoken:=next;
      If nexttoken=0 then stop:=1;
    end;
```

```
$51:begin                          { tempo }
      nexttoken:=next;
      If nexttoken=3 then
      begin
        writeln('Tempo change');
        nexttoken:=next;
        tempo:=nexttoken*65536;
        nexttoken:=next;
        Inc(tempo,nexttoken*256);
        nexttoken:=next;
        Inc(tempo,nexttoken);

        tempo:=tempo div clocktick;
        tempo:=tempo div 12;
        settimspeed(tempo);
        nexttoken:=next;
       end;
     end;
$54:begin                          { time stamp }
      nexttoken:=next;
      if nexttoken=5 then
      begin
        writeln('SMPTE');
        for i:=0 to 5 do nexttoken:=next;
      end;
     end;
$58:begin                          { time signature }
      nexttoken:=next;
      if nexttoken=4 then
      begin
        writeln('Time sign.');
        for i:=0 to 4 do nexttoken:=next;
      end;
     end;

else
   begin
     writeln('Unknown Meta event',next);
     Repeat
       nexttoken:=next;
     Until nexttoken<$80;
   end;
  end;
end;
```

```
Procedure Sysmsg;
begin
  if (nexttoken >= $f8) then
  begin
    if (nexttoken = $ff) then MetaEvent;
  end
  else
   if (nexttoken = $f0)
   then
     sysexmsg
   else
     SysCommonMsg;
end;


Procedure Chan1ByteMsg;
begin
  send(nexttoken);
  nexttoken:=next;
  while (nexttoken>=$f8) do    { real-time messages }
  begin
    send(nexttoken);
    nexttoken:=next;
  end;
  if (nexttoken < $80) then    { data byte }
  begin
    send(nexttoken);
    nexttoken:=next;
  end
  else
    Error;
end;


Procedure Chan2ByteMsg;
begin
  send(nexttoken);
  nexttoken:=next;
  while (nexttoken>=$f8) do    { real-time messages }
  begin
    send(nexttoken);
    nexttoken:=next;
  end;
```

```
      if (nexttoken<$80) then      { data byte }
      begin
        send(nexttoken);
        nexttoken:=next;
        while (nexttoken>=$f8) do  { real-time messages }
        begin
          send(nexttoken);
          nexttoken:=next;
        end;
        if (nexttoken < $80) then    { data byte }
          begin
            send(nexttoken);
            nexttoken:=next;
          end
        else
          Error;
      end
      else
        Error;
    end;


Procedure Chanmsg;
begin
  if ((nexttoken>=$C0) AND (nexttoken<$E0))
  then
    chan1ByteMsg
  else
    chan2ByteMsg;
end;


procedure MIDImsg;
begin
  if (nexttoken >= $80) then
    if (nexttoken >= $F0) then
      sysmsg
    else
      chanmsg
  else
  begin                          { running status byte }
    send(nexttoken);
    nexttoken:=next;
    if (nexttoken < $80) then    { data bytes }
    begin
```

```
      send(nexttoken);
      nexttoken:=next;
    end
    else
      error;
  end;
end;


Procedure ReadVarLength;  { calculate number of }
var value:longint;        { clock ticks }
begin
  value:=nexttoken;
  if (value and $80)=$80 then
  begin
    value:=value AND $7f;
    Repeat
      nexttoken:=next;
      value:=(value shl 7)+(nexttoken AND $7f);
    Until ((nexttoken AND $80)<>128);
  end;
  nexttoken:=next;
  counter:=value;
  while (counter>0) do;
end;

procedure MIDIstream;
begin
  readvarlength;
  MIDImsg;
end;


procedure VmidiHeader;  { determine beginning of the track }
var i:integer;
begin
  if Readpos(9)>0 then
    writeln('This is NO format 0 MIDI file !');

  curmempos:=Readpos(4)*65536;
  Inc(curmempos,ReadPos(5)*4096);
  Inc(curmempos,swap(ReadPos(6))+ReadPos(7)+8);
  Inc(curmempos,8);
end;
```

```
Procedure NewTim; interrupt;
var R : registers;
begin
  if (counter>0) then dec(counter);

  Intr(OldtimV,R);
end;


begin                          { main program }
  checkbreak:=false;
  stop:=0;

  if paramcount<>1 then
  begin
    writeln('Use: playmidi < CMF-/MIDI-file >');
    halt(1);
  end;

  result:=loadfile(paramstr(1));

  if result<>0 then
  begin
    if (result=2) then
      writeln('Not enough memory available.')
    else
      writeln('Loading error ',paramstr(1),'. ');
    halt(2);
  end;

  formattype:=check;
  if formattype=255 then
  begin
    writeln('No MIDI or CMF format. ');
    halt(3);
  end;

  if formattype=1 then         { read speed }
  begin
    clocktick:=ReadPos(13) + swap(ReadPos(12));

  end
  else
  begin
    clocktick:=ReadPos($0c) + swap(ReadPos($0d));
```

```
end;

settimer(clocktick,@newtim);

resetDSP;

if formattype=1 then        { read offset }
  Vmidiheader
else
  curmempos:=Readpos(8)+swap(Readpos(9));

Nexttoken:=next;

While (stop<>1) and not keypressed
  do MIDIstream;                        { play on }

if keypressed then ch:=readkey;


resettimer;
Writeln('That''s all...');
freemem(mempos,size);
end.
```

Listing 10.6: CMF MIDI Player in C

```
/* *********************************************
** MIDICMF.C                                 **
** Turbo C++ 2.0                             **
********************************************* */

#pragma inline
#include <stdio.h>
#include <io.h>
#include <fcntl.h>
#include <dos.h>
#include <stdlib.h>
#include <string.h>

#define port 0x220   /* base port */

#include "midi.h"
```

```
void *here;
unsigned char *header;
unsigned char *pointer;
unsigned char nexttoken;
unsigned int clocktick;
int stop=0;
long counter=0;


loadfile( char *filename )      /* loads file */
{                               /* into memory */
  int handle;
  long filesize;
  int number_of_bytes;

  if ( (handle=open(filename,O_RDONLY | O_BINARY))==-1)
    return(1);
  filesize = filelength(handle);
  if ((here=malloc(filesize))==NULL)
    return(2);
  if ((read(handle,here,filesize))==-1)
    return(1);

  close(handle);
  return(0);
}

check()    /* determine the song format */
{
  int j;
  char *type1="MThd",*type2="CTMF";
  header=(unsigned char *)here;
  j=*(header+4);
  *(header+4)=0;
  if ( (strcmp(header,type2)==0) )   /* CMF ? */
  {
    *(header+4)=j;
    return(0);
  }
  else
    if (strcmp(header,type1)==0)   /* MIDI ? */
    {
      *(header+4)=j;
      return(1);
    }
```

```
      else
        return(-1);
}

void error()
{
  printf("\nWhat you say is nonsense...\n");
  printf("%\n",nexttoken);
  exit(1);
}


void send(unsigned char token)
{
  writedat(0x38);          /* command MIDI write */
  writedat(token);         /* data byte */
}

unsigned char next()    /* read next byte */
{
  unsigned char k;
  k=*pointer;
  pointer++;
  return(k);
}



void sysexmsg()         /* a system exclusive message */
{
  send(nexttoken);              /* consists of: */
  nexttoken=next();
  while (nexttoken>=0xf8 ) /* possible real-time mesg.*/
  {
    send(nexttoken);
    nexttoken=next();
  }
  if ( nexttoken < 0x80 )    /* 1 data byte */
  {
    send(nexttoken);
    nexttoken=next();
  }
  else
    error();
  while (nexttoken != 0xf7 )  /* terminated with EOX */
```

```
    {
      while (nexttoken>=0xf8 )   /* real-time messages */
      {
        send(nexttoken);
        nexttoken=next();
      }
      while ( nexttoken < 0x80 )  /* data bytes */
      {
        send(nexttoken);
        nexttoken=next();
      }
    }
    send(nexttoken);
    nexttoken=next();
}

void sysselect()
{
    send(nexttoken);
    nexttoken=next();
    while (nexttoken>=0xf8 )    /* real-time messages */
    {
      send(nexttoken);
      nexttoken=next();
    }
    if ( nexttoken < 0x80 )     /* data byte */
    {
      send(nexttoken);
      nexttoken=next();
    }
    else
      error();
}

void syssongpos()
{
    send(nexttoken);
    nexttoken=next();
    while (nexttoken>=0xf8 )        /* real-time messages */
    {
      send(nexttoken);
      nexttoken=next();
    }
    if ( nexttoken < 0x80 )        /* data byte */
    {
```

```
      send(nexttoken);
      nexttoken=next();
      while (nexttoken>=0xf8 )    /* real-time messages */
      {
        send(nexttoken);
        nexttoken=next();
      }
      if ( nexttoken < 0x80 )     /* with data byte */
      {
        send(nexttoken);
        nexttoken=next();
      }
      else
        error();
  }
  else
    error();
}


void SysCommonMsg()
{
  if ( nexttoken==0xf6)
  {
    send(nexttoken);
    nexttoken=next();
  }
  else
    if ( nexttoken==0xf2 )
      syssongpos();
    else
      if (nexttoken==0xf3 )
      sysselect();
      else
        error();
}

void metaevent()      /* handles the different */
{                           /* meta events */
  unsigned char length;
  int i;
  long tempo;

  nexttoken=next();
  switch(nexttoken) {
```

```
  case 3:    length=next();              /* title */
             for (i=0;i<length;i++)
             putc(next(),stdout);
             nexttoken=next();
             break;

  case 0x2f:  if ((nexttoken=next())==0)
             stop=1;                    /* end of track */
             break;

  case 0x51:  if ((nexttoken=next())==3)  /* tempo */
             printf("\nTempo change");
             tempo+=((nexttoken=next())*65536);
             tempo+=((nexttoken=next())*256);
             tempo+=(nexttoken=next());
             tempo/=clocktick;
             tempo/=12;
             settimspeed(tempo);
                nexttoken=next();
             break;

  case 0x54:  if ((nexttoken=next())==5)
             printf("\nSMPTE");         /* time stamp */
             for(i=0;i<6;i++)
             nexttoken=next();
             break;

  case 0x58:  if ((nexttoken=next())==4)
             printf("\nTime sign.");
             for(i=0;i<5;i++)       /* time signature */
             nexttoken=next();
             break;

  default:    printf("\nUnknown Meta event %d",next());
                while ((nexttoken=next())<0x80);
             break;
        }
}


void sysmsg()
{
  if ( nexttoken >= 0xf8 )
  {
    if ( nexttoken == 0xff )
```

```
      metaevent();
  }
  else
    if (nexttoken == 0xf0 )
      sysexmsg();
    else
      SysCommonMsg();
}


void chan1ByteMsg()
{
  send(nexttoken);
  nexttoken=next();
  while (nexttoken>=0xf8 )        /* real-time messages */
  {
    send(nexttoken);
    nexttoken=next();
  }
  if ( nexttoken < 0x80 )    /* with data byte */
  {
    send(nexttoken);
    nexttoken=next();
  }
  else
    error();
}

void chan2ByteMsg()
{
  send(nexttoken);
  nexttoken=next();
  while (nexttoken>=0xf8 )    /* real-time messages */
  {
    send(nexttoken);
    nexttoken=next();
  }
  if ( nexttoken < 0x80 )    /* with data byte */
  {
    send(nexttoken);
    nexttoken=next();
    while (nexttoken>=0xf8 )   /* real-time messages */
    {
      send(nexttoken);
      nexttoken=next();
```

```
      }
      if ( nexttoken < 0x80 )    /* with data byte */
      {
        send(nexttoken);
        nexttoken=next();
      }
      else
        error();
  }
  else
    error();
}


void chanmsg()
{
  if ( nexttoken >= 0xC0 && nexttoken < 0xE0 )
    chan1ByteMsg();
  else
    chan2ByteMsg();
}


void MIDImsg()
{
  if (nexttoken >= 0x80 )
    if ( nexttoken >= 0xF0 )
      sysmsg();
    else
      chanmsg();
  else                           /* running status */
  {
    send(nexttoken);             /* data byte */
    nexttoken=next();
    if (nexttoken < 0x80 )       /* followed by 0 or 1 */
    {                            /* data bytes */
      send(nexttoken);
      nexttoken=next();
    }
    else
      error();
  }
}

void readvarlength()  /* read number of clock ticks */
```

```
{
  long value;

  if (( value = nexttoken) & 0x80 )
  {
    value &= 0x7f;
    do
    {
      value=(value << 7)+((nexttoken=next()) & 0x7f);
    } while ( nexttoken & 0x80);
  }
  nexttoken=next();
  counter=value;
  while(counter>0);
}

void MIDIstream()
{
  readvarlength();
  MIDImsg();
}


void Vmidiheader()  /* determine offset to the data */
{
  if ((*(header+9))>0)
    printf("\nThis is NO format 0 MIDI file !\n");
  pointer=header+((*(header+4))*65536);
  pointer+=((*(header+5))*4096);
  pointer=pointer+((*(header+6))*256)+(*(header+7))+8;
  pointer+=8;
}

void interrupt newtim()  /* decrease counter */
{
  if (counter>0)
  counter--;
  oldtim();
}


main ( int argc, char *argv[])
{
  int result,type,tel;
```

```
            if ( !(argc==2) )
            {
              printf("\nUse: playmidi < CMF-/MIDI-file > \n");
              return(-1);
            }

            if (!((result=loadfile(argv[1]))==0 ))
            {
              if (result==2)
                printf("\nNot enough memory available.\n");
              else
                printf("\nLoading error %s.\n",argv[1]);
              return(-2);
            }

            if ((type=check())==-1)
            {
              printf("\nNo MIDI or CMF format. ");
              return(-3);
            }
            if (type)       /* determine speed */
              clocktick=( *(header+13) ) + ( (*(header+12))*256);
            else
              clocktick=( *(header+0x0c) )+( (*(header+0x0d))*256);
            settimer(clocktick,newtim);

            resetDSP();

            if (type)            /* offset to the start */
              Vmidiheader();
            else
              pointer=header+(*(header+8))+( (*(header+9))*256 );
            nexttoken=next();

            while ( !stop && !kbhit() )
            MIDIstream();

            if ( kbhit() ) getch();

            resettimer();
            printf("\nThat's all...");
            free(here);
            return(0);
          }
```

CHAPTER

ELEVEN

Sound Blaster Pro's Mixer Chip

- Programming ports 2X4H and 2X5H

- Defined registers for the mixer chip

- Setting the volumes for the channels

- Filters and other settings

As you know by now, the Sound Blaster Pro has far more capabilities than its cousin the Sound Blaster. Most of these capabilities are already discussed in previous chapters. This chapter, however, is reserved for new functions not discussed earlier. Specifically, this chapter deals with functions supported by the mixer chip.

What the Mixer Chip Does

The *mixer chip* handles incoming and outgoing signals and mixes all signals into one output signal. The mixer chip handles all three input signals, from the CD-ROM, Line-in, and the mic. This way, you can hear directly what is being recorded.

Thanks to the mixer chip, you can adjust the volume for each part. Furthermore, the chip contains settings that affect recording and playback. The mixer chip is programmed through ports 2X4H and 2X5H ($X = 2$ or 4, depending on the base port).

Programming the Ports

Ports 2X4H and 2X5H are programmed the same way as they are for the FM part. A byte that selects a particular register (a variable used by the mixer chip) is written to 2X4H. The value of this register serves as a kind of index. Next, the contents of this register can be read through port 2X5H or can be assigned a new value to this register, as shown in the following "psuedocode":

```
[1] OUT 2X4H,3
[2] IN D,2X5H
[3] OUT 2X5H,9
[4] OUT 2X4H,7
[5] OUT 2X5H,D
```

This program does the following:

Register	Use
1	Selects register 3.
2	If register 1 is read through port 2X5H, the current value of this register is assigned to variable D.

Register	Use
3	This register is loaded with the new value 9.
4	Register 7 is selected.
5	Register 7 is loaded with the value of register 3.

After this program, register 3 has the value 9 and register 7 has the old value of register 3.

NOTE "Setting the Volumes" below discusses registers that are defined for the mixer chip.

You can initialize the used registers with default values. This happens when the mixer chip is reset. To do this, you first have to write a 0 to port 2X4H. The program has to wait for a short time (about 0.5 microseconds). Next you have to write a 0 to port 2X5H. After the chip is reset, all registers contain their default values and the old settings are overwritten.

Establishing Volume Settings

Every volume setting is stored in a separate register. You can change the volume of both the left and the right channel of every part. The microphone input is the only input that has no volume setting. It has none because it doesn't have stereo capability. The volume settings for the three input signals affect the recording. If the setting is at zero, the recording contains only silence.

Volume Setting Registers   All register values in Table 11.1 have the same structure. The value of the mic part is the only one that differs from the rest.

Volume Register Structure   The volume can be set at a value between 0 (silence) and 7 (maximum). However, the CT-VOICE driver and most of the other Sound Blaster Pro software allow you to set the volume at a value ranging from 0 to 15. They let you do this because these programs use bits 0 and 4, so a 4-bit value

TABLE 11.1: Registers for the Volume Settings

Part	Register Index	Default
General	22H	44H
Voice	04H	44H
FM	26H	44H
CD	28H	00H
Line	2EH	00H
Mic	0AH	00H

can be set. On the mixer chip, these bits are not used for volume settings (they are always 1). Maybe bits 0 and 4 will be used in the next versions of the Sound Blaster Pro, in which case it will be possible to set the volume from 0 to 15. Table 11.2 shows the structure of the volume registers.

TABLE 11.2: Structure of the Volume Registers

Bits	Function
b7b6b5	Left channel volume (0..7)
b3b2b1	Right channel volume (0..7)

Mic Volume Register Structure   The same goes for the mic setting: the programs use bits 2, 1, and 0 to set the volume at a value from 0 to 7. Bit 0 is always 1, so it doesn't affect the volume. Table 11.3 shows the structure of the mic volume register.

TABLE 11.3: Structure of the Mic Volume Register

Bits	Function
b2b1	Mic channel volume (0..3)

Setting the Volume of One Channel without Changing the Other

Obviously the AND, OR, and SHIFT functions have to be used if you want to set the volume of the left or the right channel without changing the value for the other channel. Using AND, OR, and SHIFT is also preferable when you are setting the volume of the mic, because future versions of the Sound Blaster Pro may use other bits of register 0AH and cannot be loaded with a fixed value.

The general algorithm to set a volume is:

1. Select the register.

2. Read the old value.

3. Clear the old value using AND.

4. If necessary, shift the new value.

5. Set the new value using OR.

6. Write the new value to the register.

Listings 11.1, 11.2, and 11.3 are examples of a short program that sets the left channel of the general volume to the value 6 without changing the setting of the right channel. For 2X4H and 2X5H, X is the selected base port; you have to replace this with the correct settings.

Listing 11.1: Assembly Example

```
MOV   AH,6
MOV   DX,2X4H     ; step 1
MOV   AL,22H
OUT   DX,AL
INC   DX          ; step 2
IN  AL,DX
AND   AL,OFH      ; step 3
MOV   CL,4        ; step 4
SHL   AH,CL
OR  AL,AH         ; step 5
OUT   DX,AL       ; step 6
```

Listing 11.2: Pascal Example

```
Var
  OldV, NewV, Help : Byte;
Begin
  Port[$2X4]:=$22;        {step 1}
  OldV:=Port[$2X5];       {step 2}
  NewV:=OldV And $0F;     {step 3}
  Help:=6 shl 4;          {step 4}
  NewV:=NewV Or Help;     {step 5}
  Port[$2X5]:=NewV;       {step 6}
End;
```

Listing 11.3: C Example

```
{
  int OldV, NewV, Help;
  outp(0x2X4,0x@@);       /* step 1 */
  OldV = inp(0x2X5);      /* step 2 */
  NewV = OldV & 0xOF;     /* step 3 */
  Help = 6 <<<< 4;        /* step 4 */
  NewV = NewV | Help;     /* step 5 */
  outp(0x2X5,NewV)        /* step 6 */
}
```

Filters and Other Settings

Besides the various volume settings, other settings are possible on the mixer chip. They are set by means of the three registers: 06H, 0CH, and 0EH.

Register 06H   Register 06H determines how the FM channels are reproduced. The settings are shown in Table 11.4

TABLE 11.4: Determining the FM Channels

Bits	Function	Settings
b6	Right channel	0 = on
		1 = off
b5	left channel	0 = on
		1 = off

If both bits are reset (=0), normal stereo reproduction is taking place. If one of the two bits is set (=1), all FM channels are reproduced through the other channel. For example, when b6 = 1 and b5 = 0 are set, everything is reproduced through the left channel. If both bits are set, no FM reproduction takes place. This way you can switch off the FM channels without changing the volume.

Register OCH Register OCH contains three functions that relate to sample recording. The functions and settings are shown in Table 11.5.

Bit 5 determines whether bit 3 is used or not. Bit 3 selects the filter type. Bits 2 and 1 allow you to determine the sample recording input. Though several input signals can be heard at the same time, only one of the three signals is recorded internally. So it is not possible to record a sample of a mixed signal of the Line and the CD-ROM.

Register OEH Register OEH contains two functions, as shown in Table 11.6.

Bit 1 is used for both recording and playing back. Bit 5 determines whether the output filter is used. Again you have to use the AND, OR, and SHIFT functions to change the various settings. Future versions of the Sound Blaster Pro may use some of the bits that are not yet used. Therefore, we advise not changing these bit values.

TABLE 11.5: Register for Sample Recording

Bits	Function	Settings
b5	Voice input filter	0 = on
		1 = off
b3	Pass filter	0 = high
		1 = low
b2b1	Voice input selection	0 = Mic input
		1 = CD-ROM
		2 = not used
		3 = line input

TABLE 11.6: Register with Two Functions

Bits	Function	Settings
b6	Output filter	0 = on
		1 = off
b1	Stereo/mono selection	0 = mono
		1 = stereo

The algorithm described in the previous section again applies to setting the various bits.

To conclude, we hope you have noticed that programming the mixer chip is quite simple, since every setting is programmed the same way.

APPENDIX

A

Sound Blaster 16 Hardware and Software

This appendix will get you acquainted with Sound Blaster's many capabilities. It explains how to install the card and looks at the software that comes with Sound Blaster 16. It shows how to install this software and briefly describes some of the third-party software and hardware available for Sound Blaster 16. This appendix also explains how to configure Sound Blaster 16 for your system.

Sound Blaster 16: An Overview

Sound Blaster 16 (SB16) is the top-of-the-line sound card from Creative Labs. The *16* in its name refers to the fact that Sound Blaster 16 can record and play back 16-bit as well as 8-bit digital sound.

The ASP Chip   Sound Blaster boasts Advanced Signal Processing (ASP), the name Creative Labs has given its proprietary digital signal-processing chip. An ASP chip can perform a number of algorithms. As such, it can create the kinds of sound effects that hardware signal-processing units create, including reverb, delay, equalization, dynamic limiting, compression, and expansion. However, creating advanced sound effects like these is only a "potential" right now because software providing the algorithms to create advanced sounds has not been written yet. To date, the ASP chip is being used only to perform data compression. In other words, the chip lets you store digital audio in less space than it would normally take.

> **NOTE**   Don't confuse data compression with *dynamic audio compression*, which is a technique for controlling the dynamic range of a sound.

How Sound Samples Are Made   Sound Blaster 16 can sample sound—that is, convert sound to digital data—and record it to a hard disk at rates from 4kHz to 44.1kHz. SB16 samples sound through an ⅛-inch mini-jack microphone input (a compatible microphone is bundled with the card) or from its ⅛-inch stereo line input. It can also sample sounds from its FM synthesizer or an attached CD-ROM drive.

The On-Board Synthesizer   Sound Blaster 16 has an on-board synthesizer that's built around the Yamaha OPL-3 four-operator FM synthesizer chip. Although the chip provides 20-voice polyphony and 20 multitimbral parts, it has a very limited sound palette and is difficult to use for anything but simple game sounds.

Wave Blaster   However, Sound Blaster 16 does have one excellent synthesizer feature: it can be connected to Creative Labs' Wave Blaster daughterboard. Wave Blaster gives SB16 virtually all the capabilities of an E-mu Proteus sample-playback synthesizer. The card costs roughly $200 more than Sound Blaster itself. Nevertheless, Wave Blaster gives you 255 professionally sampled sounds from Creative Labs' sound library. With Wave Blaster, you can turn the SB16 into a flexible and excellent-sounding synthesizer.

SB16's MIDI Interface   Sound Blaster 16 has a MIDI interface that supports both the MPU-401 dumb UART mode and the Sound Blaster standard mode. The MIDI's function is to allow PC applications to communicate with external MIDI instruments and other devices. For example, with a sequencer application running, you could play a MIDI keyboard and have the sequencer record the performance. Later, you could play it back on SB16's FM synthesizer, the Wave Blaster, the external keyboard, or any combination of the three.

However, before you can use the MIDI interface to communicate with external MIDI instruments or other devices, you have to attach the optional MIDI kit to Sound Blaster's joystick port.

Audio Outputs   For audio outputs, the Sound Blaster 16 ASP has one mini-jack output that accepts either a headphone or a stereo amplifier plug. The output can be configured as either a variable, 4-Watts-per-channel or a line-level output. Sound Blaster can drive a power amplifier or unpowered, 4-ohm speakers. You use a dial on the card's back plate to set its final output volume. The board also has both audio and data connectors to which you can attach a CD-ROM drive.

The Audio Mixer   Finally, SB16 has an *audio mixer*. To control the mixer, you can use the bundled Windows applet, the SB16 Mixer, or the SB16SET and

SB16MIX DOS applications. The mixer can accept sound from all the card's input sources—line in, the microphone, the synthesizer, a CD-ROM drive, and the PC speaker—and combine sounds into a single stereo output. While the audio mixer is combining the sounds, you can change the relative volume levels of all the sound sources, as well as lower or raise their bass, treble, or output gain.

Sound Blaster 16 Software   The SB16 card comes with software for both DOS and Windows. Most of the DOS software is meant for developers interested in designing their own software for use with SB16, but some of the DOS software is to a degree oriented toward the user. The Windows software that comes with SB16 is generally much more flexible and easier to use. It also focuses more heavily on entertainment, multimedia, music, and OLE applications.

Installing the Sound Blaster 16 Card

This part of the appendix explains how to install the Sound Blaster 16 hardware. Installing Sound Blaster 16 involves several steps:

- Making sure you have the right hardware
- Opening up your computer
- Handling the card correctly
- Attaching Wave Blaster to Sound Blaster (if you have Wave Blaster and choose to install it)
- Changing the default settings to your liking
- Placing the card in the slot
- Making joystick, stereo/audio, microphone, line input, and CD-ROM drive connections

Each step is described below.

Hardware Requirements for Sound Blaster 16

Before you install Sound Blaster 16—before you *buy* it, actually—make sure you have the right PC and peripherals for the card:

- *PC requirements.* You can use Sound Blaster 16 with most of the recent PC models: an IBM AT, 286, 386, 486; a PS/2 (model 25/30); a Tandy AT; or a 100-percent-compatible clone of any of these models.

- *Monitors.* Having a VGA monitor is nice, but you can get by with just an EGA.

- *Disk space.* You need at least 5MB of disk space for the software that comes with Sound Blaster.

- *Memory.* At least 2MB of RAM is a very good idea.

- *Operating environment.* Another very good idea is having Windows 3.1. Having Windows 3.1 isn't absolutely necessary, because if you're just going to play games, which create their own environment, you can use Windows 3.0. However, if you intend to use Sound Blaster for multimedia or to create music, Windows 3.1 will make things much more pleasant.

If your PC meets these requirements, you are ready to install the Sound Blaster 16 card.

WARNING   Using Windows 3.0 with Sound Blaster is not recommended.

Opening Up Your Computer

To install the card, the first thing to do is open your computer:

1. Turn the PC's power off, but do not disconnect its power cable—you want the PC to stay grounded.

2. Remove the screws that hold the cover. If you need help doing this, consult your computer's manual.

3. Slowly remove the PC's cover. As you remove the cover, make sure it doesn't get snagged on any cables.

4. On the inside of the PC's back panel, unscrew and remove the cover behind any unused 16-bit slot. This provides an opening for the card's back plate. When you remove the cover, be sure to save the screw. You'll need it later to anchor the Sound Blaster card to the PC.

TIP The 16-bit slots are the longer ones. Eight-bit slots are roughly half the size of 16-bit slots.

Tips for Handling Cards

Now you are ready to install the card. Before you do so, however, read the following tips to keep from damaging the card and your computer:

- Keep the card in its protective envelope whenever you pick it up or move it.

- Always hold the card by the edges. This way, you won't bend the components.

- Before touching the card, touch either the power supply in the PC or some unpainted metal surface. Do this to discharge any static electricity that may have built up in your body.

- Avoid rubbing your feet on rugs, rubbing your clothing together, or doing anything else that could cause static electricity to build up.

Follow these precautions and your Sound Blaster and PC should be safe.

WARNING By avoiding static build-up in your body, you reduce the possibility of transferring an electric charge to Sound Blaster. If static electricity discharges when the card touches the PC slot, the card or even parts of the computer could be destroyed.

Attaching Wave Blaster to Sound Blaster

If you have a Creative Labs Wave Blaster, now is the time to attach it to Sound Blaster 16. If you don't have Wave Blaster, skip ahead to the next section, "SB16 Default Settings and How to Change Them." This section explains how to connect Wave Blaster to Sound Blaster.

NOTE

If you have already installed Sound Blaster and you want to attach Wave Blaster to your SB16, disconnect all external cables from Sound Blaster before you attach Wave Blaster. As you remove the Sound Blaster card from the PC slot, be sure to follow the advice in "Tips for Handling Cards" above. Then follow the directions below for attaching Wave Blaster to Sound Blaster.

To attach Wave Blaster to Sound Blaster:

1. Insert the three plastic posts into the holes on the Wave Blaster card, as shown in Figure A.1.

2. Mount the Wave Blaster card on the Sound Blaster card by pressing the three plastic posts into the holes on the Wave Blaster card. As you do so, press the header housing on the Wave Blaster onto the header pins on the Sound Blaster.

TIP

Pressing the parts of the two cards together will probably take more pressure than you would expect. But if you're careful to align the plastic posts and header units properly, and you apply a firm, even pressure, the boards should fit together securely.

With the Wave Blaster card mounted onto the SB16, you're ready to move to the next step, considering whether or not to use Sound Blaster's default settings.

FIGURE A.1:

Connecting the Wave Blaster card
to the Sound Blaster 16 card

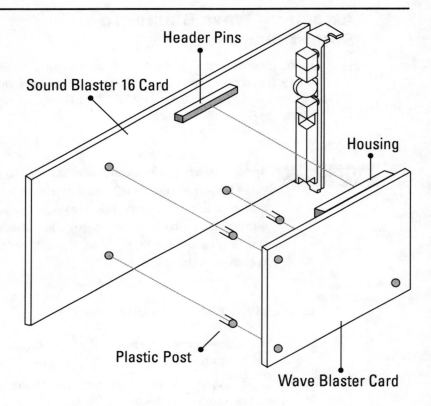

Header Pins

Sound Blaster 16 Card

Housing

Plastic Post

Wave Blaster Card

SB16 Default Settings and How to Change Them

Sound Blaster, like all expansion cards, has certain default settings to make it work with the PC in certain ways. However, you can change these default settings to suit your own needs by reconfiguring the hardware on the card. Moreover, SB16 lets you change many of its default settings by means of software as well.

The following list shows the SB16 settable parameters. All but the last two items on the list can be changed either in software or hardware; the last two can only be modified by hardware.

- IRQ (default 5)
- 8-bit DMA (default 1)

- 16-bit DMA (default 5)
- Base I/O address (default 220H to 233H)
- MIDI port base I/O address (default 330H to 331H)
- Joystick port (enable/disable)
- Audio output (amplified or line level)

There are only three reasons to change the SB16's factory defaults:

- If you want to use a joystick port that you've already installed in your PC, instead of the one on SB16.
- If you plan to connect the SB16's audio output to any kind of amplifier—including powered speakers—as opposed to connecting it to plain, ordinary, unpowered speakers.
- If an unrelated device attached to your PC—for example, a printer or modem—is already using one of SB16's IRQ, DMA, or I/O address settings and the device will conflict with the SB16. If you think such a conflict will result, you can move jumpers before you install SB16 to change its settings.

Following is a discussion of these three default settings. If you want to keep SB16's default settings and have no plans to change them, skip ahead to "Placing the Card in the Slot" later in this appendix.

Changing Joystick and Amplifier Settings

If you want to use another joystick controller card, you *have to* disable the SB16's joystick. Disabling SB16's joystick will not affect the MIDI operation of the joystick port. And if you want to use an external amplifier, you *should* bypass SB16's internal amplifier. Bypassing the internal amplifier will reduce distortion and give you greater headroom for both MIDI and audio.

NOTE IRQ, DMA, and I/O address settings are explained in Appendix B. See this appendix if you are unsure what these settings are for.

In order to disable the joystick and bypass the internal amplifier, you have to reposition jumpers on the SB16 card. *Jumpers* are small plastic and metal caps that connect pairs of pins on the card. They're easy to move from one pair of pins to another. You'll reposition one jumper for the joystick and two for the amplifier. You cannot change these defaults with software.

How to Move Jumpers   In general, the best way to move jumpers is:

1. Lay the card flat on a soft, nonconductive surface (a towel on a table is good).

2. With a pair of fine needle-nosed pliers, gently pull each jumper straight up, off the pins.

3. If necessary, reposition the jumper over a different pair of pins and push it straight down onto the pins with the pliers or with your finger.

WARNING   As you move jumpers, be careful not to bend any pins or other card components. Be sure to touch some grounded metal object to discharge static.

Disabling the Joystick Port   To disable SB16's joystick port:

- Locate jumper JYEN, as shown in Figure A.2, and remove it.

Don't reposition this jumper, just leave it off. But save it in case you decide to change your joystick setup later on.

Bypassing the Internal Amplifier   To bypass the internal amplifier with jumpers:

1. Locate jumpers OPSL and OPSR. These jumpers are near the audio outputs, as shown in Figure A.2.

2. Remove both jumpers from pins 2 and 3 (the default) and push them onto pins 1 and 2.

FIGURE A.2:

The joystick and audio amplifier jumpers on the SB16 card

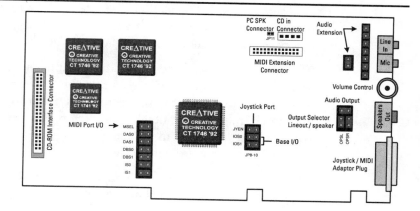

Changing the joystick and amplifier defaults is a fairly simple operation in the installation stage. Remember, however, that if you want to change these settings in the future, you will have to disconnect all wires, remove the card from the PC, and go through all this rigmarole again. This tiresome necessity brings up the third reason for changing settings: conflicts.

Changing IRQ, DMA, and I/O Address Settings

Besides joystick and amplifier settings, you can also change Sound Blaster's IRQ, DMA, and I/O address settings. It's important to realize that, in most cases, you won't know whether the SB16 will conflict with other devices—and hence whether you need to change the defaults—until you have installed and used SB16. Most people don't even know what an IRQ or DMA is, and even if they do, who remembers the IRQ setting of their modem anyway?

> **NOTE**   See Appendix B if you need information about what IRQ, DMA, and I/O address settings do.

Experience teaches us that the best strategy is to install the card with its default settings and try it out. If you do discover a conflict, you can still leave the jumpers alone and override SB16's IRQ, DMA, and I/O address settings with the installation or setup software. Even if you're certain there will be a conflict, you can still ignore the jumpers and change defaults while you install the SB16 software.

Changing DMA, IRQ, and I/O address settings with the software is easier, faster, and more documentable. Clearly, using the software is the recommended method for changing these values. And using the software does not require you to pull the SB16 out of the PC and put it back on again. For all these reasons, we suggest that you leave the hardware in its factory configuration, finish installing the card, and then make any changes with software.

However, if you want to move jumpers, read the Sound Blaster manual. And read Appendix B as well, so you know what you're getting into.

Placing the Card into the Slot

Once your joystick and amplifier are set to your liking, it's time to put the SB16 in its slot.

At one end of the Sound Blaster card is a metal plate, called the *back plate,* with various jacks on it. On one of the long sides of the card, as shown in Figure A.3, is the *connector tab,* a series of small, gold-colored metal rectangles. The connector tab is the part of the card that you insert into the PC's expansion slot. The gold rectangles on the connector tab are contacts by which the card is connected electronically to the computer.

To install Sound Blaster 16 in your PC:

1. Touch the PC power supply or another unpainted metal surface. Do this to discharge any static electricity you may be carrying.

2. Pick up the card and touch the power supply again, just to be sure.

3. Hold the SB16 card so its connector tab is directly over the slot into which you want to insert it. At this point, the back plate of the card should be facing the rear of the PC.

4. Gently but firmly insert the Sound Blaster connector tab into the PC slot.

FIGURE A.3:

The Sound Blaster 16 card back plate connections and connector tab

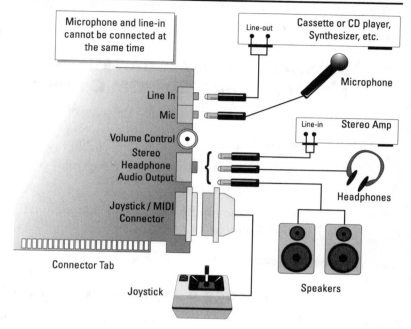

Microphone and line-in cannot be connected at the same time

Line-out

Cassette or CD player, Synthesizer, etc.

Line In

Mic

Volume Control

Stereo Headphone Audio Output

Joystick / MIDI Connector

Connector Tab

Microphone

Line-in   Stereo Amp

Headphones

Speakers

Joystick

WARNING   Do not push the card hard enough to break anything. If the card doesn't slide in easily, pull it out and make sure nothing is obstructing the slot, the back plate, or any other part of the card. Then try again—gently. Breaking things in here can be very expensive.

The back plate should be seated firmly against the card opening you made earlier in the back of the PC.

5. Move the top of the back plate so it lines up with the hole from which you re-moved the screw earlier. You removed this screw when you removed the PC cover.

6. Using the screw, fasten Sound Blaster's back plate to the PC.

The final part of the hardware installation has to do with connecting Sound Blaster 16 to the outside world.

Joystick, Stereo/Audio, Microphone, Line Input, and CD-ROM Connections

As shown in Figure A.3, the back plate of the SB16 card has, from bottom to top:

- The 15-pin joystick D-connector port
- The stereo audio output, a ⅛-inch mini-jack
- The volume dial
- The audio inputs, first the microphone and then the line level input, both ⅛-inch mini-jacks

Following is information about how to make connections to these ports.

Connecting a Joystick to Sound Blaster

The Joystick port is a standard port for connecting any analog joystick with a 15-pin sub-D connector. Sound Blaster supports all the standard PC software that uses any analog joystick. If you already have a joystick port on your PC, either remove the old one or disable SB16's.

NOTE See "Changing Joystick and Amplifier Settings" earlier in this appendix for information about disabling the Sound Blaster joystick.

To connect a joystick to Sound Blaster:

- Simply plug the joystick's D-connector into the SB16 port.

The MIDI Kit   The Joystick port also connects to the optional MIDI kit, so you can add MIDI In and Out ports to SB16. To use the port for both MIDI and a joystick:

- Attach the MIDI kit, and then plug the joystick into the through-connector of the MIDI kit.

Using Two Joysticks   To use two joysticks with the SB16, you need a joystick splitter cable. Creative Labs sells one and maintains that its cable is the only one that is guaranteed to work properly. It's probably worth the small extra cost to get the Creative Labs model and not deal with the many fly-by-night companies that populate the computer business.

Connecting Stereo Audio Output to Sound Blaster

The stereo audio output connection is made through an ⅛" mini-jack (see Figure A.3). Using this jack, Sound Blaster can send stereo audio output to a pair of powered or unpowered speakers, a stereo amplifier, or a pair of stereo headphones. If you're going to use an amplifier, be sure to set the audio jumpers correctly. Otherwise, just plug your unpowered speakers or headphones into the jack, and you're set.

NOTE   For information about setting the audio jumpers, see "Changing Joystick and Amplifier Settings" earlier in this appendix.

Connecting a Microphone

You can plug the microphone that comes with Sound Blaster 16 directly into the card's microphone input, but using Sound Blaster's microphone is guaranteed to produce poor-quality recordings. Almost any microphone you buy will work better than the one that comes with Sound Blaster. It will last a lot longer as well (the switch on mine didn't work). However, you have to get an adapter plug or cable to plug any but the cheesiest microphone into SB16's mini-jack.

Experiment first. The Sound Blaster microphone is optimized for voice, and if you intend to record voices only, you're okay. But if you record sound with a broader frequency bandwidth, such as music, the sound will distort badly.

Line Input

Connect the Line Input jack to any line-level source of sound you want to record with Sound Blaster, including a tape or CD player, a radio, a TV, or an electronic instrument such as a synthesizer. For Sound Blaster, you'll need a splitter cable in order to mix the signals of two mono plugs from the source into a single stereo plug.

Remember, consumer equipment such as stereos and CD players usually require RCA plugs, and professional equipment such as synthesizers have ¼-inch plugs. Sound Blaster, of course, uses a one-prong stereo mini-plug. Keep these conversions in mind as you shop for a splitter cable.

Connecting to a CD-ROM Drive

To connect to an internal or external CD-ROM drive, follow the directions in the player's manual. A CD-ROM drive typically requires two connections:

- One to the SB16's SCSI port in order to transfer computer files from the CD-ROM to the PC
- One to the SB16 audio mixer in order to route CD sound (Red Book audio) from the CD-ROM to SB16

Installing Sound Blaster 16 Software

One of the nicest things about the Sound Blaster 16 is the installation and setup software Creative Labs includes with the card. With only minimal input from the user, four programs do all the technical dirty work, including reconfiguring the defaults, installing both DOS and Windows drivers, and even testing the card. Moreover, you can change IRQ, DMA, and I/O addresses after you make the card settings. You'll appreciate the fact that you can change IRQ, DMA, and I/O settings if you install some new device later that causes a conflict with Sound Blaster. With earlier versions of Sound Blaster, you had to remove the card to readjust these settings.

The four software installation programs are:

INSTALL.EXE	The Installation program. This program installs the Sound Blaster 16 software on your hard disk and alters the CONFIG.SYS and AUTOEXEC.BAT files accordingly.
SBCONFIG.EXE	The Configuration program. This program sets the card's IRQ, DMA, and I/O settings.

| TESTSB16.EXE | The Test program. This program lets you test your card's sound capabilities. |
| WINSETUP.EXE | The Windows Setup program. This program installs Windows drivers and modifies your SYSTEM.INI file to make the SB16 work in Windows. |

You should already have installed the card in an expansion slot. The following discusses how to install the SB16 software and set the card up.

INSTALL for Installing Sound Blaster

To run INSTALL.EXE, follow these steps:

1. Boot your PC in MS-DOS.

2. Put SB16 disk #1 into your floppy drive. (We'll assume you use drive B:.)

3. At the DOS prompt, type **B:INSTALL** and press Enter.

4. Follow the instructions the program gives you.

TIP   Before you begin the installation, read the README file first for any late-breaking changes (don't be disappointed if there aren't any).

As the INSTALL program runs, you'll spend most of your time watching it write things to your hard disk. If you've followed our advice and not changed any IRQ, DMA, or I/O address settings, you can just answer "yes" to all questions. When you see the "Software Installation Completed" screen:

5. Press any key.

6. Exit the program.

The software is now on your hard disk in a directory called SB16. Your CONFIG.SYS and AUTOEXEC.BAT files have been modified to accommodate Sound Blaster 16.

SBCONFIG for the IRQ, DMA, and I/O Address Settings

The Configuration program sets the card's IRQ, DMA, and I/O address settings. To run this program:

1. At the DOS prompt, type **CD SB16** to move to the SB16 directory.

2. At the SB16 prompt, type **SBCONFIG** and press Enter.

3. Follow the instructions the program gives.

If you're accepting the defaults, just press Enter or S and Enter, as the program explains. You can change settings by pressing the arrow keys. When the program asks to reboot the system, answer yes.

The SB16 should now be set up to work in DOS. When the computer is back up, you can test the card.

TEST for Testing Your Card's Sound Capabilities

The Test program let's you find out what kinds of sounds your Sound Blaster can produce. To run the Test program, follow these steps:

1. At the DOS prompt, type **CD SB16** to move to the SB16 directory.

2. At the SB16 prompt, type **TESTSB16** and press Enter.

3. Follow the instructions the program gives.

After it does some of its own testing, the program will let you see if the card really works by presenting you with a display that gives you options for playing short sounds that test all the card's sound capabilities. You can play any of four files that are included on the disk:

- Two MIDI files are included. One MIDI file uses the 2-operator FM synthesizer and the other uses the 4-operator FM synthesizer.

- Two digital audio files are included. One of the audio files plays back in 8-bit sound and the other plays back in 16-bit sound.

Select an option and press Enter to play the 2-to-3-second test sounds. If you don't hear anything, check all your connections.

If You Don't Hear Anything... If you still don't hear anything, it is probably because your SB16 settings are in conflict with those of another device in your PC. Unfortunately, you're in for some tedious work:

- Look up the settings of your other devices in their respective manuals, write them down, and see if their settings match those of the SB16. If settings match, go back to the SBCONFIG program and start changing the settings. If you aren't sure whether a setting matches, start changing the SB16 settings. Go through the IRQ settings first, then the DMA and finally the address settings. You'll have to change one setting, test the card, change another setting, test the card again, and so on until SB16 can produce sounds or until you run out of options.

- If the above technique doesn't work, start removing the other cards in your PC one at a time. Turn the computer off first, pull a card, reboot, and try the Test program again. At best, SB16 will work after you pull a card. Then all you have to do is figure out the card's settings and change them or change the settings on the SB16 so the two cards don't conflict. At worst, you'll pull all the cards and discover that the Sound Blaster still doesn't work. If this happens, check the card on another computer or call Creative Labs. You might have a defective card, although this doesn't happen often.

TIP   Some computers have problems playing 16-bit audio. The SB16 *Getting Started* manual documents the procedure for resolving this problem quite well.

WINSETUP for Setting the Windows Drivers

The WINSETUP program installs Windows drivers and modifies your SYS-TEM.INI file to make the SB16 work in Windows.

As we've mentioned before, you can take best advantage of Sound Blaster 16 and its software if Windows 3.1 is installed on your PC. If you are already using Windows 3.1 and you have successfully set up and tested Sound Blaster in DOS, you can set up the SB16's Windows drivers. Follow these steps:

1. Start Windows.

2. Open the Program Manager.

3. From the File menu, choose Run.

4. In the dialog box, type **C:\SB16\WINAPPL\WINSETUP** and click OK.

5. When the program is finished, restart Windows.

Installing Wave Blaster Software

If you installed Creative Labs' Wave Blaster daughterboard on your Sound Blaster 16, you must install its software as well. Follow these steps:

1. Start your PC in DOS.

2. Put Wave Blaster disk #1 in your floppy drive (we'll assume this is drive B).

3. Type **B:** to enter the B drive directory.

4. Type **INSTALL** and press Enter.

The install program creates a directory called WAVEBLST and installs in it all the files necessary to run the Wave Blaster.

TIP

> By installing the Wave Blaster daughterboard onto the SB16, you will improve the sound quality of your SB16's MIDI performances enormously. See "The Wave Blaster" later in this appendix for a thorough discussion of the Wave Blaster.

Testing Wave Blaster   To test the Wave Blaster, run the DEMO.BAT program:

1. Type **CD WAVEBLST** to enter the Wave Blaster directory.
2. At the DOS prompt, type **DEMO** and press Enter.

The program DEMO.BAT will play a demo tune on the Wave Blaster.

Routing MIDI Data to the Wave Blaster   To play the Wave Blaster in Windows, you have to use the windows MIDI Mapper to get MIDI data from a sequencer or other MIDI application to the Wave Blaster (and not the OPL-3). To set up the MIDI Mappers to get MIDI data for the Wave Blaster:

1. Open the Windows Control Panel.
2. Open the MIDI Mapper icon.

Notice that the MIDI Mapper defaults to SB16 Ext FM, which means that it is set to use the OPL-3 FM chip. You want to change this:

3. Click on the arrow to the right of the SB16 Ext FM setting.
4. From the drop-down list, choose Extended MIDI.

Now any MIDI data generated by a Windows application will be routed to the Wave Blaster. Instead of hearing the OPL-3 when you play a MIDI file or any MIDI sequence, you'll hear sampled instrumental sounds with a very high degree of fidelity, dynamic range, and other qualities that create a gratifying musical experience.

Installing CD-ROM Software

Installing a CD-ROM drive in your PC to work with the SB16 opens up a lot of possibilities, and we recommend it heartily. In order for your PC to read CD-ROM data, the setup program that comes with your CD-ROM drive installs MSCDEX.EXE and modifies the CONFIG.SYS file so it can load MSCDEX.EXE at startup. A DOS device driver residing in the directory with MSCDEX.EXE tells DOS that the CD-ROM drive exists.

To play CD-ROM audio, your PC needs the MCICDA.DRV driver that comes with Windows 3.1. You can install it with the Control Panel and drivers icon, where you'll see it listed as [MCI] CD Audio. Read your CD-ROM and Windows manuals to learn how to install MCICDA.DRV.

Sound Blaster 16 Enhancements

Sound Blaster 16 possesses a remarkable set of functions that weren't available on any single card at any price just a few years ago. For example, SB16's ability to record and play 16-bit digital audio offers tremendous opportunities for all sorts of applications, from creating your own recordings to enjoying commercial multimedia titles.

To take advantage of the SB16 hardware, of course, you need software to operate it. The SB16 comes with a number of DOS and Windows programs that serve the creative potential of the card. However, most of the DOS programs are quite limited and so unintuitive as to discourage creativity. As for Windows, a few of the Windows programs are useful, but even the best are less than inspiring, or lack the full functionality that could let you take complete creative advantage of the card.

The good news is that some excellent third-party software is available for Sound Blaster 16. A good MIDI sequencer or digital audio recording/editing application can help the user who wants to create music and record digital audio with Sound Blaster 16. Many game, multimedia, educational, and other programs use the SB16's sound to great advantage as well.

This said, let's look at the more capable of the bundled Sound Blaster applications.

The Wave Blaster

Unfortunately, the SB16 uses the dreadful Yamaha OPL-3 synthesizer chip. The sounds produced by this chip may once have been acceptable as novelties and for computer games, but are so lacking in dynamics, color, variation, and sonic complexity as to make them boring. In light of the OPL-3's limitations, the most brilliant aspect of the SB16 is its ability to substitute Creative Labs' Wave Blaster for the OPL-3.

The Wave Blaster (WB) is an optional SB16 daughterboard loaded with 4MB of the same digital samples used in the superb-sounding E-mu Proteus. The Proteus is a professional sample-playback synthesizer whose well-programmed acoustic and synthesized instrumental sounds—melodic as well as percussive—are used in studios everywhere. The WB's on-board ROM contains 383 different sounds, providing up to 32-note polyphony. It can respond individually and simultaneously on all 16 MIDI channels, and defaults to the General MIDI instrument and percussion maps.

By installing the Wave Blaster daughterboard onto the SB16, you will improve the sound quality of your SB16's MIDI performances enormously. The OPL-3 chip can still function, but after you hear the Wave Blaster you'll never want to hear the Yamaha sounds again.

The Control Panel

In the Wave Blaster, sounds are arranged according to the General MIDI instrument map, making them compatible with thousands of MIDI files available both commercially and from bulletin board systems. In addition, you can customize the Wave Blaster in many ways by using the Wave Blaster Control Panel, shown in Figure A.4. The Wave Blaster Control Panel is found in the Sound Blaster 16 Program Group.

Following are some basic instructions for using the Wave Blaster Control Panel:

- To turn any of the sixteen Wave Blaster MIDI channels on and off, click in the box to the left of the channel.

- To lock any given sound to a specific MIDI channel, click in the M (for "mute") column.

- To set channel volumes and pan positions, simply click and drag the Volume or Pan sliders left or right.

FIGURE A.4:

The Wave Blaster Control Panel lets you control sounds and other parameters.

Establishing Global Settings

Clicking on the Global button (the one that looks like a globe) brings up the Global Settings window shown in Figure A.5. Here, you can set a number of overall parameters:

- To set master tuning, transposition, or pitch bend ranges, move the respective slider left or right.

- To change the Wave Blaster's velocity curve (which gives a sound different responses to the force with which you strike a key on a MIDI keyboard connected to the SB16), click one of the five Velocity buttons.

- To choose one of the four MIDI modes or four General MIDI options, click any one of the buttons in those panels. These set many sophisticated mapping and prioritization schema in the Wave Blaster. Setting these modes and options requires a sound knowledge of MIDI and synthesizers, however.

FIGURE A.5:
The Wave Blaster's Global Settings screen lets you configure Wave Blaster's response to MIDI.

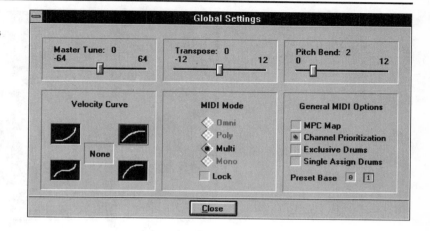

The Bank Arranger for Creating New Sounds

Click the Bank button to access WB's Bank Arranger. The Bank Arranger shows you—and lets you load and arrange—the sounds produced by all the instruments to create entirely new banks of patches.

To use the Bank Arranger:

1. Open any instrument bank in both the Instrument Bank and Available Instrument Preset windows.

2. Substitute a bank from the Available window for any bank in the Instrument Bank window. To do this, select a bank in each window and click the arrow button. This will give the Wave Blaster an entirely different set of sounds.

Creative WaveStudio

Within its rather limited scope, Creative WaveStudio is a surprisingly capable digital audio editor. As shown in Figure A.6, it graphically displays WAV files. With the WAV files displayed, you can move quickly to various points in the file by clicking and dragging on the overview window. Except for its lack of an Undo command, a rather serious oversight, Creative WaveStudio is an excellent tool. With it, you can create short audio clips and even mix two clips.

FIGURE A.6:
Creative WaveStudio lets you record and edit digital audio.

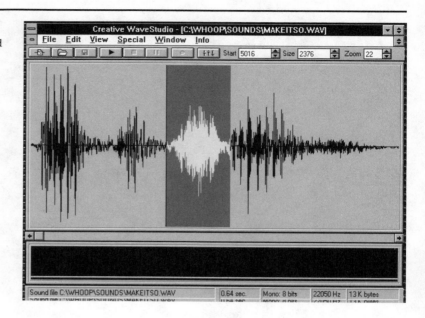

In its main window, the program displays a waveform, a menu bar, and a set of buttons. You can click on buttons to start, stop, or pause Creative WaveStudio's recording and playback functions. You can tell where you are in a file by looking at the three readouts that show the beginning and end of your selection. Scroll buttons let you change a selection's size and location, and you can also drag across a readout value and type in a different number to change sizes and locations. Changes in the readout are reflected in the selection. As shown in Figure A.7, the display window can hold a number of files.

Zooming

The information bar at the bottom of the screen shows the file's duration, sample rate, size, and format. You can zoom in and out to view only a few cycles or the entire sample:

- To zoom out and simultaneously select the entire file, double-click in the overview screen.

FIGURE A.7:
Creative WaveStudio lets you work
with many files at once.

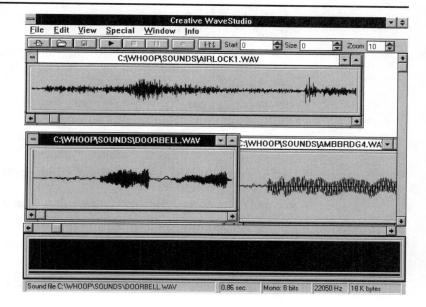

- To select part of a sample, drag across a section in the Preview window at the bottom of the screen. The section you dragged across will appear in the main window. Unfortunately, the zoom factor doesn't change when you do this. To see your file, you have to change the zoom factor manually.

Editing a File

Click and drag the mouse to select a section of a file. The Edit menu offers the following options for working with part of a file:

Option	Use
Cut	Cuts part of a selection and places it on the Clipboard so you can paste it elsewhere.
Copy	Copies part of a selection to the Clipboard so you can place it elsewhere.
Paste	Places the selection on the Clipboard at a new location in the file.

Option	Use
Paste	Combines the two sounds. This menu also lets you
Mix	delete a selection or crop a file—that is, delete everything but the selection.

The Special Menu   The Special menu lets you insert a silent section in a file, convert a selection to silence, fade in or out, or make a selection play backwards. For example, the Rap! command places a copy of a selection immediately before the original to create a stutter effect. With the Rap! command, you can create echoes and amplify a sound's volume (but not lower it) up to 500 percent.

The Mixer Button   Clicking on the Mixer button starts the Sound Blaster 16 Mixer Control program. The Sound Blaster 16 Mixer is covered in the next section.

Mixing Sound Sources with the SB16 Mixer

The Sound Blaster 16 Mixer lets you set the volume of the card's microphone, line, CD, and other inputs simply by moving sliders on the screen. You can also adjust the gain and the master output volume, and turn each source on and off by clicking buttons on the right side of the window. The settings you make in this window will be in effect for every application that you use.

TIP   Being able to turn off input sources is helpful. For example, if you aren't using a microphone you can turn that input off to reduce some of the noise in the circuit. Set both Gain controls to x4 for the best balance between signal volume and noise.

Soundo'LE

Object Linking and Embedding (OLE) is a new technology that lets you copy and paste data "objects" created in one application into documents created by another application. You can, for instance, digitize your voice with Creative Soundo'LE, then cut and paste the sound into a spreadsheet. An icon appearing in the spreadsheet represents your voice. When someone clicks on this icon, they will hear your voice. The document in which you record the sound is called the *source* document, and the document into which you paste the object is called the *destination* document.

Creative Soundo'LE is designed to let you use OLE technology. You record sounds in Soundo'LE just as you do in Creative WaveStudio: click on the record button, speak into the microphone, and click stop when you're finished. However, because it has no editing functions, a better approach would be to record in WaveStudio, edit the recording to your satisfaction, and open the resulting file in Soundo'LE.

To insert a Soundo'LE recording into a document:

1. Open the document into which you want to insert a sound.

2. Choose Insert Object from whatever menu offers it.

3. Choose Soundo'LE. The Soundo'LE window will open.

4. From Soundo'LE's File menu, select an object and click OK.

5. From Soundo'LE's File menu, choose Update (the destination application).

6. Return to your destination application.

7. Double-click on the Soundo'LE icon in your destination document and it will play back.

If you want more information on OLE technology, read the Microsoft Windows manuals.

APPENDIX

B

DMAs, IRQs, and I/O Addresses

This appendix explains what DMA channels, IRQ numbers, and I/O addresses are for. It explains how they interact with the Sound Blaster card as well.

Understanding DMA Channels

When the Sound Blaster (SB16) records and plays digital audio, it uses a Direct Memory Access (DMA) channel in the PC to move audio between itself and the PC's RAM. SB16 does this in order to bypass the PC's main processor and move the data at speeds required for digital audio.

The Sound Blaster uses two of the PC AT's six DMA channels: one (defaulting to channel 1) for 8-bit audio and a second (defaulting to channel 5) for 16-bit audio. Other devices, some of which may be connected to your PC, use DMA channels too. Both floppy and hard disk drives typically use DMA channels 2 or 3, and the following devices often use channel 1:

- SCSI controller cards
- Network cards
- Backup tape controller cards
- Scanner cards
- PostScript and other printer cards

Because digital audio requires huge amounts of data to be transferred at one time, it is important to set your Sound Blaster to a DMA channel that won't be used by another device while you are playing or recording audio. If you won't be using SCSI devices or network, printer, and other controller cards as you play or record sound, the default should be okay in any case.

You'll know you have a DMA conflict if you hear a hissing sound when you try to play audio, or if it doesn't play at all. If you're using Sound Blaster 16 and you have a DMA conflict, run the Setup program again and reset the DMA parameters. The Setup program will revise your system files to accommodate the new settings. If you're using Sound Blaster Pro, remove the card and change the DMA setting. If you are using another version of Sound Blaster, you have to go to your other devices and change their DMA settings.

Understanding IRQ Levels

When a device attached to your PC wants the computer's CPU to perform some function, it requests the processor to interrupt what it is doing and instead do the job at hand. This "job" could be receiving a MIDI note, writing to a floppy disk, interpreting a keyboard instruction, or any of a number of things. To keep track of these requests, the devices connected to your PC have individual *interrupt numbers*. This way, whenever the processor gets an interrupt request (an IRQ) from two or more devices at once, it knows that it should attend to the lower numbers first.

Table B.1 shows the most common IRQ settings for 80×86 PC peripherals.

TABLE B.1: Common IRQ Settings for 80×86 PC Peripherals

IRQ	Device
0	Timer
1	Keyboard
2	Used with IRQ9
3	Serial Port 2: COM2 and 4 (modem)
4	Serial Port 1: COM1 and 3 (serial mouse)
5	Parallel Printer 2
6	Floppy Drives
7	Parallel Printer 1
8	Clock
9	IRQ2 for 80×86 computers
10	Not assigned
11	Not assigned
12	Not assigned
13	80×87 Coprocessor
14	Hard Disk
15	Not assigned

IRQ levels are set at the factory to what the manufacturer believes is the card's best chance of avoiding conflicts. The Sound Blaster 16 defaults to IRQ5. The default for Sound Blaster is IRQ7.

Understanding I/O Addresses

Every device in your PC has an Input/Output (I/O) address that helps it communicate with the computer. The I/O address is a number that connects all a device's connectors to the PC slot, and lets the PC differentiate among its various installed devices. When your PC's central processing unit (CPU) wants to send or receive data to or from your Sound Blaster or another device, it "broadcasts" the device's Input/Output address. When the device hears its address being broadcast, it knows the CPU has a message for it, and it listens. The devices that are set to other addresses simply ignore the broadcast. Obviously, no address can be used by more than one device.

Some devices, including the Sound Blaster, use a *range* of addresses. For example, a device that uses ten address locations, set to, say, a "base" I/O address of 330, will use up all the addresses from 330 to 339. In addition, the Sound Blaster and other devices that perform more than one function will have a different base address (and range, if necessary) for each function.

TIP   I/O addresses are expressed in *hexadecimal notation,* a numbering system used widely in computers and organized on a base of sixteen (as opposed to the decimal system's base of 10). Hex numbers use the letters *A* through *F* to express numbers 10 through 15, so you'll see numbers like 23FH, or 30DH, for example. The *H* after a number indicates that it is a hex number. You may also see hex figures preceded by a dollar sign ($220). The *H* and the *$* only tell you that the number is in hex; they don't affect the number's actual value.

Sound Blaster has one base address for its overall functions and another specifically for its MIDI port. The overall base address default is 220H with a range that goes to 233H; the MIDI port has a base address of 330H and a range of two addresses that goes to 331H.

Creative Labs counsels Sound Blaster users against changing the card's addresses. They are rarely used by other devices and are programmed into a lot of the games and other software that support the Sound Blaster. We also advise against changing I/O addresses if only because not changing them cuts down on the messing around you have to do.

APPENDIX

c

Sound Blaster Port Addresses

Table C.1 shows the port addresses for registers that control various parts of the Sound Blaster. Table C.2 shows the same for the Sound Blaster Pro. The possible base ports for the Sound Blaster are 210H, 220H, 230H, 240H, 250H, and 260H. The possible base ports for the Sound Blaster Pro are 220H and 240H.

TABLE C.1: Port Chart of the Sound Blaster

Port*	Description	Access
200H–207H	Analog joystick port	Read/write
Port + 00H	C/MS 1..6 register data	Write
Port + 01H	C/MS 1..6 register selection	Write
Port + 02H	C/MS 7..12 register data	Write
Port + 03H	C/MS 7..12 register	Write
Port + 06H	DSP reset	Write
Port + 08HFM	Register selection and status	Write and read
Port + 09H	FM register data	Write
Port + 0AH	DSP read data	Read
Port + 0CH	DSP give command or data and buffer status	Write and read
Port + 0EH	DSP data available status	Read
388H	FM register selection and status	Write and read
389H	FM register data	Write

* "Port" in this table refers to the base port.

TABLE C.2: Port Chart of the Sound Blaster Pro

Port*	Description	Access
200H–207H	Analog joystick port	Read/write
Port + 00H	Left FM register selection and status	Write and read
Port + 01H	Left FM register data	Write
Port + 02H	Right FM register selection and status	Write and read
Port + 03H	Right FM register data	Write

TABLE C.2: Port Chart of the Sound Blaster Pro (continued)

Port*	Description	Access
Port + 04H	Mixer chip register selection	Write
Port + 05H	Mixer chip register data	Write and read
Port + 06H	DSP reset	Write
Port + 08H	Both FM register selection and status	Write and read
Port + 09H	Both FM register data	Write
Port + 0AH	DSP read data	Read
Port + 0CH	DSP give command or data and buffer status	Write and read
Port + 0EH	DSP data available status	Read
Port + 10H	CD-ROM command and data register	Write and read
Port + 11H	CD-ROM status register	Read
Port + 12H	CD-ROM reset register	Write
Port + 13H	CD-ROM access register	Write
388H	FM register selection and status	Write and read

* "Port" in this table refers to the base port.

APPENDIX

D

Mixer Chip Registers

T his appendix shows registers for controlling the operation of the mixer chip. Table D.1 shows the general registers, and Table D.2 shows the input choices. Following is a description of the abbreviations used in Table D.1:

Abbreviation	Meaning
XX	Not defined
l.	Left
r.	Right
vol.	Volume
FINP	Input filter
TFIL	Input filter type
FOUT	Output filter
ST	Stereo/mono mode

TABLE D.1: General Registers

Register	Bit 7	Bit 6	Bit 5	Bit 4	Bit 3	Bit 2	Bit 1	Bit 0
00H	Data reset							
02H	DSP volume l.			XX	DSP volume r.			XX
0AH	XX	XX	XX	XX	XX	Mic vol.		XX
0CH	XX	XX	FINP	XX	TFIL	Select		XX
0EH	XX	XX	FOUT	XX	XX	XX	ST	XX
22H	General vol.			XX	General vol.			XX
26H	FM volume l.			XX	FM volume r.			XX
28H	CD volume l.			XX	CD volume r.			XX
2EH	Line volume l.			XX	Line volume r.			XX

TABLE D.2: Input Choices

Select	Input Choice
0	Microphone
1	CD-ROM
3	Line

APPENDIX

E

DSP Commands

This appendix discusses all DSP commands. Some commands are beyond the scope of this book but are mentioned anyway to give you an idea of what they are used for. Port 2XCH is used to write to the DSP; port 2XAH is used to read the DSP.

Play Commands

Following are DSP Play commands.

10H, 8 bits directly

1. Give command 10H.
2. Send a data byte.
3. Repeat steps 1 and 2 at a constant speed.

14H, 8 bits via DMA

1. Set DMA controller and take over IRQ interrupt.
2. Set the sampling rate (see command 40H).
3. Give command 14H.
4. Send the least significant byte of the length of sample block 1.
5. Send the most significant byte of the length of sample block 1.
6. The sample output starts immediately after step 5; at the end the DSP generates an interrupt via the set IRQ interrupt. Blocks with a maximum length of 64KB can be sent via the DMA. Thus, larger samples must be cut into smaller blocks.

91H, High-speed 8 bits via DMA (Pro)

1. Set DMA controller and take over IRQ interrupt.
2. Set the sampling rate (see command 40H).
3. Give command 48H.
4. Send the least significant byte of the length of sample block 1.

5. Send the most significant byte of the length of sample block 1.

6. Give command 91H.

7. The sample output starts after step 6; at the end the DSP generates an interrupt via the set IRQ interrupt. Blocks with a maximum length of 64KB can be sent via the DMA. Thus, larger samples must be cut into smaller blocks.

NOTE Commands 48H and 91H are only supported by the Sound Blaster Pro. These commands have to be used to play back samples at a higher sampling rate.

Commands for Playing Compressed Samples

Following are a list of commands for playing compressed samples.

16H, 2-bit compression via DMA

The same method applies to this command as to command 14H.

17H, 2-bit compression via DMA with reference byte

The same method applies to this command as to command 14H. The first byte of the sample data is the reference byte; this byte contains normal 8-bit sample data. If you play back different sample blocks, command 16H must be used for the next blocks because these sample blocks don't include a reference byte.

74H, 4-bit compression via DMA

See command 16H.

75H, 4-bit compression via DMA with reference byte

See command 17H.

76H, 2.6-bit compression via DMA

See command 16H.

77H, 2.6-bit compression via DMA with reference byte

See command 17H.

Recording Commands

Following are DSP Recording commands.

20H, Direct recording

1. Give command 20H.

2. Read a data byte and store it.

3. Repeat step 1 and 2 at a constant speed.

24H, Recording via DMA

1. Set DMA controller and take over IRQ interrupt.

2. Set the sampling rate (see command 40H).

3. Give command 24H.

4. Send the least significant byte of the length of sample block 1.

5. Send the most significant byte of the length of sample block 1.

6. The sample input starts immediately after step 5; at the end the DSP generates an interrupt via the set IRQ interrupt. Blocks with a maximum length of 64KB can be read via the DMA. Thus, larger samples must be recorded as smaller blocks.

99H, High-speed 8 bits via DMA (Pro)

1. Set DMA controller and take over IRQ interrupt.

2. Set the sampling rate (see command 40H).

3. Give command 48H.

4. Send the least significant byte of the length of sample block 1.

5. Send the most significant byte of the length of sample block 1.

6. Give command 99H.

7. The sample input starts after step 6; at the end the DSP generates an interrupt via the set IRQ interrupt. Blocks with a maximum length of 64KB can be read via the DMA. Thus, larger samples must be recorded as smaller blocks.

NOTE   Commands 48H and 99H are only supported by the Sound Blaster Pro. These commands have to be used to record samples at a higher sampling rate.

Speaker Commands

Following are the Speaker commands.

D1H, Turn on speaker connection

After this command, the signals of the DSP are sent to the amplifier that is present on the card. This command takes about 112 milliseconds.

D3H, Turn off speaker connection

After this command, the DSP doesn't send any signals to the amplifier. The DSP needs 220 milliseconds at most to execute this command.

D8H, Ask speaker setting

1. Give command D8H.

2. Read one byte from the DSP. If this byte has the value 0, the speaker is off. If the byte has the value 255, the speaker is on.

NOTE This command is only supported by the Sound Blaster Pro.

Other DSP Commands

Following are the remainder of the DSP commands.

40H, Set sampling rate

1. Give command 40H.

2. Send the byte that results from the following formula:

```
256 -1,000,000 / sampling rate
```

48H, Set block length

Refer to commands 91H and 99H for the use of this command.

80H, Set a silence block

1. Take over IRQ interrupt.

2. Set the sampling rate (see command 40H).

3. Give command 80H.

4. Send the least significant byte of the length of silence block 1.

5. Send the most significant byte of the length of silence block 1.

6. At the end the DSP generates an interrupt via the set IRQ.

D0H, Stop DMA

Stops any DMA input or output between the DSP and the memory.

D4H, Continue DMA

In case the DMA operation was stopped, you can continue the DMA operation by giving this command.

E1H, Ask version

1. Give command E1H.
2. Read the most significant version number.
3. Read the least significant version number.

DSP MIDI Commands

Following are descriptions of the DSP MIDI commands.

30H, Direct MIDI input

1. Give command 30H.
2. Check whether bit 7 of port 2XEH is set (=1).
3. Read the MIDI code.
4. Repeat steps 2 and 3.

31H, MIDI input via interrupt

1. Take over IRQ interrupt.
2. Give command 31H.
3. If a MIDI code is passed on, the DSP generates an interrupt.
4. The interrupt routine has to read and has to store the MIDI code.
5. Read port 2XEH once and end the interrupt.

32H, Direct MIDI input with time stamp

1. Give command 32H.

2. Check whether bit 7 of port 2XEH is set (=1).

3. Read the least significant byte of the time stamp.

4. Read the middle byte of the time stamp.

5. Read the most significant byte of the time stamp.

6. Read the MIDI code.

7. Repeat steps 2 through 6.

Steps 3 through 5 result in a 24-bit value indicating a time in milliseconds. This is the number of milliseconds that passed after command 32H was sent.

33H, MIDI input with time stamp via interrupt

This command works the same way as command 31H, only this time the interrupt routine has to read four bytes. The first three bytes contain the time stamp and the last byte contains the actual MIDI code.

34H, Direct MIDI UART mode

After this command, MIDI codes can be both sent and read. You can write a MIDI code directly to the DSP without first having to send command 38H.

35H, MIDI UART mode via interrupt

This command has the same effect as the previous command, except that the MIDI input takes place via the interrupt (see command 31H).

36H, Direct MIDI UART mode with time stamp

This command works the same way as command 34H. However, to read MIDI code the same conditions apply to this command as to command 32H.

37H, MIDI UART mode with time stamp via interrupt

Again, reading takes place via an interrupt. Just as at command 33H, the interrupt has to read both the MIDI code and the time stamp.

For the UART modes, the DSP makes use of a 64-byte buffer, so the DSP can store MIDI codes in the buffer when MIDI input is too fast. This way, the DSP can remember no more then 64 codes without a time stamp or 16 codes with a time stamp.

38H, Send a MIDI code

1. Give command 38H.
2. Read port 22CH.
3. Repeat step 2 until bit 7 is reset (=0).
4. Write a MIDI code.

NOTE   MIDI UART and time stamp are only supported by the Sound Blaster Pro. The DSP has to be reset (via port 2X6H) if you want to disable the UART mode.

APPENDIX

F

ID Codes for MIDI Instrument Manufacturers

Table F.1 lists the ID codes for various MIDI instrument manufacturers. These codes are used in system exclusive messages, the MIDI messages that are only applicable to a system made by one manufacturer.

NOTE See Chapter 10 for more information about system exclusive messages.

TABLE F.1: Codes for MIDI Instrument Manufacturers

Decimal	Hexadecimal	Manufacturer's ID
0	00	For general use
1	01	Sequential Circuits
2	02	Big Briar
3	03	Octave Plateau
4	04	Moog
5	05	Passport Designs
6	06	Lexicon
7	07	Kurzweil
8	08	CBS/Fender
9	09	Steinway & Sons
10	0A	Delta Lab Research
11	0B	Sound Composition System
12	0C	General Electro Music
13	0D	Techmar
15	0F	Ensoniq
16	10	Oberheim
17	11	Paia Electronics
18	12	Simmons
19	13	Gentle Electric

TABLE F.1: Codes for MIDI Instrument Manufacturers (continued)

Decimal	Hexadecimal	Manufacturer's ID
20	14	Fairlight
22	16	Lowery
32	20	Bon Tempi
33	21	SIEL
34	22	Ircam
35	23	Synthaxe
36	24	Hohner
37	25	Crumar
38	26	Solton
39	27	Jellinghaus
44	2C	Peter Struven
57	39	Soundcraft Electronics
62	3E	Waldorf
64	40	Kawai
65	41	Roland
66	42	Korg
67	43	Yamaha
68	44	Casio
70	46	Kamiya Studio
71	47	Akai
72	48	Japan Victor
73	49	Meishosa
78	4E	TEAC
80	50	Matsushita
81	51	Fostex

APPENDIX

G

MIDI Status and Data Bytes

Table G.1 lists the byte values of various MIDI messages.

TABLE G.1: MIDI Status and Data Bytes

Status Byte			Data Bytes	
First Byte Value	**Function**		**Second Byte Value**	**Third Byte Value**
80 128	Channel 1	Note off	Note Number	Note Velocity
81 129	Channel 2	"	(0–127)	(0–127)
82 130	Channel 3	"	"	"
83 131	Channel 4	"	"	"
84 132	Channel 5	"	"	"
85 133	Channel 6	"	"	"
86 134	Channel 7	"	"	"
87 135	Channel 8	"	"	"
88 136	Channel 9	"	"	"
89 137	Channel 10	"	"	"
8A 138	Channel 11	"	"	"
8B 139	Channel 12	"	"	"
8C 140	Channel 13	"	"	"
8D 141	Channel 14	"	"	"
8E 142	Channel 15	"	"	"
8F 143	Channel 16	"	"	"
90 144	Channel 1	Note on	Note Number	Note Velocity
91 145	Channel 2	"	(0–127)	(0–127)
92 146	Channel 3	"	"	"
93 147	Channel 4	"	"	"
94 148	Channel 5	"	"	"
95 149	Channel 6	"	"	"
96 150	Channel 7	"	"	"
97 151	Channel 8	"	"	"
98 152	Channel 9	"	"	"

TABLE G.1: MIDI Status and Data Bytes (continued)

Status Byte			Data Bytes	
First Byte Value	Function		Second Byte Value	Third Byte Value
99 153	Channel 10	"	"	"
9A 154	Channel 11	"	"	"
9B 155	Channel 12	"	"	"
9C 156	Channel 13	"	"	"
9D 157	Channel 14	"	"	"
9E 158	Channel 15	"	"	"
9F 159	Channel 16	"	"	"
A0 160	Channel 1	Polyphonic	Note number	Aftertouch
A1 161	Channel 2	Aftertouch	(0–127)	Pressure
A2 162	Channel 3	"	"	(0–127)
A3 163	Channel 4	"	"	"
A4 164	Channel 5	"	"	"
A5 165	Channel 6	"	"	"
A6 166	Channel 7	"	"	"
A7 167	Channel 8	"	"	"
A8 168	Channel 9	"	"	"
A9 169	Channel 10	"	"	"
AA 170	Channel 11	"	"	"
AB 171	Channel 12	"	"	"
AC 172	Channel 13	"	"	"
AD 173	Channel 14	"	"	"
AE 174	Channel 15	"	"	"
AF 175	Channel 16	"	"	"
B0 176	Channel 1	Control/	*	*
B1 177	Channel 2	Mode Change	"	"

TABLE G.1: MIDI Status and Data Bytes (continued)

Status Byte			Data Bytes	
First Byte Value	**Function**		**Second Byte Value**	**Third Byte Value**
B2 178	Channel 3	"	"	"
B3 179	Channel 4	"	"	"
B4 180	Channel 5	"	"	"
B5 181	Channel 6	"	"	"
B6 182	Channel 7	"	"	"
B7 183	Channel 8	"	"	"
B8 184	Channel 9	"	"	"
B9 185	Channel 10	"	"	"
BA 186	Channel 11	"	"	"
BB 187	Channel 12	"	"	"
BC 188	Channel 13	"	"	"
BD 189	Channel 14	"	"	"
BE 190	Channel 15	"	"	"
BF 191	Channel 16	"	"	"
C0 192	Channel 1	Program	Program	None
C1 193	Channel 2	Change	Number	"
C2 194	Channel 3	"	(0–127)	"
C3 195	Channel 4	"	"	"
C4 196	Channel 5	"	"	"
C5 197	Channel 6	"	"	"
C6 198	Channel 7	"	"	"
C7 199	Channel 8	"	"	"
C8 200	Channel 9	"	"	"
C9 201	Channel 10	"	"	"
CA 202	Channel 11	"	"	"
CB 203	Channel 12	"	"	"

TABLE G.1: MIDI Status and Data Bytes (continued)

Status Byte			Data Bytes	
First Byte Value	**Function**		**Second Byte Value**	**Third Byte Value**
CC 204	Channel 13	"	"	"
CD 205	Channel 14	"	"	"
CE 206	Channel 15	"	"	"
CF 207	Channel 16	"	"	"
D0 208	Channel 1	Channel	Aftertouch	None
D1 209	Channel 2	Aftertouch	Pressure	"
D2 210	Channel 3	"	(0–127)	"
D3 211	Channel 4	"	"	"
D4 212	Channel 5	"	"	"
D5 213	Channel 6	"	"	"
D6 214	Channel 7	"	"	"
D7 215	Channel 8	"	"	"
D8 216	Channel 9	"	"	"
D9 217	Channel 10	"	"	"
DA 218	Channel 11	"	"	"
DB 219	Channel 12	"	"	"
DC 220	Channel 13	"	"	"
DD 221	Channel 14	"	"	"
DE 222	Channel 15	"	"	"
DF 223	Channel 16	"	"	"
E0 224	Channel 1	Pitch Wheel	Pitch Wheel	Pitch Wheel
E1 225	Channel 2	"	LSB	MSB
E2 226	Channel 3	"	(0–127)	(0–127)
E3 227	Channel 4	"	"	"
E4 228	Channel 5	"	"	"
E5 229	Channel 6	"	"	"

TABLE G.1: MIDI Status and Data Bytes (continued)

Status Byte			Data Bytes	
First Byte Value	**Function**		**Second Byte Value**	**Third Byte Value**
E6 230	Channel 7	"	"	"
E7 231	Channel 8	"	"	"
E8 232	Channel 9	"	"	"
E9 233	Channel 10	"	"	"
EA 234	Channel 11	"	"	"
EB 235	Channel 12	"	"	"
EC 236	Channel 13	"	"	"
ED 237	Channel 14	"	"	"
EE 238	Channel 15	"	"	"
EF 239	Channel 16	"	"	"
F0 240	System Exclusive	**	**	
F1 241	System Common	Not defined?	?	
F2 242	System Common	Song Position Pointer	LSB	MSB
F3 243	System Common	Song Select	Song number (0–127)	None
F4 244	System Common	Not defined?	?	
F5 245	System Common	Not defined?	?	
F6 246	System Common	Tune Request	None	None
F7 247	System Common	End of SysEx (EOX)	"	"
F8 248	System Real Time	Timing Clock	"	"
F9 249	System Real Time	Not defined	"	"
FA 250	System Real Time	Start	"	"
FB 251	System Real Time	Continue	"	"
FC 252	System Real Time	Stop	"	"
FD 253	System Real Time	Not defined	"	"

TABLE G.1: MIDI Status and Data Bytes (continued)

Status Byte			Data Bytes	
First Byte Value	Function		Second Byte Value	Third Byte Value
FE 254	System Real Time	Active Sensing	"	"
FF 255	System Real Time	System Reset	"	"
* See Appendix F				
** The system-exclusive second byte is the manufacturer's ID. It is followed by several data bytes and terminated by an EOX (F7).				

INDEX

Note to the Reader: Throughout this index, **boldfaced** page numbers indicate primary discussions of a topic. *Italicized* page numbers indicate illustrations. Page numbers followed by a "t" indicate a table.

Symbols & Numbers

(pound sign), for sharps, 41
@ (at sign), for flats, 41
\ (vertical sign), for measures, 41
8-bit expansion slot, *13*, 450
9-voice setting, in FM chip, 29
11-voice setting, in FM chip, 29
16-bit digital audio, 466
16-bit expansion slot, *13*, 13, 450

A

Accidentals (Sequencer Plus Junior Note Edit menu), 68
acoustic instruments, MIDI versions, 82
Active Sense message (MIDI), 378, 389
active voice, function to return, 156
ADC (analog-to-digital converter), 29–30
Add (Sequencer Plus Junior View menu), 67

Additional Information block type, 262
additive synthesis, 103–105, *104*, 186, 191
AdLib card, xiii
    BNK format, **113–116**
    FM chip support, 29
    INS instrument format, **109**, **111–112**
    instrument files and instrument banks, 109
    ports, 176
    ROL file format, **147–150**
    SOUND.COM driver, 129
Advanced Signal Processing (ASP) chip, 446
aftertouch effects, 372
Aftertouch function (MIDI), 377
All Notes OFF message, 378, 386
AM setting, 108, 183
amplifier
    changing settings, 453–455
    connecting, 459
Amplify (Vedit Effect menu), 59
amplitude, 27, 29, 222
amplitude vibrato, 108

C

G

H

I

J

N

T

W

X

Y

Z

MAKE A GOOD COMPUTER EVEN BETTER.

POCKET-SIZED PC EXPERTISE.

550 pp. ISBN: 756-8.

The *PC User's es-sen'-tial, ac-ces'sible Pocket Dictionary* is the most complete, most readable computer dictionary available today. With over 2,000 plain-language entries, this inexpensive handbook offers exceptional coverage of computer industry terms at a remarkably affordable price.

In this handy reference you'll find plenty of explanatory tables and figures, practical tips, notes, and warnings, and in-depth entries on the most essential terms. You'll also appreciate the extensive cross-referencing, designed to make it easy for you to find the answers you need.

Presented in easy-to-use alphabetical order, *The PC User's es-sen'-tial, ac-ces'-si-ble Pocket Dictionary* covers every conceivable computer-related topic. Ideal for home, office, and school use, it's the only computer dictionary you need!

SYBEX. Help Yourself.

2021 Challenger Drive
Alameda, CA 94501
1-510-523-8233
1-800-227-2346

SYBEX

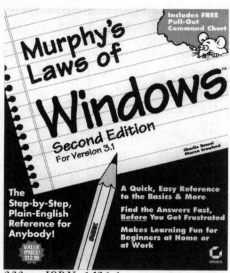

THE PERFECT WAY TO MASTER WORDPERFECT FOR WINDOWS.

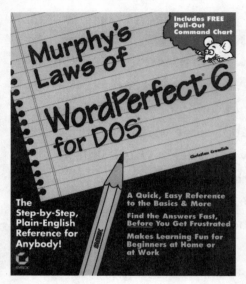

THE WORLD'S BEST SELLING WORD PROCESSING SERIES.

Your Guide to DOS Dominance.

1000 pp. ISBN:1442-3

DOS 6.2 can save you hundreds of dollars in hardware and software purchases. *Mastering DOS 6.2 (Special Edition)* shows you how.

Whether you're a beginner or expert, whether you use DOS or Windows, *Mastering DOS 6.2 (Special Edition)* will help you make the most of the new DOS utilities. Find out how to protect your computer work with ScanDisk, Backup, Undelete and Anti-Virus. Get a complete overview of disk caching and disk defragmenting. Discover the secret of expanding your memory by typing a single command.

You'll even find out about the new DOS utility DoubleSpace that will double the available space on your hard disk.

SYBEX. Help Yourself.

2021 Challenger Drive
Alameda, CA 94501
1-800-227-2346

SYBEX

JEST FOR DOS.

YOUR GUIDE TO A WORLD OF CONVENIENCE.

321 pp. ISBN: 798-3.

Finally there's a guide that helps you fulfill the promises of computer convenience you've always heard about —*Exploring the World of Online Services.*

With the help of this book, you can discover the myriad conveniences you can enjoy by using your computer and a modem. Find out how to send electronic mail and messages, or tap into over 5,500 public online databases. Get money-saving advice for choosing modems and communication software, and for saving money on your online bills.

Online veterans will especially enjoy the in-depth coverage of WinCIM, the new Windows version of the CompuServe Information Manager (CIM), and the in-depth discussion of a range of online service providers.

SYBEX. Help Yourself.

2021 Challenger Drive
Alameda, CA 94501
800-227-2346

SYBEX